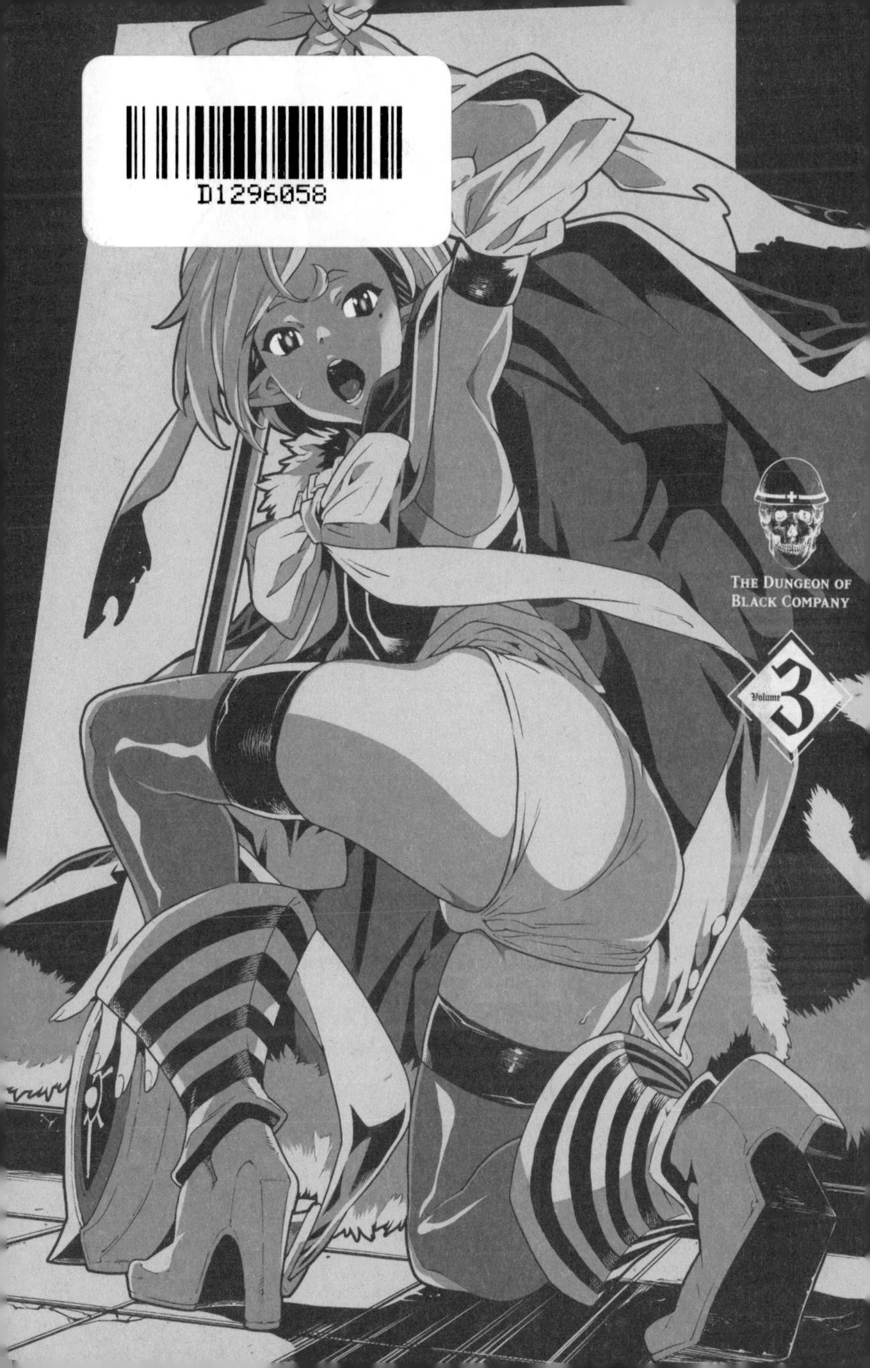
THE DUNGEON OF
BLACK COMPANY
Volume 3

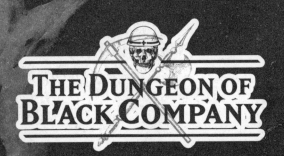

THE DUNGEON OF BLACK COMPANY

CHARACTER

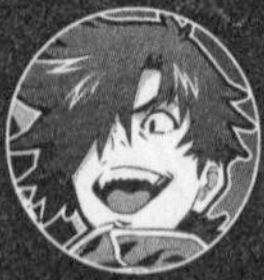

NINOMIYA KINJI

A selfish and unscrupulous young man. Suddenly summoned into a different world, he is forced to work for a black company.

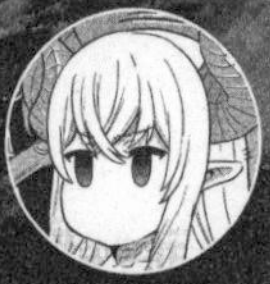

RIM

Though she looks like a cute little girl, she is actually a huge, voracious monster that dwells in the dungeon. She follows Ninomiya in exchange for food.

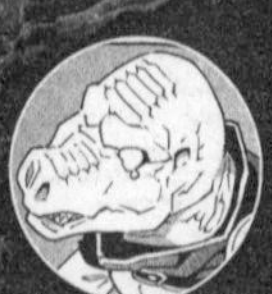

WANIBE

A pathetic lizardman. He gets himself caught up in all kinds of hijinks after signing on for Ninomiya's schemes. A rather pitiful guy well-suited to work as a minion.

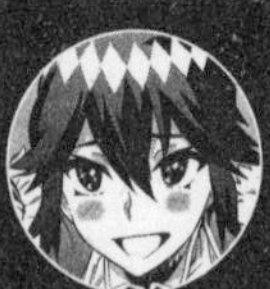

SHIA

An unfortunate girl with a strong work ethic and even stronger knack for battle. Her deeds have earned her the title of Hero. Now that she's wised up a bit, she's thrown in with Ninomiya.

STORY

Ninomiya Kinji thought he'd finally made it to the cushy NEET lifestyle of his dreams, but no sooner did he leave the rat race than he found himself summoned to another world! There, he was forced to work in a monster-infested dungeon for a notorious sweatshop operation: the Raiza'ha Mining Corporation. Yet through his sheer deviousness and indomitable will, he was able to rise through the ranks. Wrangling along his roommate Wanibe and the monster girl Rim, he formed the Dungeon Black Company, aiming to overthrow his employers. After enlisting the aid of Company Hero Shia, he defeated the Majin, the Lord of the Dungeon. Soon afterward, he and Rim discovered a strange device and found themselves propelled to parts unknown...

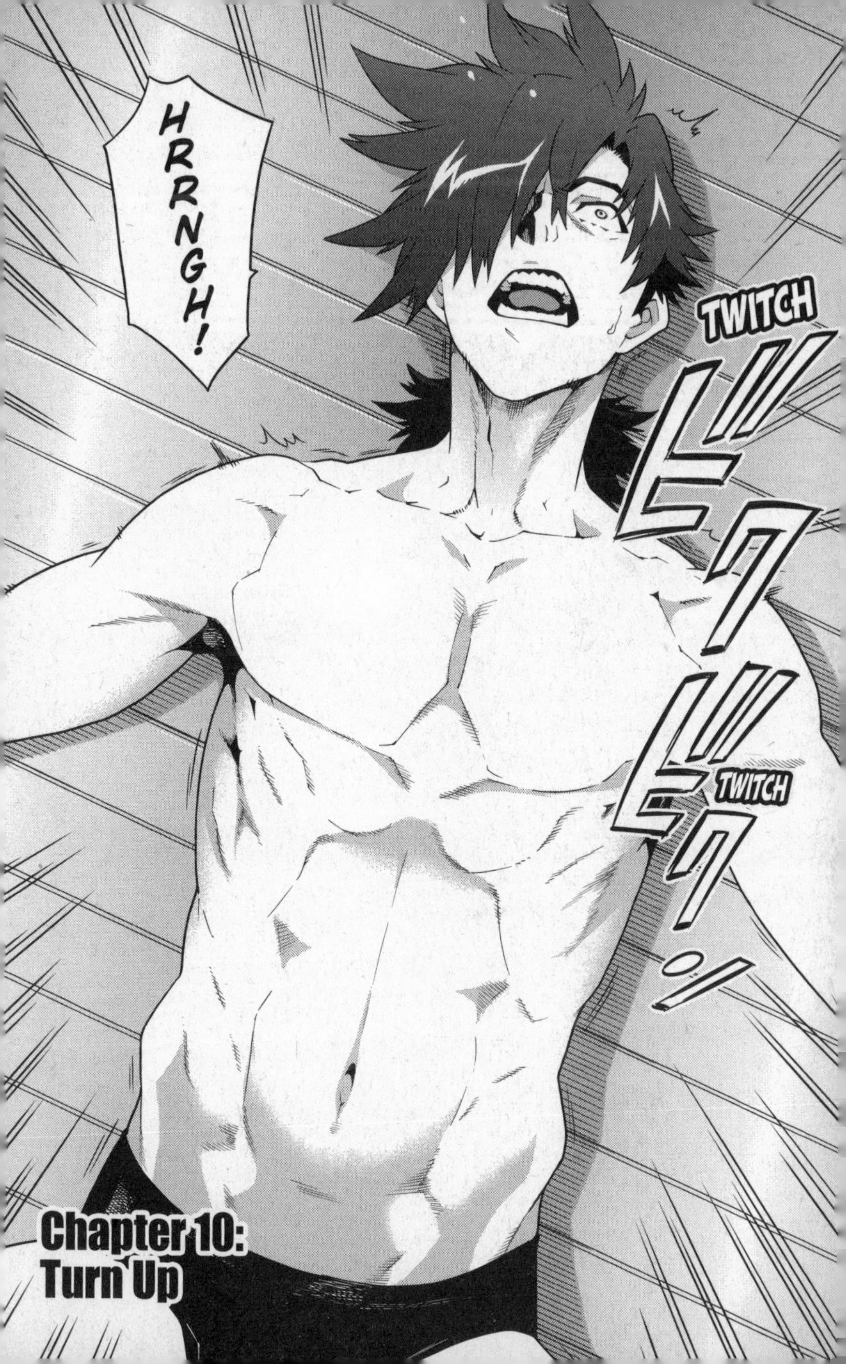
TWITCH
ビクッビクッ
TWITCH
HRRNGH!
Chapter 10: Turn Up

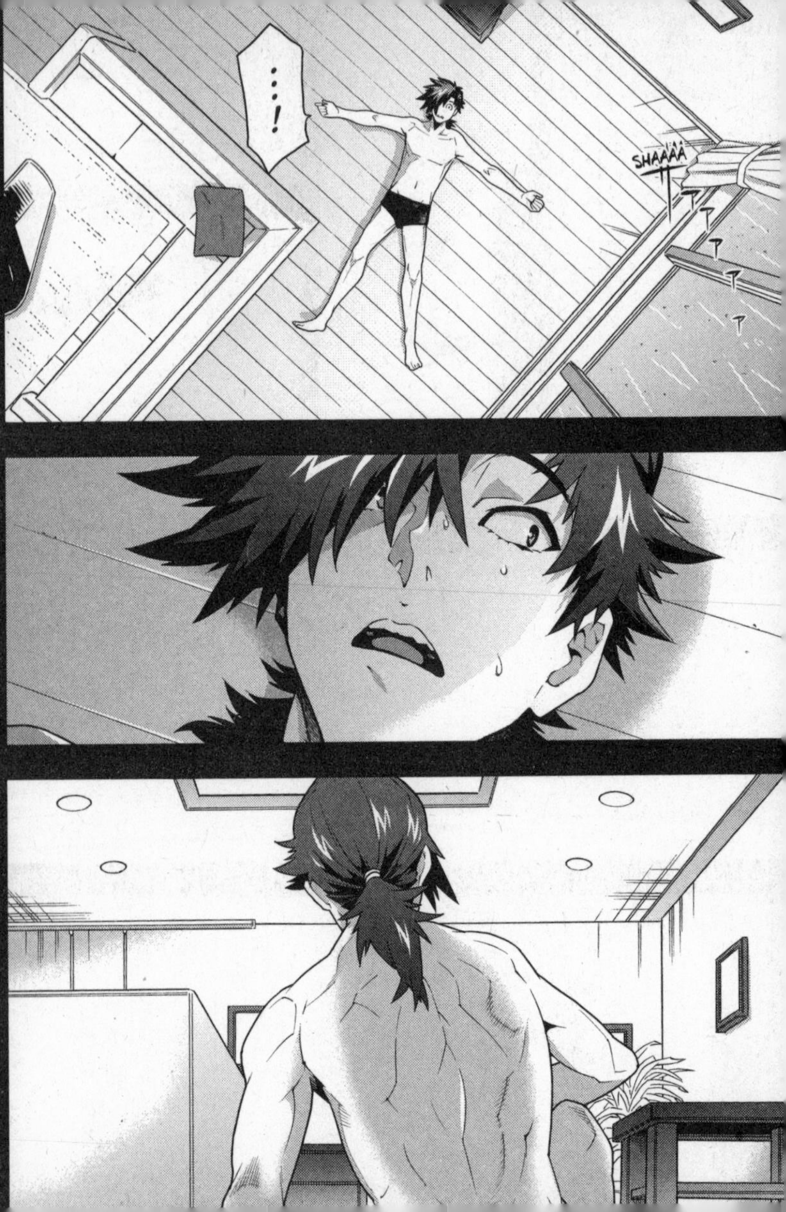
...!
SHAAAA

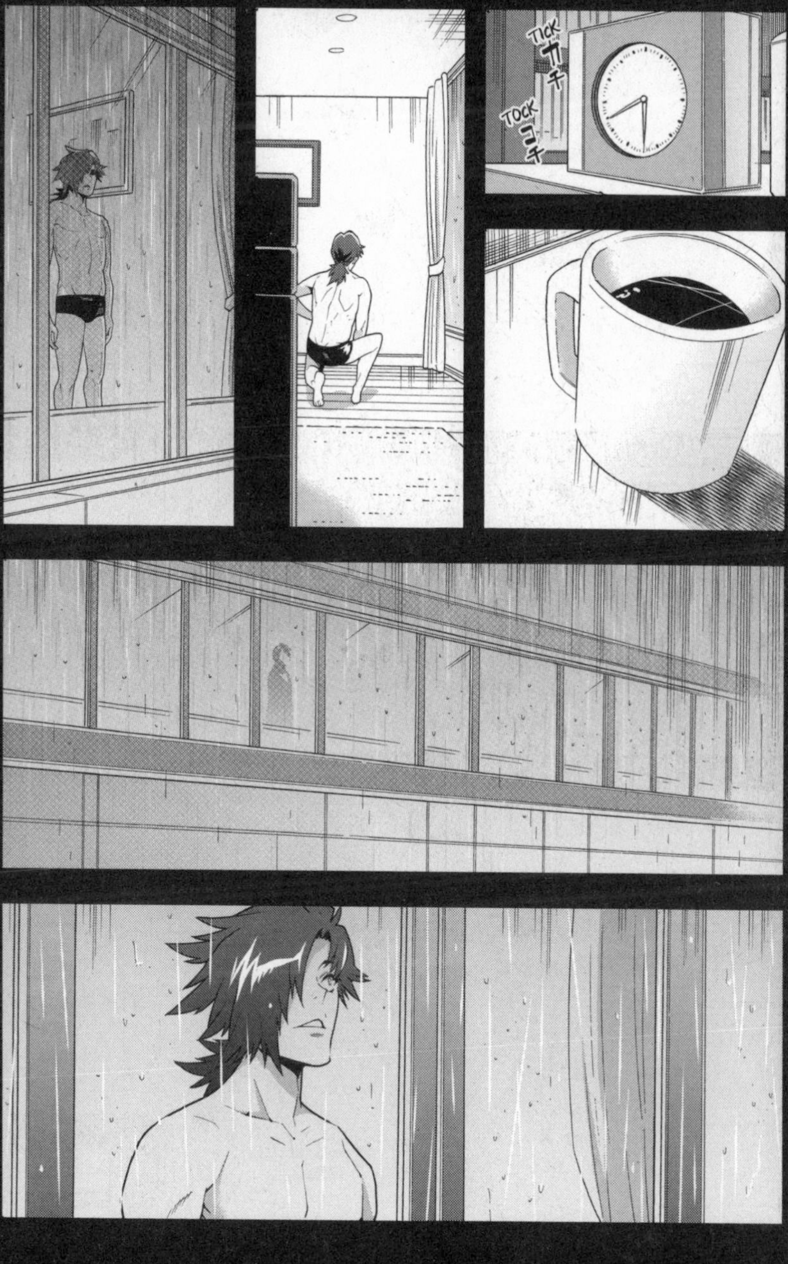
TICK
ガチ
TOCK
コチ

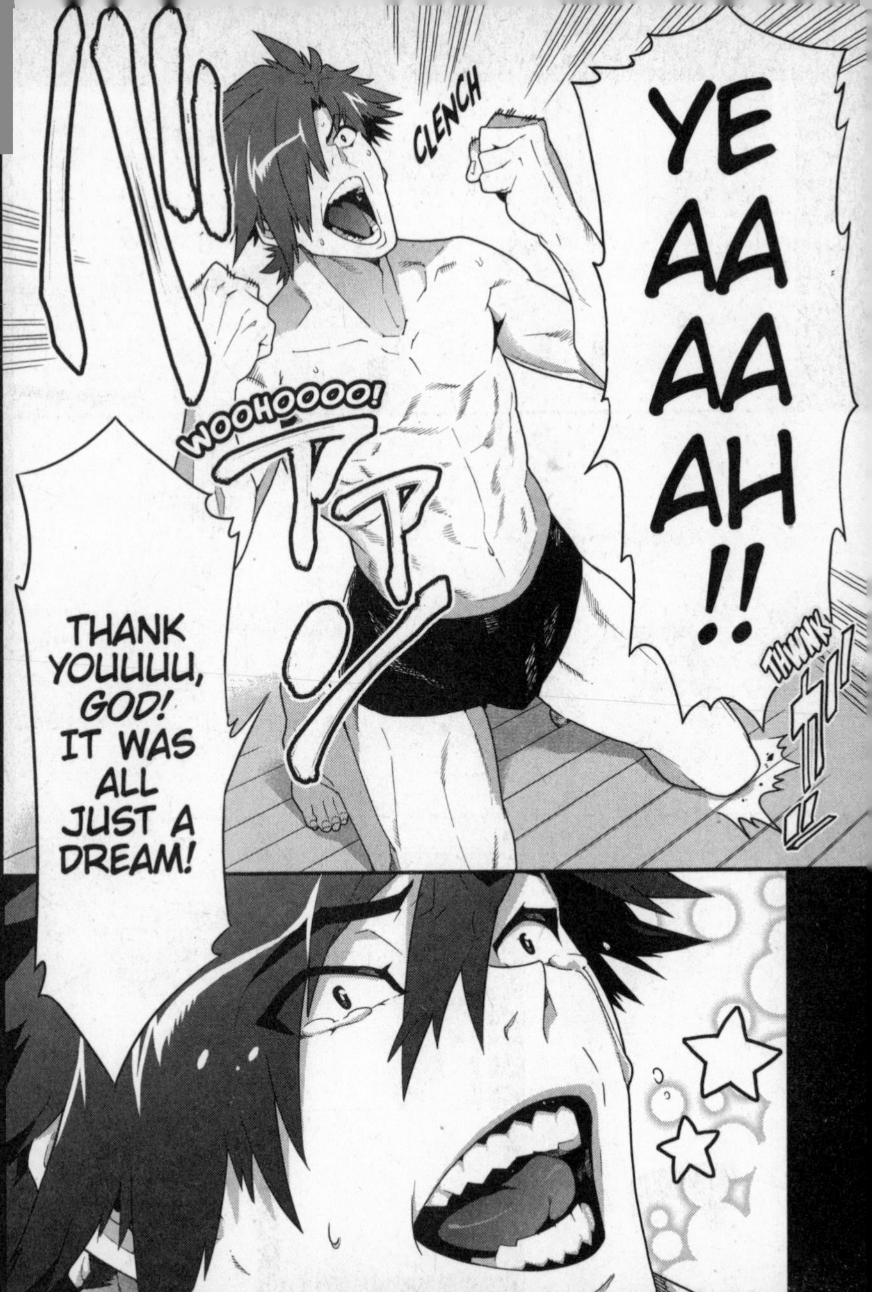
YEAAAAAAH!!
CLENCH
THWNK
WOOHOOOO!
THANK YOUUUU, GOD! IT WAS ALL JUST A DREAM!

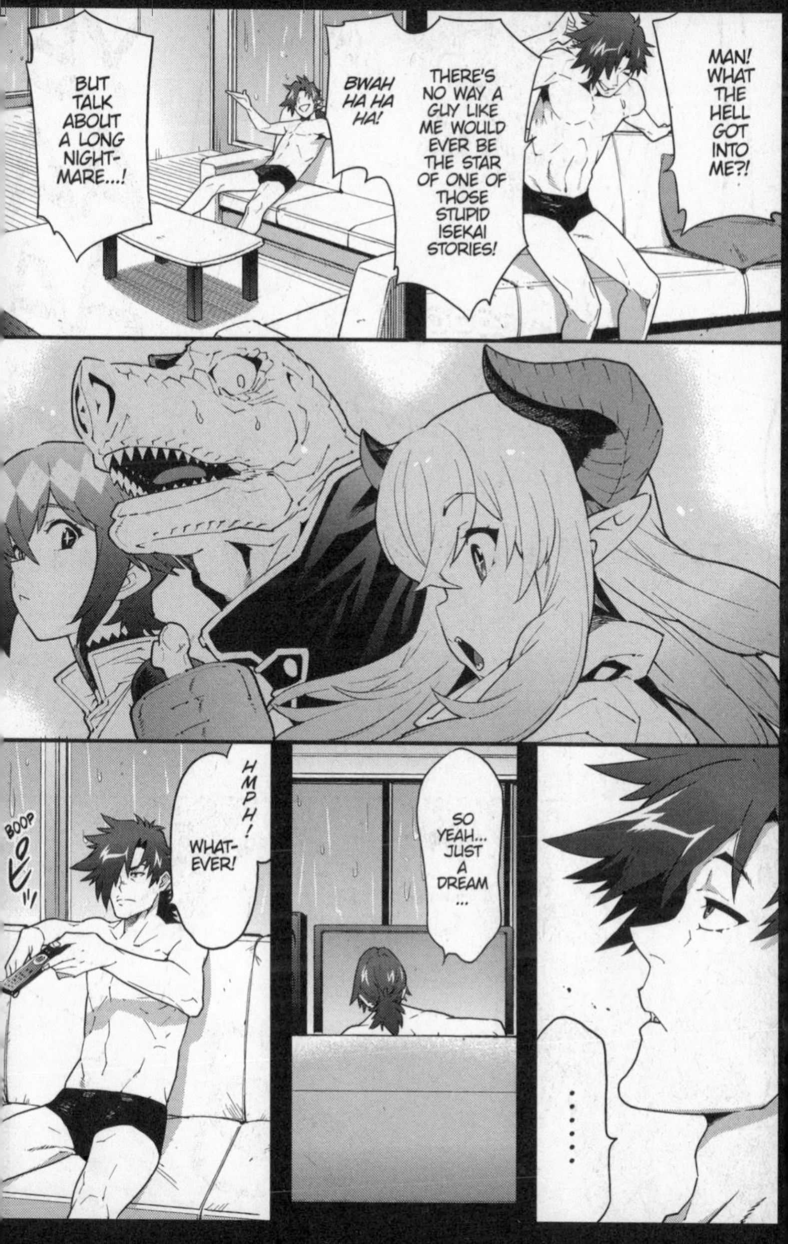
MAN! WHAT THE HELL GOT INTO ME?!
THERE'S NO WAY A GUY LIKE ME WOULD EVER BE THE STAR OF ONE OF THOSE STUPID ISEKAI STORIES!
BWAH HA HA HA!
BUT TALK ABOUT A LONG NIGHT-MARE...!
......
SO YEAH... JUST A DREAM...
HMPH! WHAT-EVER!
BOOP

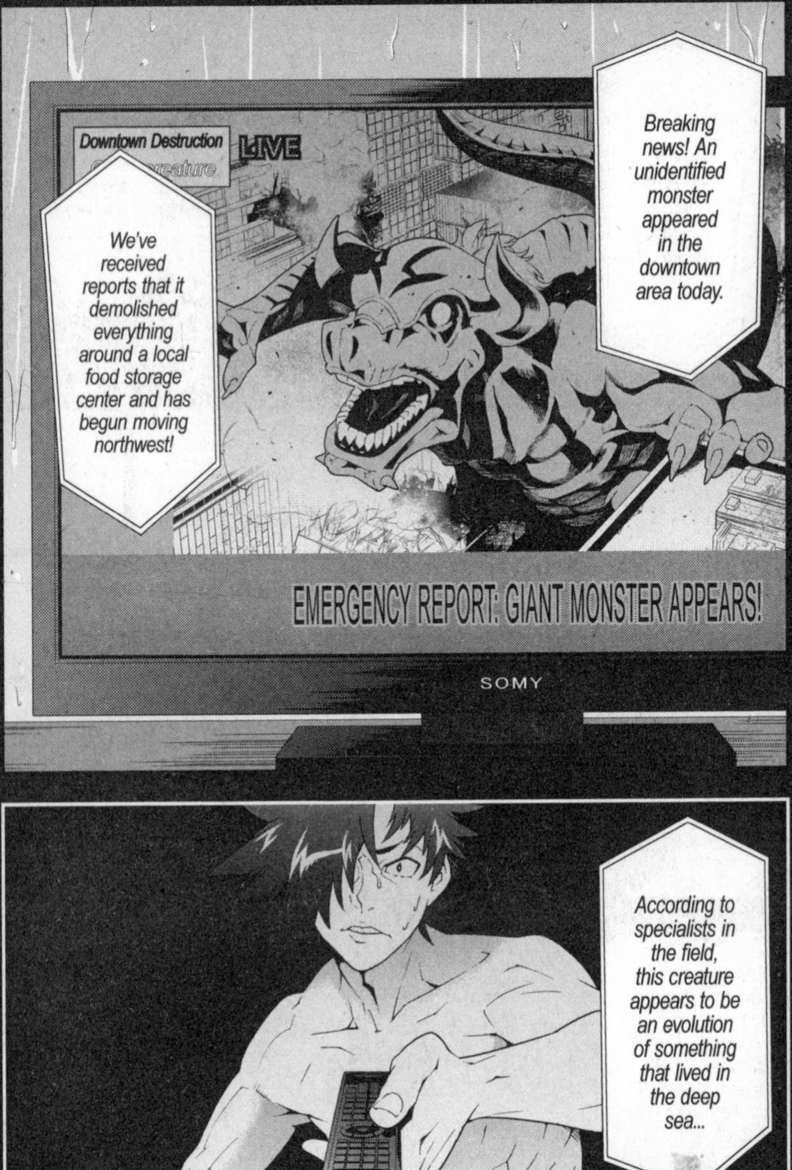
Breaking news! An unidentified monster appeared in the downtown area today.
Downtown Destruction
LIVE
We've received reports that it demolished everything around a local food storage center and has begun moving northwest!
EMERGENCY REPORT: GIANT MONSTER APPEARS!
SOMY
According to specialists in the field, this creature appears to be an evolution of something that lived in the deep sea...

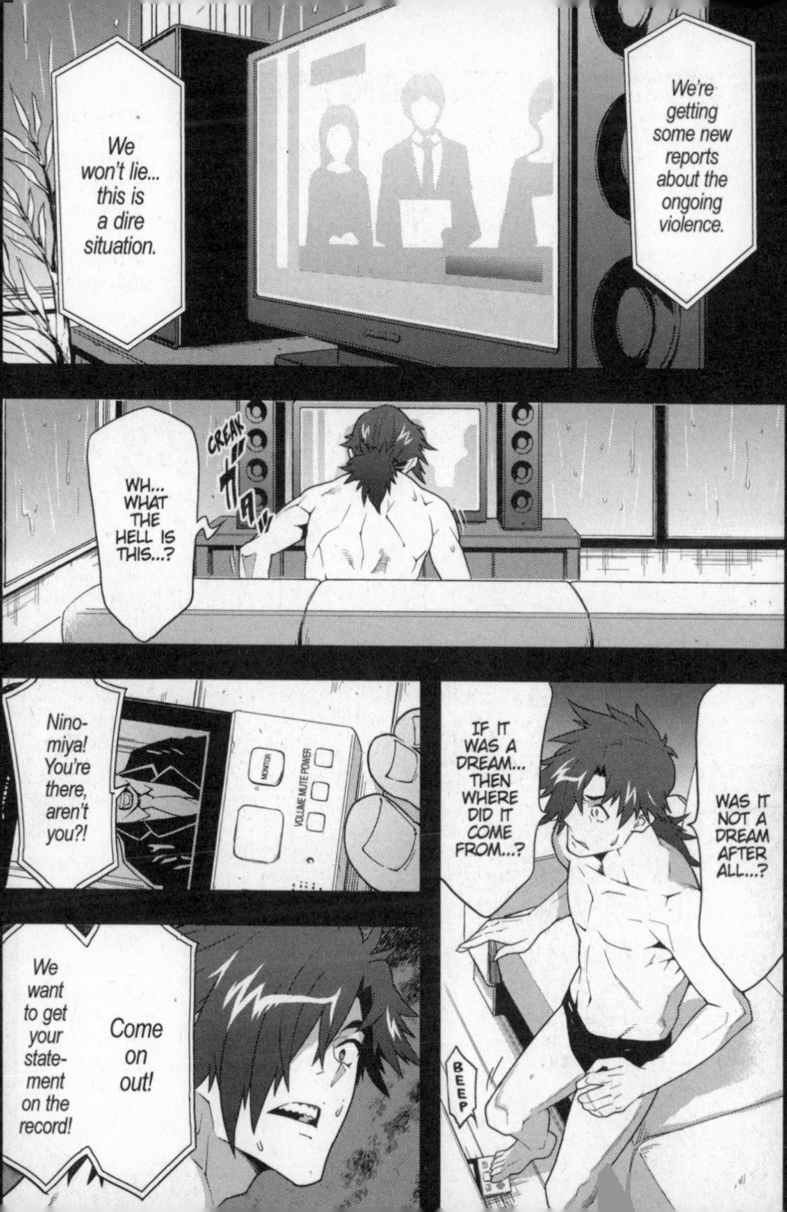
We're getting some new reports about the ongoing violence.
We won't lie... this is a dire situation.
CREAK
WH... WHAT THE HELL IS THIS...?
WAS IT NOT A DREAM AFTER ALL...?
IF IT WAS A DREAM... THEN WHERE DID IT COME FROM...?
BEEP
Nino-miya! You're there, aren't you?!
MONITOR
VOLUME MUTE POWER
Come on out!
We want to get your state-ment on the record!

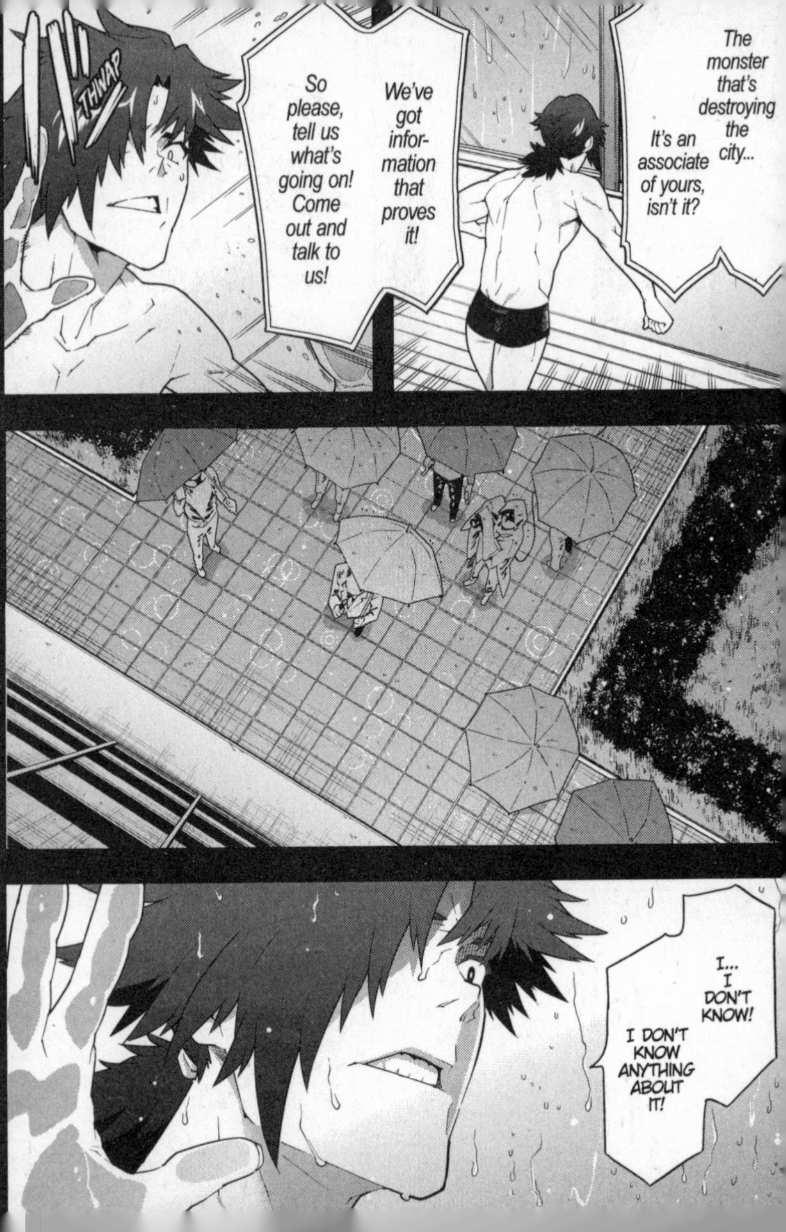

The monster that's destroying the city...
It's an associate of yours, isn't it?
We've got information that proves it!
So please, tell us what's going on! Come out and talk to us!
THWAP
I... I DON'T KNOW!
I DON'T KNOW ANYTHING ABOUT IT!

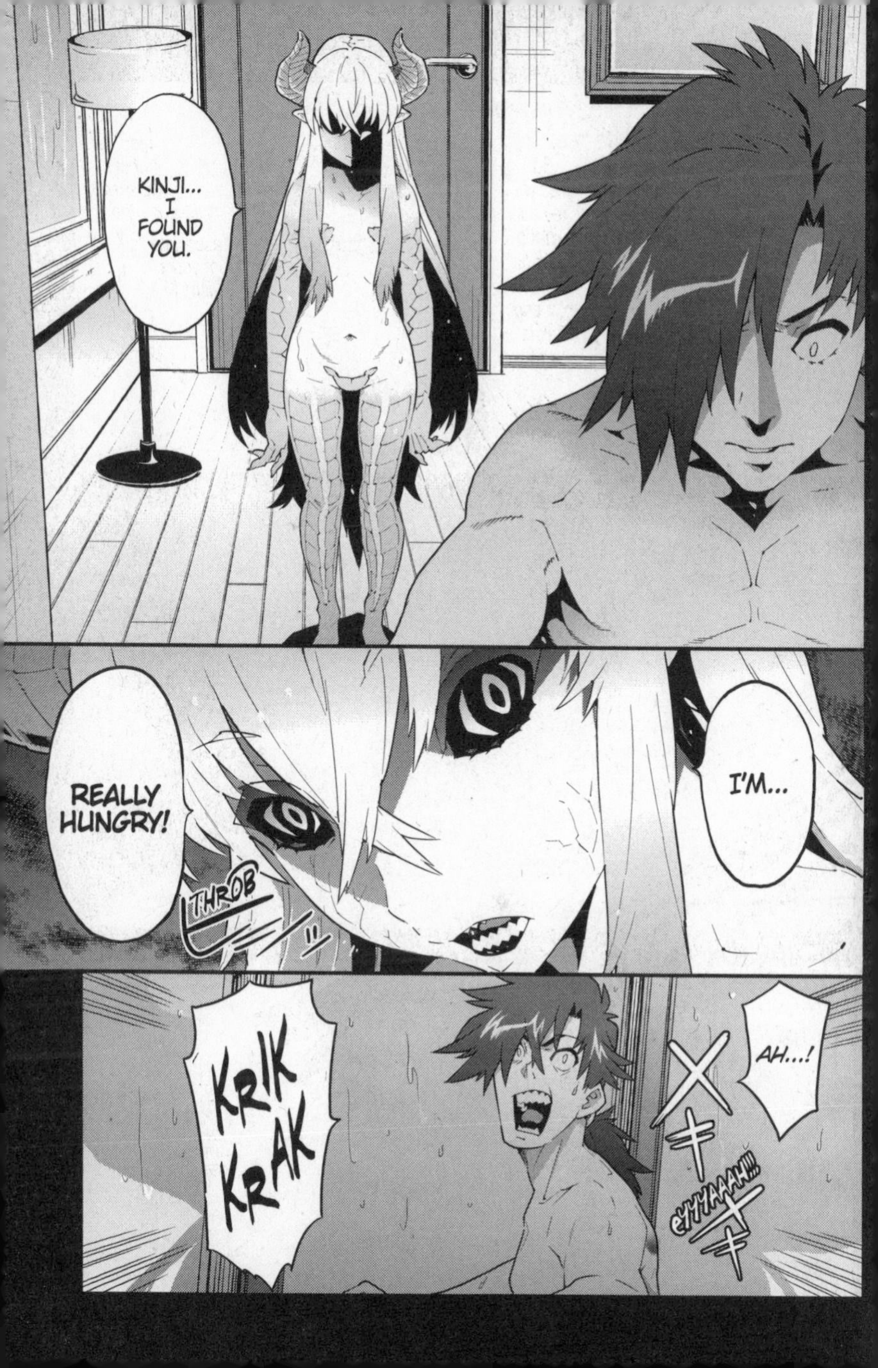
KINJI... I FOUND YOU.
I'M...
REALLY HUNGRY!
THROB
AH...!
KRIK KRAK
EYYYAAAH!!!

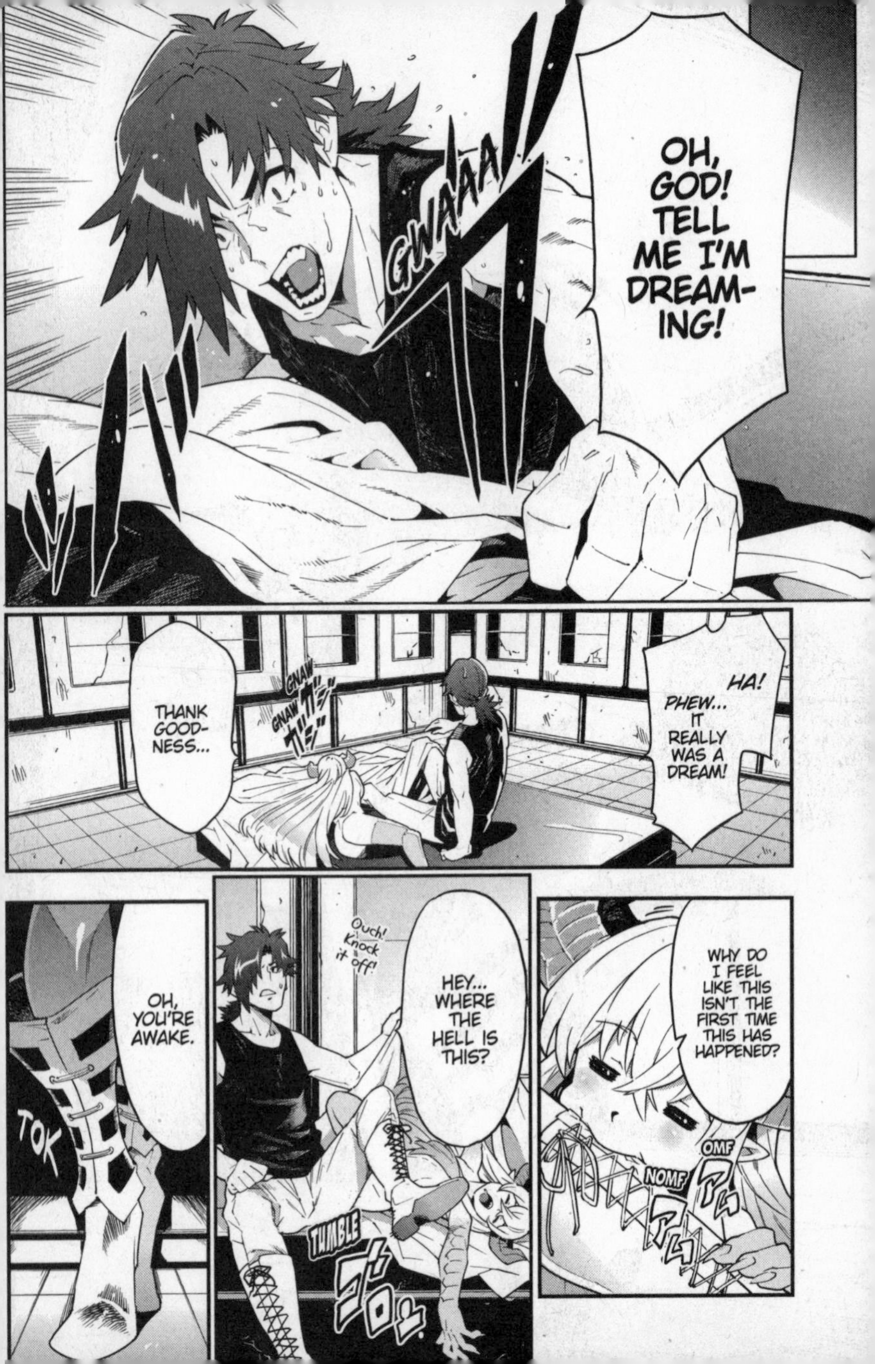
OH, GOD! TELL ME I'M DREAMING!
GWAAA!!
HA! PHEW... IT REALLY WAS A DREAM!
GNAW GNAW
THANK GOODNESS...
WHY DO I FEEL LIKE THIS ISN'T THE FIRST TIME THIS HAS HAPPENED?
OMF
NOMF
HEY... WHERE THE HELL IS THIS?
Ouch! Knock it off!
TUMBLE
OH, YOU'RE AWAKE.
TOK

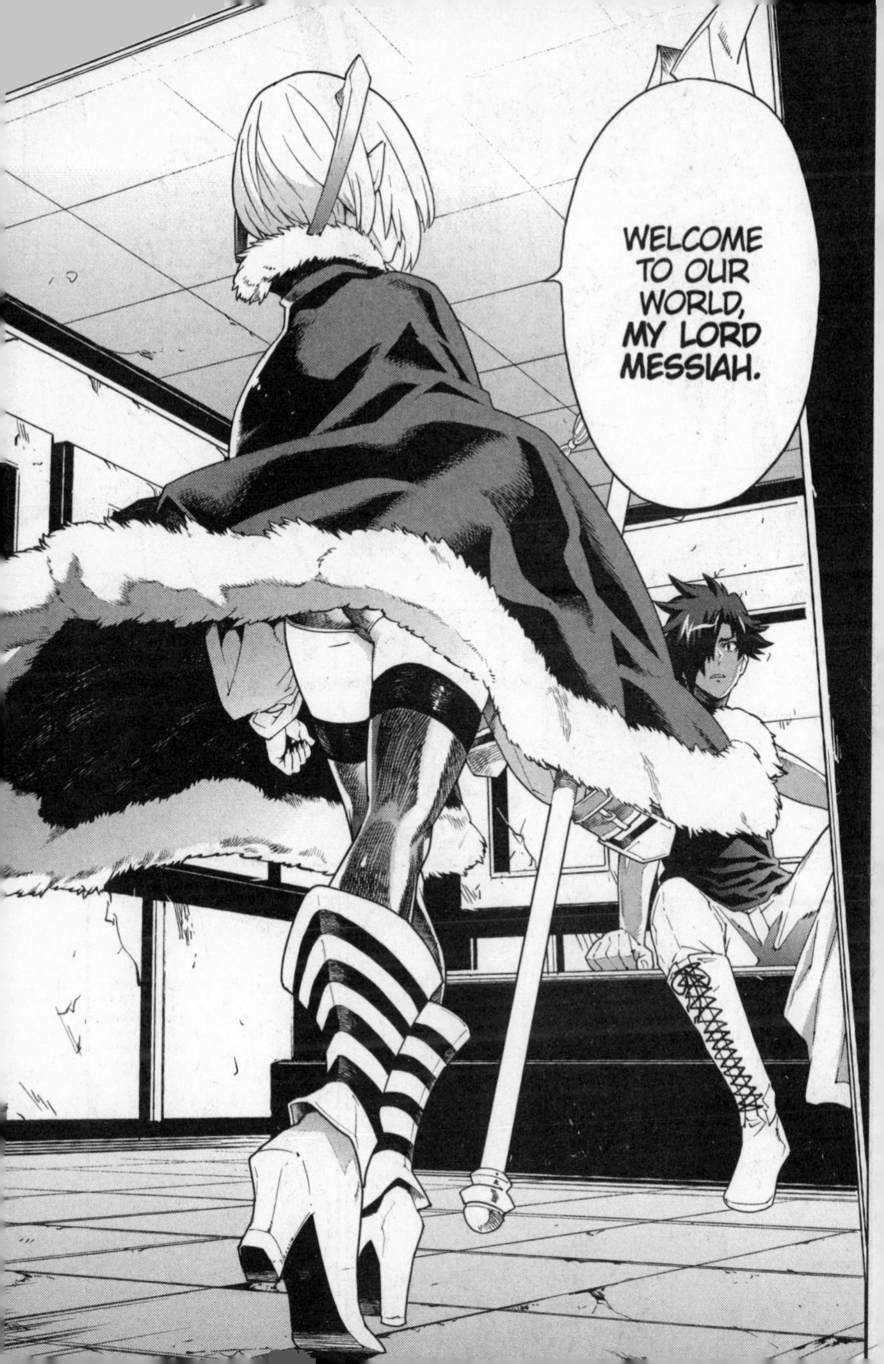
WELCOME TO OUR WORLD, MY LORD MESSIAH.

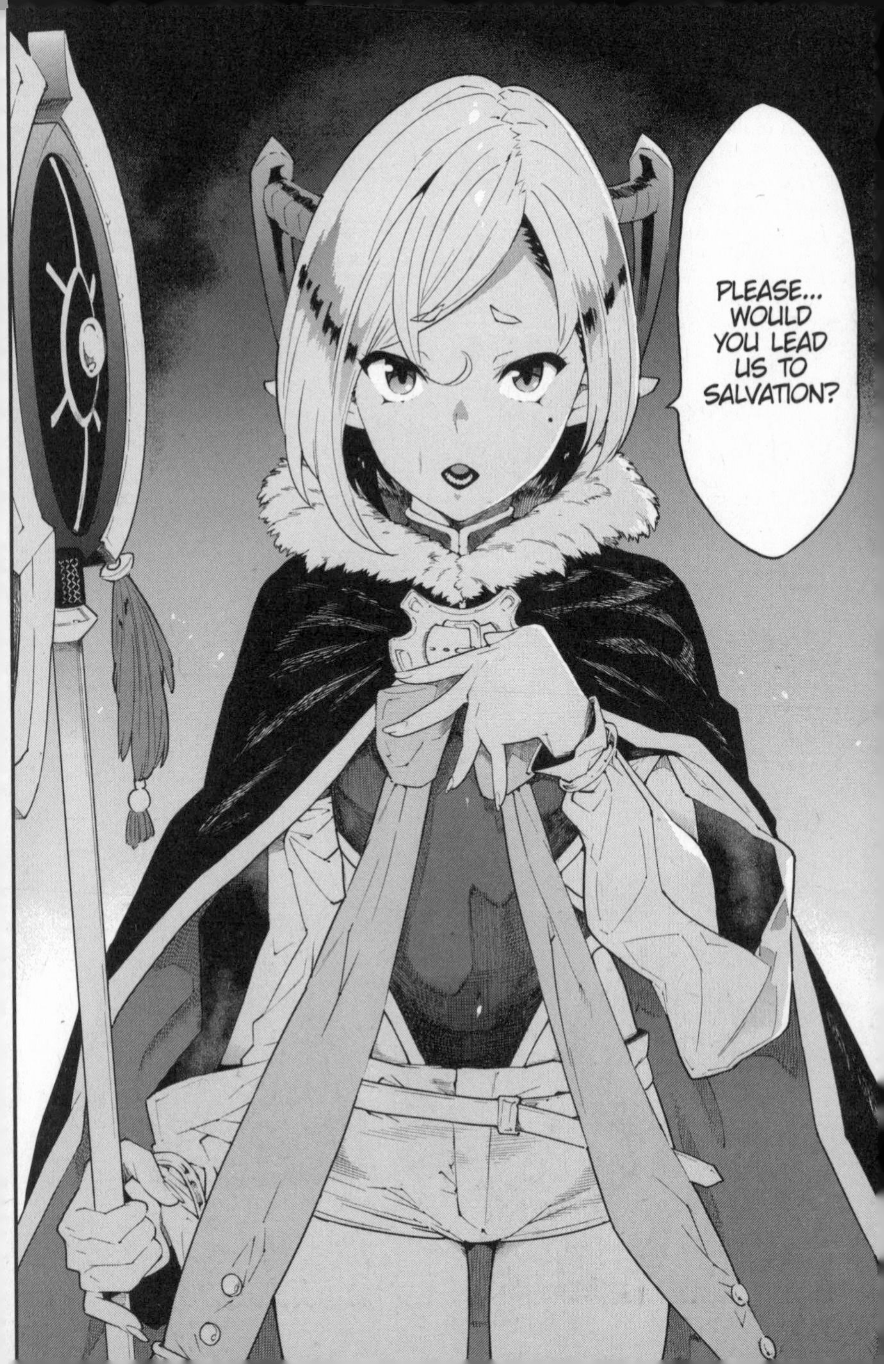
PLEASE... WOULD YOU LEAD US TO SALVATION?

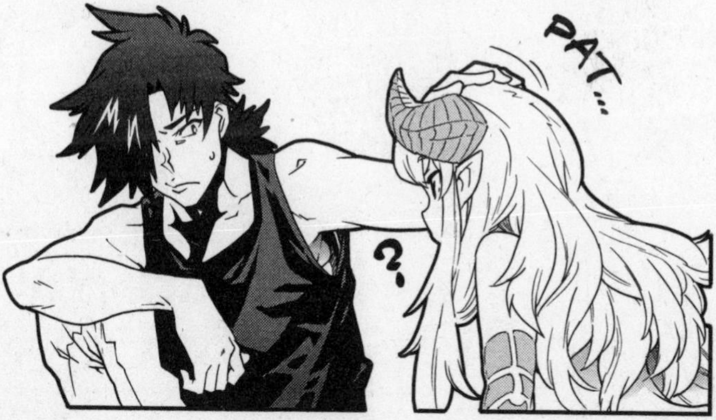
PAT...
?

THE DUNGEON OF
BLACK COMPANY

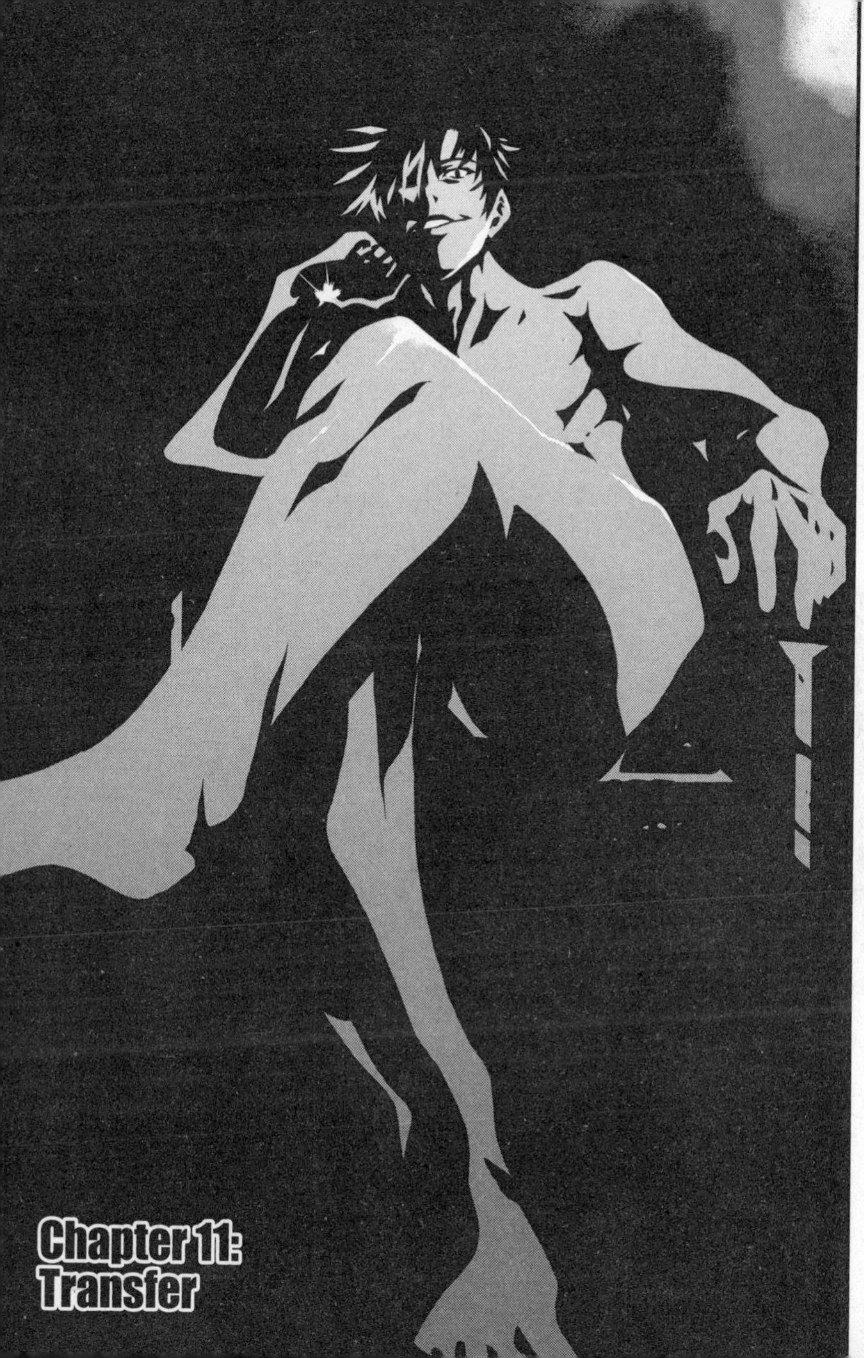

Chapter 11: Transfer

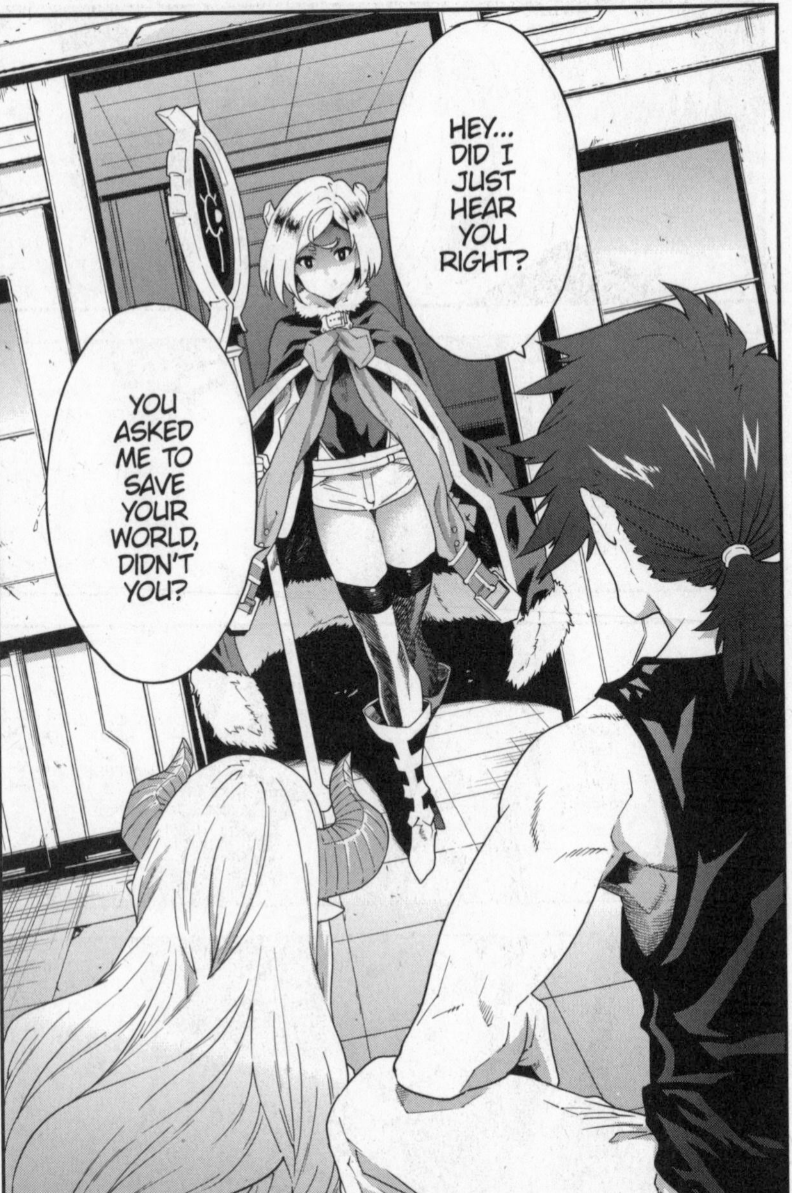
HEY... DID I JUST HEAR YOU RIGHT?
YOU ASKED ME TO SAVE YOUR WORLD, DIDN'T YOU?

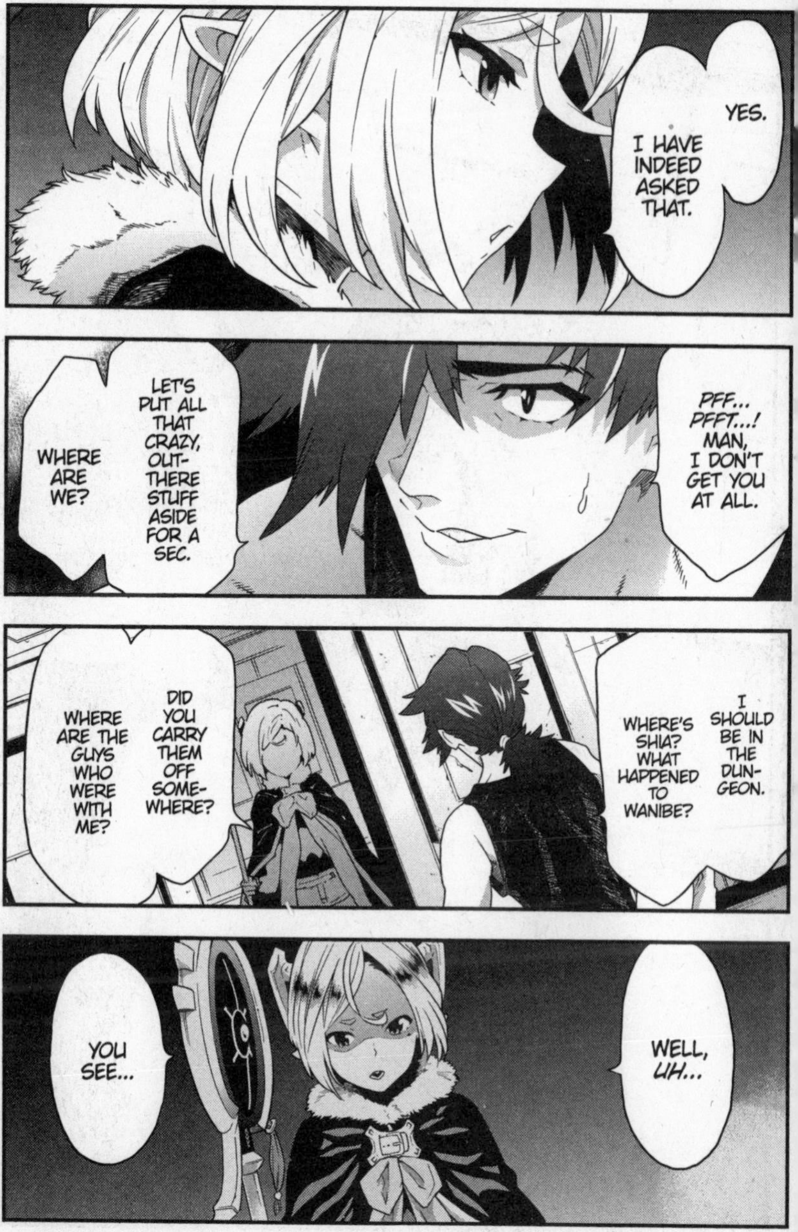
YES.
I HAVE INDEED ASKED THAT.
PFF... PFFT...! MAN, I DON'T GET YOU AT ALL.
LET'S PUT ALL THAT CRAZY, OUT-THERE STUFF ASIDE FOR A SEC.
WHERE ARE WE?
I SHOULD BE IN THE DUNGEON.
WHERE'S SHIA? WHAT HAPPENED TO WANIBE?
DID YOU CARRY THEM OFF SOMEWHERE?
WHERE ARE THE GUYS WHO WERE WITH ME?
WELL, UH...
YOU SEE...

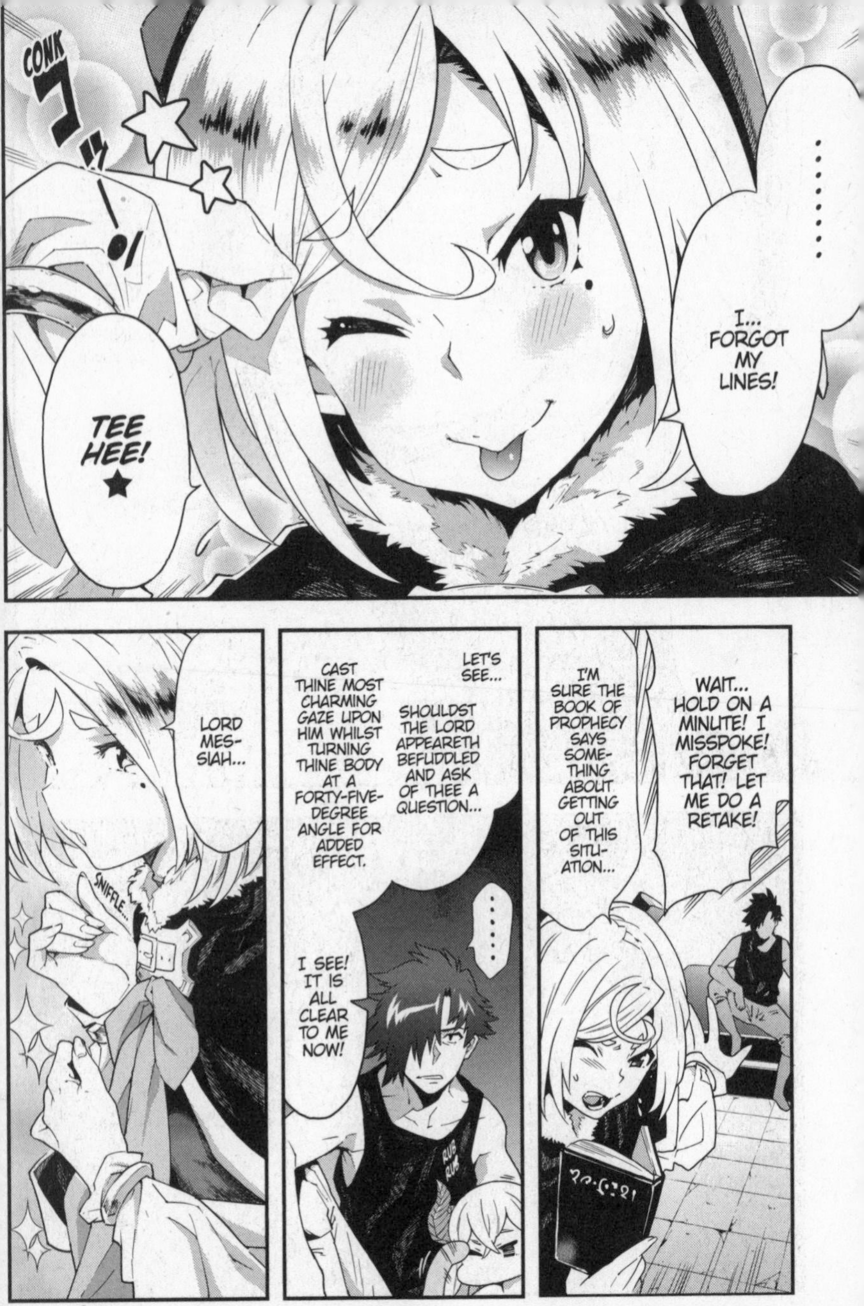
CONK
……
I... FORGOT MY LINES!
TEE HEE! ★
WAIT... HOLD ON A MINUTE! I MISSPOKE! FORGET THAT! LET ME DO A RETAKE!
I'M SURE THE BOOK OF PROPHECY SAYS SOMETHING ABOUT GETTING OUT OF THIS SITUATION...
LET'S SEE...
SHOULDST THE LORD APPEARETH BEFUDDLED AND ASK OF THEE A QUESTION...
CAST THINE MOST CHARMING GAZE UPON HIM WHILST TURNING THINE BODY AT A FORTY-FIVE-DEGREE ANGLE FOR ADDED EFFECT.
……
I SEE! IT IS ALL CLEAR TO ME NOW!
RUB RUB
LORD MESSIAH...
SNIFFLE...

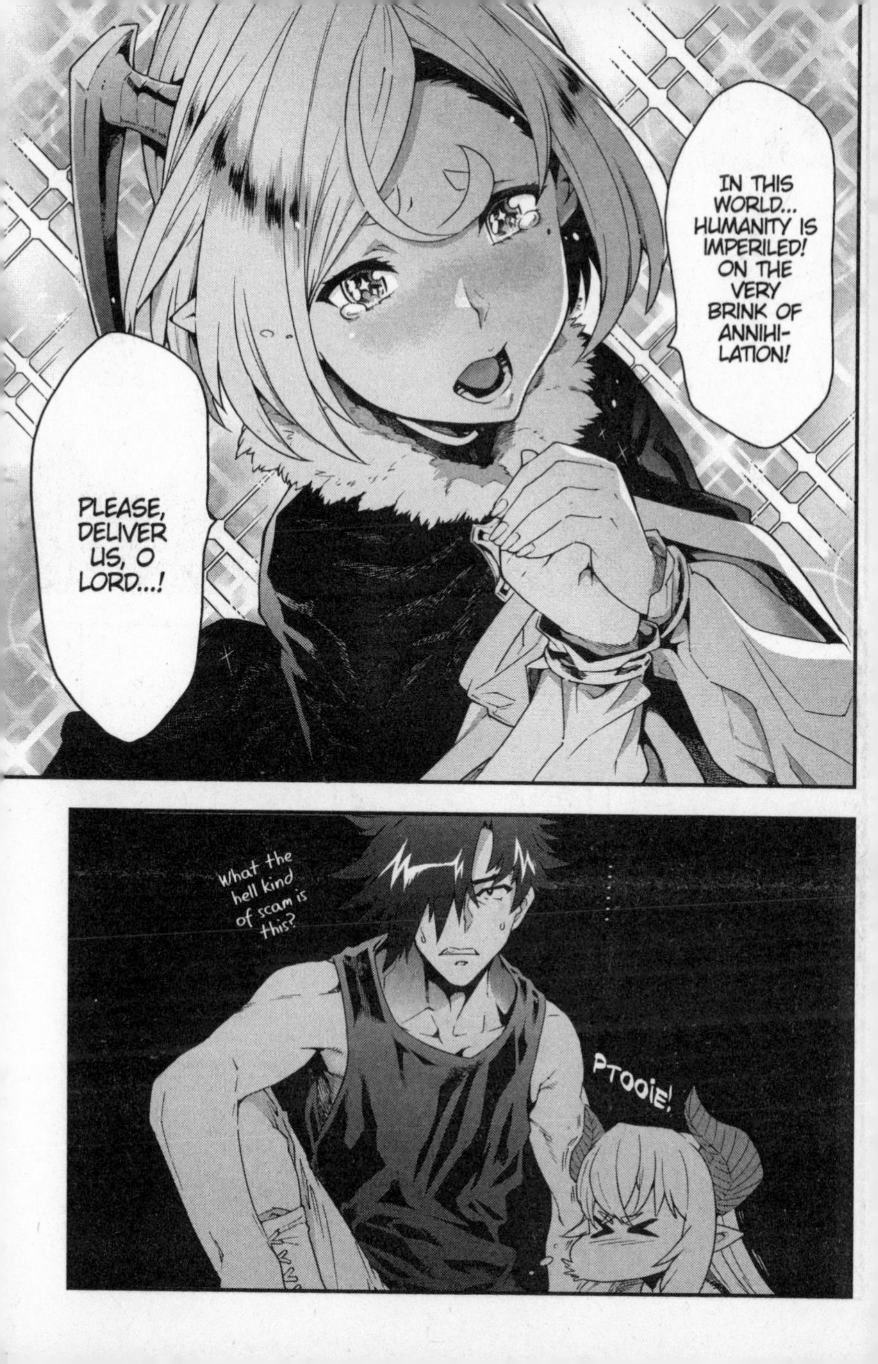
IN THIS WORLD... HUMANITY IS IMPERILED! ON THE VERY BRINK OF ANNIHI-LATION!
PLEASE, DELIVER US, O LORD...!
PTOOIE!
What the hell kind of scam is this?

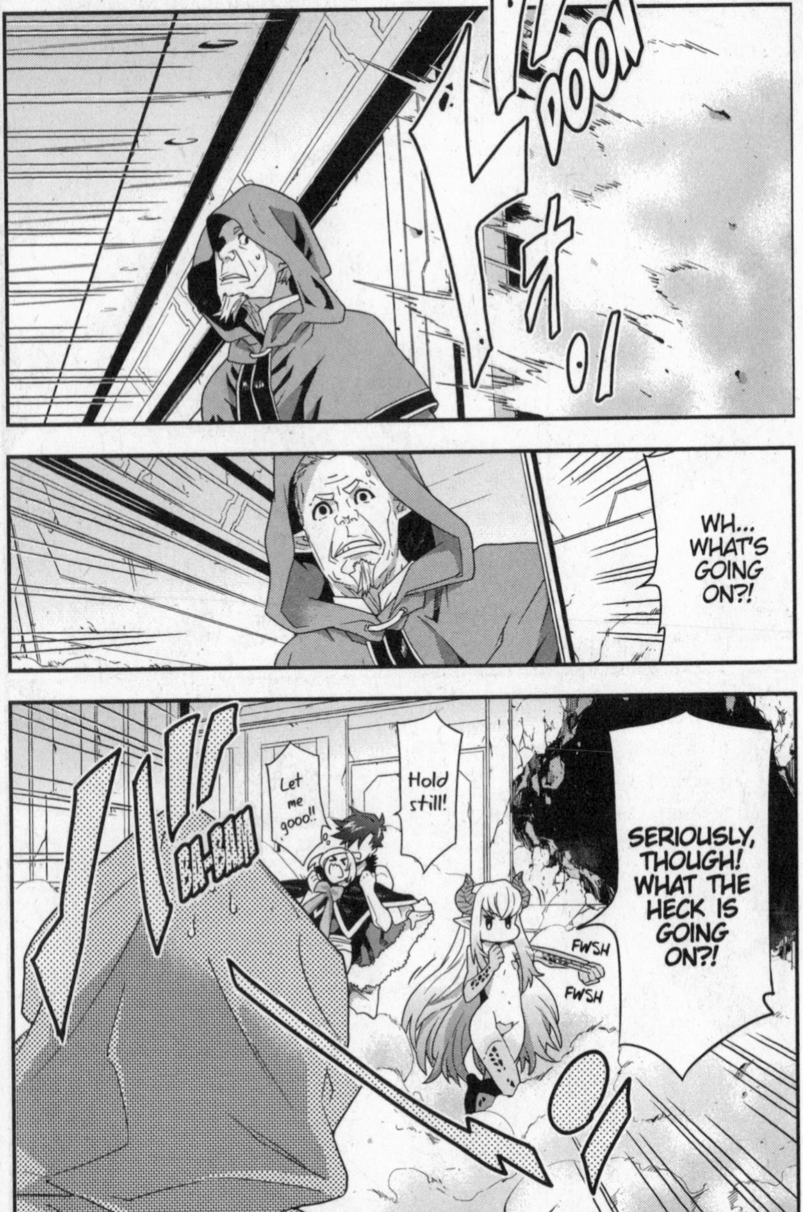
DOOON
WH... WHAT'S GOING ON?!
SERIOUSLY, THOUGH! WHAT THE HECK IS GOING ON?!
Hold still!
Let me gooo!!
FWSH
FWSH
BA-BAM

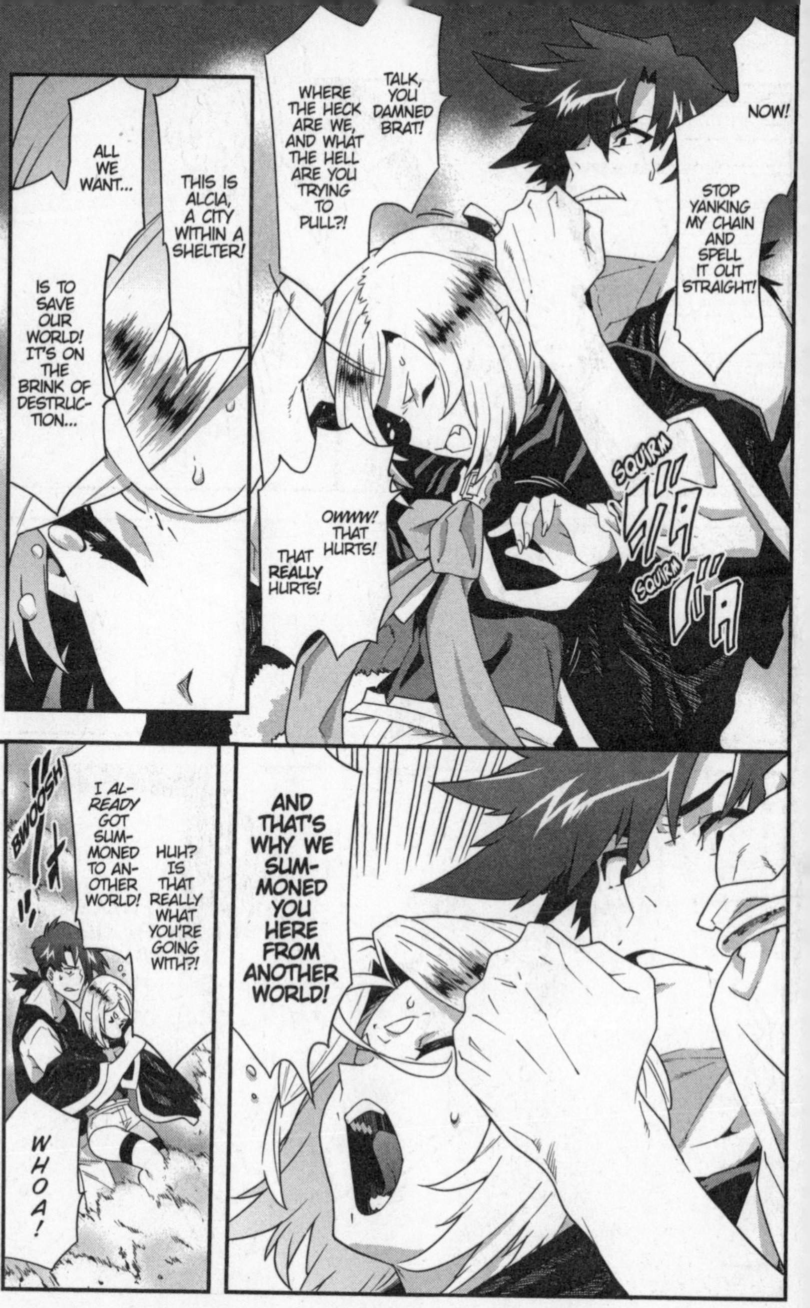
NOW!
STOP YANKING MY CHAIN AND SPELL IT OUT STRAIGHT!
TALK, YOU DAMNED BRAT!
WHERE THE HECK ARE WE, AND WHAT THE HELL ARE YOU TRYING TO PULL?!
SQUIRM
SQUIRM
OWWW! THAT HURTS!
THAT REALLY HURTS!
THIS IS ALCIA, A CITY WITHIN A SHELTER!
ALL WE WANT...
IS TO SAVE OUR WORLD! IT'S ON THE BRINK OF DESTRUCTION...
AND THAT'S WHY WE SUMMONED YOU HERE FROM ANOTHER WORLD!
HUH? IS THAT REALLY WHAT YOU'RE GOING WITH?!
I ALREADY GOT SUMMONED TO ANOTHER WORLD!
BWOOSH
WHOA!

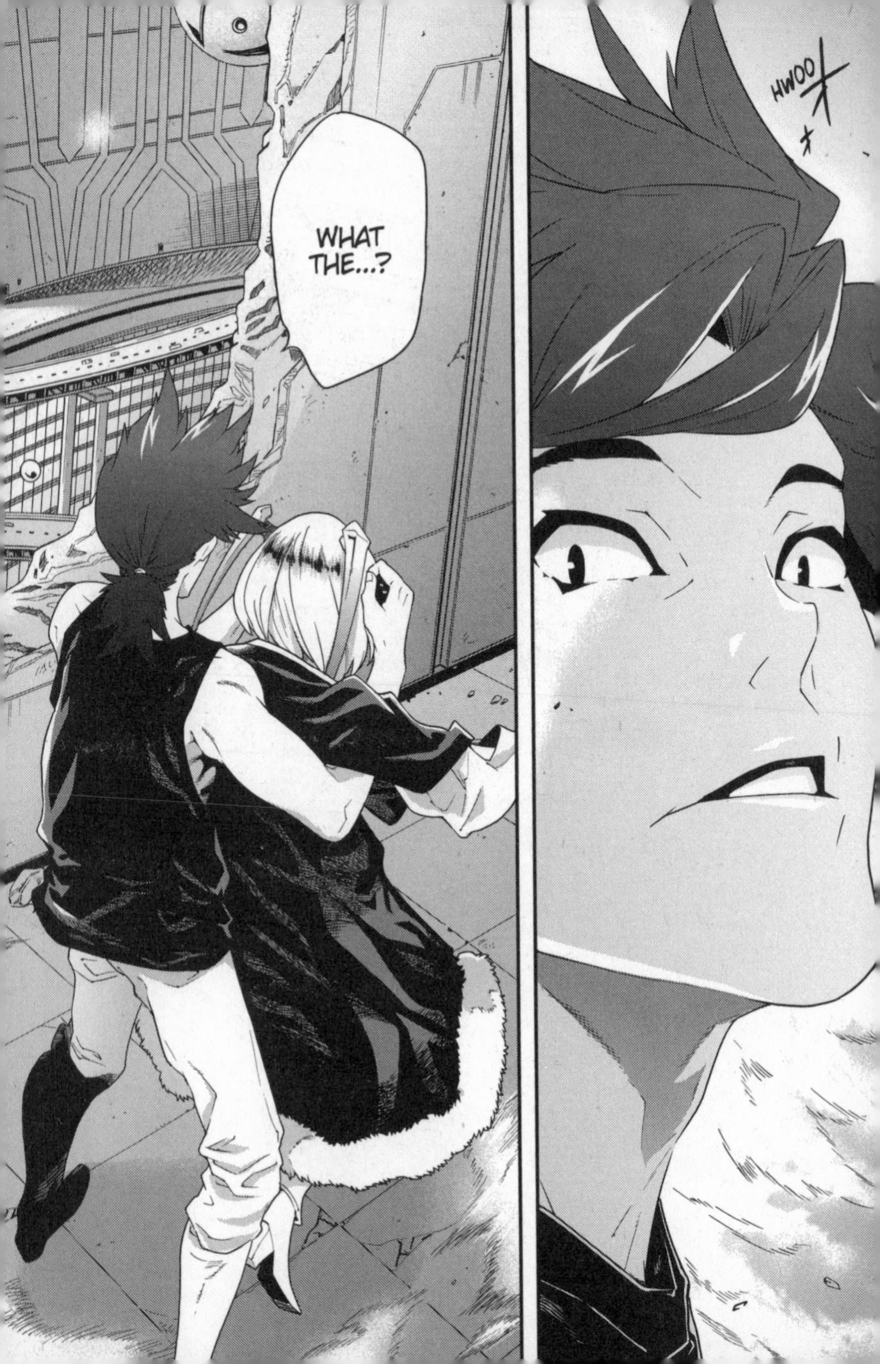
HWOO
WHAT THE...?

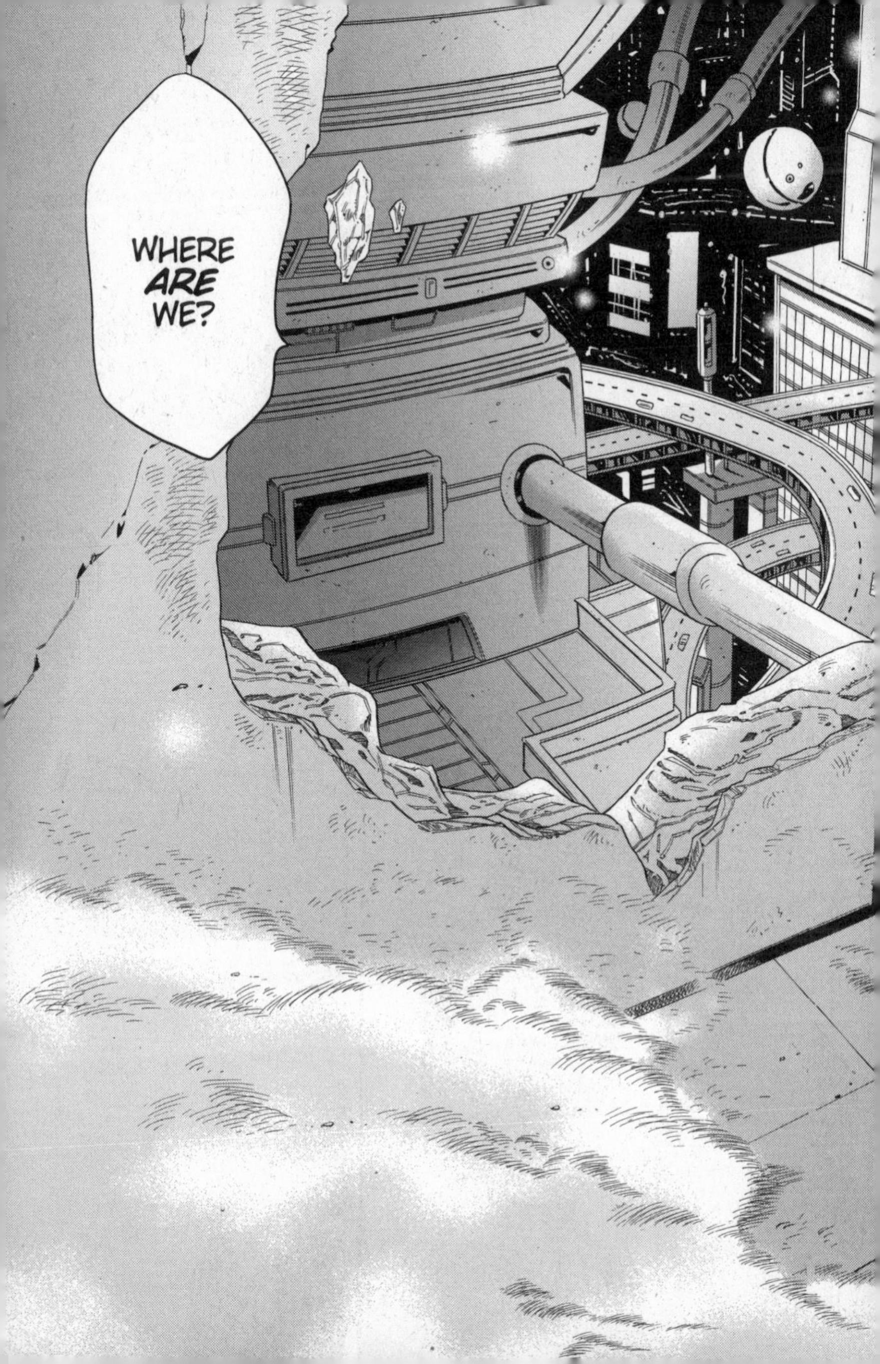
WHERE ARE WE?

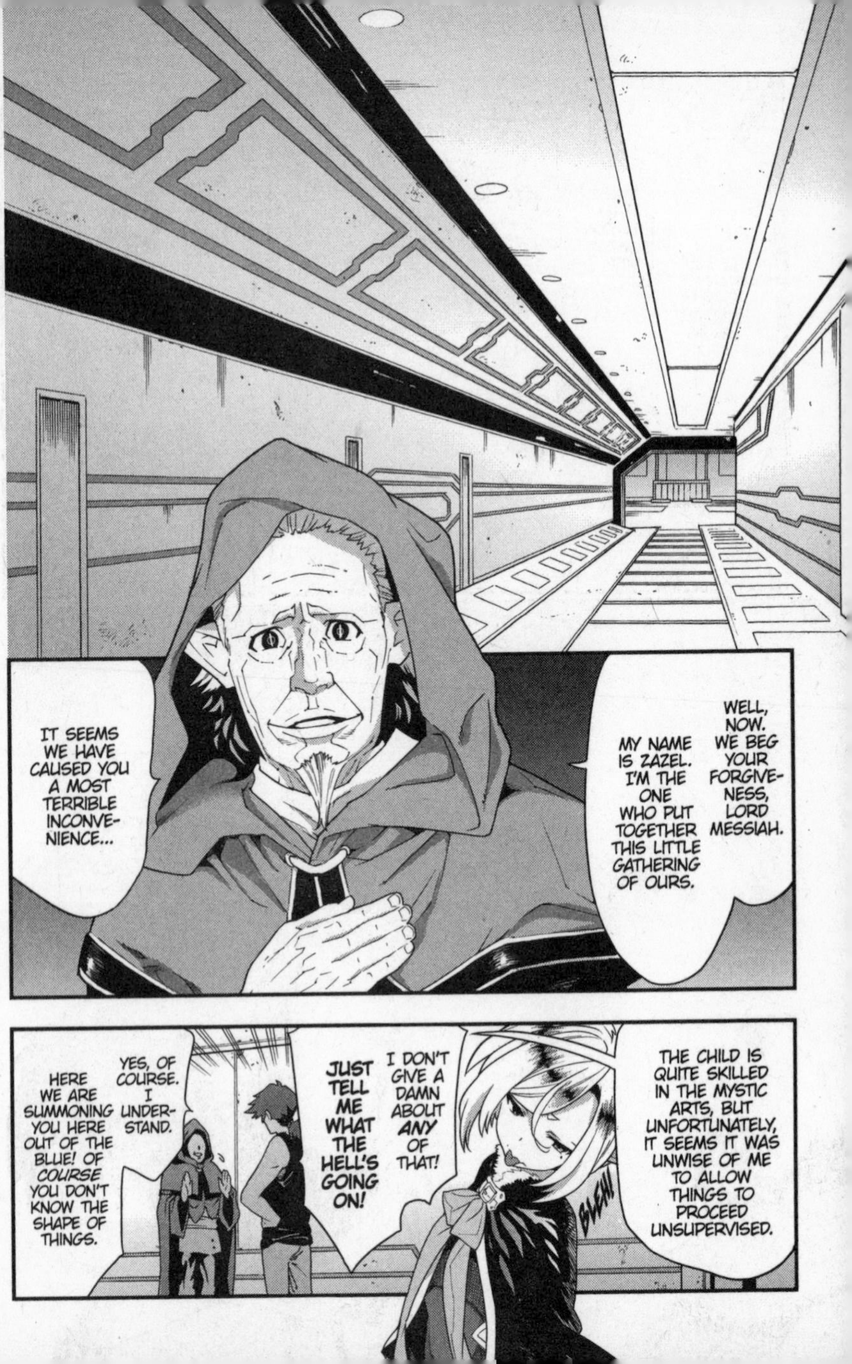
WELL, NOW. WE BEG YOUR FORGIVENESS, LORD MESSIAH.
MY NAME IS ZAZEL. I'M THE ONE WHO PUT TOGETHER THIS LITTLE GATHERING OF OURS.
IT SEEMS WE HAVE CAUSED YOU A MOST TERRIBLE INCONVENIENCE...
THE CHILD IS QUITE SKILLED IN THE MYSTIC ARTS, BUT UNFORTUNATELY, IT SEEMS IT WAS UNWISE OF ME TO ALLOW THINGS TO PROCEED UNSUPERVISED.
BLEH!
I DON'T GIVE A DAMN ABOUT *ANY* OF THAT!
JUST TELL ME WHAT THE HELL'S GOING ON!
YES, OF COURSE. I UNDERSTAND.
HERE WE ARE SUMMONING YOU HERE OUT OF THE BLUE! OF *COURSE* YOU DON'T KNOW THE SHAPE OF THINGS.

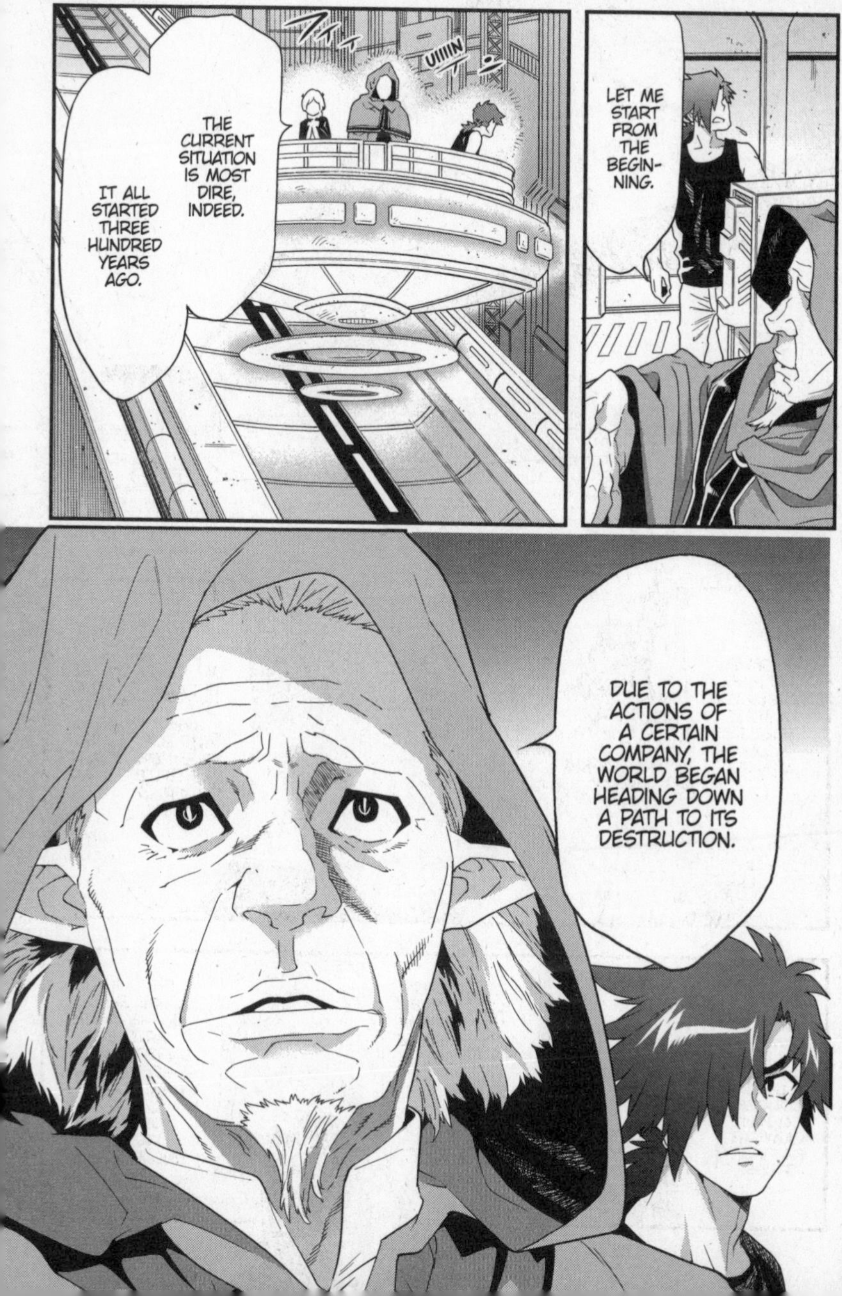
LET ME START FROM THE BEGIN-NING.
UIIIIN
THE CURRENT SITUATION IS MOST DIRE, INDEED.
IT ALL STARTED THREE HUNDRED YEARS AGO.
DUE TO THE ACTIONS OF A CERTAIN COMPANY, THE WORLD BEGAN HEADING DOWN A PATH TO ITS DESTRUCTION.

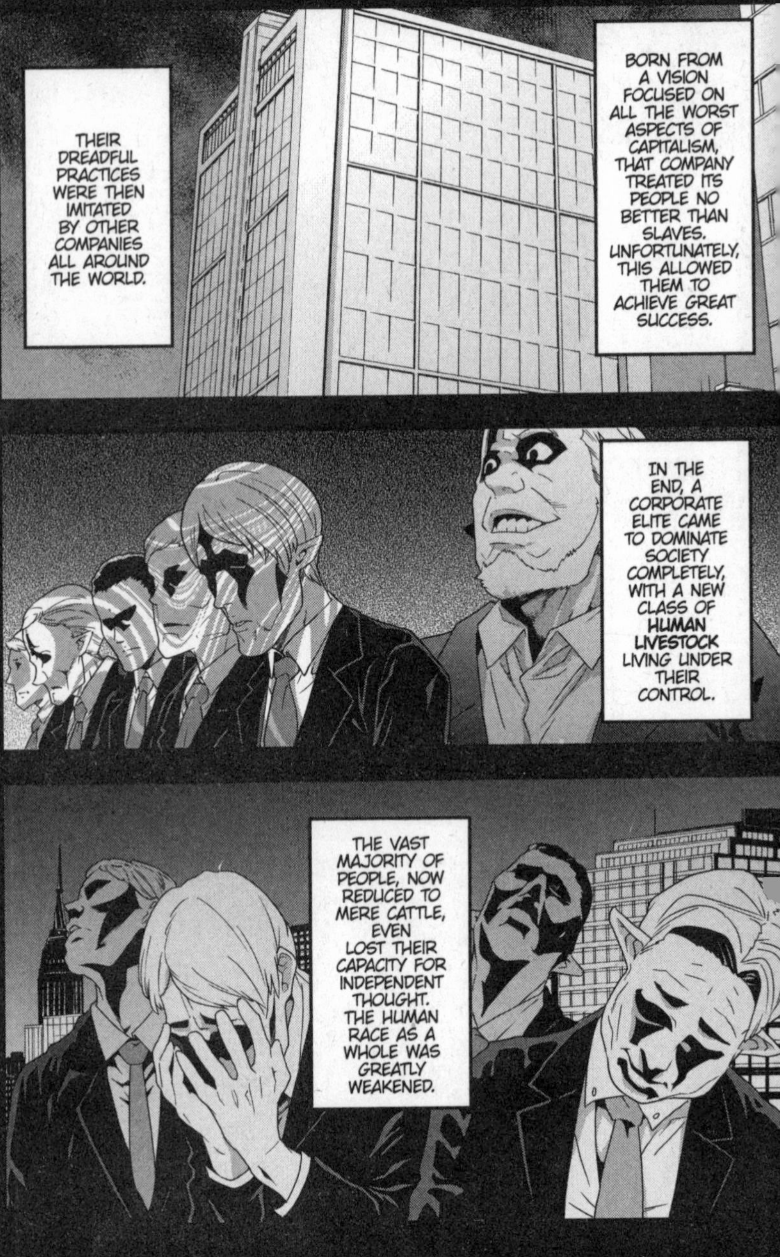
BORN FROM A VISION FOCUSED ON ALL THE WORST ASPECTS OF CAPITALISM, THAT COMPANY TREATED ITS PEOPLE NO BETTER THAN SLAVES. UNFORTUNATELY, THIS ALLOWED THEM TO ACHIEVE GREAT SUCCESS.
THEIR DREADFUL PRACTICES WERE THEN IMITATED BY OTHER COMPANIES ALL AROUND THE WORLD.
IN THE END, A CORPORATE ELITE CAME TO DOMINATE SOCIETY COMPLETELY, WITH A NEW CLASS OF **HUMAN LIVESTOCK** LIVING UNDER THEIR CONTROL.
THE VAST MAJORITY OF PEOPLE, NOW REDUCED TO MERE CATTLE, EVEN LOST THEIR CAPACITY FOR INDEPENDENT THOUGHT. THE HUMAN RACE AS A WHOLE WAS GREATLY WEAKENED.

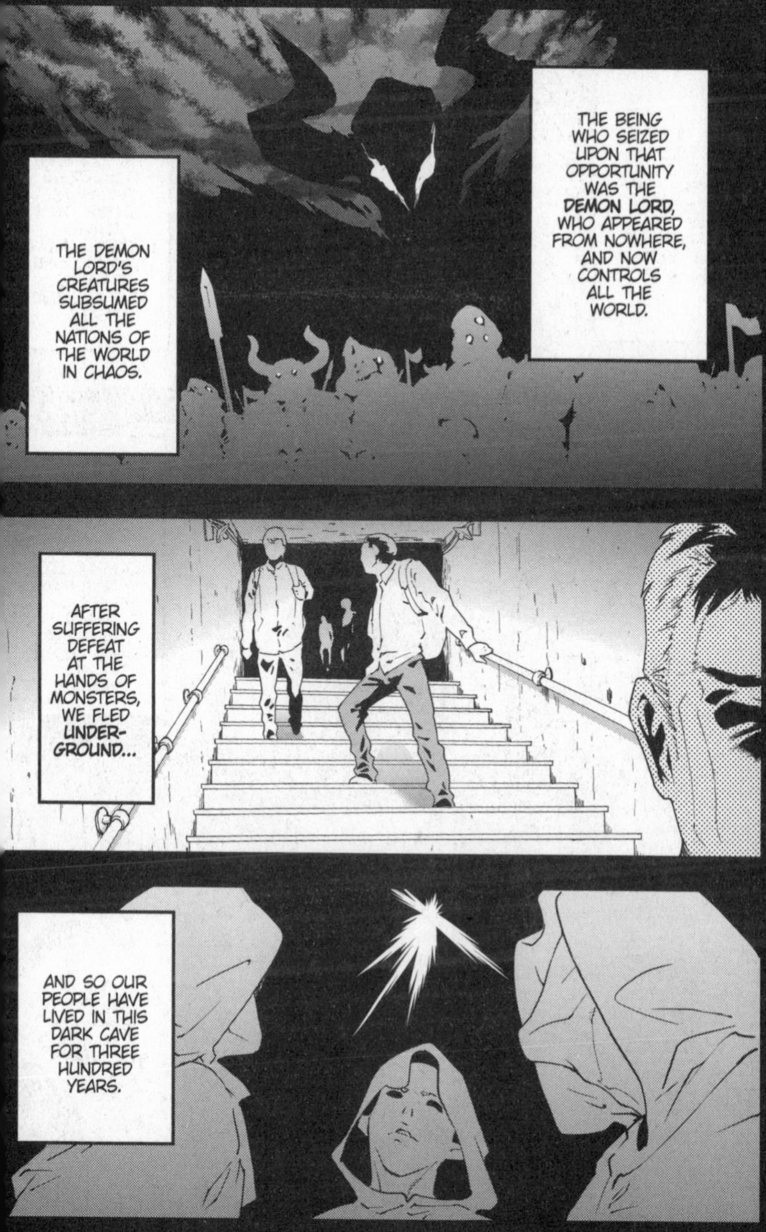
THE BEING WHO SEIZED UPON THAT OPPORTUNITY WAS THE **DEMON LORD**, WHO APPEARED FROM NOWHERE, AND NOW CONTROLS ALL THE WORLD.
THE DEMON LORD'S CREATURES SUBSUMED ALL THE NATIONS OF THE WORLD IN CHAOS.
AFTER SUFFERING DEFEAT AT THE HANDS OF MONSTERS, WE FLED **UNDER-GROUND...**
AND SO OUR PEOPLE HAVE LIVED IN THIS DARK CAVE FOR THREE HUNDRED YEARS.

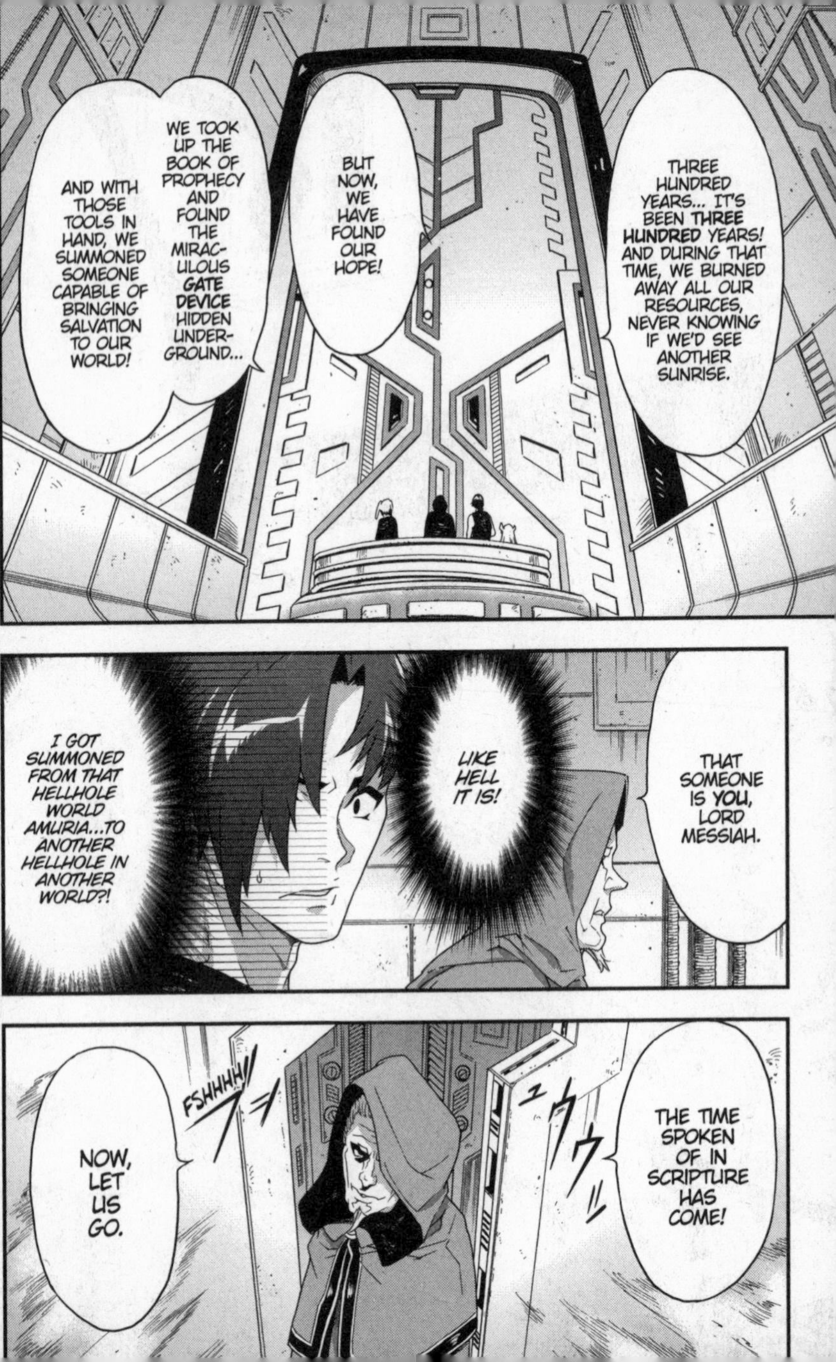
THREE HUNDRED YEARS... IT'S BEEN THREE HUNDRED YEARS! AND DURING THAT TIME, WE BURNED AWAY ALL OUR RESOURCES, NEVER KNOWING IF WE'D SEE ANOTHER SUNRISE.
BUT NOW, WE HAVE FOUND OUR HOPE!
WE TOOK UP THE BOOK OF PROPHECY AND FOUND THE MIRACULOUS GATE DEVICE HIDDEN UNDERGROUND...
AND WITH THOSE TOOLS IN HAND, WE SUMMONED SOMEONE CAPABLE OF BRINGING SALVATION TO OUR WORLD!
THAT SOMEONE IS YOU, LORD MESSIAH.
LIKE HELL IT IS!
I GOT SUMMONED FROM THAT HELLHOLE WORLD AMURIA...TO ANOTHER HELLHOLE IN ANOTHER WORLD?!
THE TIME SPOKEN OF IN SCRIPTURE HAS COME!
FSHHHH!!
NOW, LET US GO.

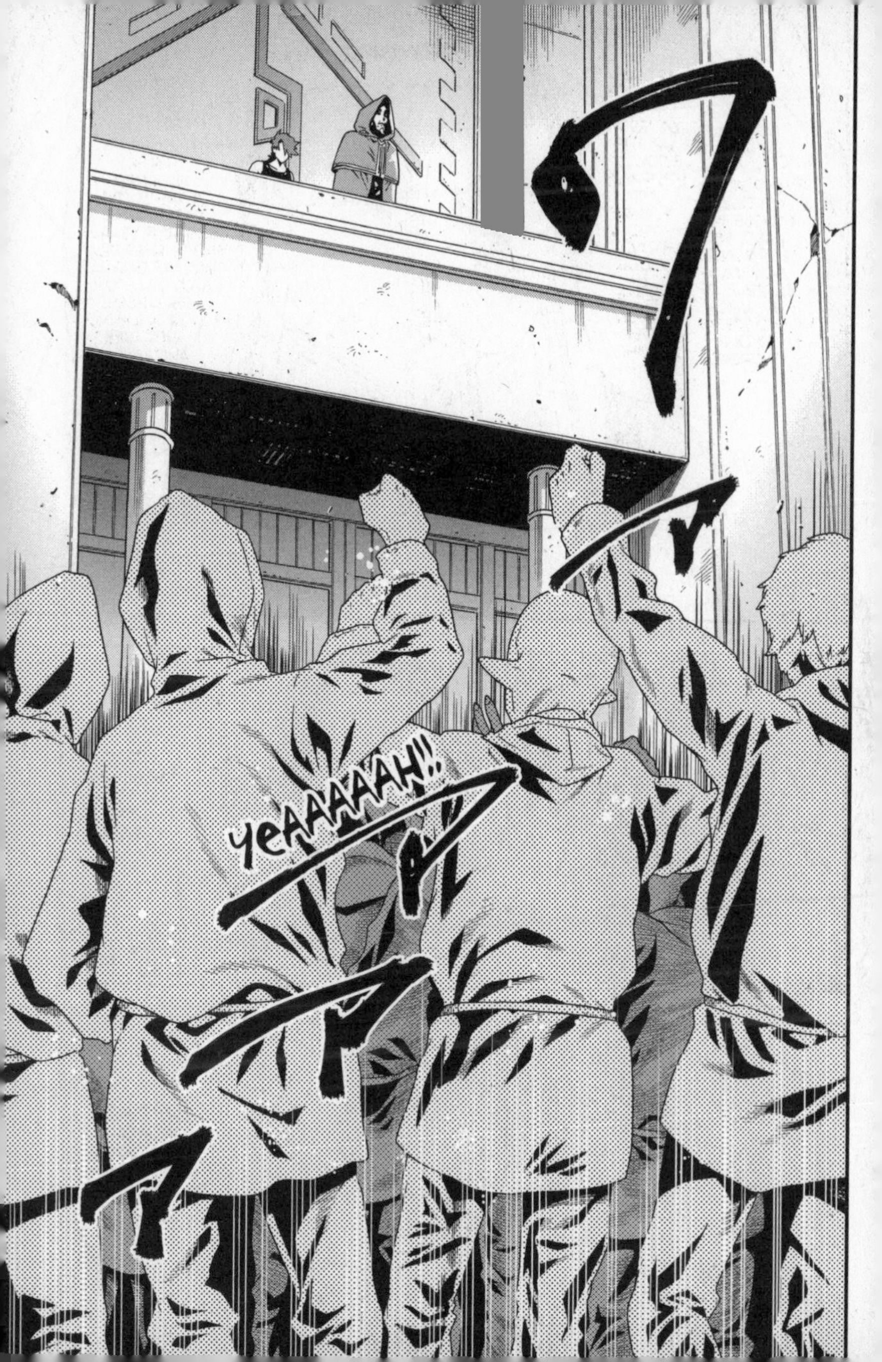
YeAAAAAH!!

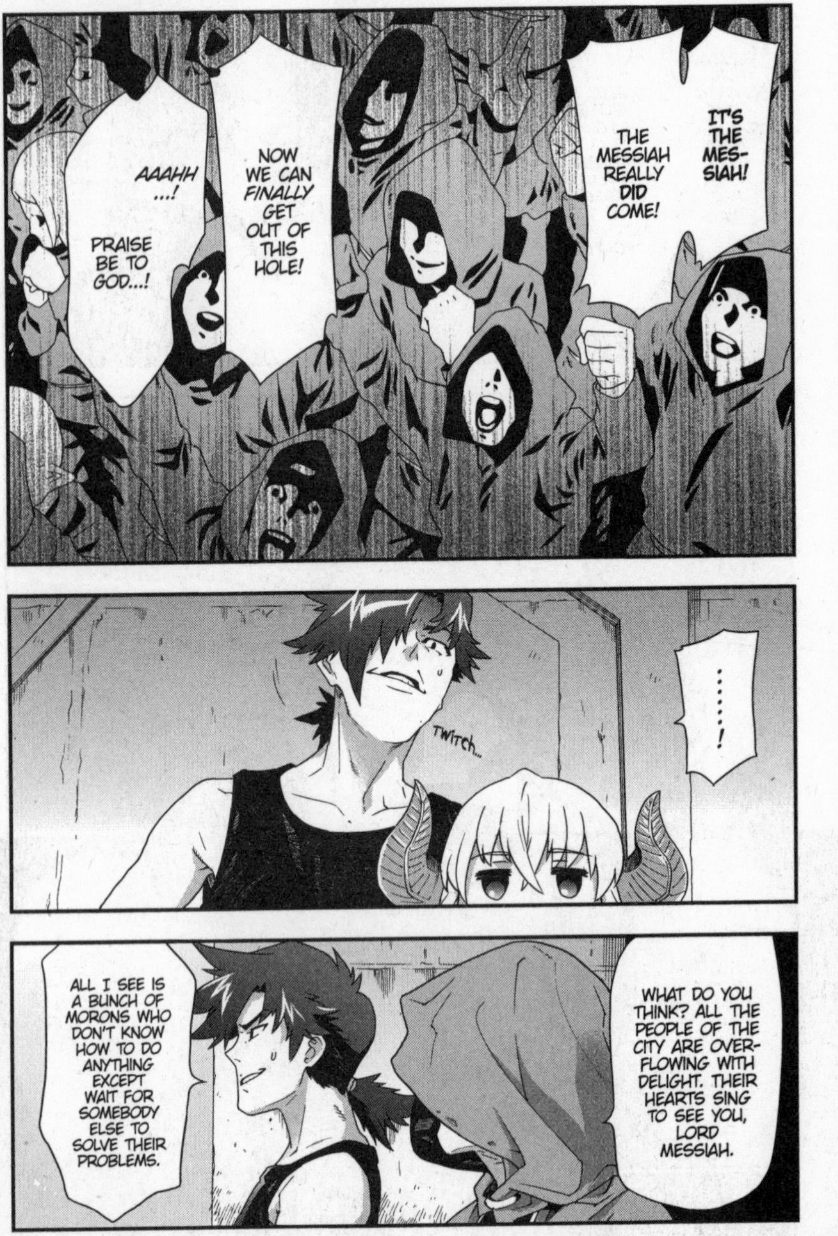
IT'S THE MES-SIAH!
THE MESSIAH REALLY DID COME!
NOW WE CAN FINALLY GET OUT OF THIS HOLE!
AAAHH ...!
PRAISE BE TO GOD...!
......!
Twitch...
WHAT DO YOU THINK? ALL THE PEOPLE OF THE CITY ARE OVER-FLOWING WITH DELIGHT. THEIR HEARTS SING TO SEE YOU, LORD MESSIAH.
ALL I SEE IS A BUNCH OF MORONS WHO DON'T KNOW HOW TO DO ANYTHING EXCEPT WAIT FOR SOMEBODY ELSE TO SOLVE THEIR PROBLEMS.

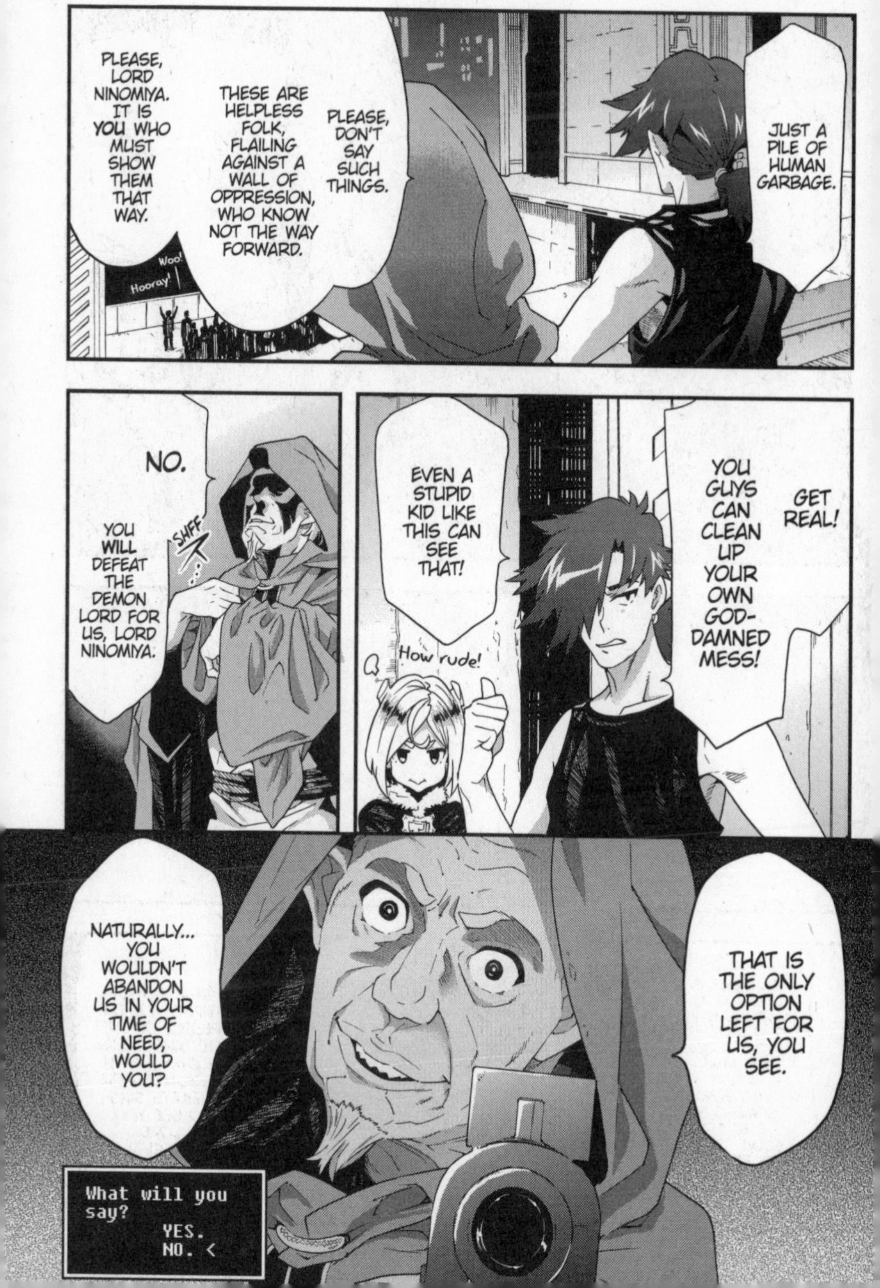
JUST A PILE OF HUMAN GARBAGE.
PLEASE, DON'T SAY SUCH THINGS.
THESE ARE HELPLESS FOLK, FLAILING AGAINST A WALL OF OPPRESSION, WHO KNOW NOT THE WAY FORWARD.
PLEASE, LORD NINOMIYA. IT IS YOU WHO MUST SHOW THEM THAT WAY.
Woo!
Hooray!
GET REAL!
YOU GUYS CAN CLEAN UP YOUR OWN GOD-DAMNED MESS!
EVEN A STUPID KID LIKE THIS CAN SEE THAT!
How rude!
NO.
SHFF
YOU WILL DEFEAT THE DEMON LORD FOR US, LORD NINOMIYA.
THAT IS THE ONLY OPTION LEFT FOR US, YOU SEE.
NATURALLY... YOU WOULDN'T ABANDON US IN YOUR TIME OF NEED, WOULD YOU?
What will you say?
YES.
NO. <

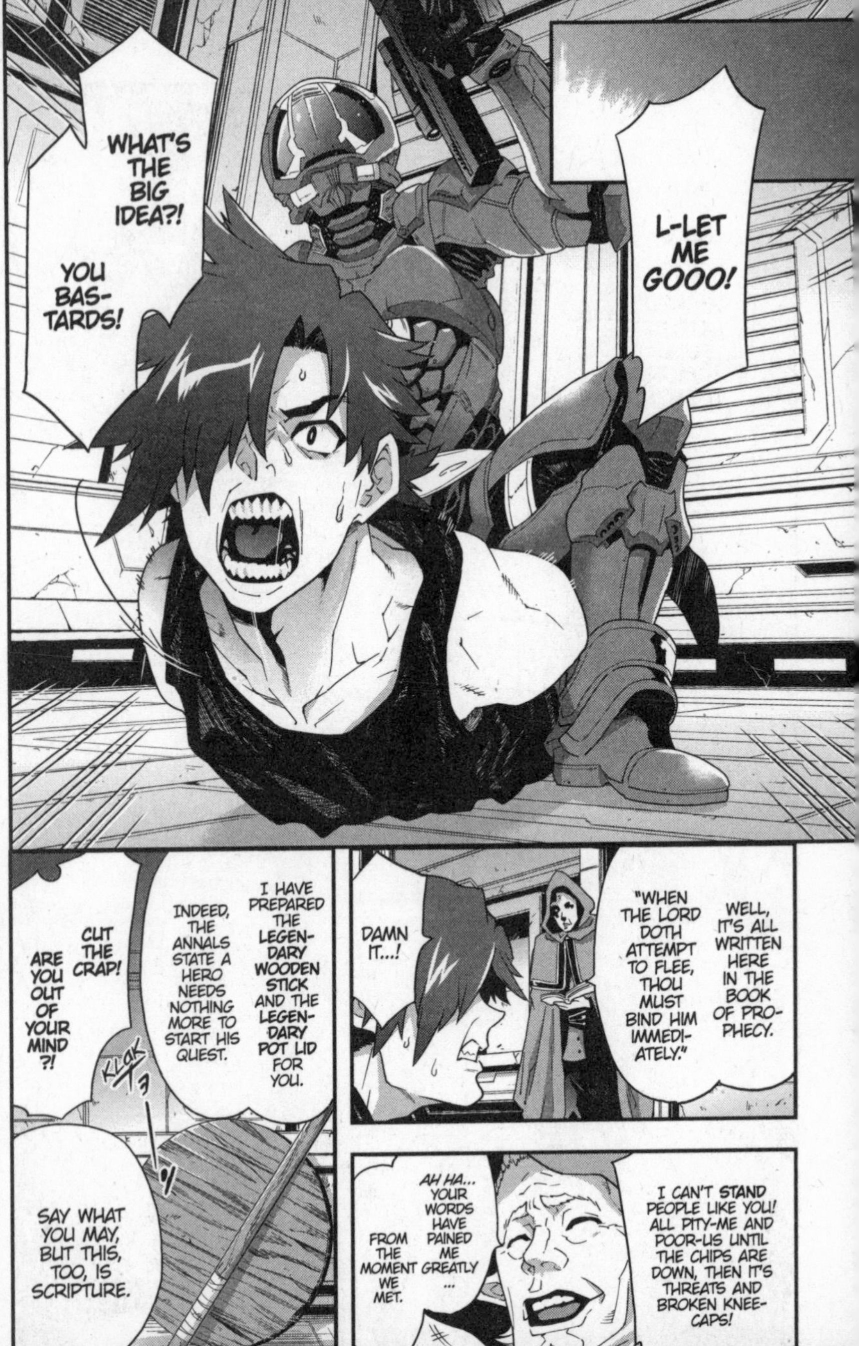
L-LET ME GOOO!
WHAT'S THE BIG IDEA?!
YOU BASTARDS!
WELL, IT'S ALL WRITTEN HERE IN THE BOOK OF PROPHECY.
"WHEN THE LORD DOTH ATTEMPT TO FLEE, THOU MUST BIND HIM IMMEDIATELY."
DAMN IT...!
I HAVE PREPARED THE LEGENDARY WOODEN STICK AND THE LEGENDARY POT LID FOR YOU.
INDEED, THE ANNALS STATE A HERO NEEDS NOTHING MORE TO START HIS QUEST.
CUT THE CRAP!
ARE YOU OUT OF YOUR MIND?!
KLAK
SAY WHAT YOU MAY, BUT THIS, TOO, IS SCRIPTURE.
I CAN'T STAND PEOPLE LIKE YOU! ALL PITY-ME AND POOR-US UNTIL THE CHIPS ARE DOWN, THEN IT'S THREATS AND BROKEN KNEECAPS!
AH HA... YOUR WORDS HAVE PAINED ME GREATLY...
FROM THE MOMENT WE MET.

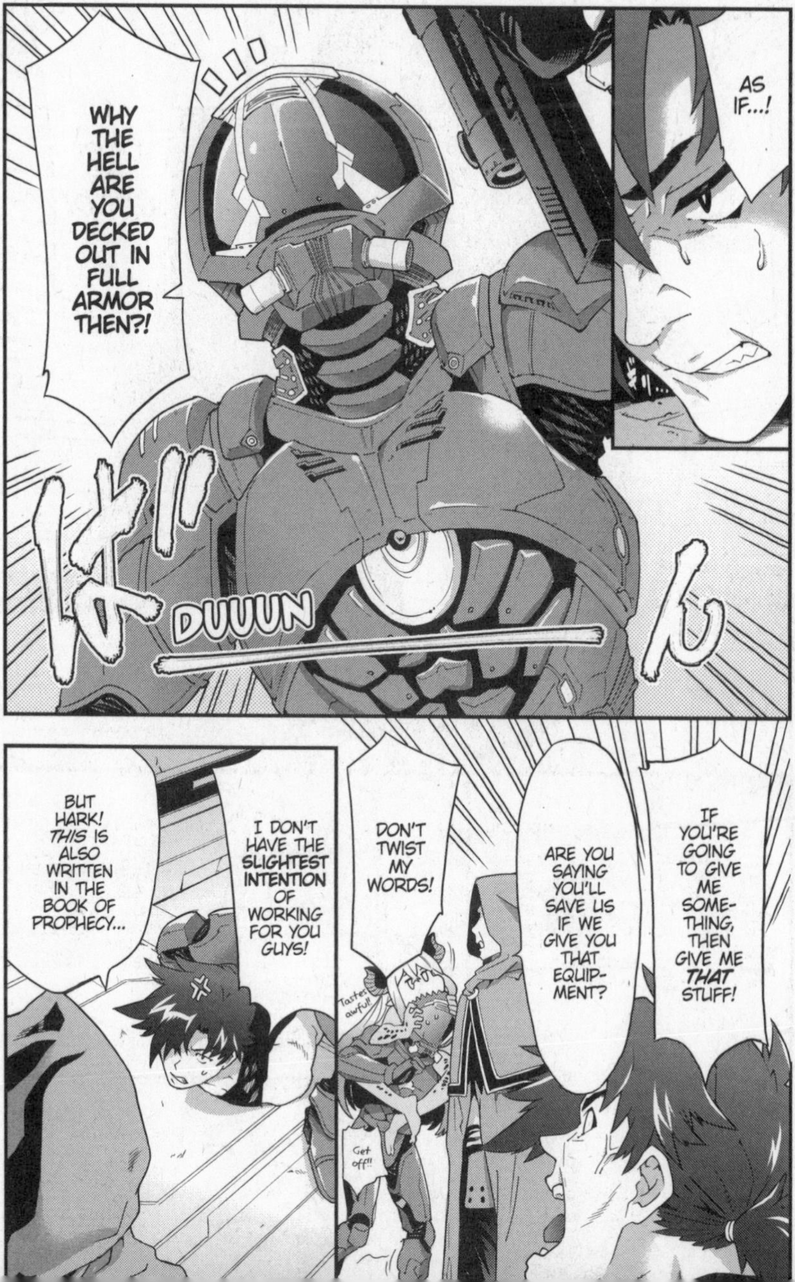
AS IF...!
...
WHY THE HELL ARE YOU DECKED OUT IN FULL ARMOR THEN?!
DUUUN
IF YOU'RE GOING TO GIVE ME SOMETHING, THEN GIVE ME *THAT* STUFF!
ARE YOU SAYING YOU'LL SAVE US IF WE GIVE YOU THAT EQUIPMENT?
DON'T TWIST MY WORDS!
Tastes awful!
Get off!!
I DON'T HAVE THE **SLIGHTEST INTENTION** OF WORKING FOR YOU GUYS!
BUT HARK! *THIS* IS ALSO WRITTEN IN THE BOOK OF PROPHECY...

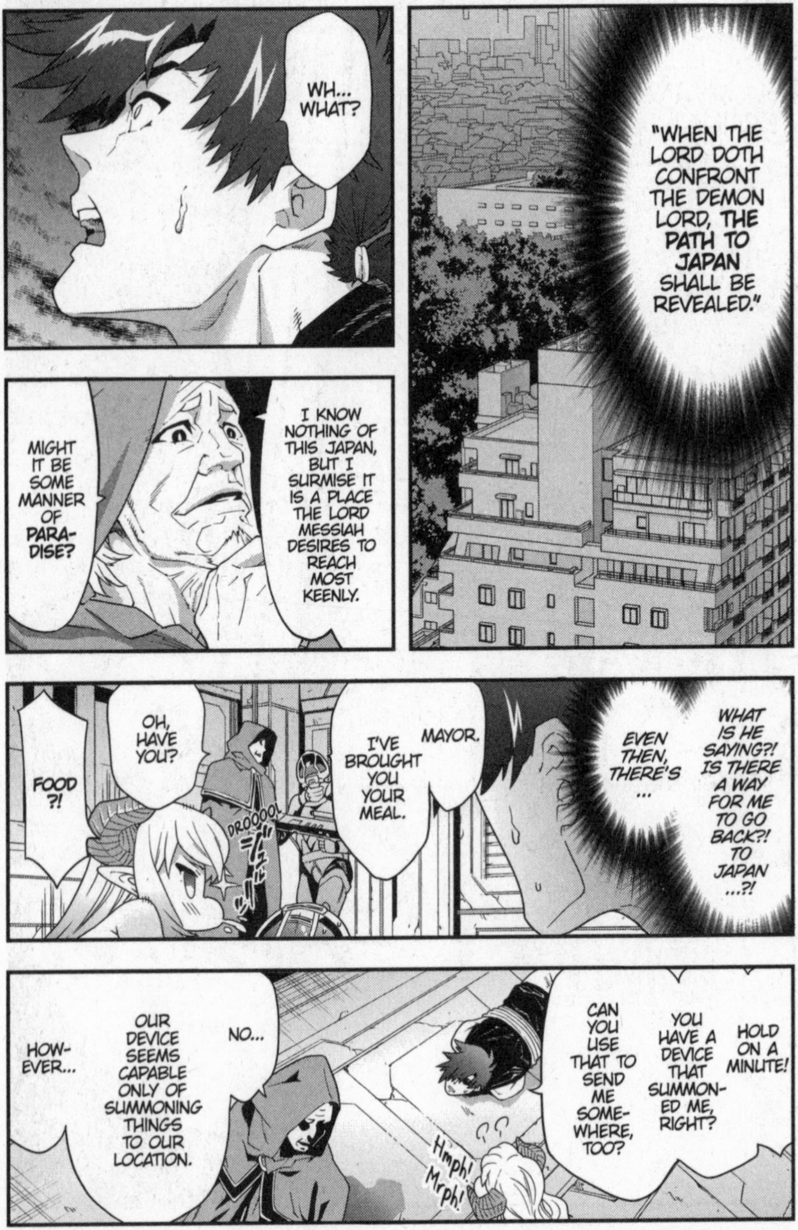
"WHEN THE LORD DOTH CONFRONT THE DEMON LORD, THE PATH TO JAPAN SHALL BE REVEALED."
WH... WHAT?
I KNOW NOTHING OF THIS JAPAN, BUT I SURMISE IT IS A PLACE THE LORD MESSIAH DESIRES TO REACH MOST KEENLY.
MIGHT IT BE SOME MANNER OF PARA-DISE?
WHAT IS HE SAYING?! IS THERE A WAY FOR ME TO GO BACK?! TO JAPAN ...?!
EVEN THEN, THERE'S ...
MAYOR.
I'VE BROUGHT YOU YOUR MEAL.
OH, HAVE YOU?
FOOD ?!
DROOOOL
HOLD ON A MINUTE!
YOU HAVE A DEVICE THAT SUMMON-ED ME, RIGHT?
CAN YOU USE THAT TO SEND ME SOME-WHERE, TOO?
Hmph! Mrph!
NO...
OUR DEVICE SEEMS CAPABLE ONLY OF SUMMONING THINGS TO OUR LOCATION.
HOW-EVER...

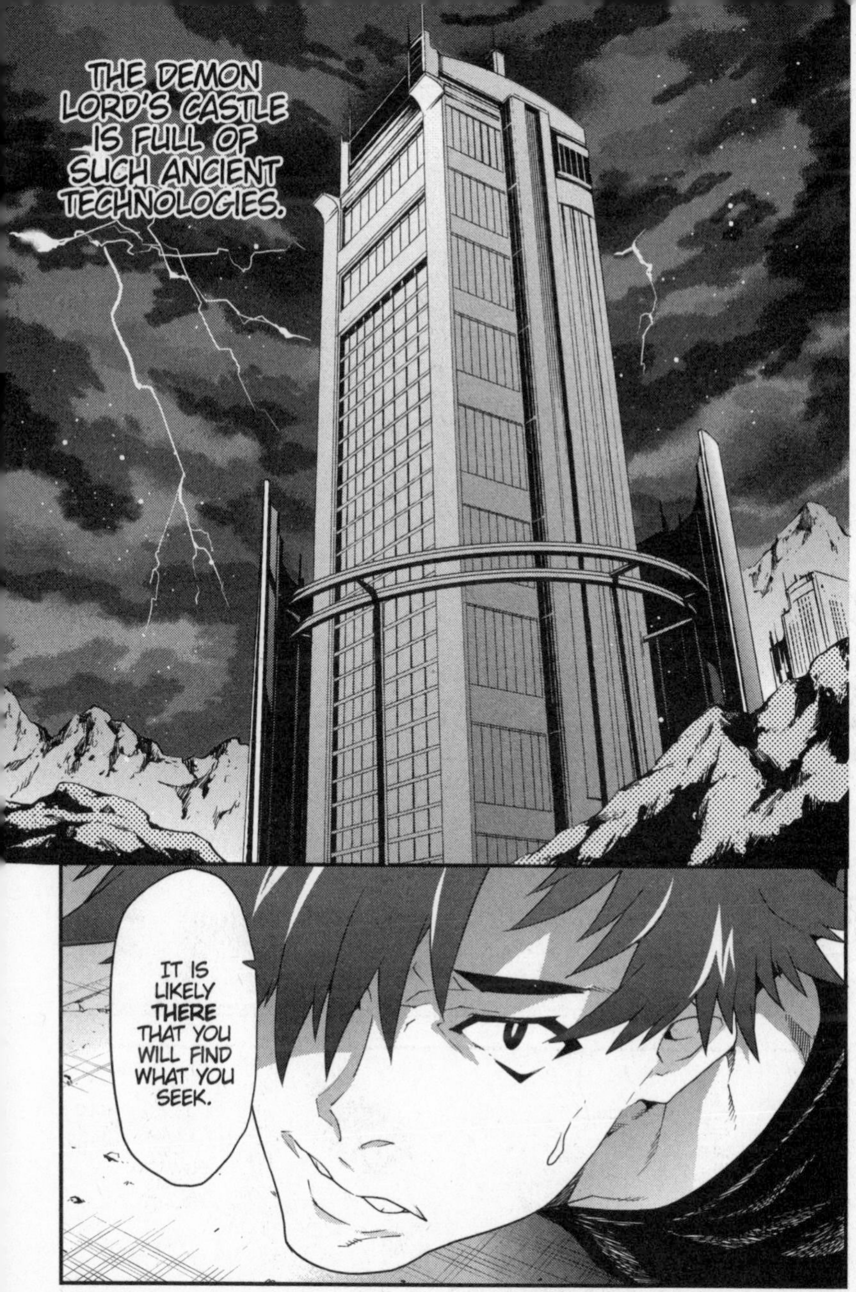
THE DEMON LORD'S CASTLE IS FULL OF SUCH ANCIENT TECHNOLOGIES.
IT IS LIKELY THERE THAT YOU WILL FIND WHAT YOU SEEK.

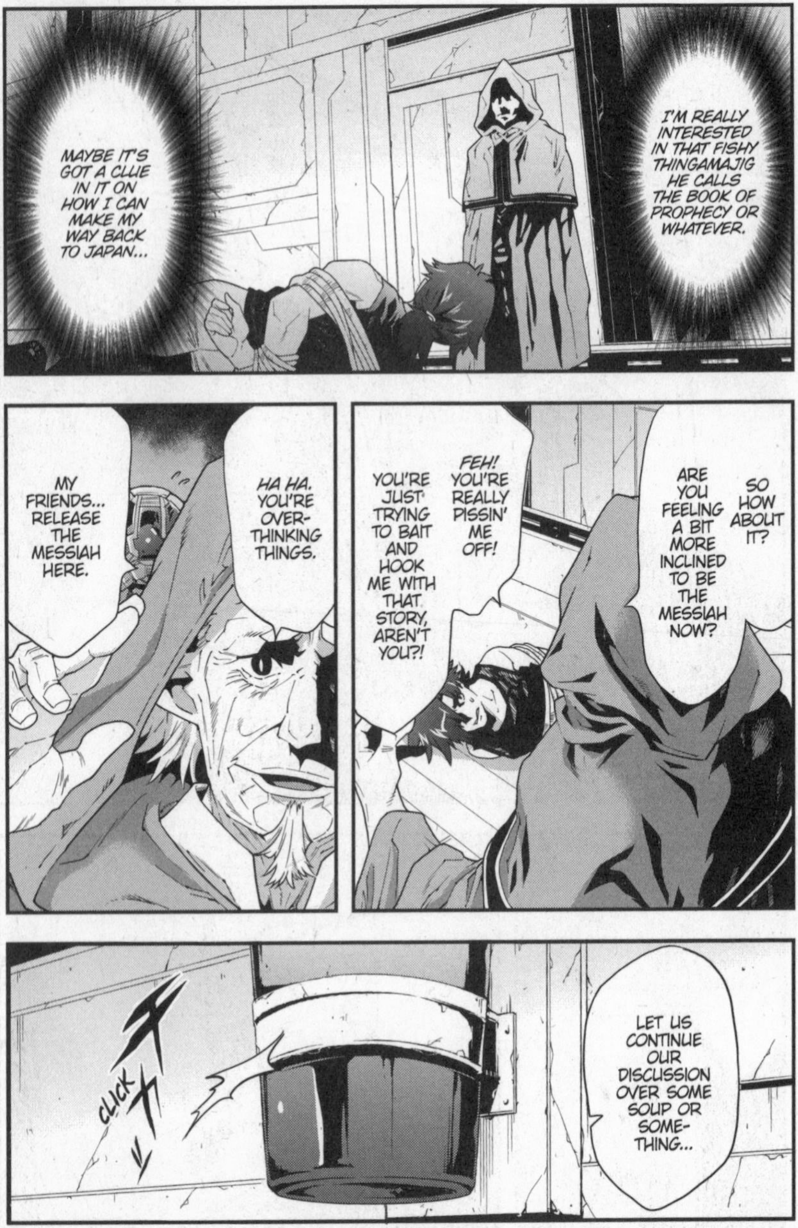
I'M REALLY INTERESTED IN THAT FISHY THINGAMAJIG HE CALLS THE BOOK OF PROPHECY OR WHATEVER.
MAYBE IT'S GOT A CLUE IN IT ON HOW I CAN MAKE MY WAY BACK TO JAPAN...
SO HOW ABOUT IT?
ARE YOU FEELING A BIT MORE INCLINED TO BE THE MESSIAH NOW?
FEH! YOU'RE REALLY PISSIN' ME OFF!
YOU'RE JUST TRYING TO BAIT AND HOOK ME WITH THAT STORY, AREN'T YOU?!
HA HA. YOU'RE OVER-THINKING THINGS.
MY FRIENDS... RELEASE THE MESSIAH HERE.
LET US CONTINUE OUR DISCUSSION OVER SOME SOUP OR SOME-THING...
CLICK

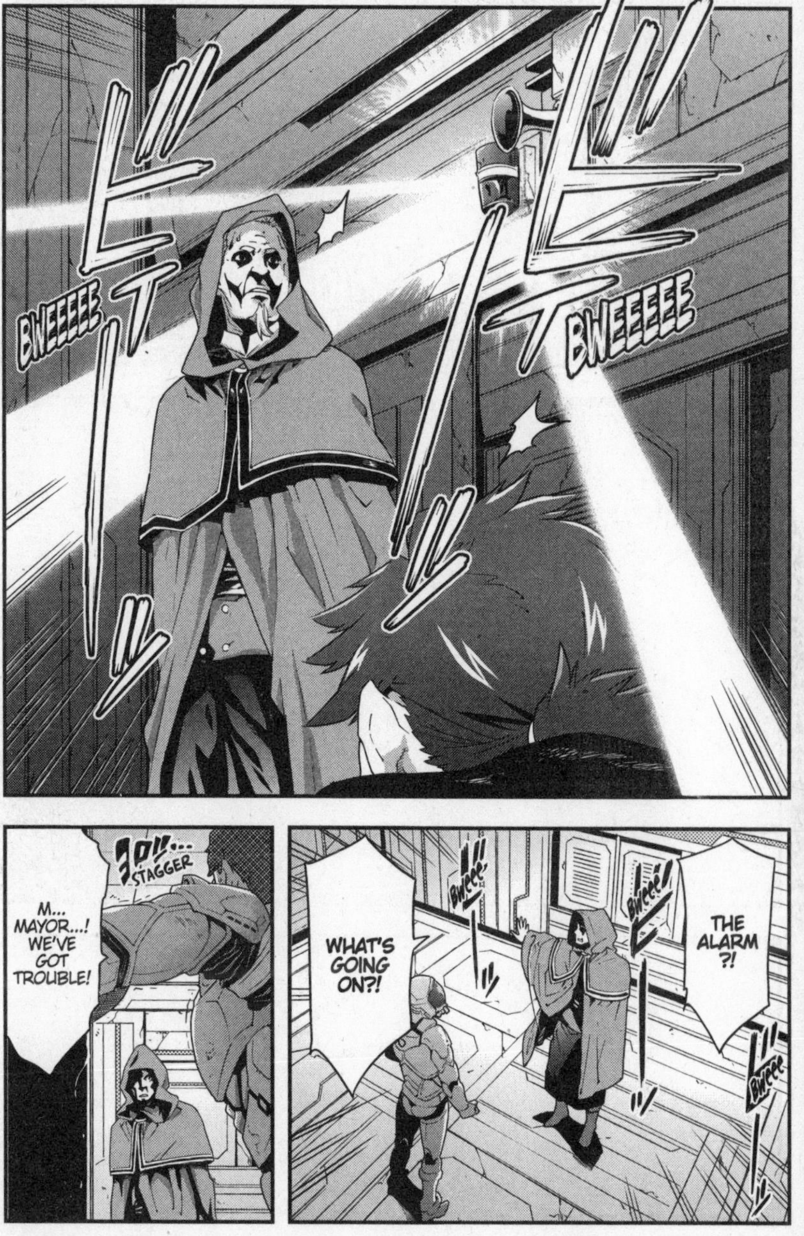
BWEEEEE
BWEEEEE
Bweee
THE ALARM ?!
Bweee
WHAT'S GOING ON?!
Bweee
STAGGER
M... MAYOR...! WE'VE GOT TROUBLE!

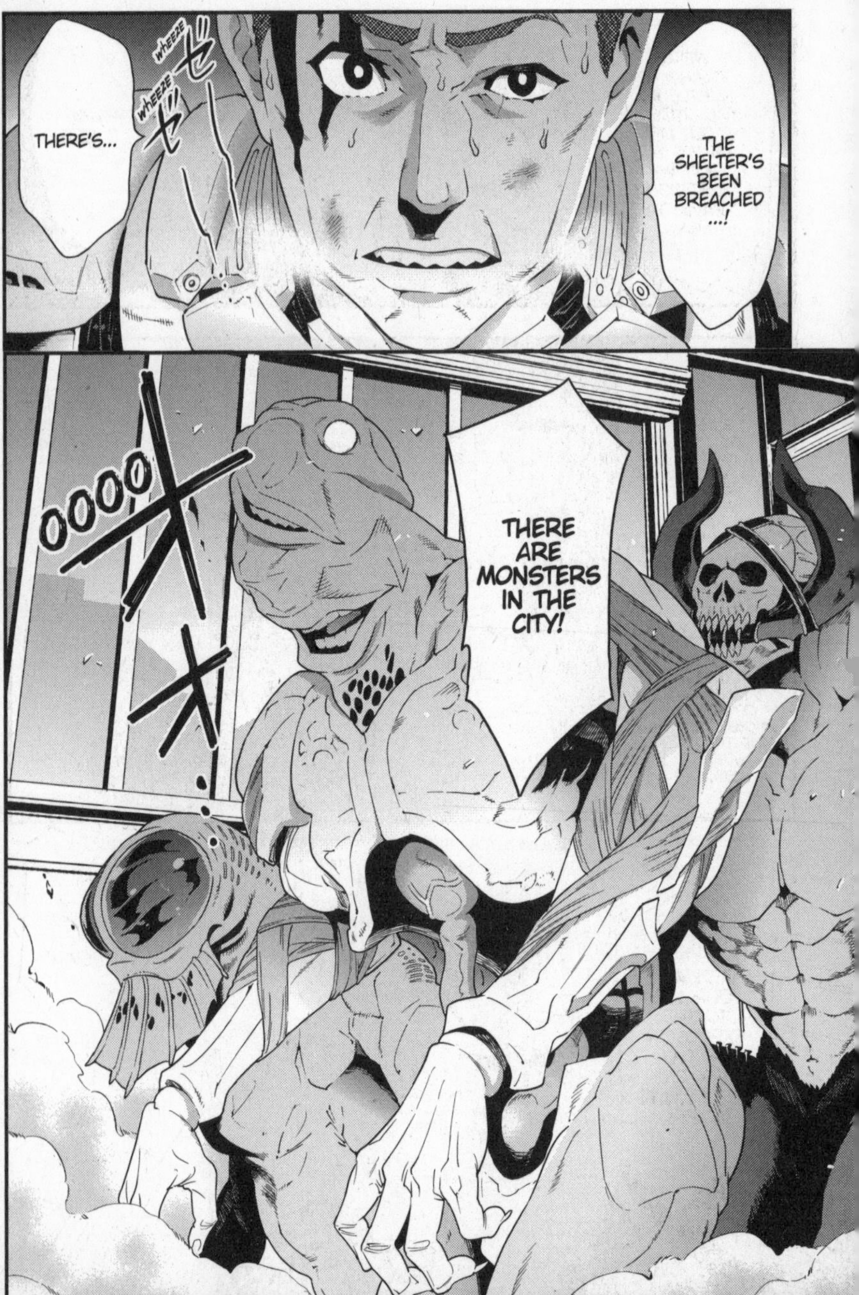
THE SHELTER'S BEEN BREACHED ....!
wheeze
wheeze
THERE'S...
THERE ARE MONSTERS IN THE CITY!
OOOO

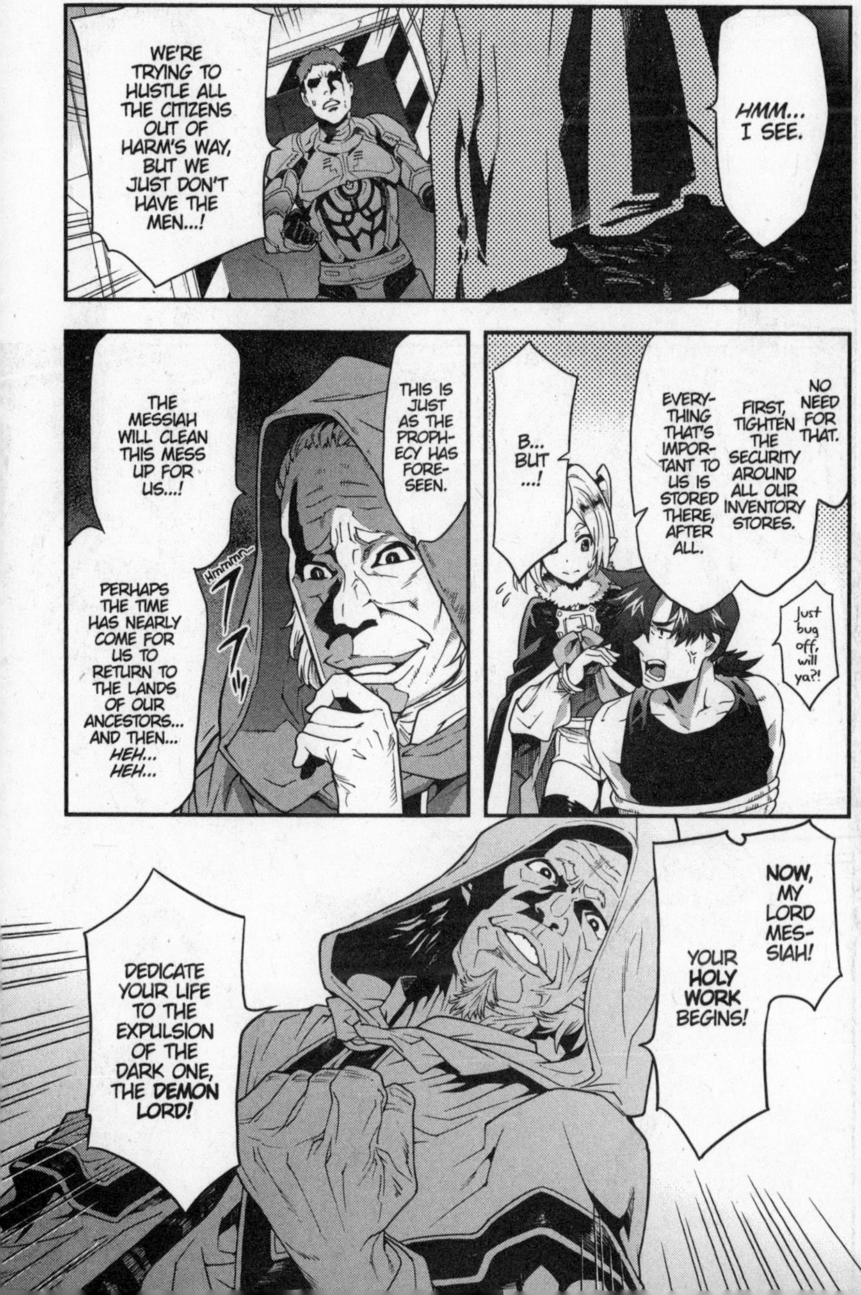
HMM... I SEE.
WE'RE TRYING TO HUSTLE ALL THE CITIZENS OUT OF HARM'S WAY, BUT WE JUST DON'T HAVE THE MEN...!
NO NEED FOR THAT.
FIRST, TIGHTEN THE SECURITY AROUND ALL OUR INVENTORY STORES.
EVERYTHING THAT'S IMPORTANT TO US IS STORED THERE, AFTER ALL.
B... BUT ...!
Just bug off, will ya?!
THIS IS JUST AS THE PROPHECY HAS FORESEEN.
THE MESSIAH WILL CLEAN THIS MESS UP FOR US...!
Hmmmm...
PERHAPS THE TIME HAS NEARLY COME FOR US TO RETURN TO THE LANDS OF OUR ANCESTORS... AND THEN... HEH... HEH...
NOW, MY LORD MESSIAH!
YOUR HOLY WORK BEGINS!
DEDICATE YOUR LIFE TO THE EXPULSION OF THE DARK ONE, THE DEMON LORD!

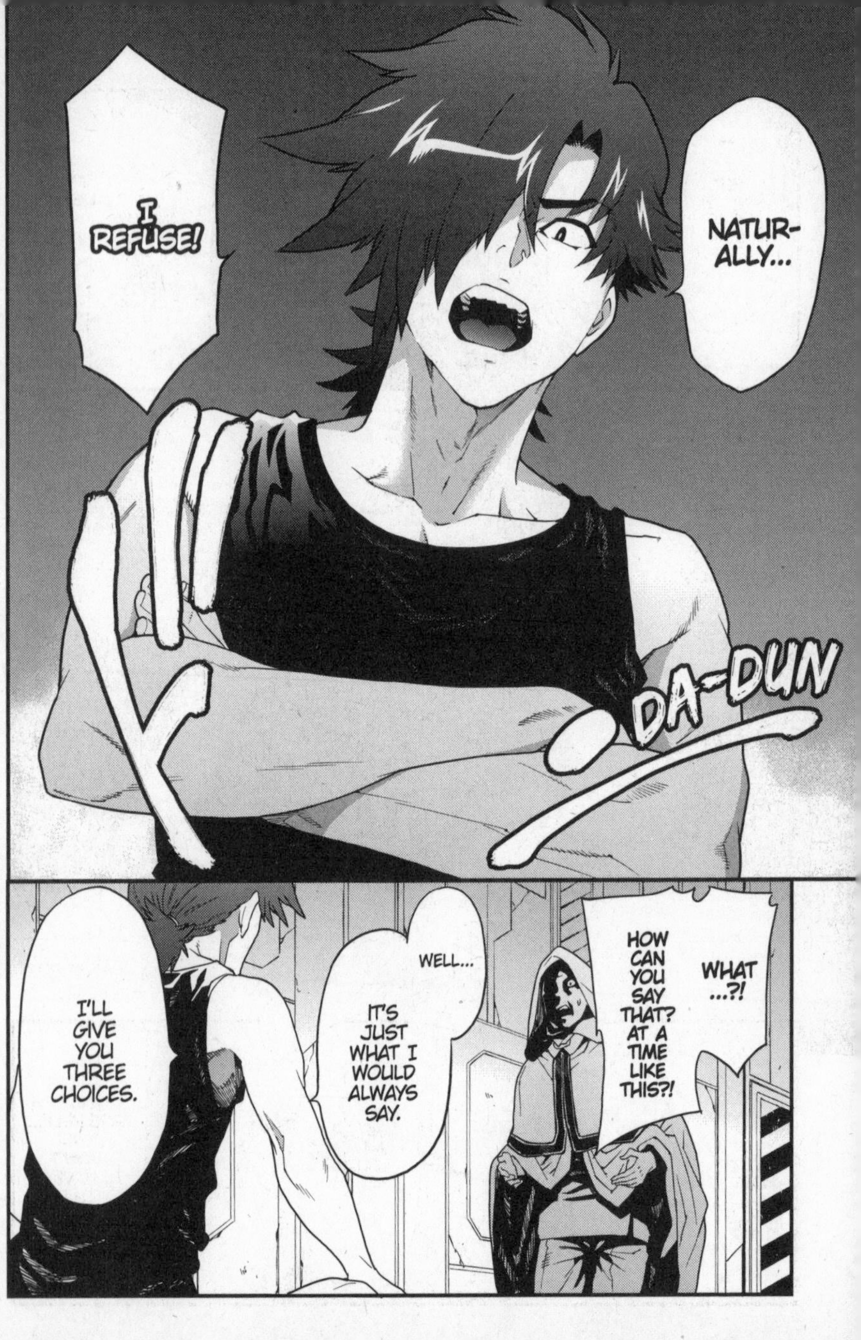
NATUR-ALLY...
I REFUSE!
DA-DUN
WHAT ...?!
HOW CAN YOU SAY THAT? AT A TIME LIKE THIS?!
WELL...
IT'S JUST WHAT I WOULD ALWAYS SAY.
I'LL GIVE YOU THREE CHOICES.

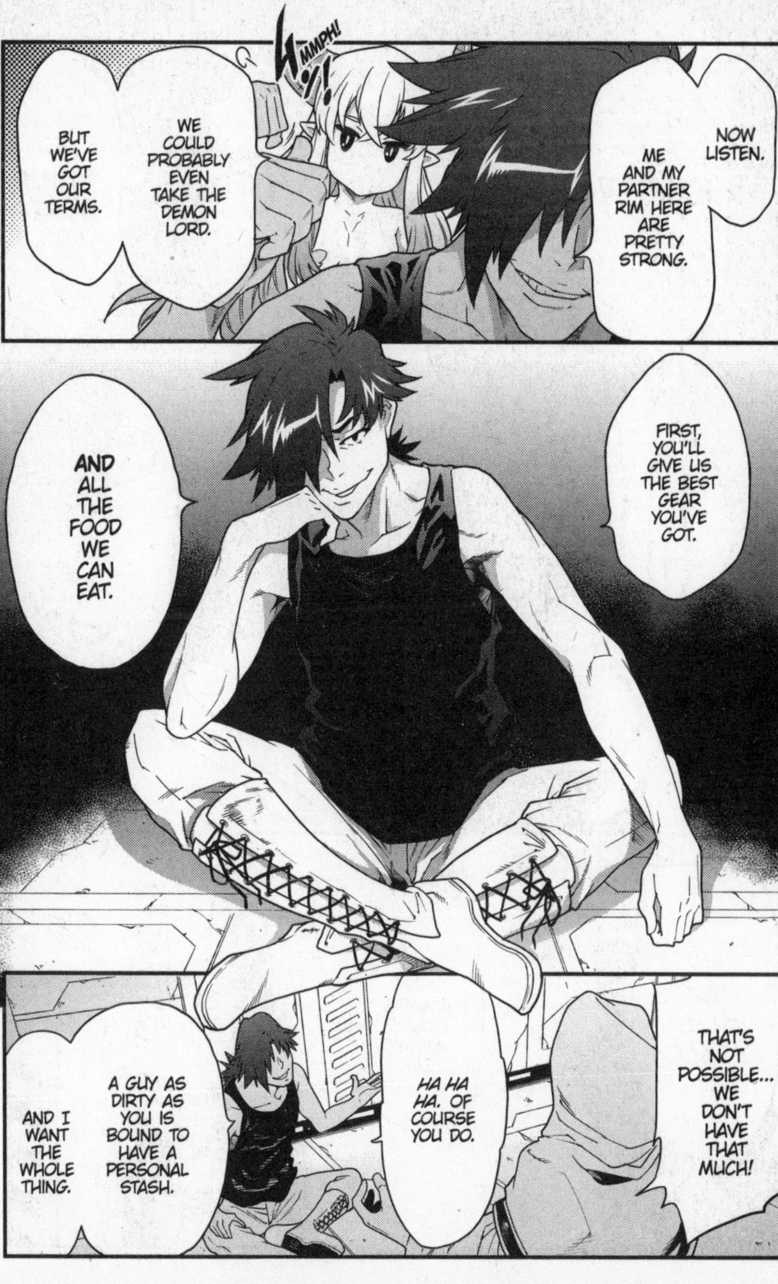
NOW LISTEN.
ME AND MY PARTNER RIM HERE ARE PRETTY STRONG.
MMPH!
WE COULD PROBABLY EVEN TAKE THE DEMON LORD.
BUT WE'VE GOT OUR TERMS.
FIRST, YOU'LL GIVE US THE BEST GEAR YOU'VE GOT.
AND ALL THE FOOD WE CAN EAT.
THAT'S NOT POSSIBLE... WE DON'T HAVE THAT MUCH!
HA HA HA. OF COURSE YOU DO.
A GUY AS DIRTY AS YOU IS BOUND TO HAVE A PERSONAL STASH.
AND I WANT THE WHOLE THING.

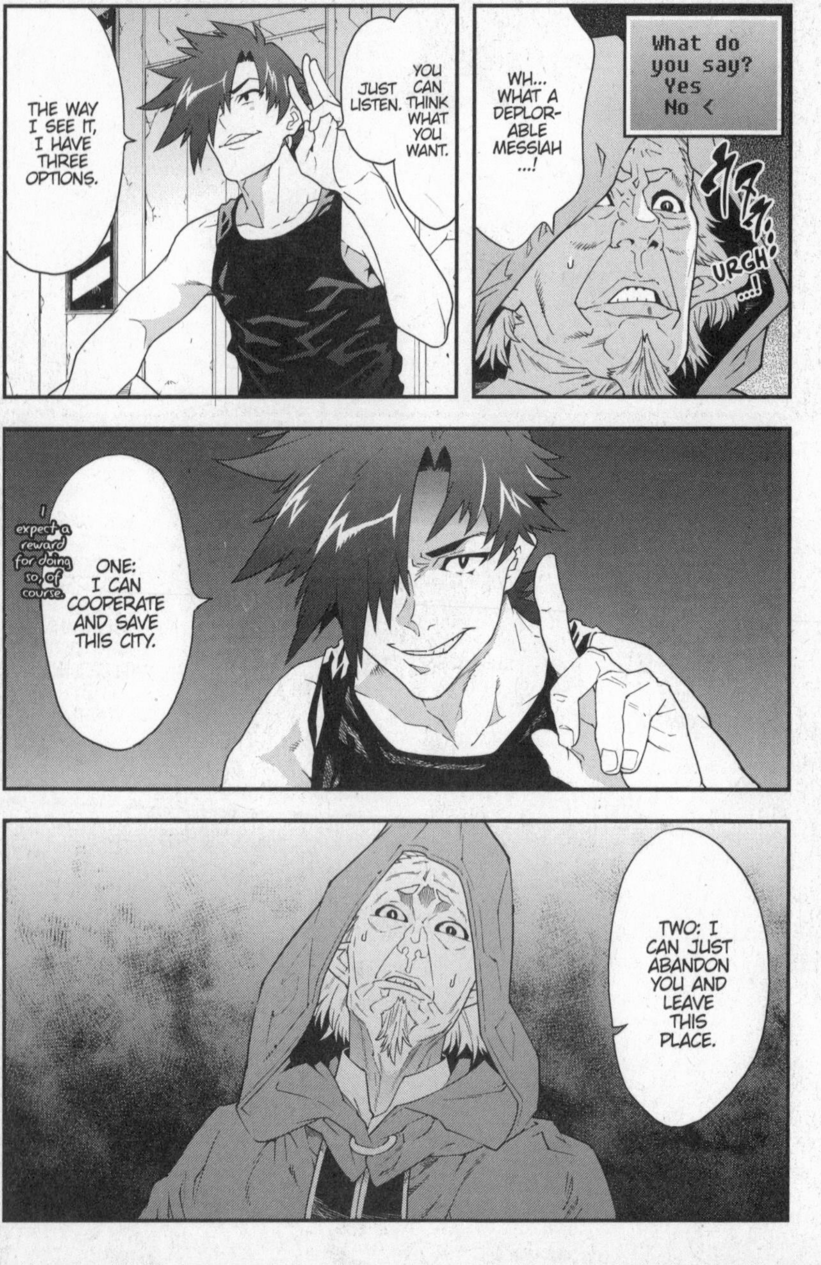
What do you say?
Yes
No <
WH... WHAT A DEPLORABLE MESSIAH ...!
URGH ...!
YOU CAN THINK WHAT YOU WANT.
JUST LISTEN.
THE WAY I SEE IT, I HAVE THREE OPTIONS.
ONE: I CAN COOPERATE AND SAVE THIS CITY.
I expect a reward for doing so, of course.
TWO: I CAN JUST ABANDON YOU AND LEAVE THIS PLACE.

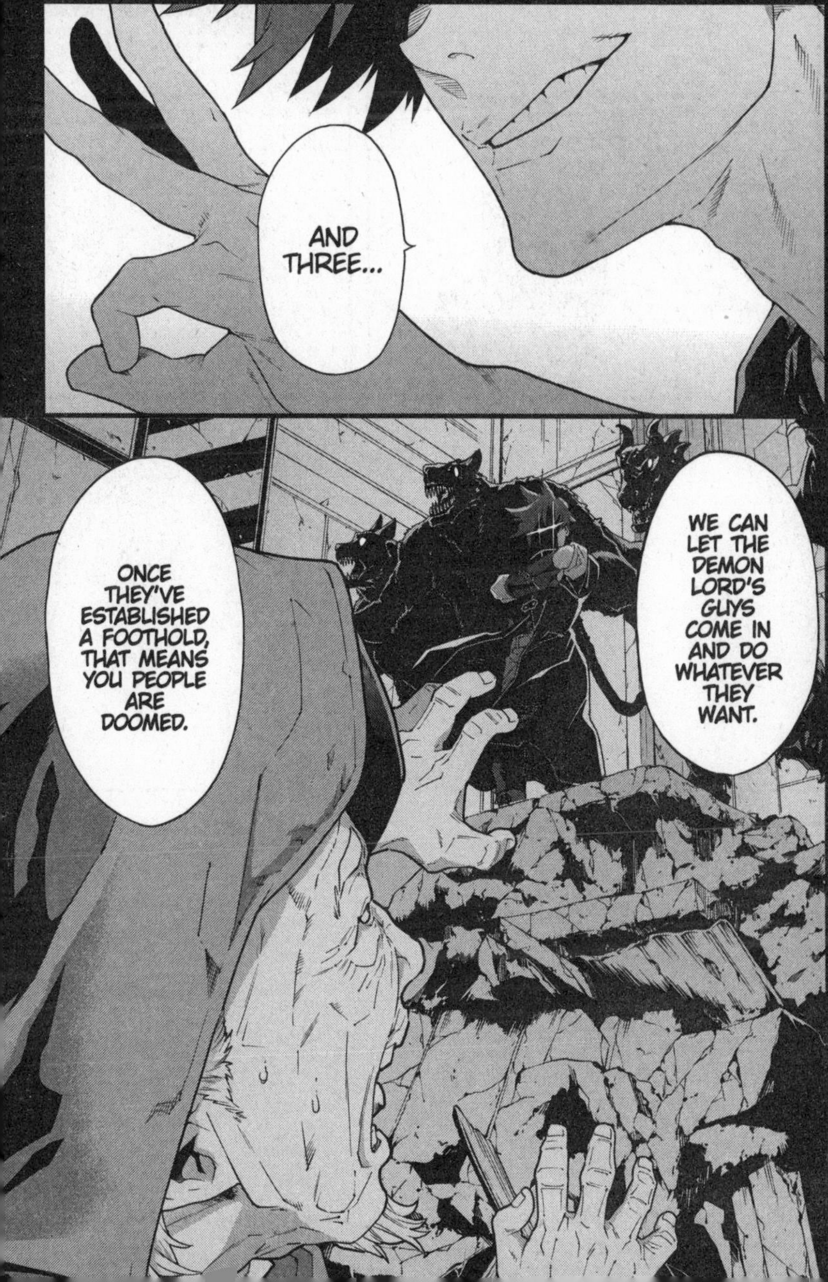
AND THREE...
WE CAN LET THE DEMON LORD'S GUYS COME IN AND DO WHATEVER THEY WANT.
ONCE THEY'VE ESTABLISHED A FOOTHOLD, THAT MEANS YOU PEOPLE ARE DOOMED.

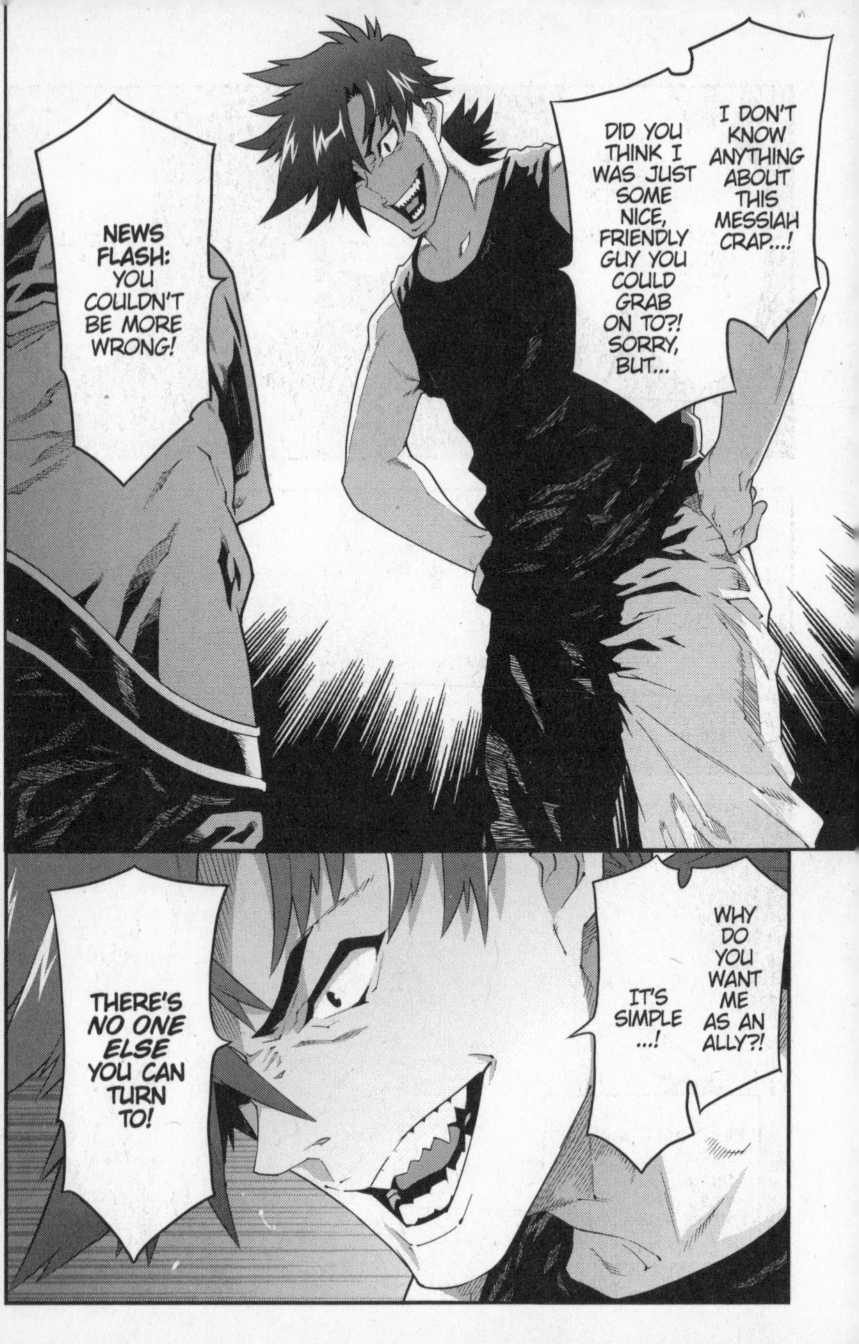
I DON'T KNOW ANYTHING ABOUT THIS MESSIAH CRAP...!
DID YOU THINK I WAS JUST SOME NICE, FRIENDLY GUY YOU COULD GRAB ON TO?! SORRY, BUT...
NEWS FLASH: YOU COULDN'T BE MORE WRONG!
WHY DO YOU WANT ME AS AN ALLY?!
IT'S SIMPLE ...!
THERE'S *NO ONE ELSE* YOU CAN TURN TO!

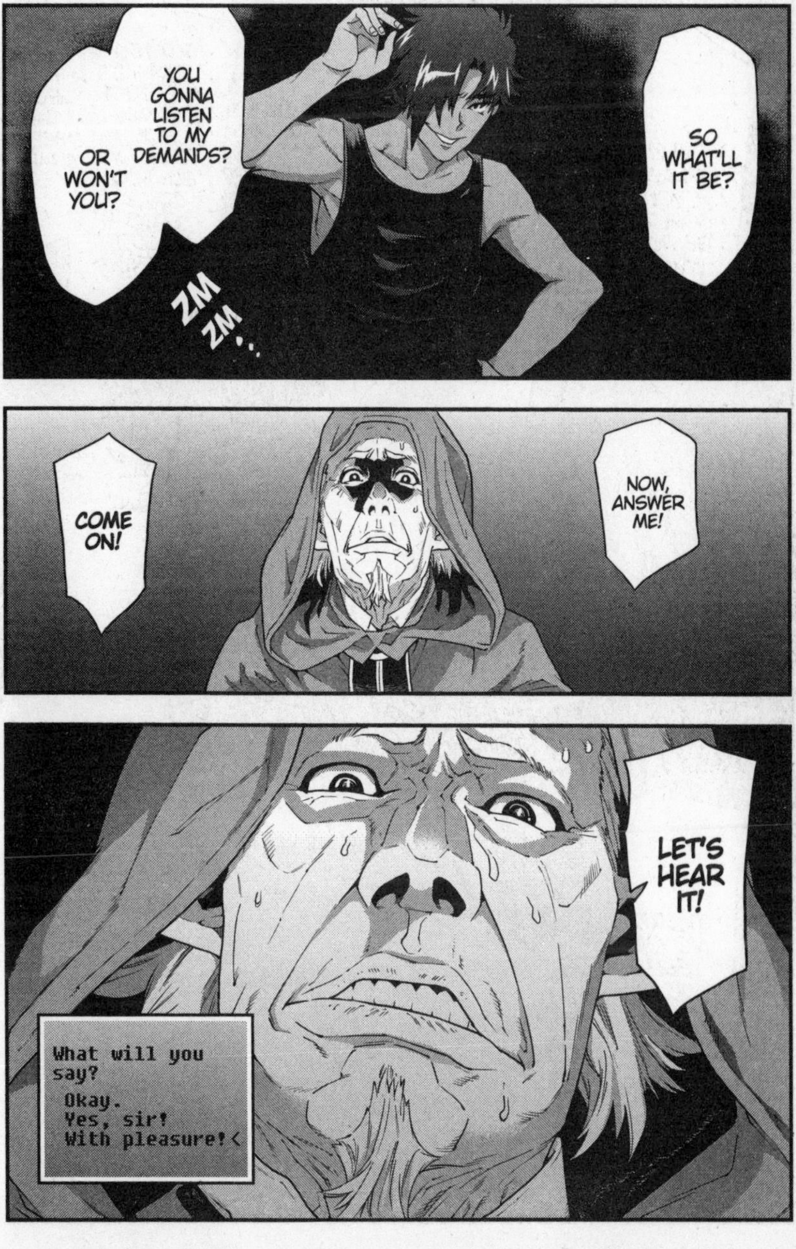
SO WHAT'LL IT BE?
YOU GONNA LISTEN TO MY DEMANDS?
OR WON'T YOU?
ZM ZM...
NOW, ANSWER ME!
COME ON!
LET'S HEAR IT!
What will you say?
Okay.
Yes, sir!
With pleasure!<

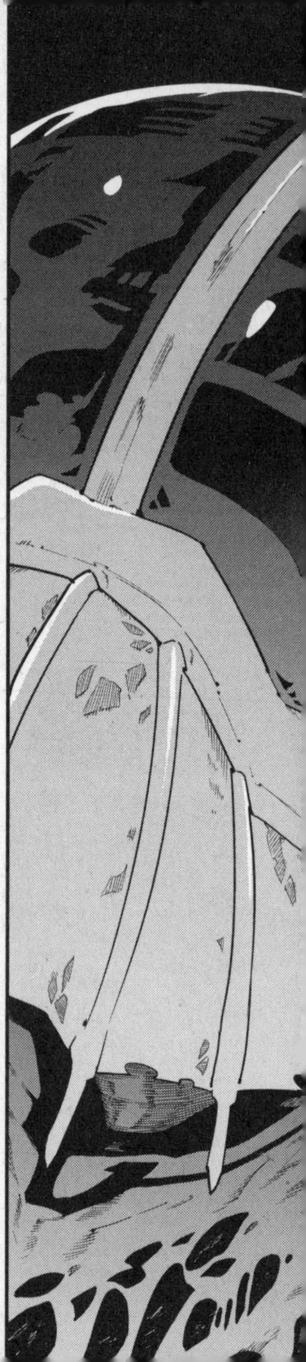
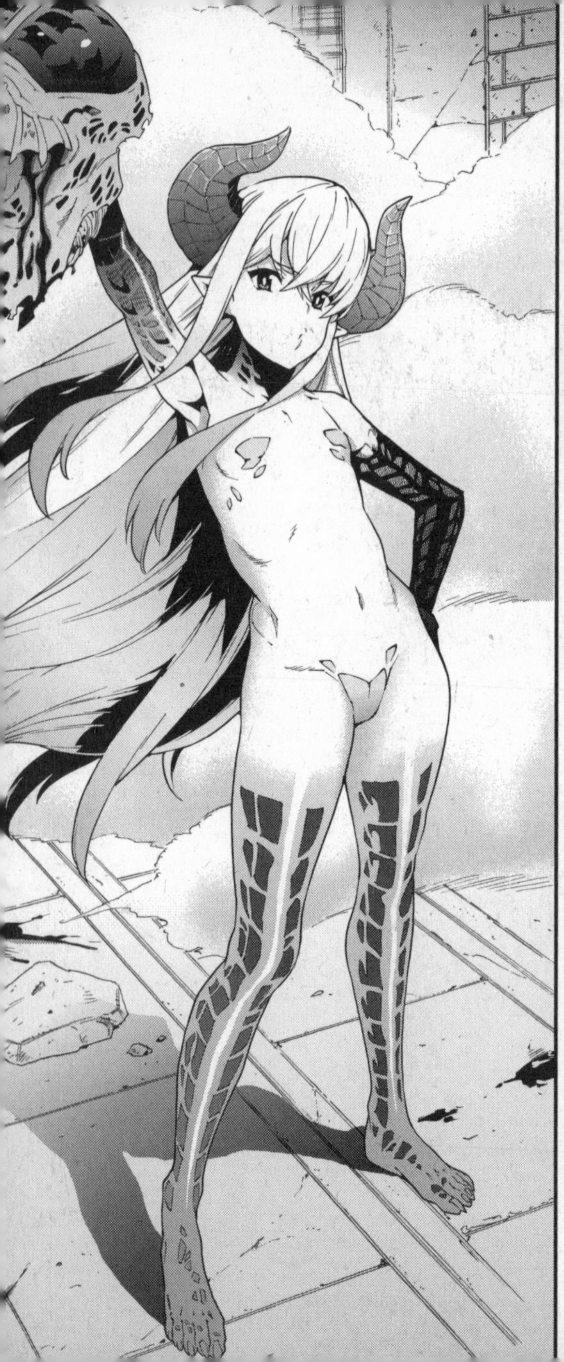

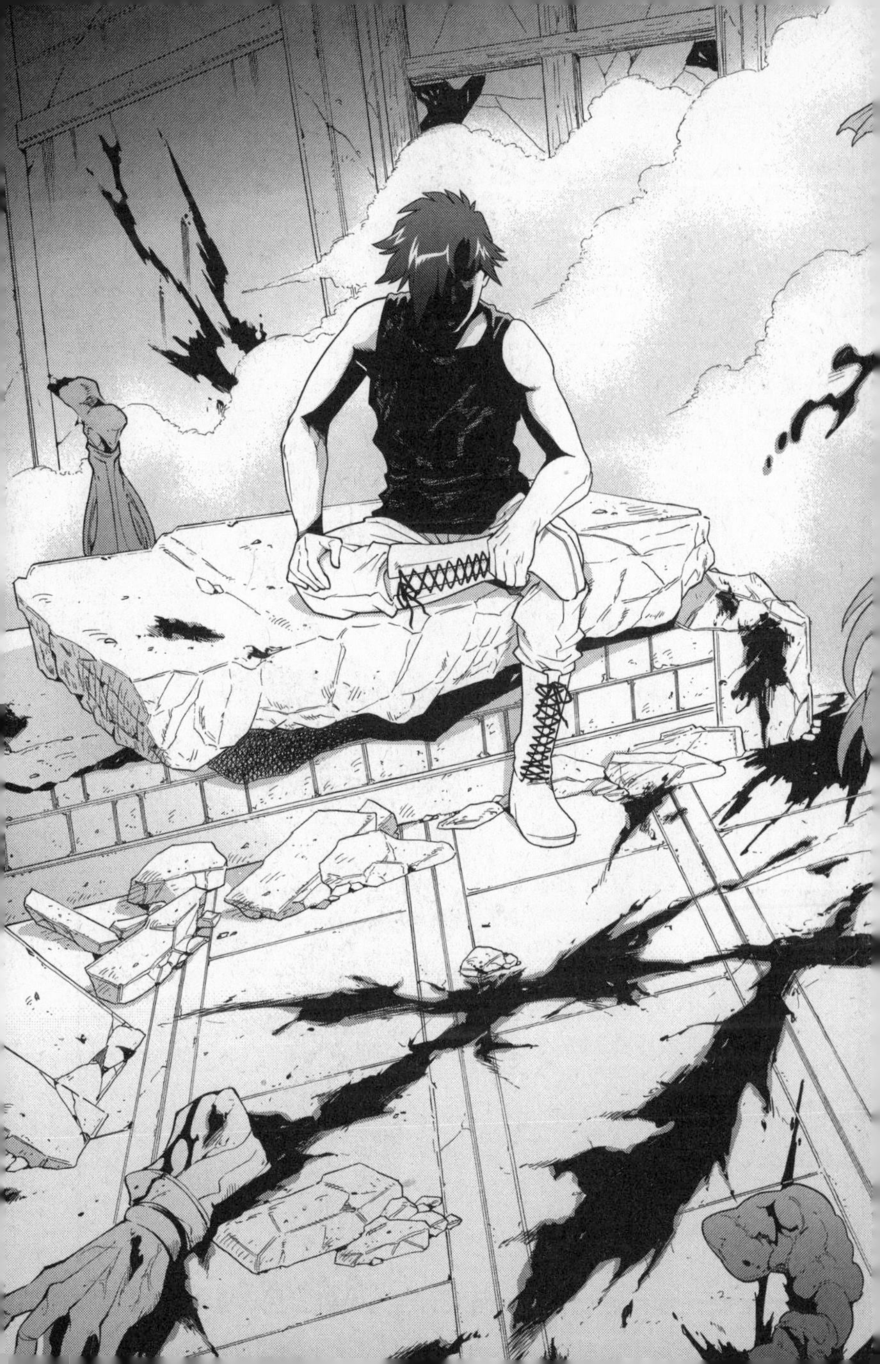

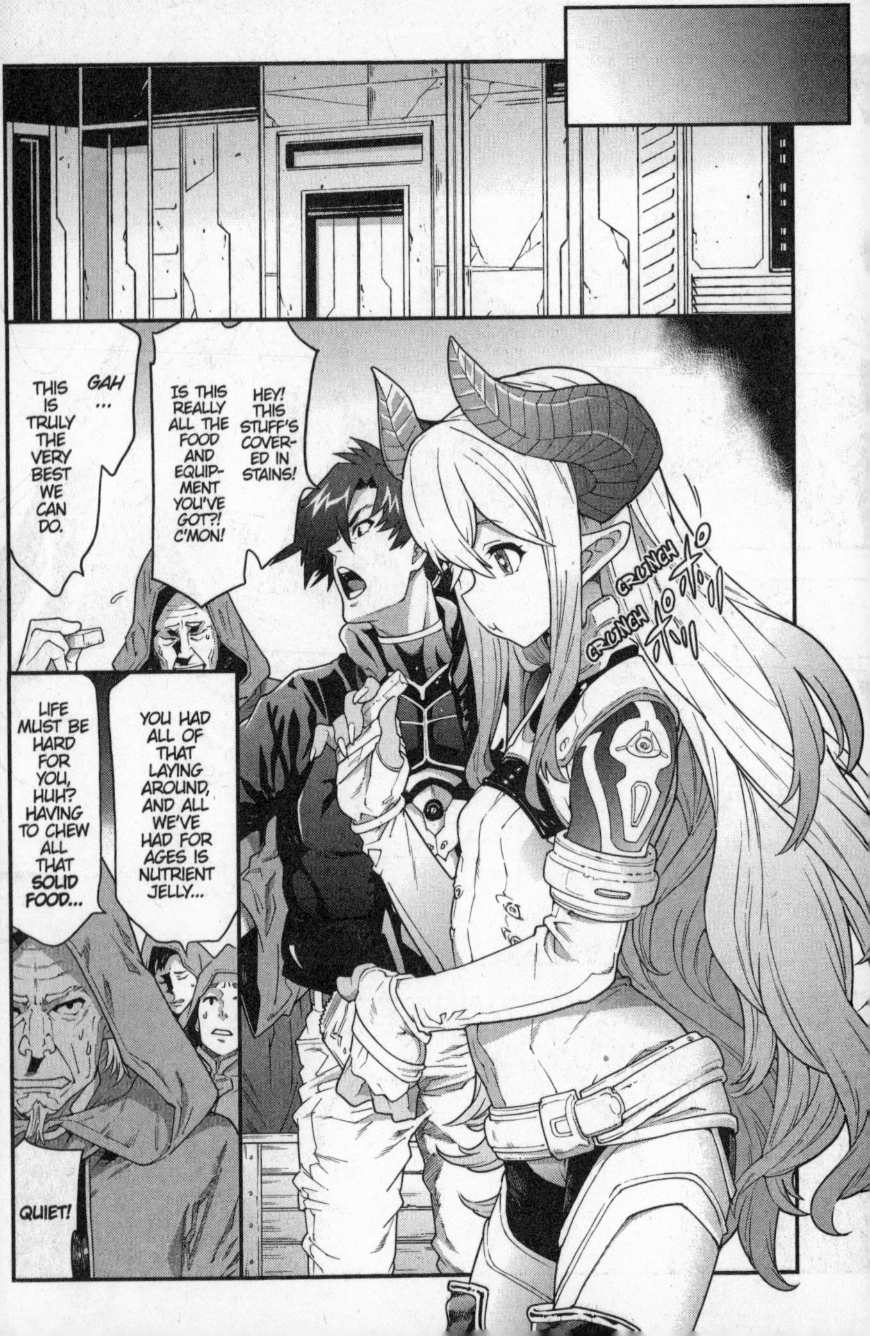
HEY! THIS STUFF'S COVERED IN STAINS!
IS THIS REALLY ALL THE FOOD AND EQUIPMENT YOU'VE GOT?! C'MON!
GAH...
THIS IS TRULY THE VERY BEST WE CAN DO.
CRUNCH
CRUNCH
YOU HAD ALL OF THAT LAYING AROUND, AND ALL WE'VE HAD FOR AGES IS NUTRIENT JELLY...
LIFE MUST BE HARD FOR YOU, HUH? HAVING TO CHEW ALL THAT SOLID FOOD...
QUIET!

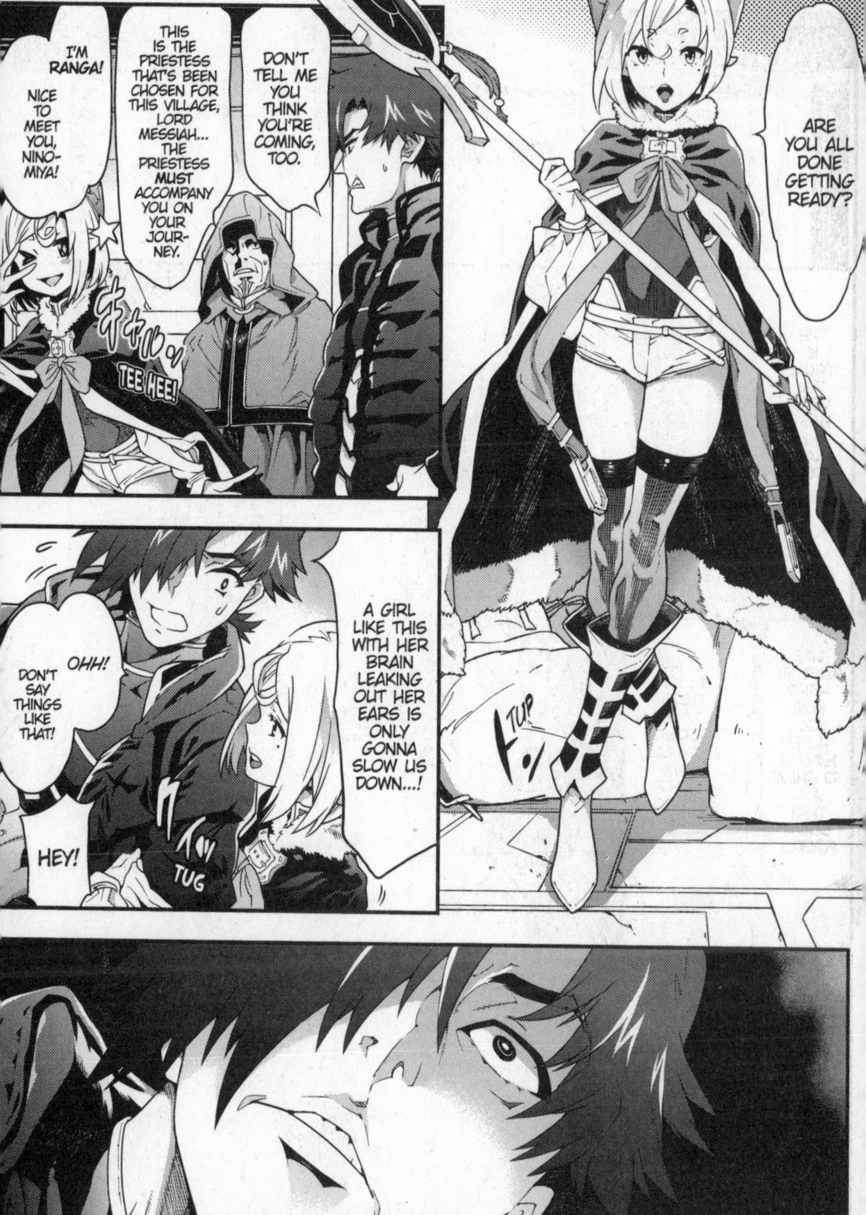
ARE YOU ALL DONE GETTING READY?
TUP
DON'T TELL ME YOU THINK YOU'RE COMING, TOO.
THIS IS THE PRIESTESS THAT'S BEEN CHOSEN FOR THIS VILLAGE, LORD MESSIAH... THE PRIESTESS MUST ACCOMPANY YOU ON YOUR JOURNEY.
I'M RANGA!
NICE TO MEET YOU, NINOMIYA!
TEE HEE!
A GIRL LIKE THIS WITH HER BRAIN LEAKING OUT HER EARS IS ONLY GONNA SLOW US DOWN...!
OHH!
DON'T SAY THINGS LIKE THAT!
TUG
HEY!

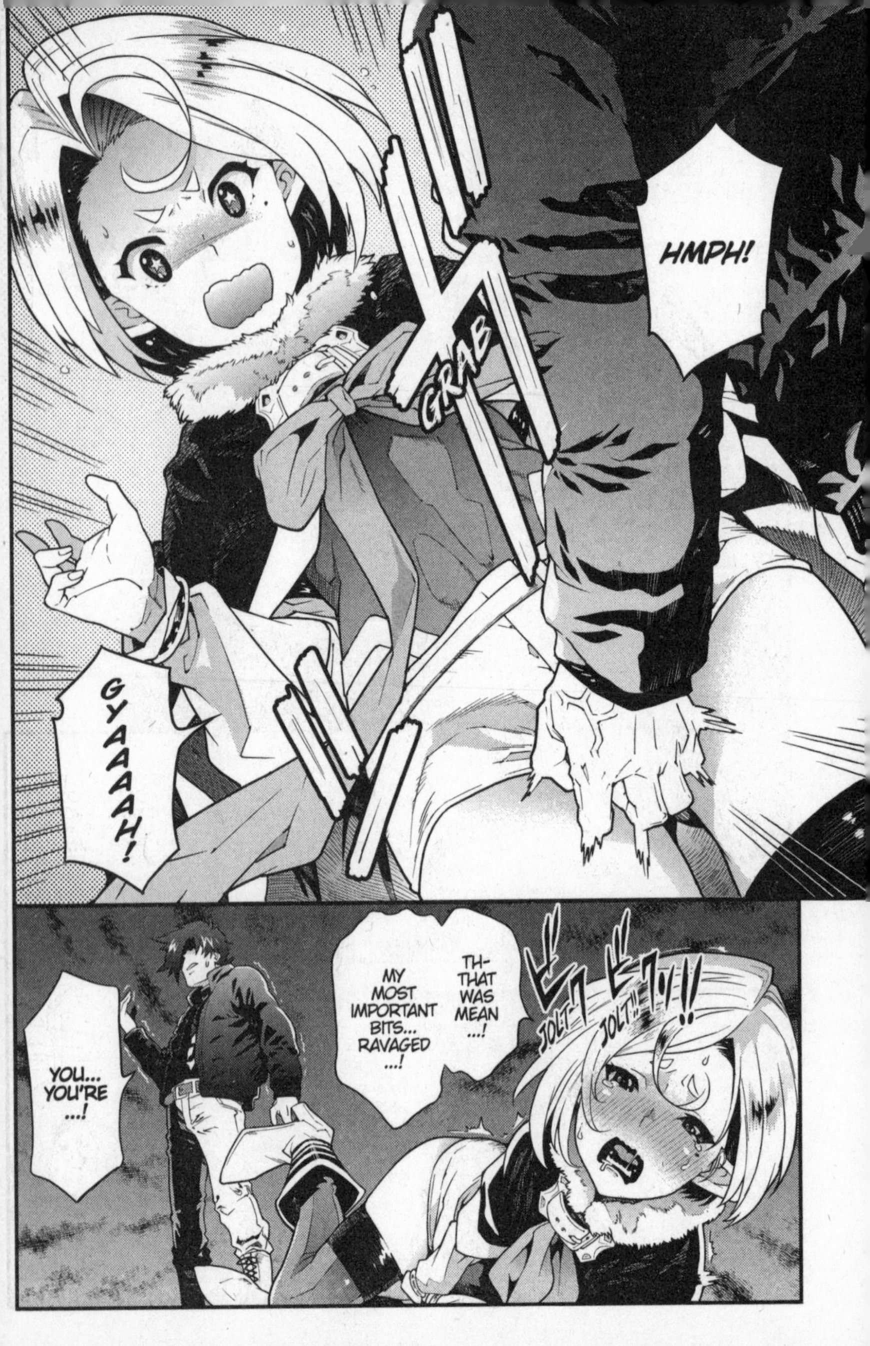
HMPH!
GRAB
GYAAAAH!
JOLT! JOLT!!
TH-THAT WAS MEAN...!
MY MOST IMPORTANT BITS... RAVAGED...!
YOU... YOU'RE...!

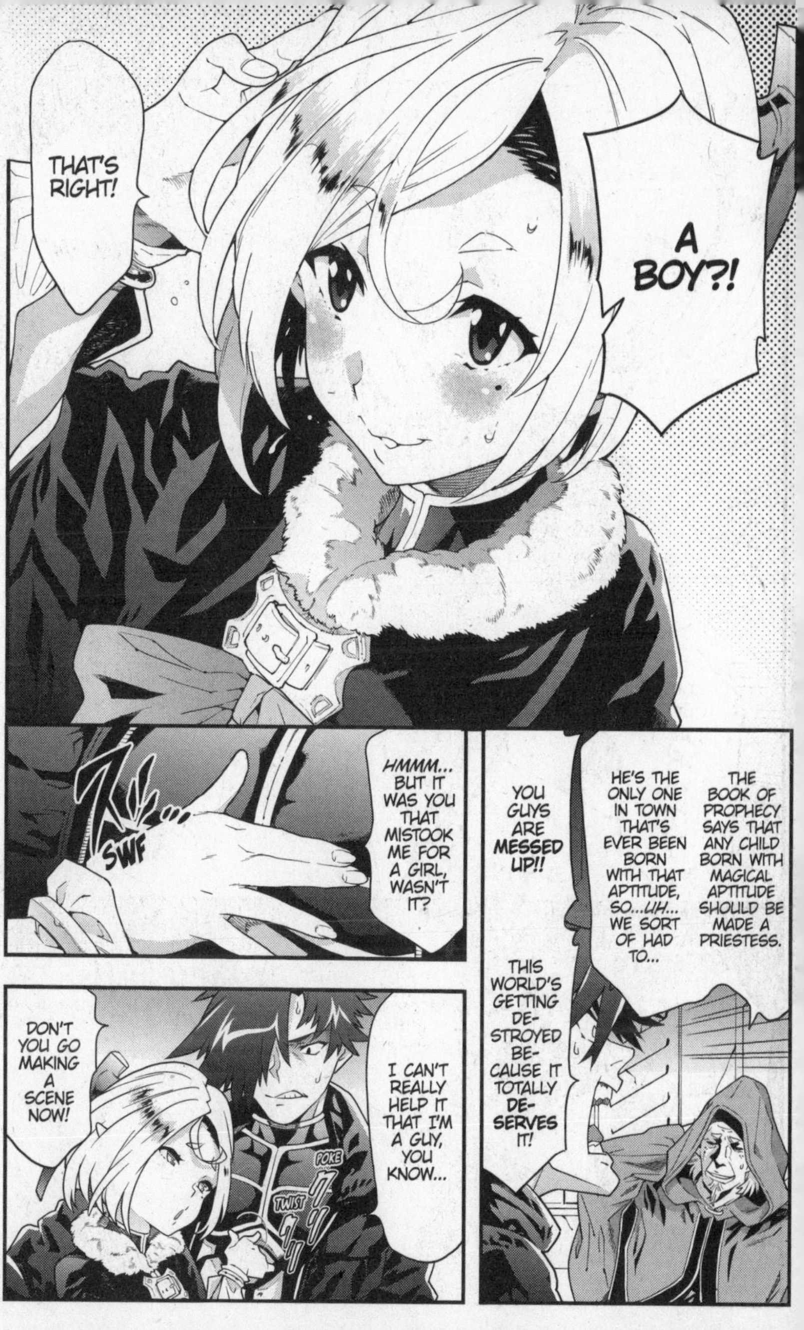
A BOY?!
THAT'S RIGHT!
THE BOOK OF PROPHECY SAYS THAT ANY CHILD BORN WITH MAGICAL APTITUDE SHOULD BE MADE A PRIESTESS.
HE'S THE ONLY ONE IN TOWN THAT'S EVER BEEN BORN WITH THAT APTITUDE, SO...UH... WE SORT OF HAD TO...
YOU GUYS ARE MESSED UP!!
HMMM... BUT IT WAS YOU THAT MISTOOK ME FOR A GIRL, WASN'T IT?
SWF
THIS WORLD'S GETTING DE-STROYED BE-CAUSE IT TOTALLY DE-SERVES IT!
I CAN'T REALLY HELP IT THAT I'M A GUY, YOU KNOW...
DON'T YOU GO MAKING A SCENE NOW!
POKE
TWIST

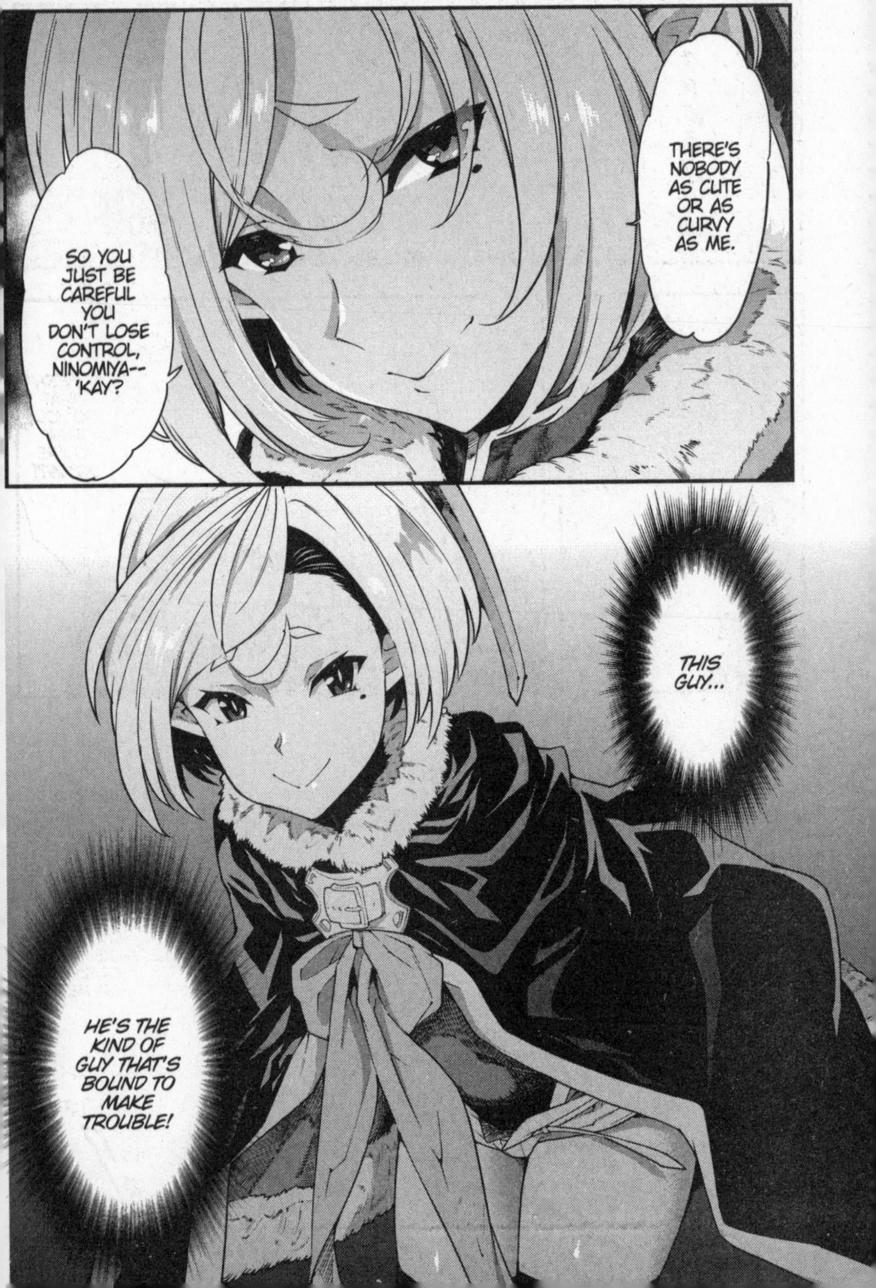
THERE'S NOBODY AS CUTE OR AS CURVY AS ME.
SO YOU JUST BE CAREFUL YOU DON'T LOSE CONTROL, NINOMIYA--'KAY?
THIS GUY...
HE'S THE KIND OF GUY THAT'S BOUND TO MAKE TROUBLE!

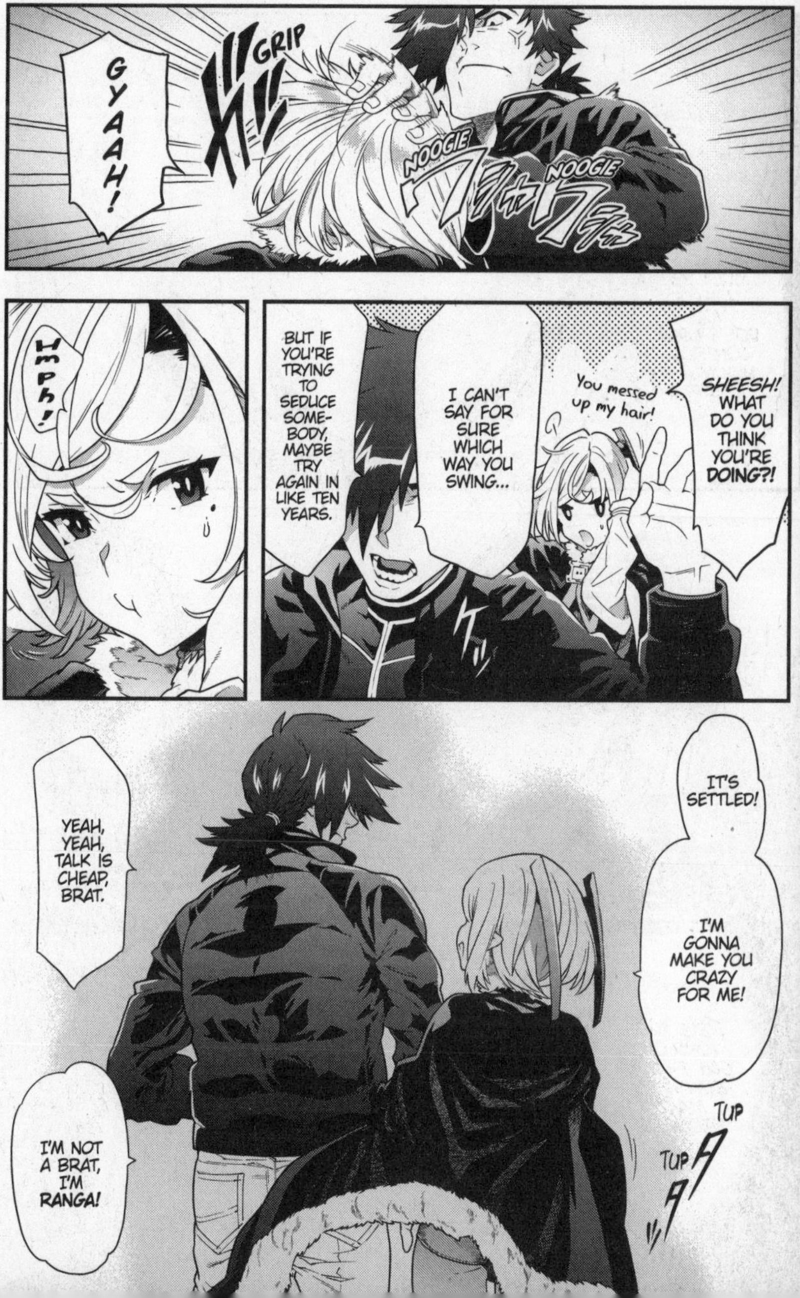
GRIP
NOOGIE
NOOGIE
GYAAH!
SHEESH! WHAT DO YOU THINK YOU'RE DOING?!
You messed up my hair!
I CAN'T SAY FOR SURE WHICH WAY YOU SWING...
BUT IF YOU'RE TRYING TO SEDUCE SOMEBODY, MAYBE TRY AGAIN IN LIKE TEN YEARS.
Umph!
IT'S SETTLED!
I'M GONNA MAKE YOU CRAZY FOR ME!
TUP
TUP
YEAH, YEAH, TALK IS CHEAP, BRAT.
I'M NOT A BRAT, I'M RANGA!

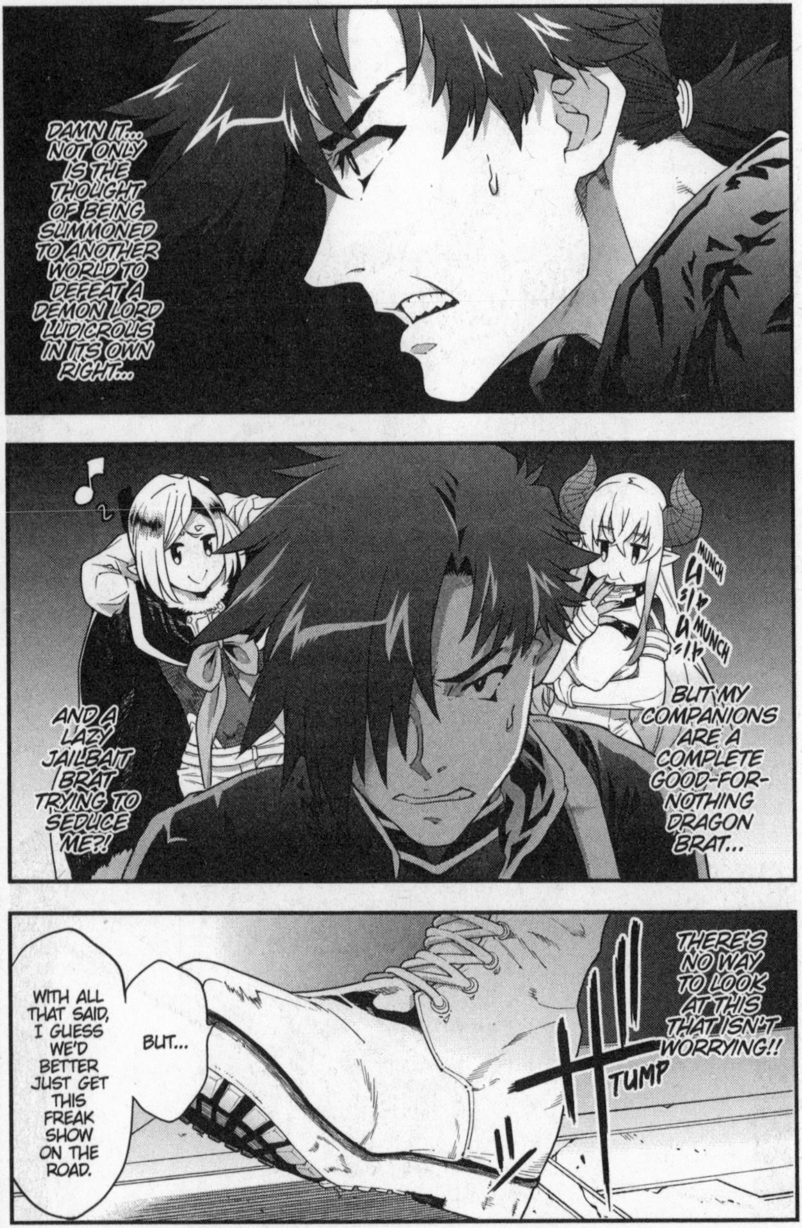
DAMN IT... NOT ONLY IS THE THOUGHT OF BEING SUMMONED TO ANOTHER WORLD TO DEFEAT A DEMON LORD LUDICROUS IN ITS OWN RIGHT...
MUNCH
MUNCH
BUT MY COMPANIONS ARE A COMPLETE GOOD-FOR-NOTHING DRAGON BRAT...
AND A LAZY JAILBAIT BRAT TRYING TO SEDUCE ME?!
THERE'S NO WAY TO LOOK AT THIS THAT ISN'T WORRYING!!
TUMP
BUT...
WITH ALL THAT SAID, I GUESS WE'D BETTER JUST GET THIS FREAK SHOW ON THE ROAD.

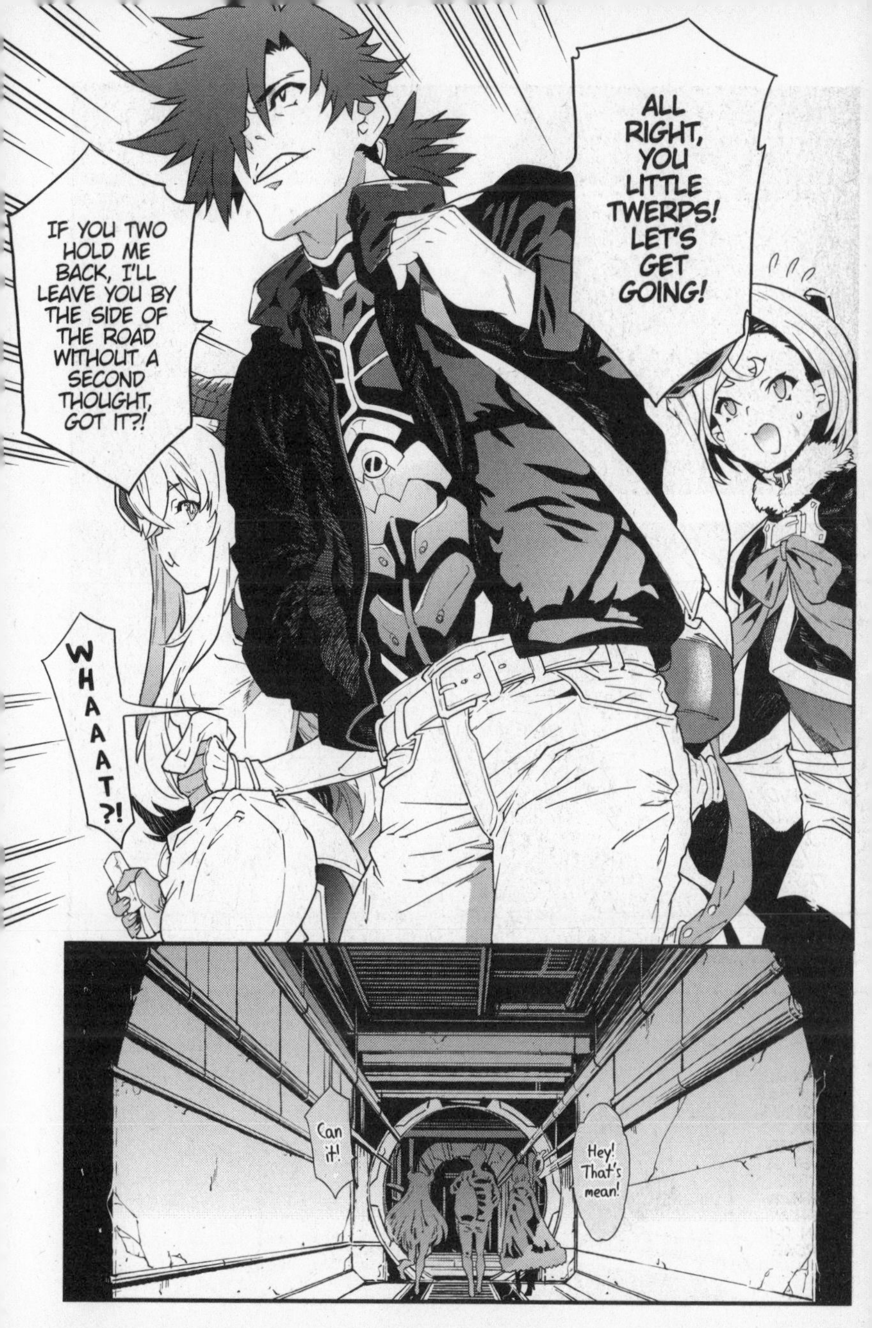
ALL RIGHT, YOU LITTLE TWERPS! LET'S GET GOING!
IF YOU TWO HOLD ME BACK, I'LL LEAVE YOU BY THE SIDE OF THE ROAD WITHOUT A SECOND THOUGHT, GOT IT?!
WHAAAAT?!
Hey! That's mean!
Can it!

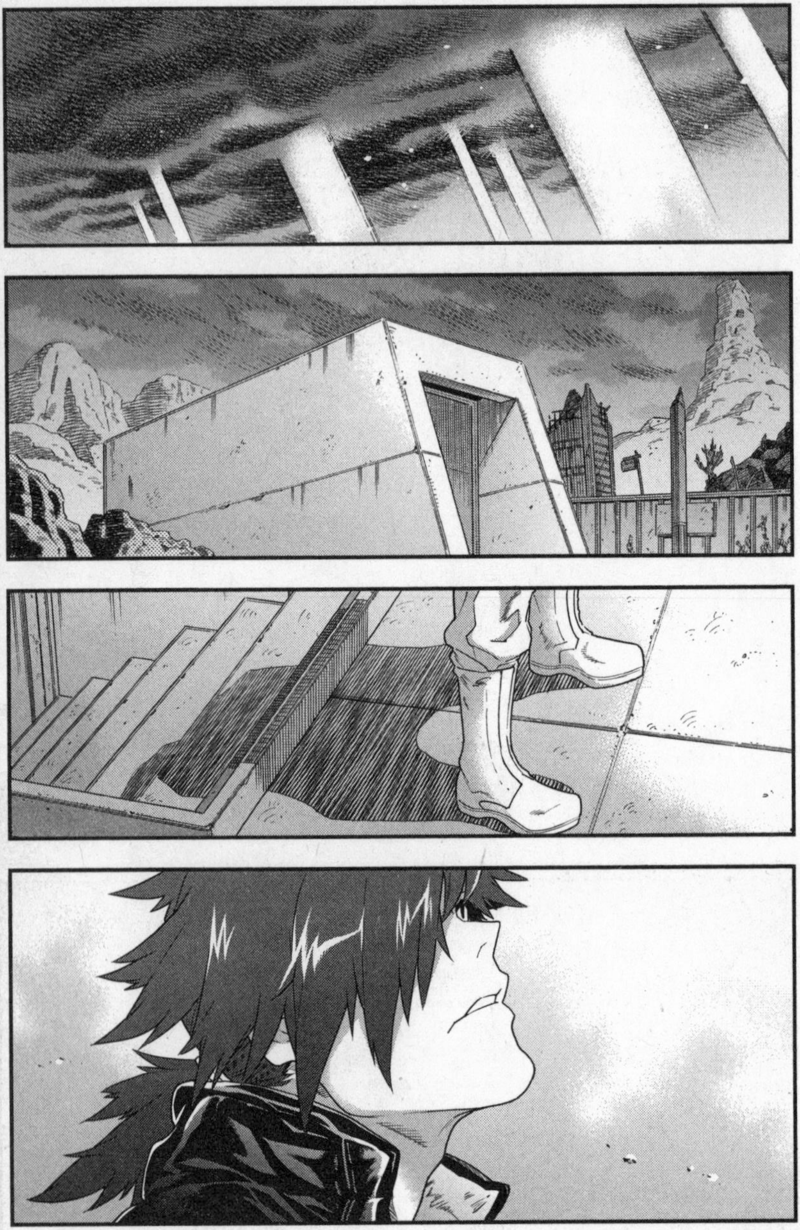

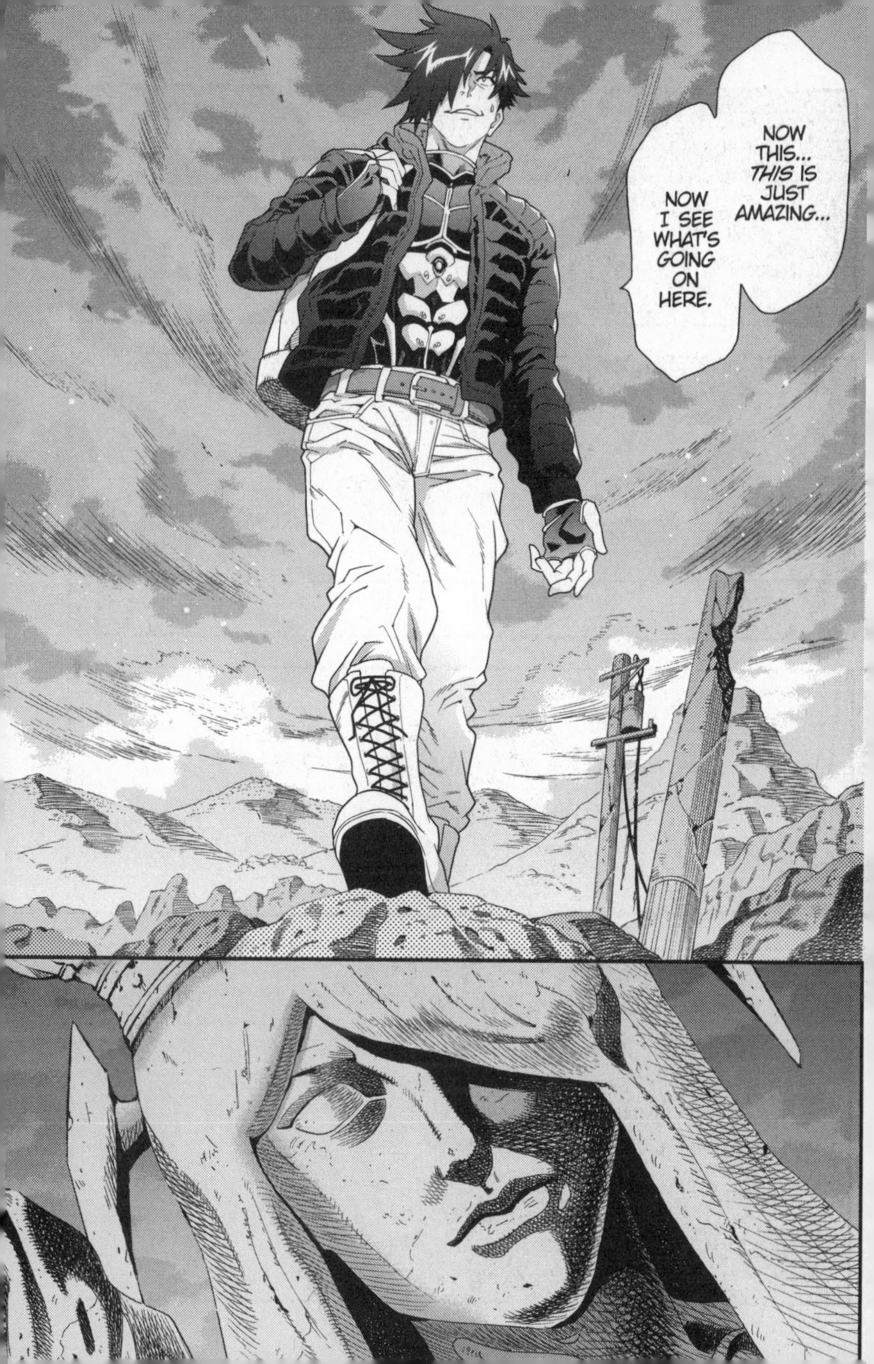
NOW THIS... *THIS* IS JUST AMAZING...
NOW I SEE WHAT'S GOING ON HERE.

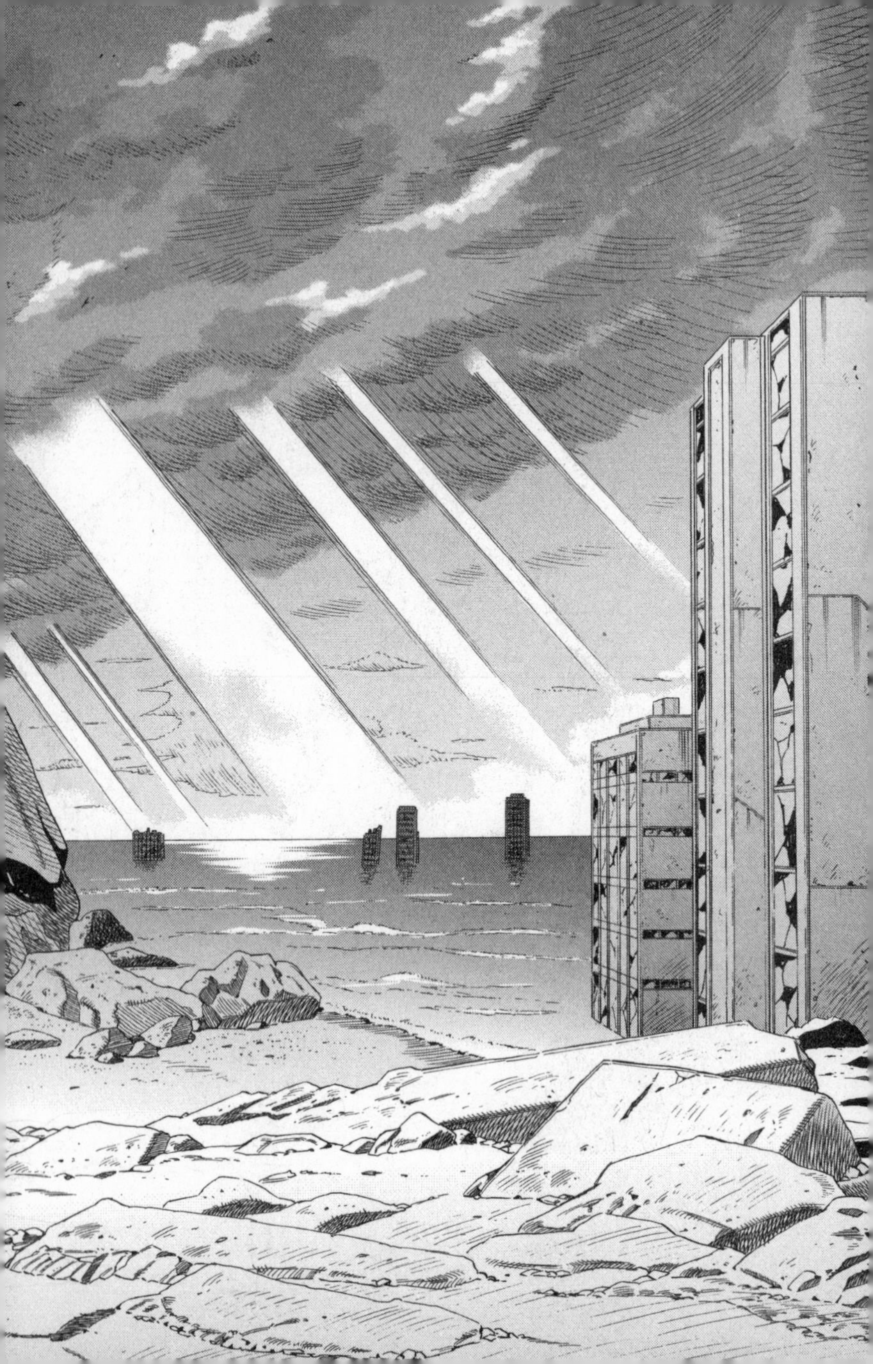

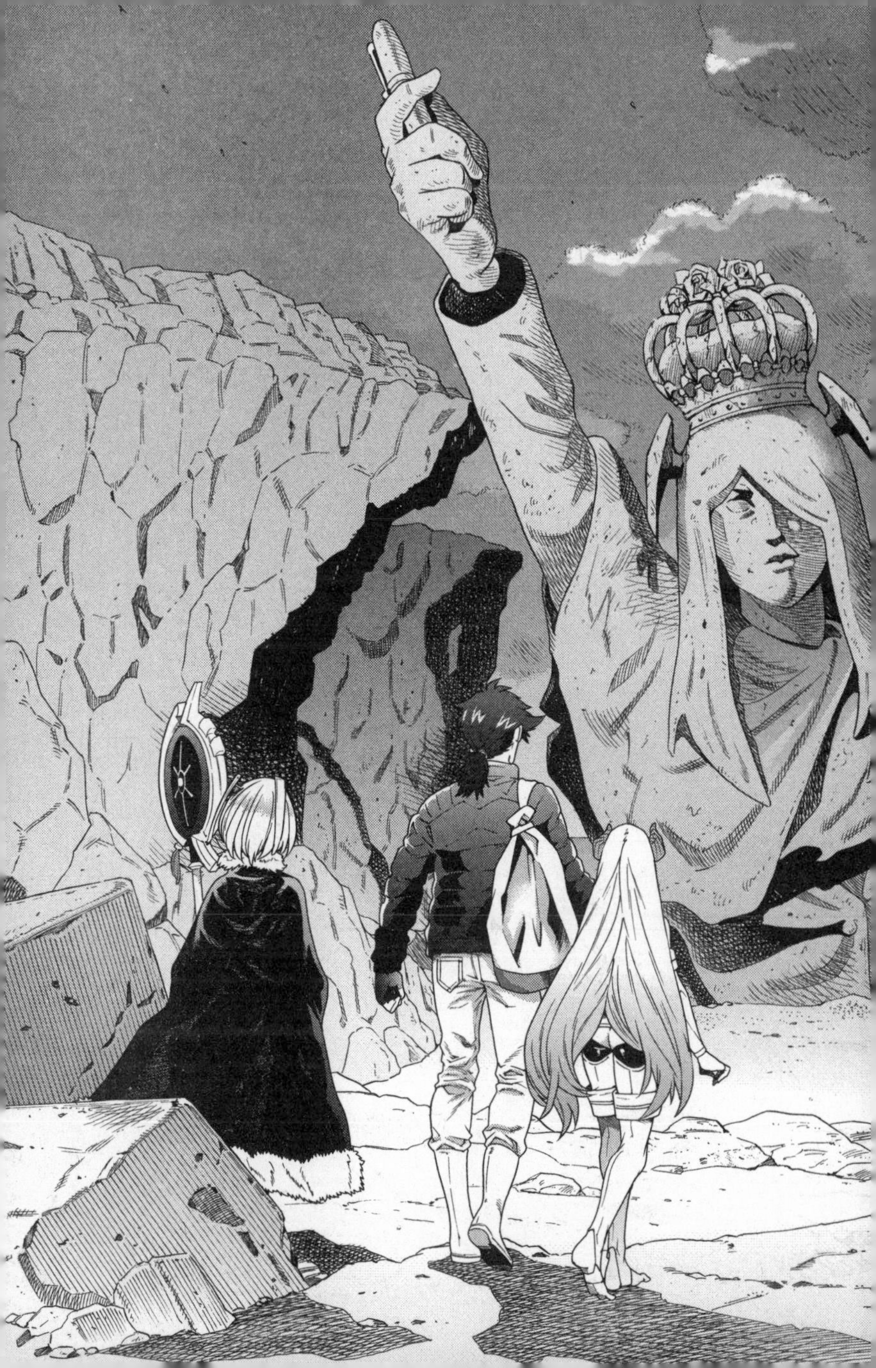

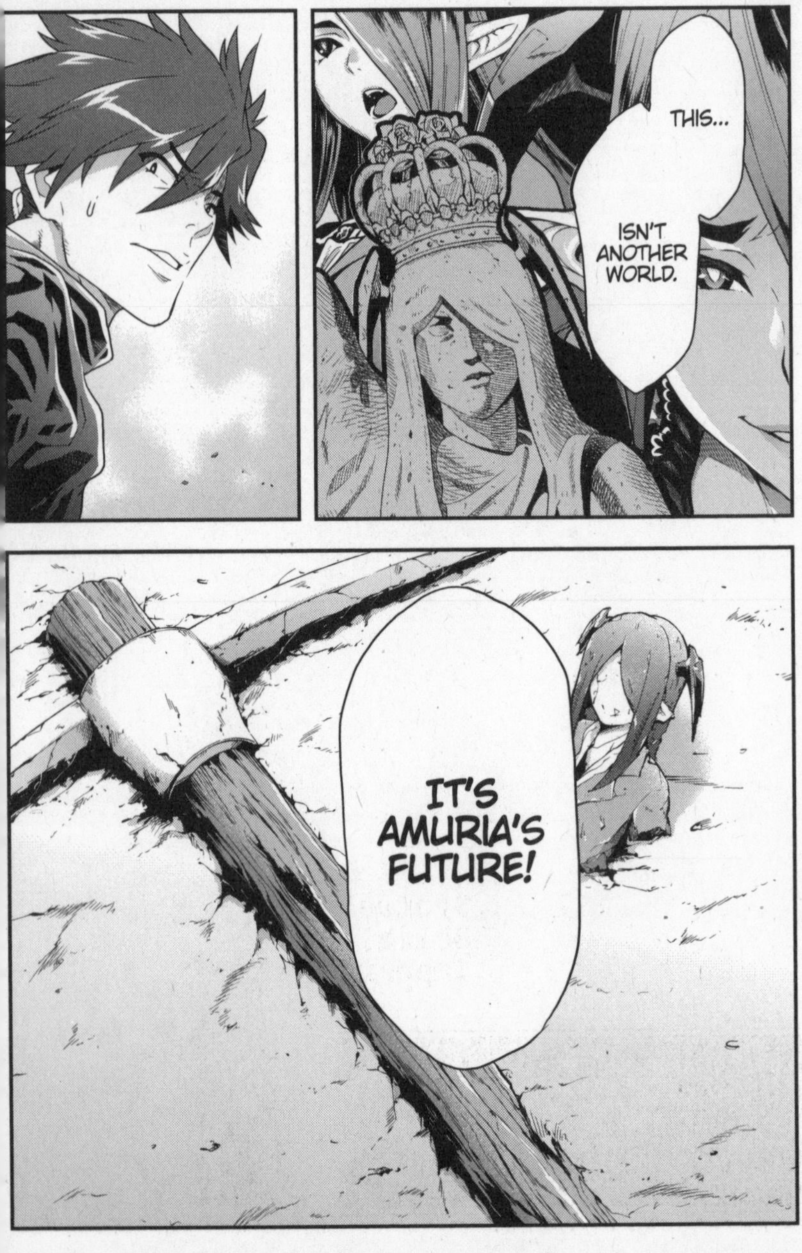
THIS...
ISN'T ANOTHER WORLD.
IT'S AMURIA'S FUTURE!

Statue of Belza the Impartial

A giant statue built to pray for
(curse) all people (other than her)
to be treated equally and fairly (as
livestock). On the pedestal's plaque
are engraved some words of praise
(scribbles and scrawlings) to
Raiza'ha's prosperity.

THE DUNGEON OF
BLACK COMPANY

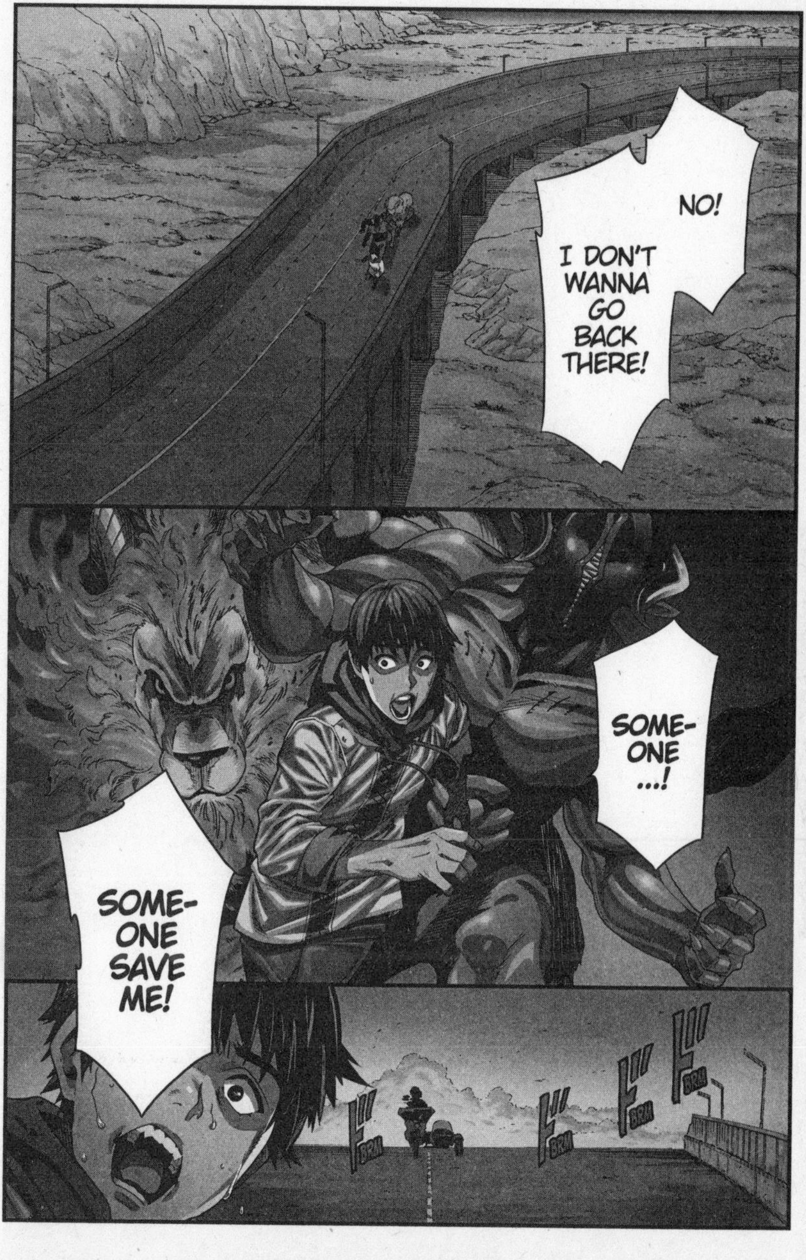
NO!
I DON'T WANNA GO BACK THERE!
SOME-ONE ...!
SOME-ONE SAVE ME!

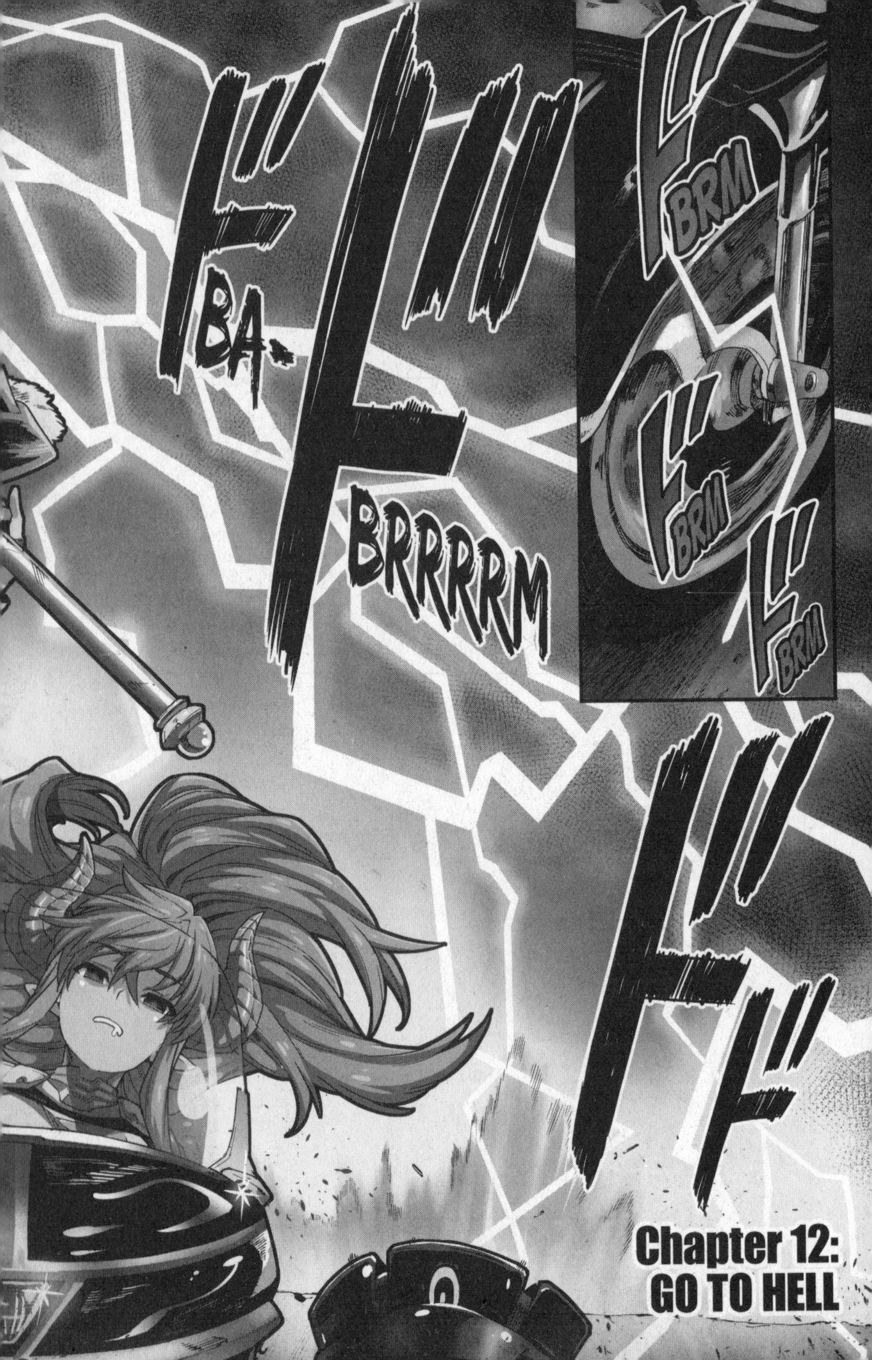
BRM
BRM
BRM
BA-BRRRRM
Chapter 12:
GO TO HELL

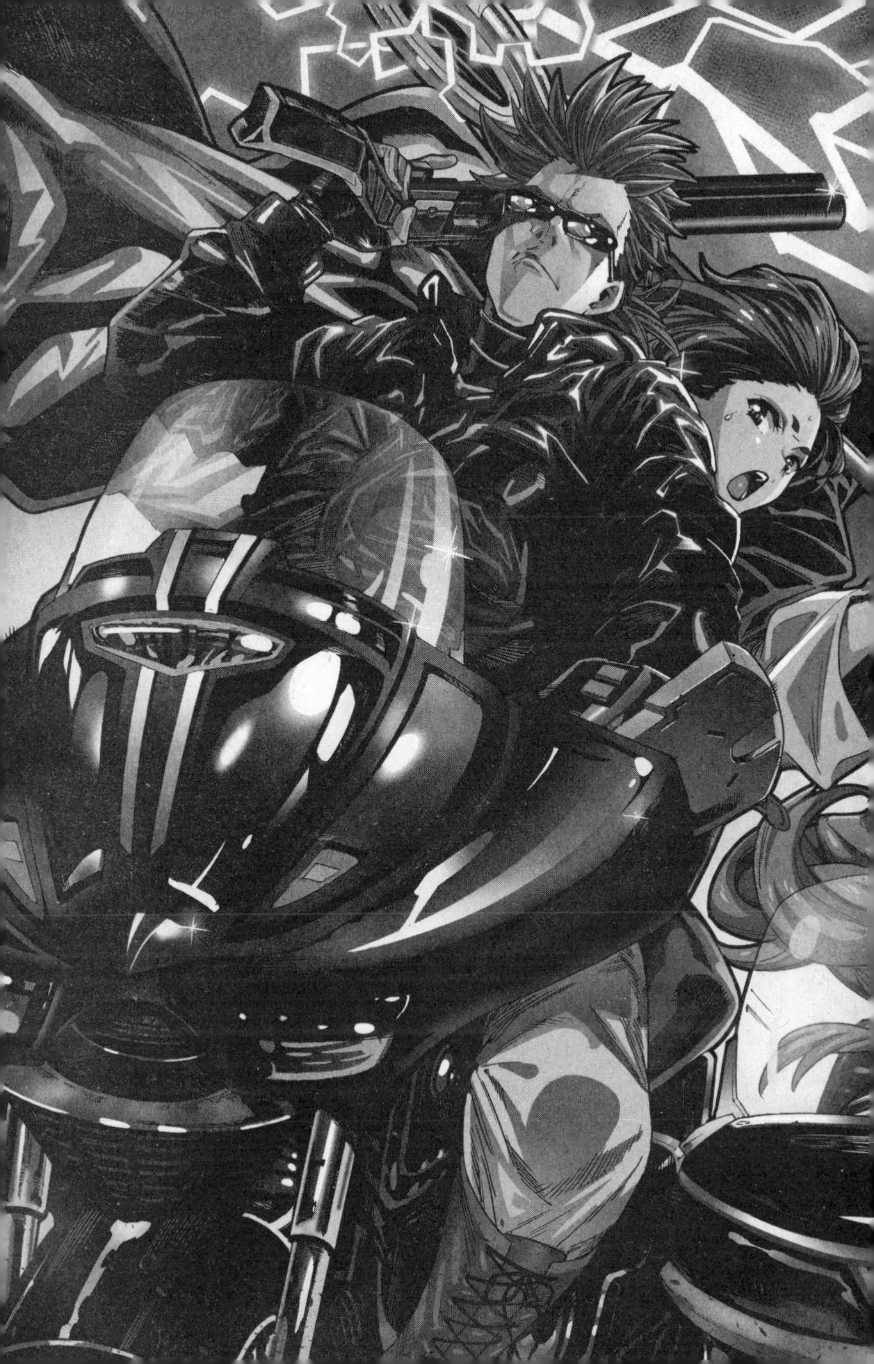

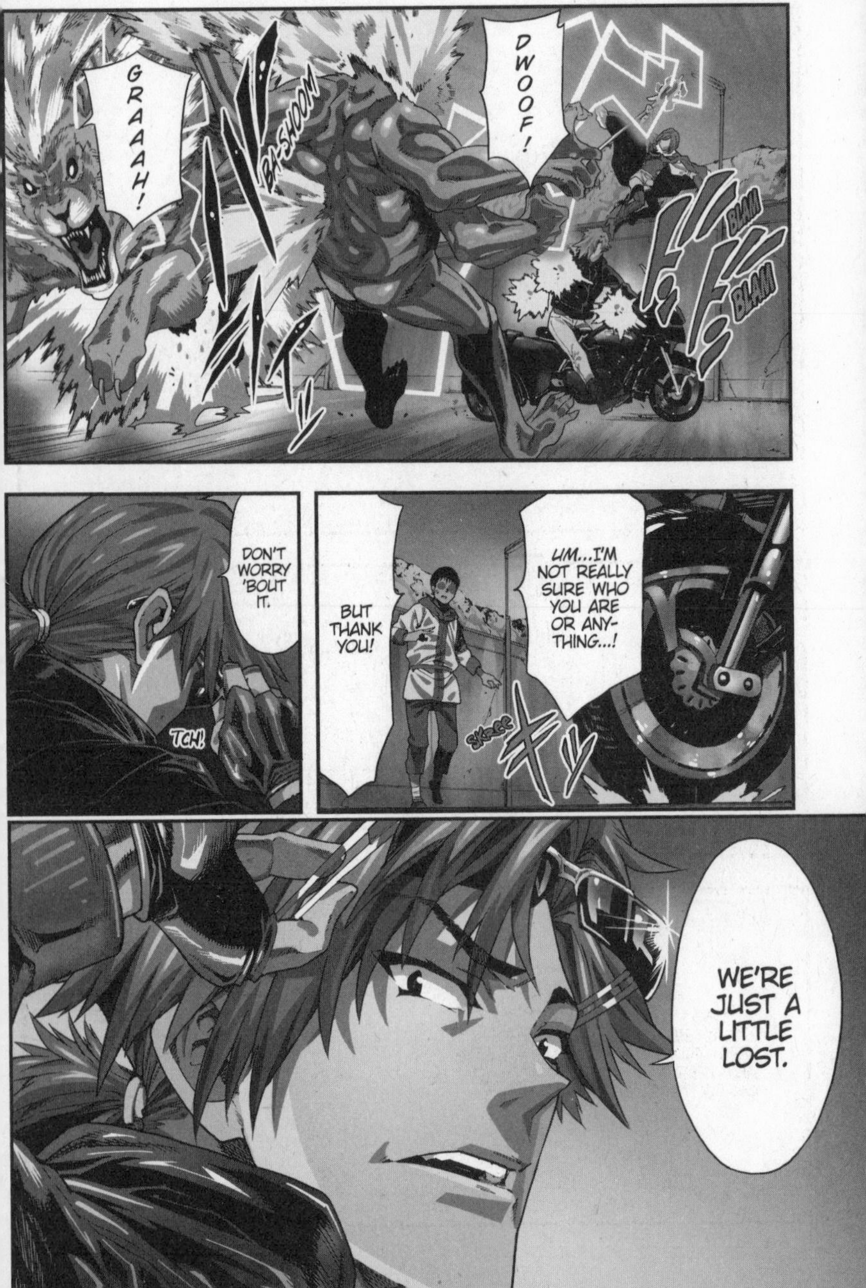
DWOOF!
BLAM
BLAM
BA-SHOOM
GRAAAH!
UM...I'M NOT REALLY SURE WHO YOU ARE OR ANY-THING...!
BUT THANK YOU!
SKREE
DON'T WORRY 'BOUT IT.
TCH!
WE'RE JUST A LITTLE LOST.

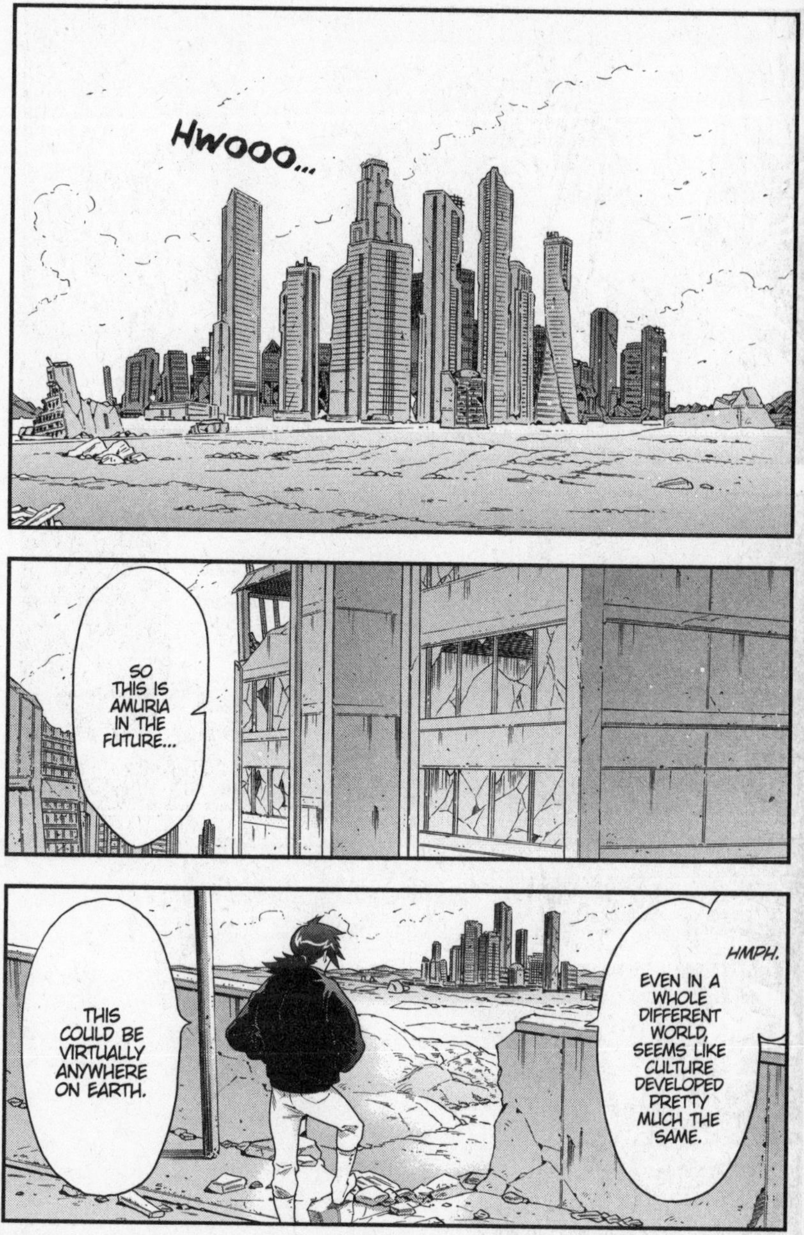
HWOOO...
SO THIS IS AMURIA IN THE FUTURE...
HMPH.
EVEN IN A WHOLE DIFFERENT WORLD, SEEMS LIKE CULTURE DEVELOPED PRETTY MUCH THE SAME.
THIS COULD BE VIRTUALLY ANYWHERE ON EARTH.

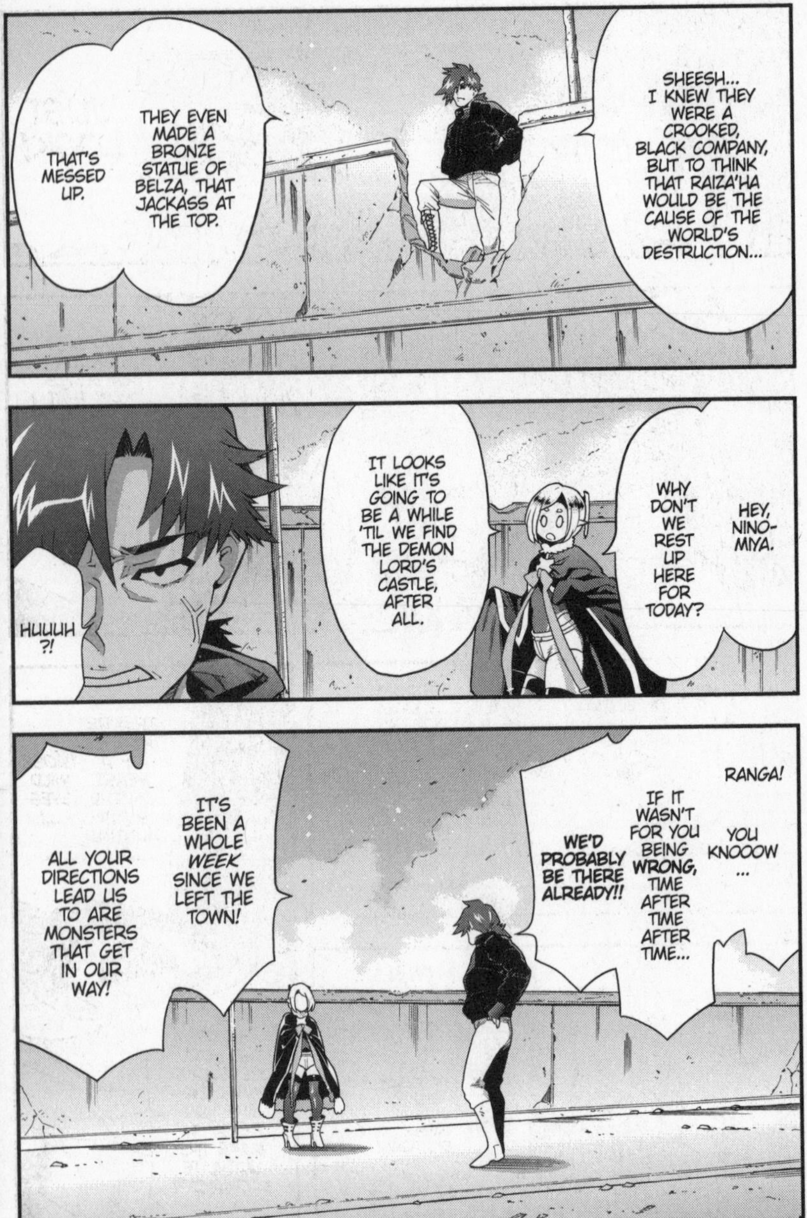
SHEESH... I KNEW THEY WERE A CROOKED, BLACK COMPANY, BUT TO THINK THAT RAIZA'HA WOULD BE THE CAUSE OF THE WORLD'S DESTRUCTION...
THEY EVEN MADE A BRONZE STATUE OF BELZA, THAT JACKASS AT THE TOP.
THAT'S MESSED UP.
HEY, NINO-MIYA.
WHY DON'T WE REST UP HERE FOR TODAY?
IT LOOKS LIKE IT'S GOING TO BE A WHILE 'TIL WE FIND THE DEMON LORD'S CASTLE, AFTER ALL.
HUUUH ?!
RANGA!
YOU KNOOOW ...
IF IT WASN'T FOR YOU BEING *WRONG*, TIME AFTER TIME AFTER TIME...
WE'D PROBABLY BE THERE ALREADY!!
IT'S BEEN A WHOLE *WEEK* SINCE WE LEFT THE TOWN!
ALL YOUR DIRECTIONS LEAD US TO ARE MONSTERS THAT GET IN OUR WAY!

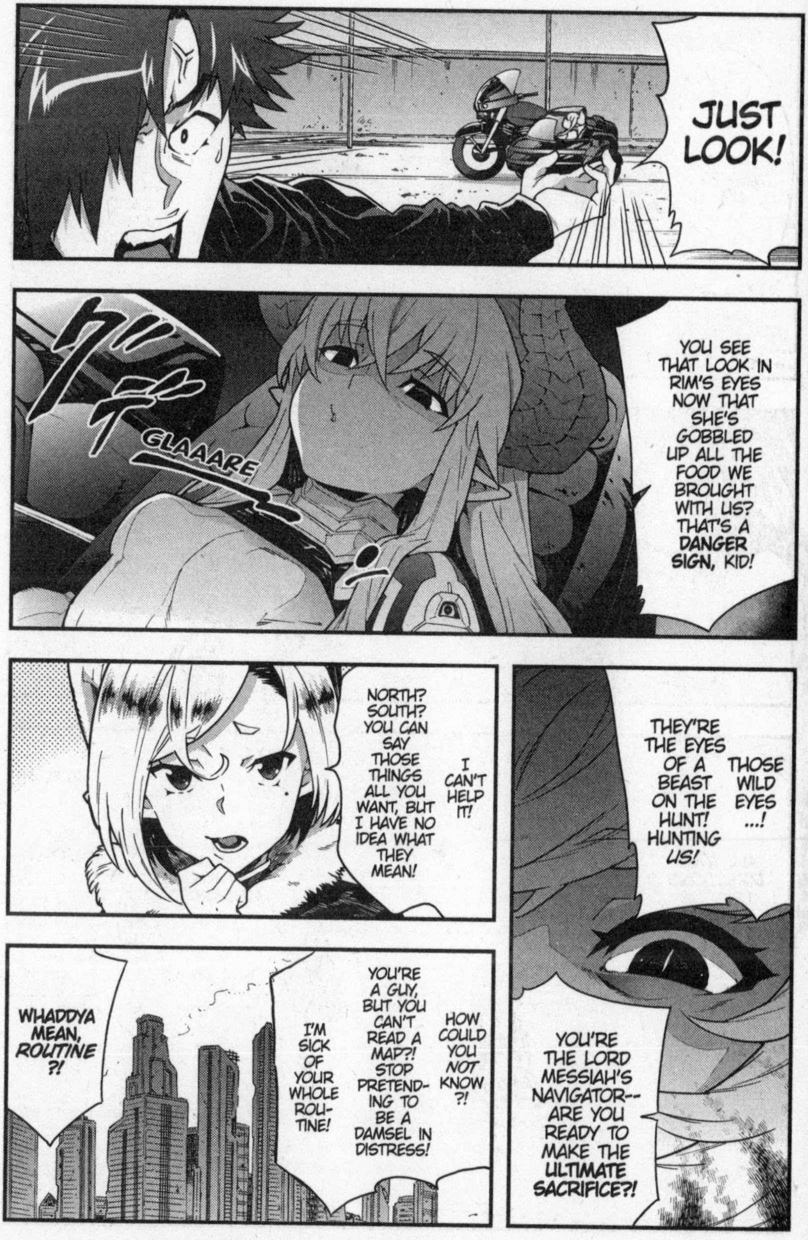
JUST LOOK!
YOU SEE THAT LOOK IN RIM'S EYES NOW THAT SHE'S GOBBLED UP ALL THE FOOD WE BROUGHT WITH US? THAT'S A DANGER SIGN, KID!
GLAAARE
THOSE WILD EYES ...!
THEY'RE THE EYES OF A BEAST ON THE HUNT! HUNTING US!
YOU'RE THE LORD MESSIAH'S NAVIGATOR-- ARE YOU READY TO MAKE THE ULTIMATE SACRIFICE?!
NORTH? SOUTH? YOU CAN SAY THOSE THINGS ALL YOU WANT, BUT I HAVE NO IDEA WHAT THEY MEAN!
I CAN'T HELP IT!
HOW COULD YOU NOT KNOW ?!
YOU'RE A GUY, BUT YOU CAN'T READ A MAP?! STOP PRETENDING TO BE A DAMSEL IN DISTRESS!
I'M SICK OF YOUR WHOLE ROUTINE!
WHADDYA MEAN, ROUTINE ?!

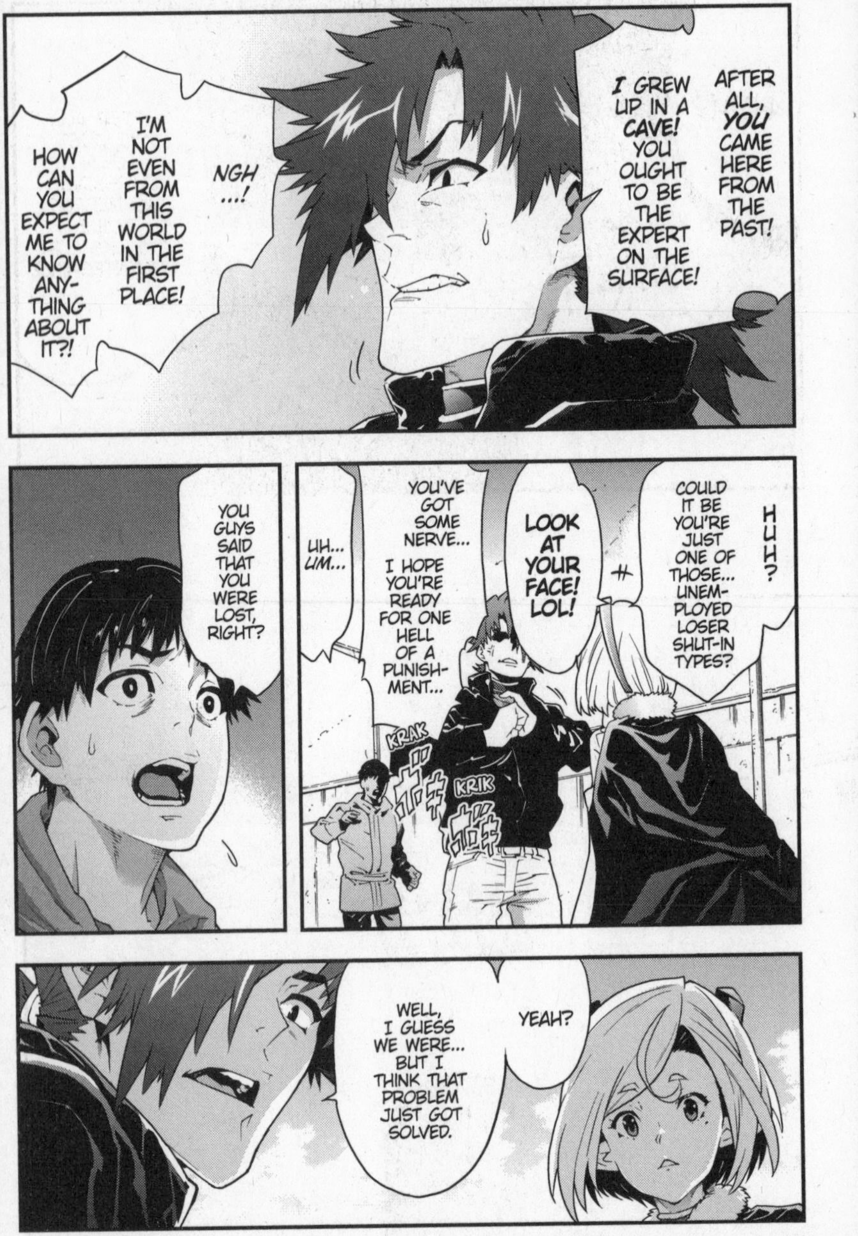
AFTER ALL, YOU CAME HERE FROM THE PAST!
I GREW UP IN A CAVE! YOU OUGHT TO BE THE EXPERT ON THE SURFACE!
NGH...!
I'M NOT EVEN FROM THIS WORLD IN THE FIRST PLACE!
HOW CAN YOU EXPECT ME TO KNOW ANY-THING ABOUT IT?!
HUH?
COULD IT BE YOU'RE JUST ONE OF THOSE... UNEMPLOYED LOSER SHUT-IN TYPES?
LOOK AT YOUR FACE! LOL!
YOU'VE GOT SOME NERVE...
I HOPE YOU'RE READY FOR ONE HELL OF A PUNISHMENT...
UH... UM...
KRAK
KRIK
YOU GUYS SAID THAT YOU WERE LOST, RIGHT?
YEAH?
WELL, I GUESS WE WERE... BUT I THINK THAT PROBLEM JUST GOT SOLVED.

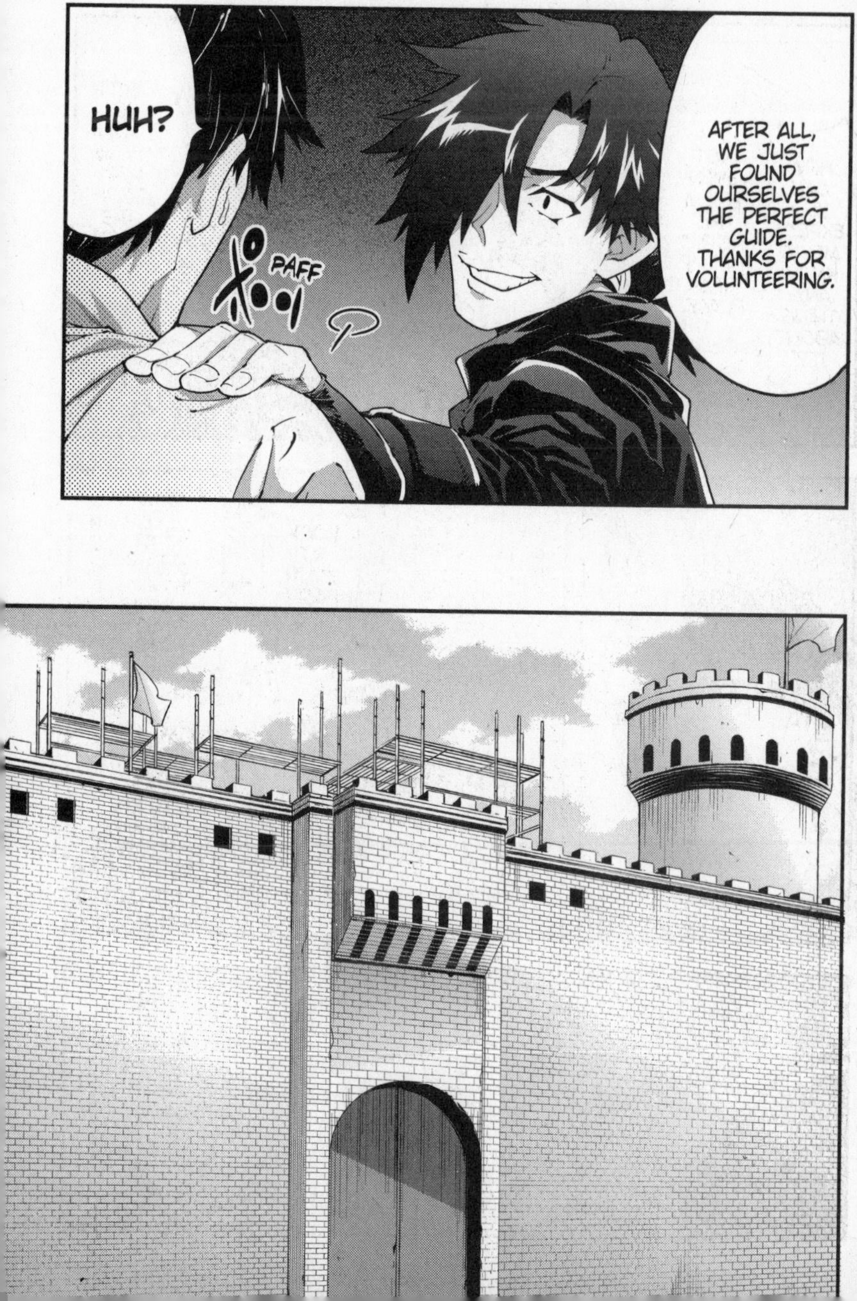
AFTER ALL, WE JUST FOUND OURSELVES THE PERFECT GUIDE. THANKS FOR VOLUNTEERING.
HUH?
PAFF

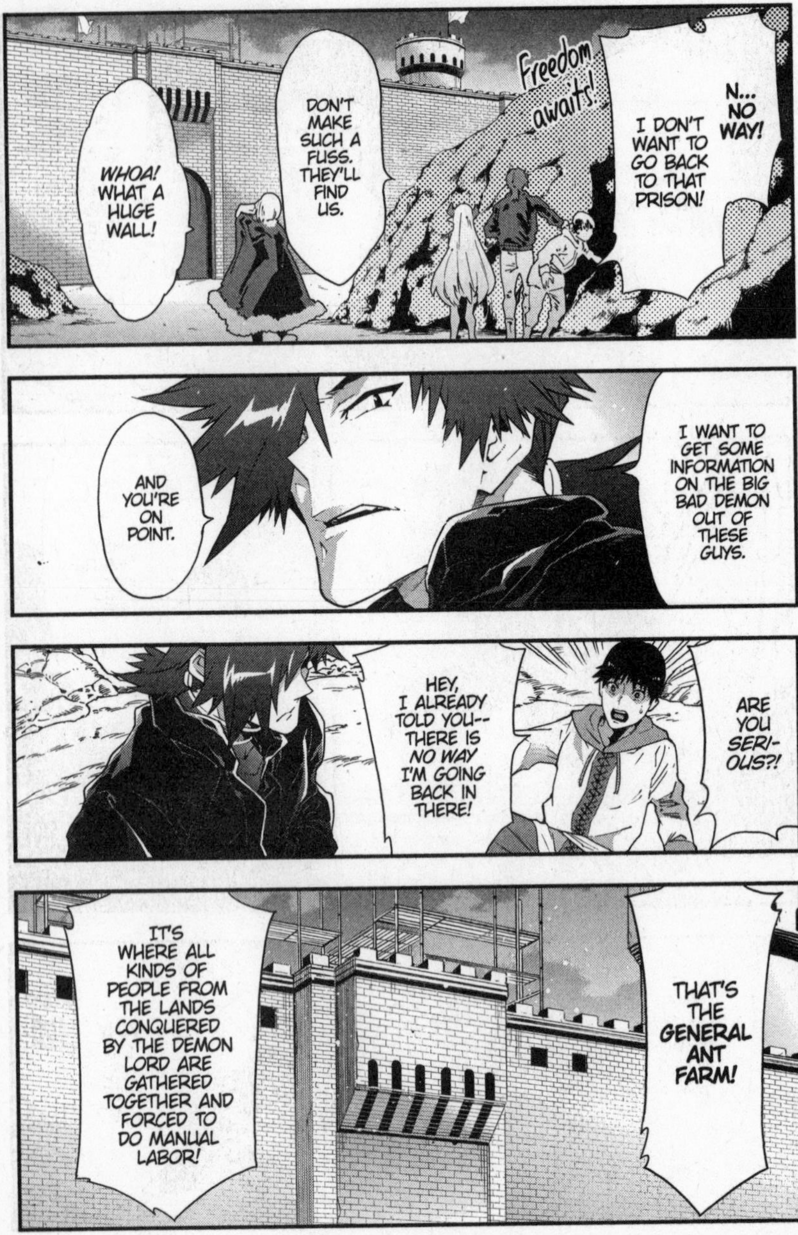
N... NO WAY!
I DON'T WANT TO GO BACK TO THAT PRISON!
Freedom awaits!
DON'T MAKE SUCH A FUSS. THEY'LL FIND US.
WHOA! WHAT A HUGE WALL!
I WANT TO GET SOME INFORMATION ON THE BIG BAD DEMON OUT OF THESE GUYS.
AND YOU'RE ON POINT.
ARE YOU SERI-OUS?!
HEY, I ALREADY TOLD YOU-- THERE IS NO WAY I'M GOING BACK IN THERE!
THAT'S THE GENERAL ANT FARM!
IT'S WHERE ALL KINDS OF PEOPLE FROM THE LANDS CONQUERED BY THE DEMON LORD ARE GATHERED TOGETHER AND FORCED TO DO MANUAL LABOR!

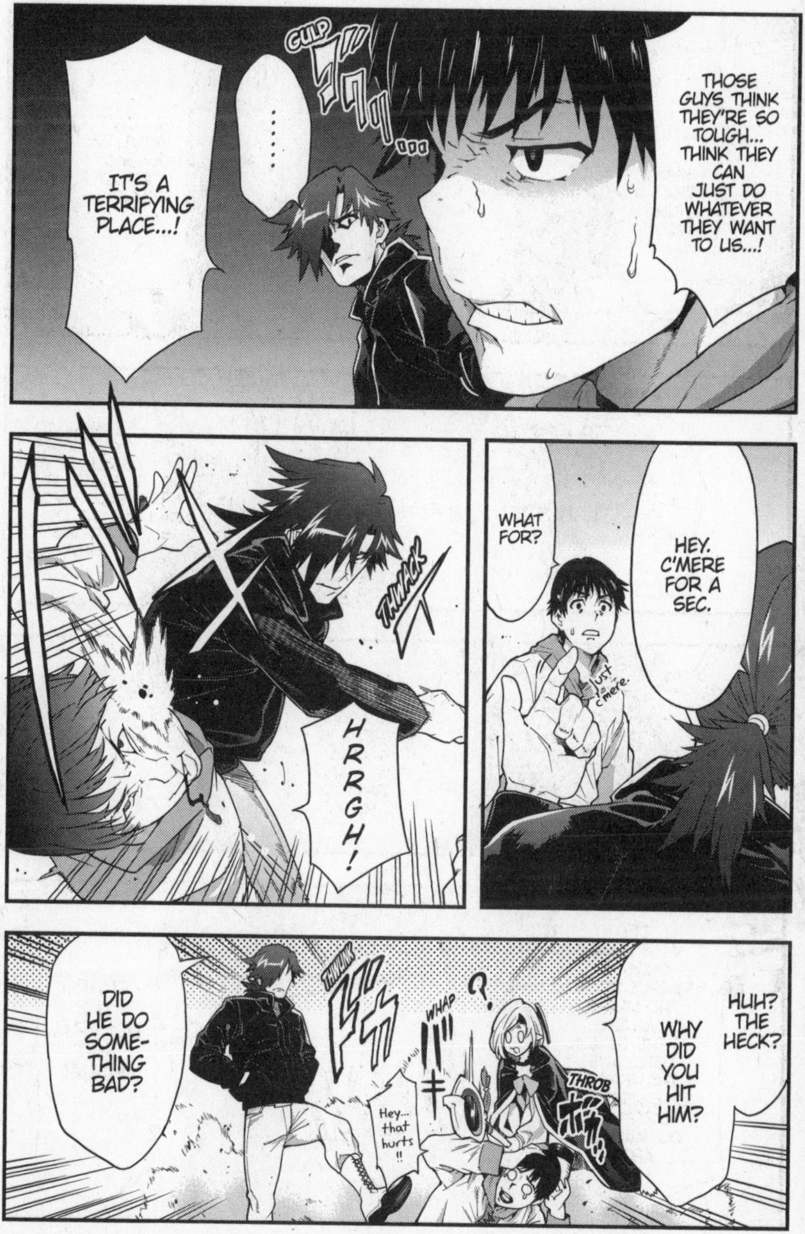
THOSE GUYS THINK THEY'RE SO TOUGH... THINK THEY CAN JUST DO WHATEVER THEY WANT TO US...!
GULP
......
IT'S A TERRIFYING PLACE...!
HEY. C'MERE FOR A SEC.
WHAT FOR?
Just c'mere.
THWACK
HRRGH!
HUH? THE HECK?
WHY DID YOU HIT HIM?
THROB
Hey... that hurts!!
WHAP
THWUNK
DID HE DO SOME-THING BAD?

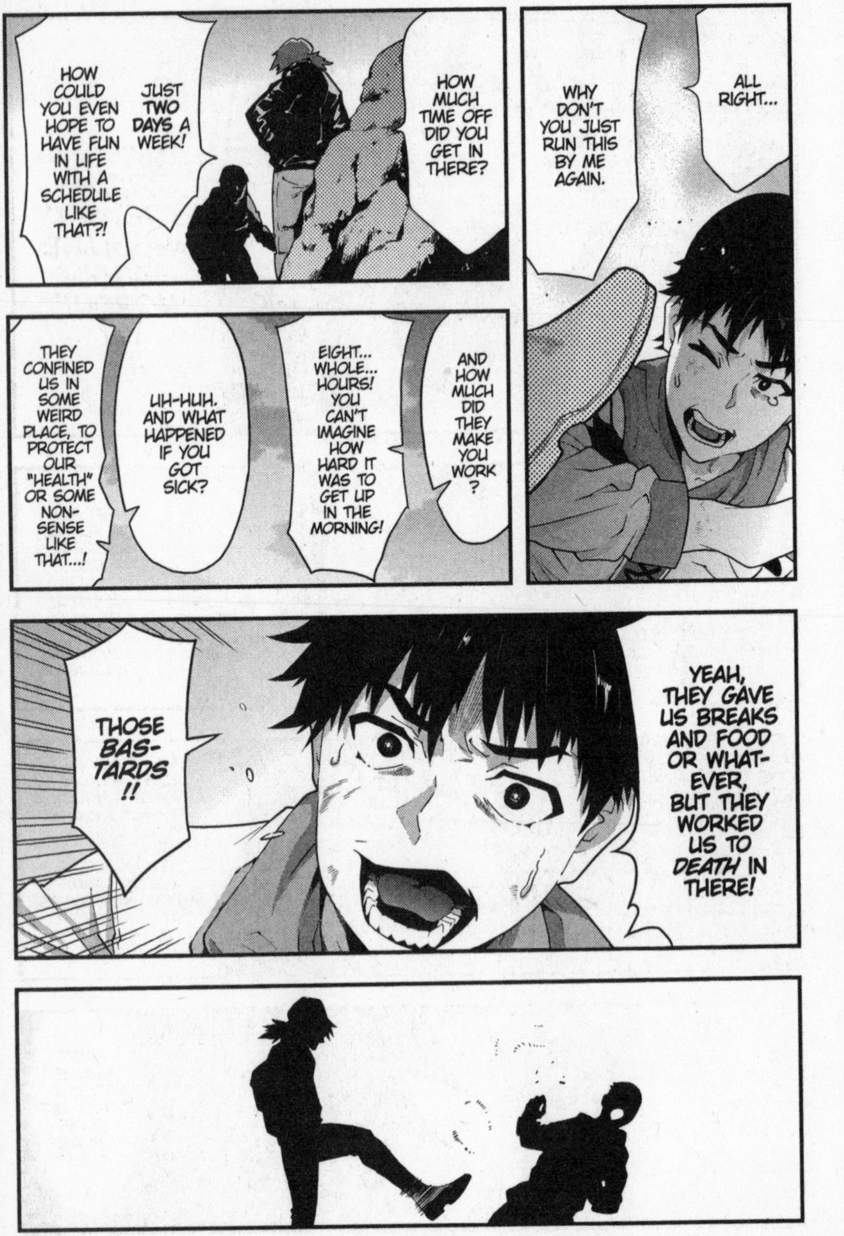
ALL RIGHT...
WHY DON'T YOU JUST RUN THIS BY ME AGAIN.
HOW MUCH TIME OFF DID YOU GET IN THERE?
JUST TWO DAYS A WEEK!
HOW COULD YOU EVEN HOPE TO HAVE FUN IN LIFE WITH A SCHEDULE LIKE THAT?!
AND HOW MUCH DID THEY MAKE YOU WORK?
EIGHT... WHOLE... HOURS! YOU CAN'T IMAGINE HOW HARD IT WAS TO GET UP IN THE MORNING!
UH-HUH. AND WHAT HAPPENED IF YOU GOT SICK?
THEY CONFINED US IN SOME WEIRD PLACE, TO PROTECT OUR "HEALTH" OR SOME NON-SENSE LIKE THAT...!
YEAH, THEY GAVE US BREAKS AND FOOD OR WHAT-EVER, BUT THEY WORKED US TO *DEATH* IN THERE!
THOSE *BAS-TARDS* !!

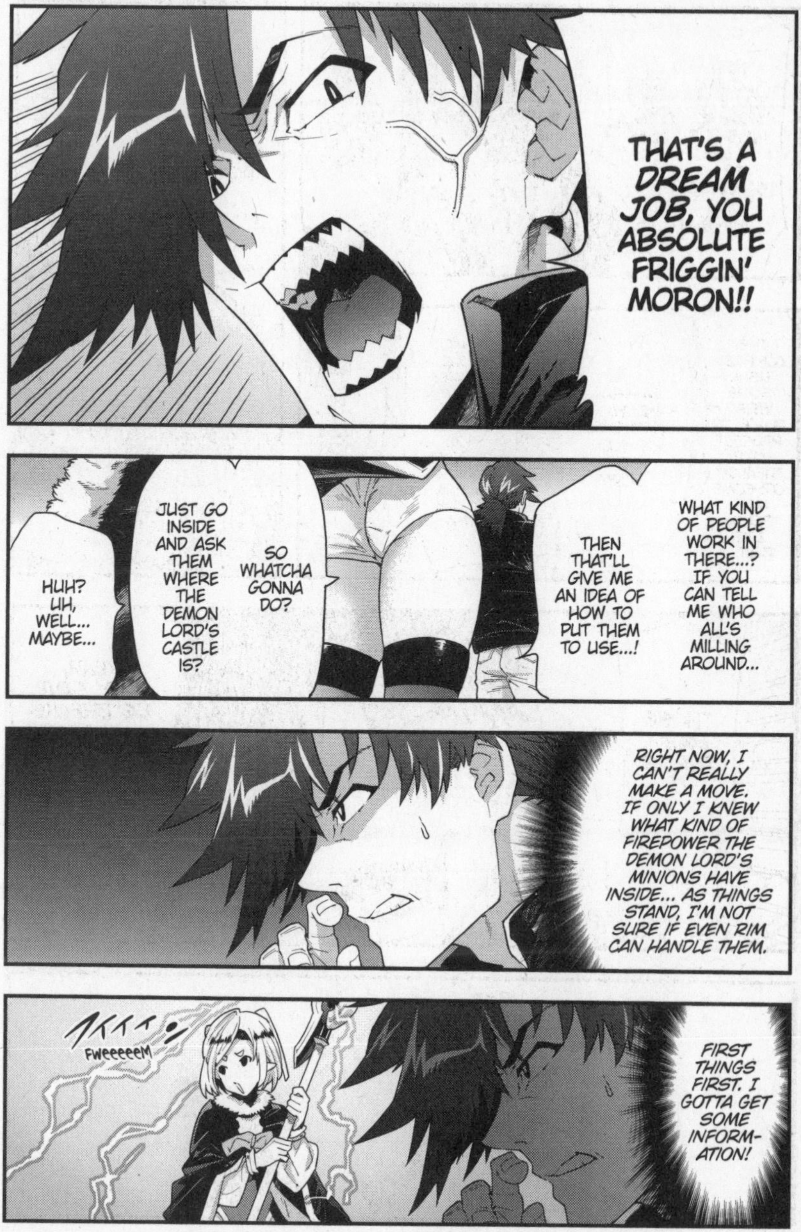

THAT'S A DREAM JOB, YOU ABSOLUTE FRIGGIN' MORON!!
WHAT KIND OF PEOPLE WORK IN THERE...? IF YOU CAN TELL ME WHO ALL'S MILLING AROUND...
THEN THAT'LL GIVE ME AN IDEA OF HOW TO PUT THEM TO USE...!
SO WHATCHA GONNA DO?
JUST GO INSIDE AND ASK THEM WHERE THE DEMON LORD'S CASTLE IS?
HUH? UH, WELL... MAYBE...
RIGHT NOW, I CAN'T REALLY MAKE A MOVE. IF ONLY I KNEW WHAT KIND OF FIREPOWER THE DEMON LORD'S MINIONS HAVE INSIDE... AS THINGS STAND, I'M NOT SURE IF EVEN RIM CAN HANDLE THEM.
FIRST THINGS FIRST. I GOTTA GET SOME INFORMATION!
FweeeeeM

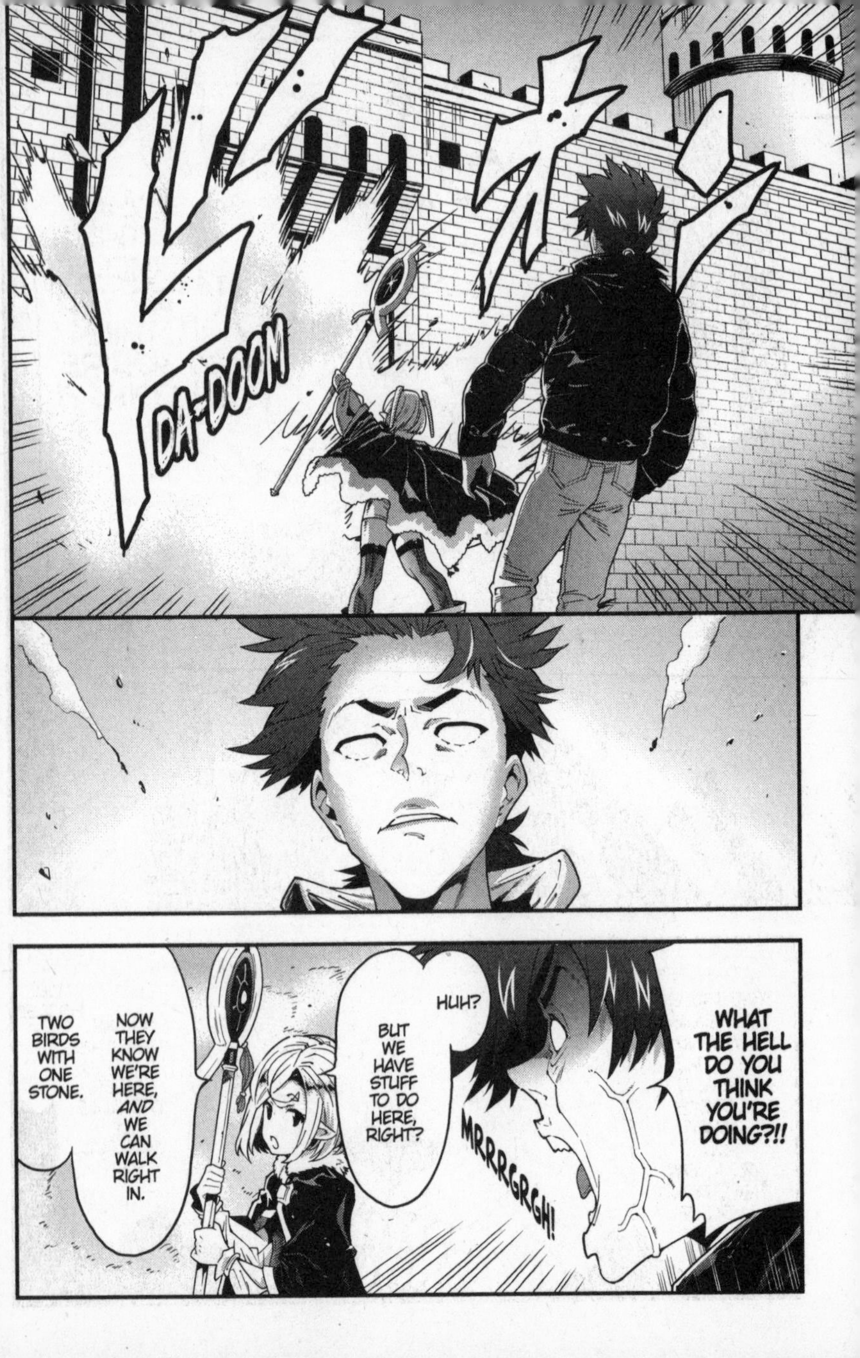
DA-DOOM
WHAT THE HELL DO YOU THINK YOU'RE DOING?!!
MRRRGRGH!
HUH?
BUT WE HAVE STUFF TO DO HERE, RIGHT?
NOW THEY KNOW WE'RE HERE, AND WE CAN WALK RIGHT IN.
TWO BIRDS WITH ONE STONE.

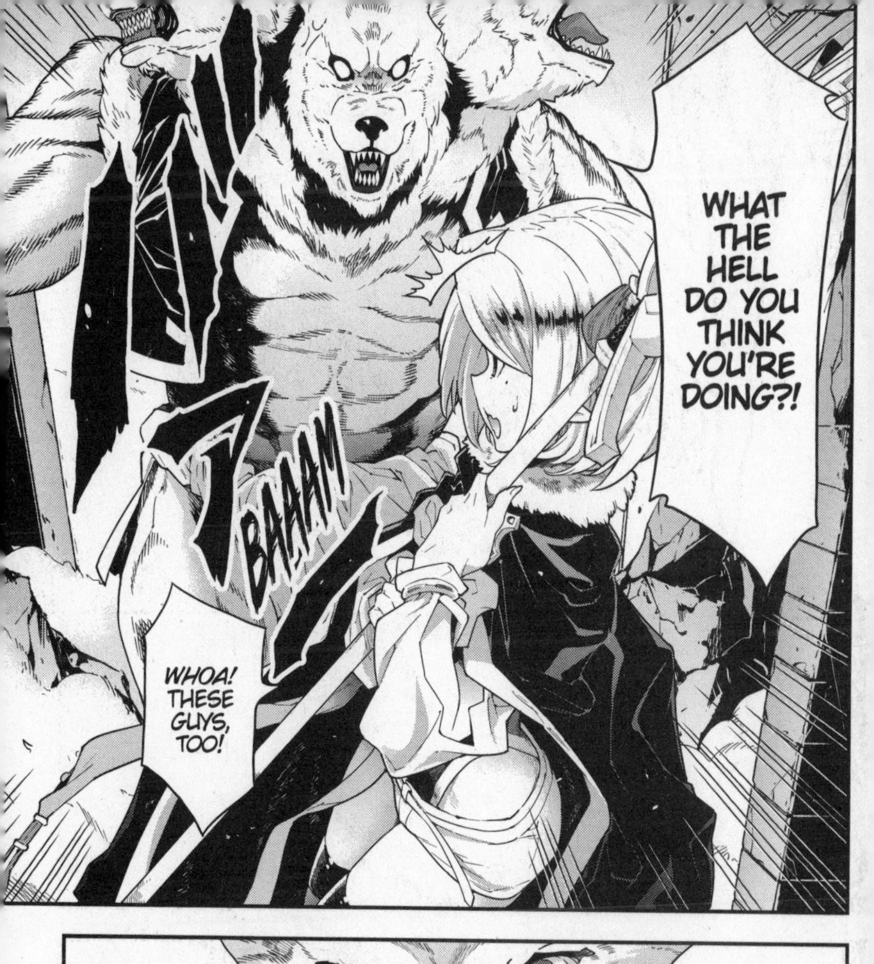
WHAT THE HELL DO YOU THINK YOU'RE DOING?!
BAAAM
WHOA! THESE GUYS, TOO!

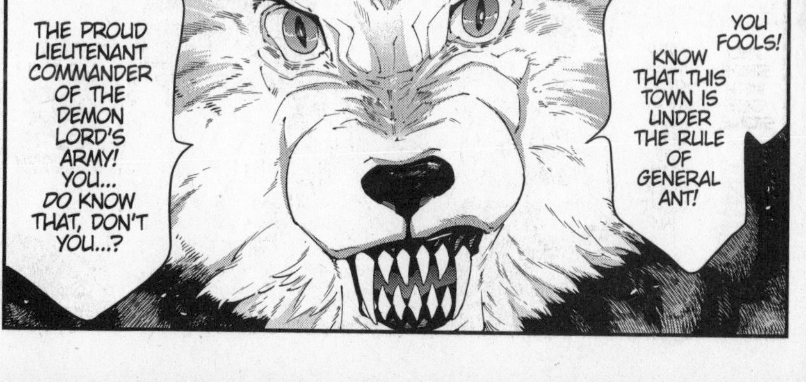
YOU FOOLS!
KNOW THAT THIS TOWN IS UNDER THE RULE OF GENERAL ANT!
THE PROUD LIEUTENANT COMMANDER OF THE DEMON LORD'S ARMY! YOU... DO KNOW THAT, DON'T YOU...?

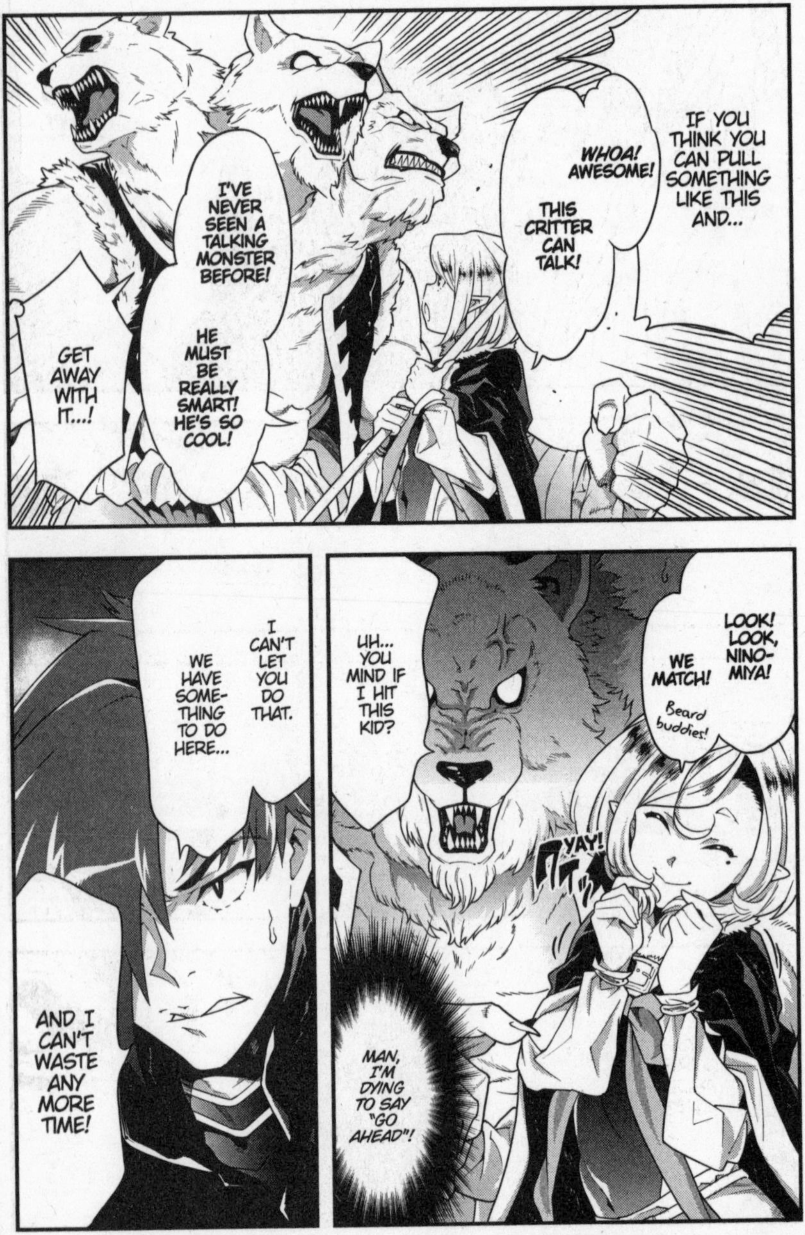
IF YOU THINK YOU CAN PULL SOMETHING LIKE THIS AND...
WHOA! AWESOME!
THIS CRITTER CAN TALK!
I'VE NEVER SEEN A TALKING MONSTER BEFORE!
HE MUST BE REALLY SMART! HE'S SO COOL!
GET AWAY WITH IT...!
LOOK! LOOK, NINO-MIYA!
WE MATCH!
Beard buddies!
YAY!
UH... YOU MIND IF I HIT THIS KID?
MAN, I'M DYING TO SAY "GO AHEAD"!
I CAN'T LET YOU DO THAT.
WE HAVE SOME-THING TO DO HERE...
AND I CAN'T WASTE ANY MORE TIME!

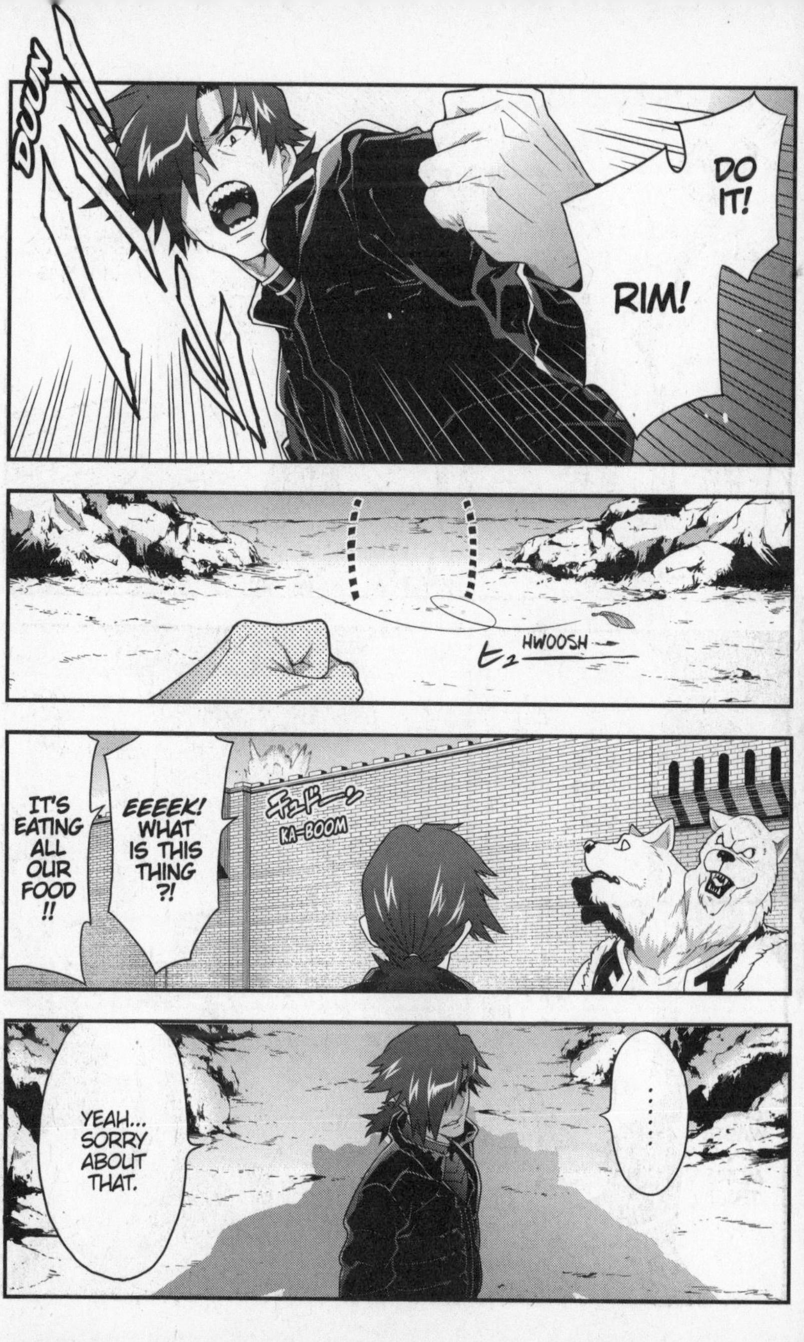
DUUN
DO IT!
RIM!
HWOOSH
KA-BOOM
EEEEK! WHAT IS THIS THING ?!
IT'S EATING ALL OUR FOOD !!
......
YEAH... SORRY ABOUT THAT.

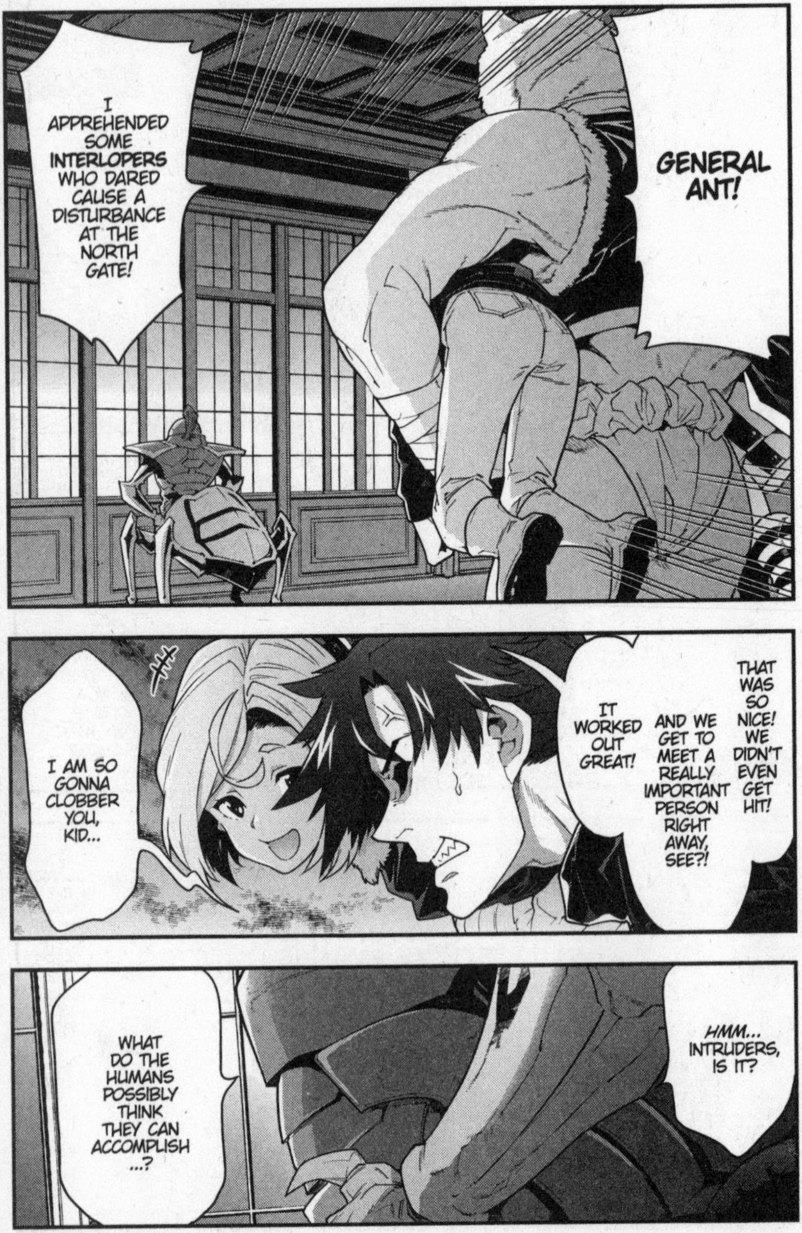
GENERAL ANT!
I APPREHENDED SOME INTERLOPERS WHO DARED CAUSE A DISTURBANCE AT THE NORTH GATE!
THAT WAS SO NICE! WE DIDN'T EVEN GET HIT!
AND WE GET TO MEET A REALLY IMPORTANT PERSON RIGHT AWAY, SEE?!
IT WORKED OUT GREAT!
I AM SO GONNA CLOBBER YOU, KID...
HMM... INTRUDERS, IS IT?
WHAT DO THE HUMANS POSSIBLY THINK THEY CAN ACCOMPLISH ...?

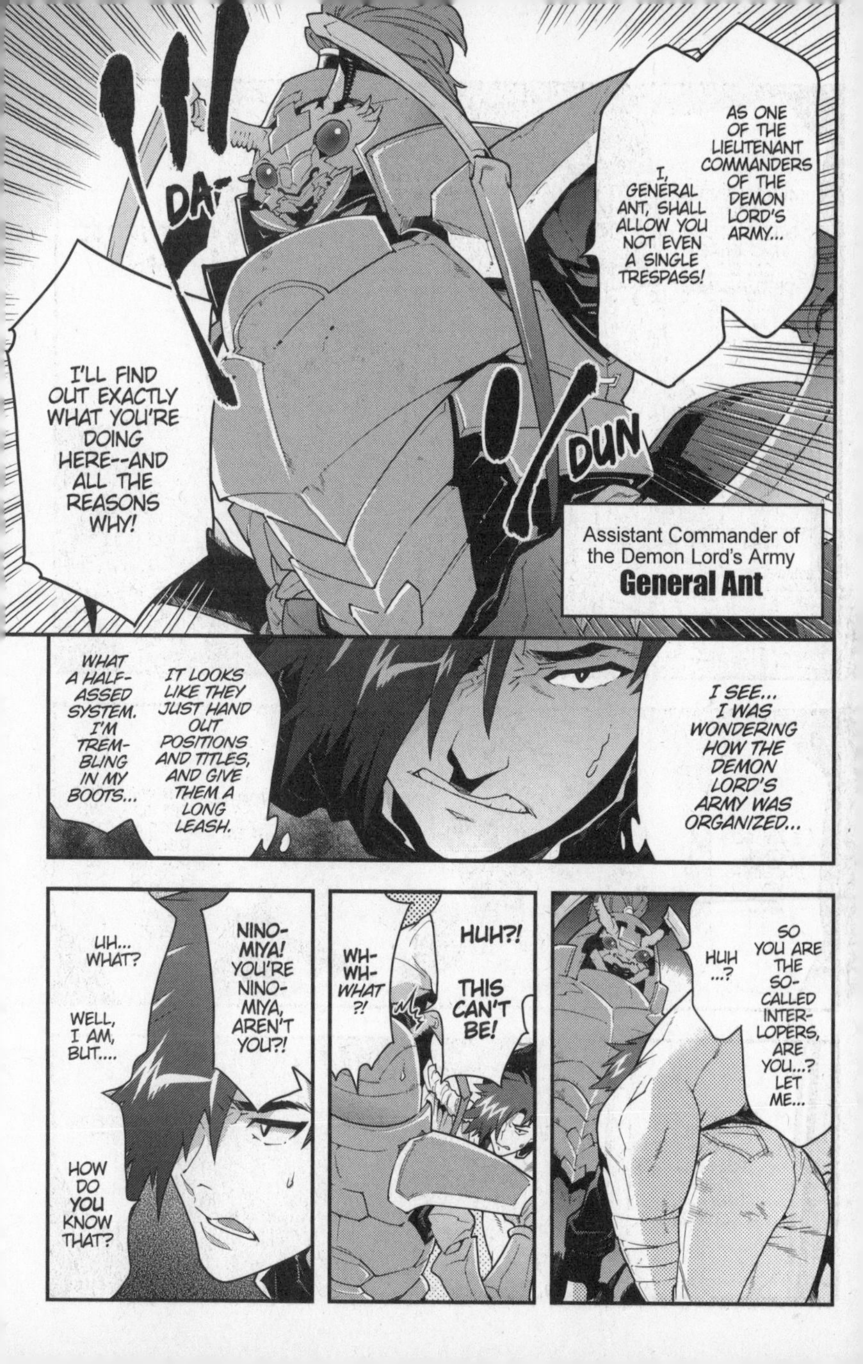
AS ONE OF THE LIEUTENANT COMMANDERS OF THE DEMON LORD'S ARMY...
I, GENERAL ANT, SHALL ALLOW YOU NOT EVEN A SINGLE TRESPASS!
DA
DUN
Assistant Commander of the Demon Lord's Army
General Ant
I'LL FIND OUT EXACTLY WHAT YOU'RE DOING HERE--AND ALL THE REASONS WHY!
I SEE... I WAS WONDERING HOW THE DEMON LORD'S ARMY WAS ORGANIZED...
IT LOOKS LIKE THEY JUST HAND OUT POSITIONS AND TITLES, AND GIVE THEM A LONG LEASH.
WHAT A HALF-ASSED SYSTEM. I'M TREMBLING IN MY BOOTS...
SO YOU ARE THE SO-CALLED INTERLOPERS, ARE YOU...? LET ME...
HUH ...?
HUH?!
THIS CAN'T BE!
WH-WH-WHAT?!
NINOMIYA! YOU'RE NINOMIYA, AREN'T YOU?!
UH... WHAT?
WELL, I AM, BUT....
HOW DO YOU KNOW THAT?

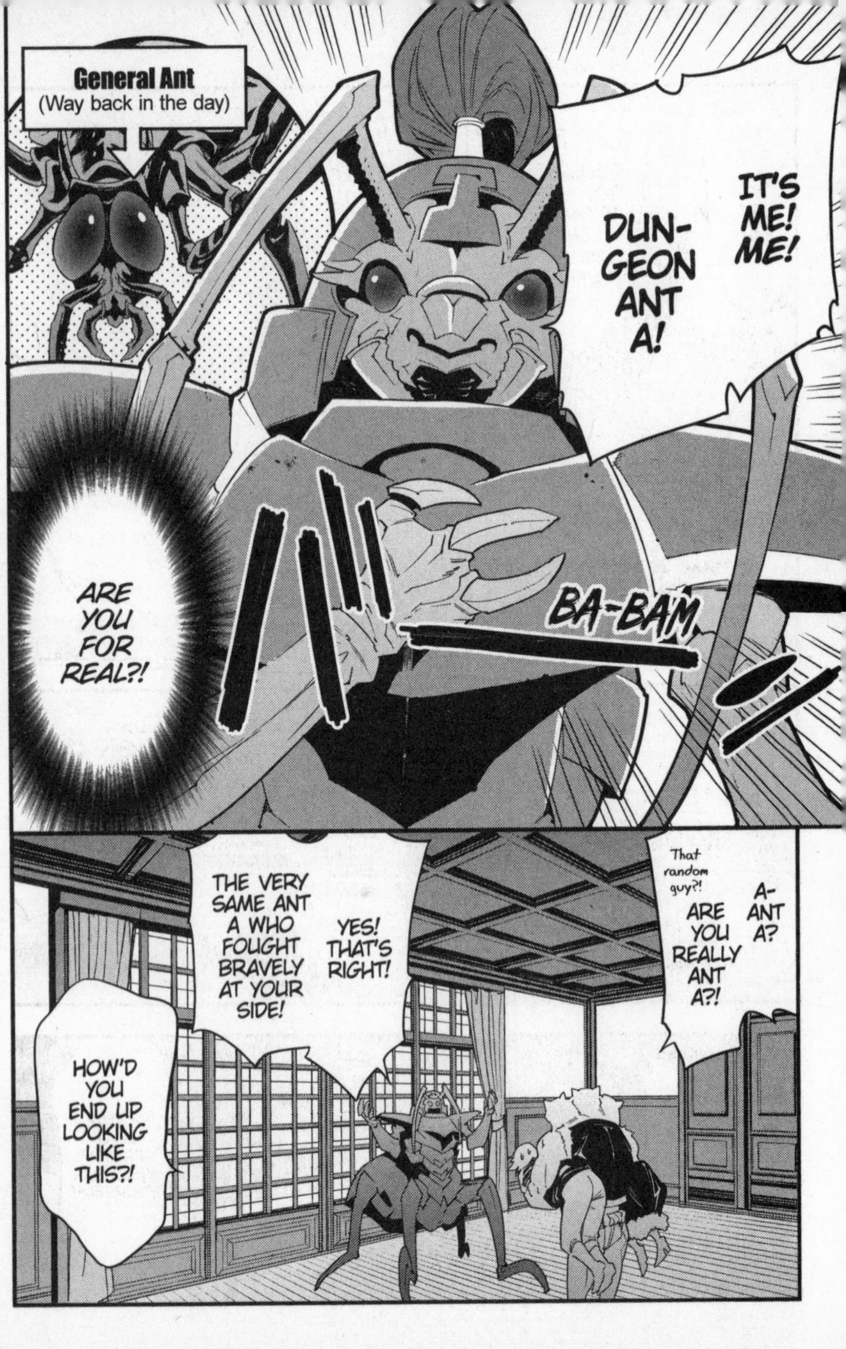
IT'S ME! ME!
DUNGEON ANT A!
General Ant
(Way back in the day)
BA-BAM
ARE YOU FOR REAL?!
That random guy?!
A-ANT A?
ARE YOU REALLY ANT A?!
YES! THAT'S RIGHT!
THE VERY SAME ANT A WHO FOUGHT BRAVELY AT YOUR SIDE!
HOW'D YOU END UP LOOKING LIKE THIS?!

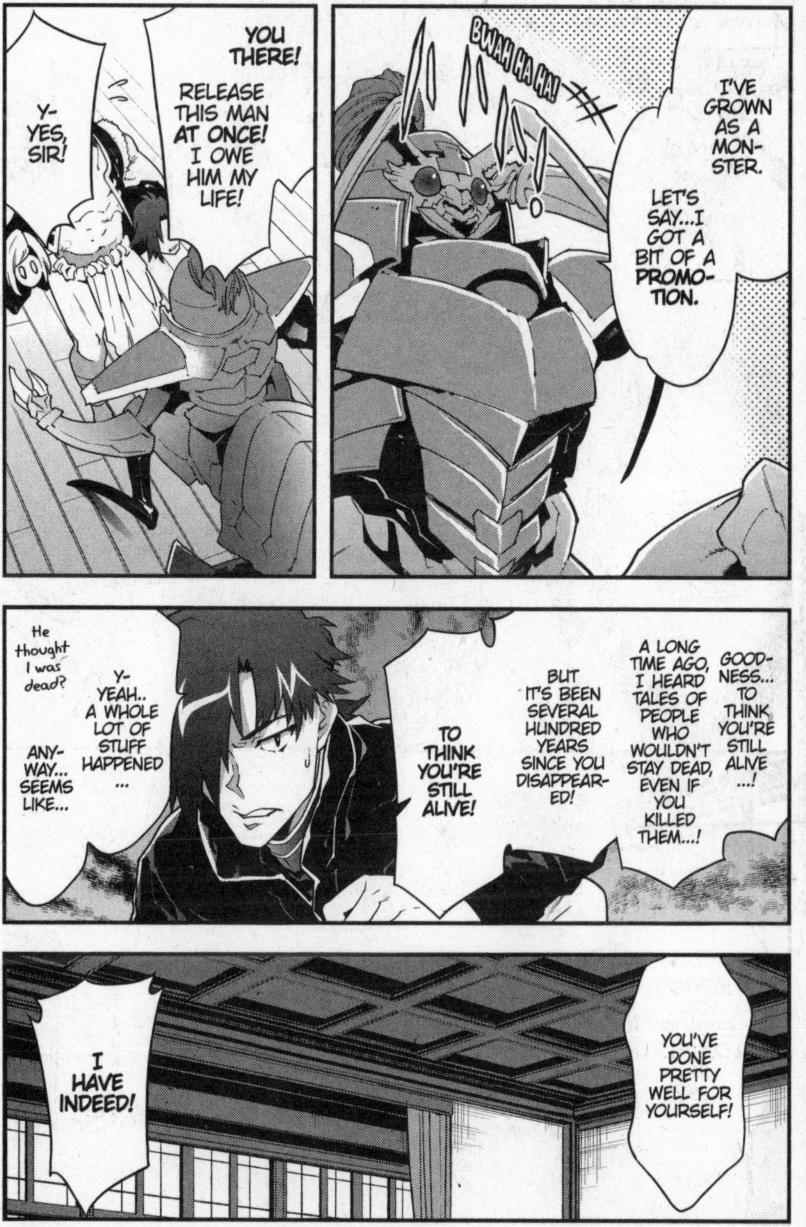
BWAH HA HA!
I'VE GROWN AS A MONSTER.
LET'S SAY...I GOT A BIT OF A PROMOTION.
YOU THERE!
RELEASE THIS MAN AT ONCE! I OWE HIM MY LIFE!
Y-YES, SIR!
GOODNESS... TO THINK YOU'RE STILL ALIVE ...!
A LONG TIME AGO, I HEARD TALES OF PEOPLE WHO WOULDN'T STAY DEAD, EVEN IF YOU KILLED THEM...!
BUT IT'S BEEN SEVERAL HUNDRED YEARS SINCE YOU DISAPPEARED!
TO THINK YOU'RE STILL ALIVE!
Y-YEAH.. A WHOLE LOT OF STUFF HAPPENED ...
He thought I was dead?
ANYWAY... SEEMS LIKE...
YOU'VE DONE PRETTY WELL FOR YOURSELF!
I HAVE INDEED!

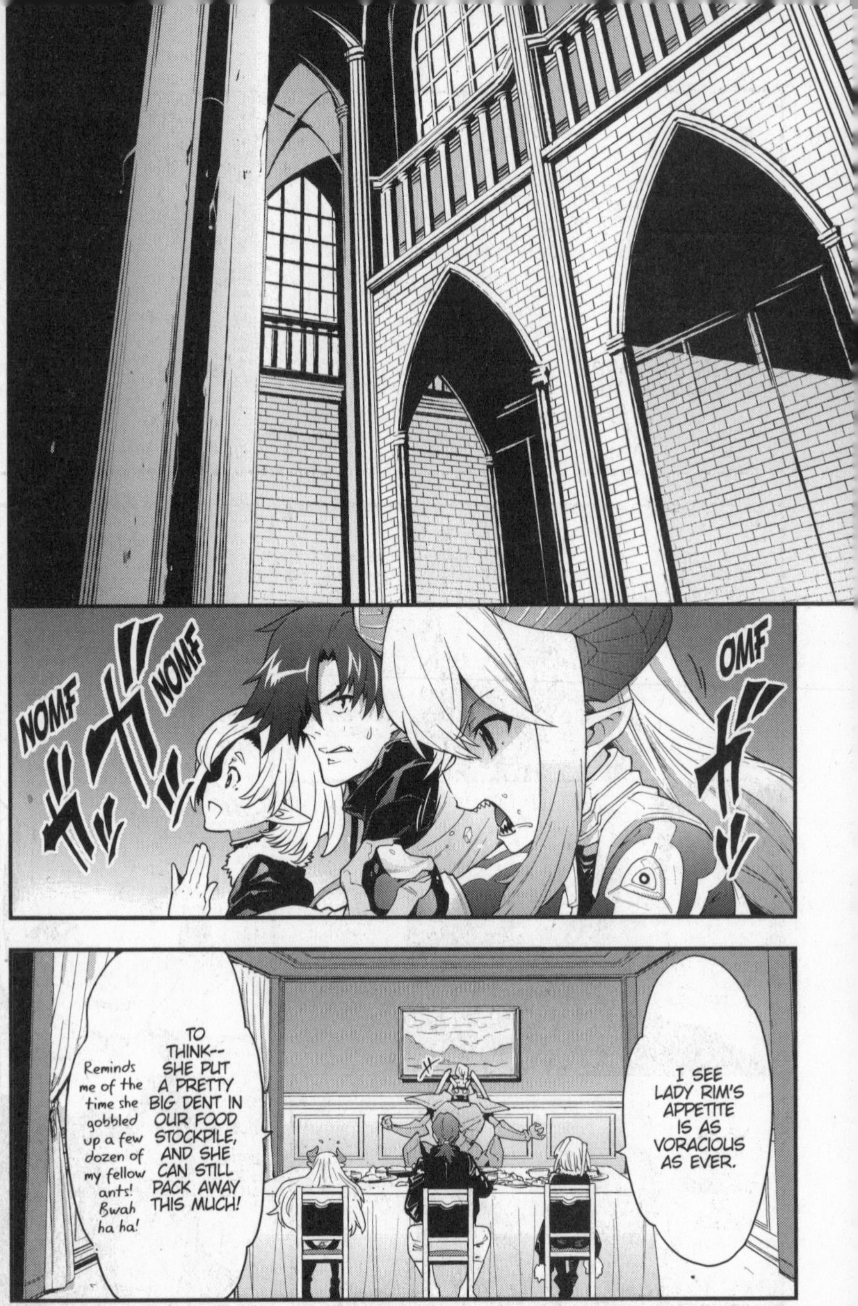
OMF
NOMF
NOMF
I SEE LADY RIM'S APPETITE IS AS VORACIOUS AS EVER.
TO THINK-- SHE PUT A PRETTY BIG DENT IN OUR FOOD STOCKPILE, AND SHE CAN STILL PACK AWAY THIS MUCH!
Reminds me of the time she gobbled up a few dozen of my fellow ants! Bwah ha ha!

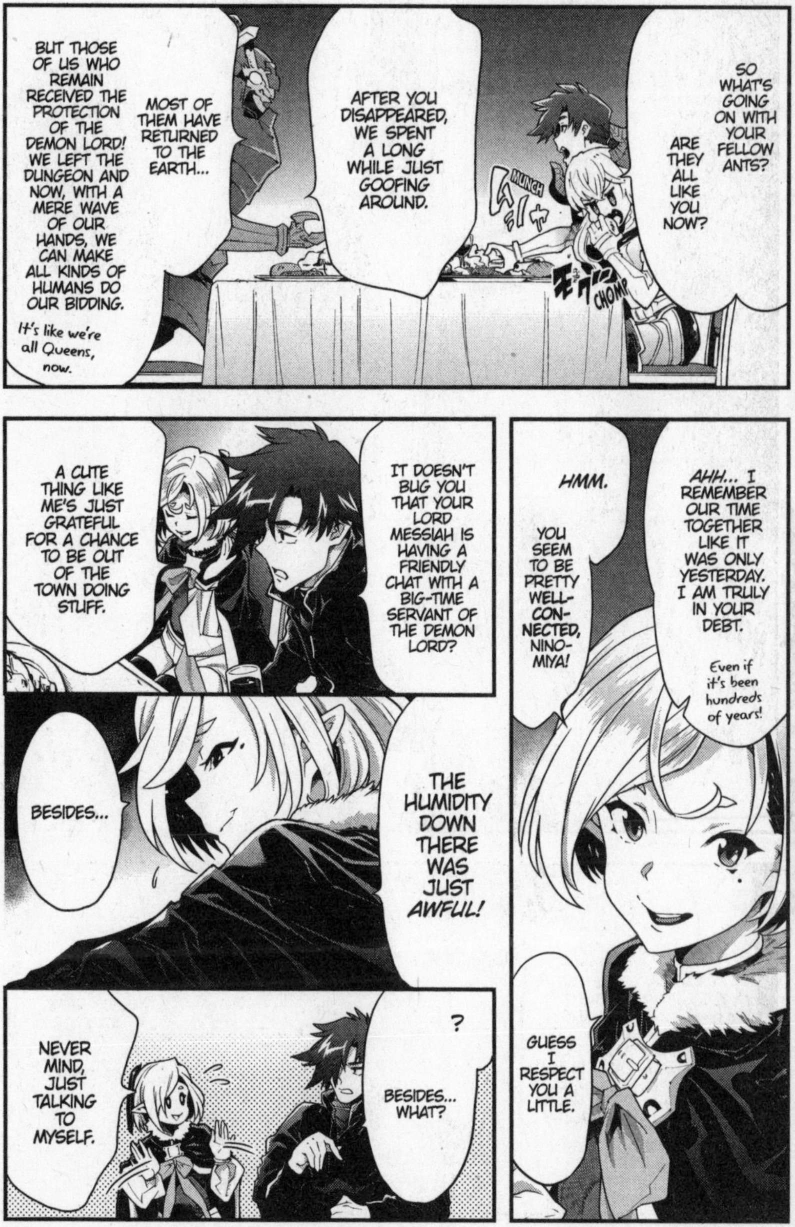
SO WHAT'S GOING ON WITH YOUR FELLOW ANTS?
ARE THEY ALL LIKE YOU NOW?
MUNCH
CHOMP
AFTER YOU DISAPPEARED, WE SPENT A LONG WHILE JUST GOOFING AROUND.
MOST OF THEM HAVE RETURNED TO THE EARTH...
BUT THOSE OF US WHO REMAIN RECEIVED THE PROTECTION OF THE DEMON LORD! WE LEFT THE DUNGEON AND NOW, WITH A MERE WAVE OF OUR HANDS, WE CAN MAKE ALL KINDS OF HUMANS DO OUR BIDDING.
It's like we're all Queens, now.
AHH... I REMEMBER OUR TIME TOGETHER LIKE IT WAS ONLY YESTERDAY. I AM TRULY IN YOUR DEBT.
Even if it's been hundreds of years!
HMM.
YOU SEEM TO BE PRETTY WELL-CONNECTED, NINOMIYA!
GUESS I RESPECT YOU A LITTLE.
IT DOESN'T BUG YOU THAT YOUR LORD MESSIAH IS HAVING A FRIENDLY CHAT WITH A BIG-TIME SERVANT OF THE DEMON LORD?
A CUTE THING LIKE ME'S JUST GRATEFUL FOR A CHANCE TO BE OUT OF THE TOWN DOING STUFF.
THE HUMIDITY DOWN THERE WAS JUST *AWFUL!*
BESIDES...
?
BESIDES... WHAT?
NEVER MIND, JUST TALKING TO MYSELF.

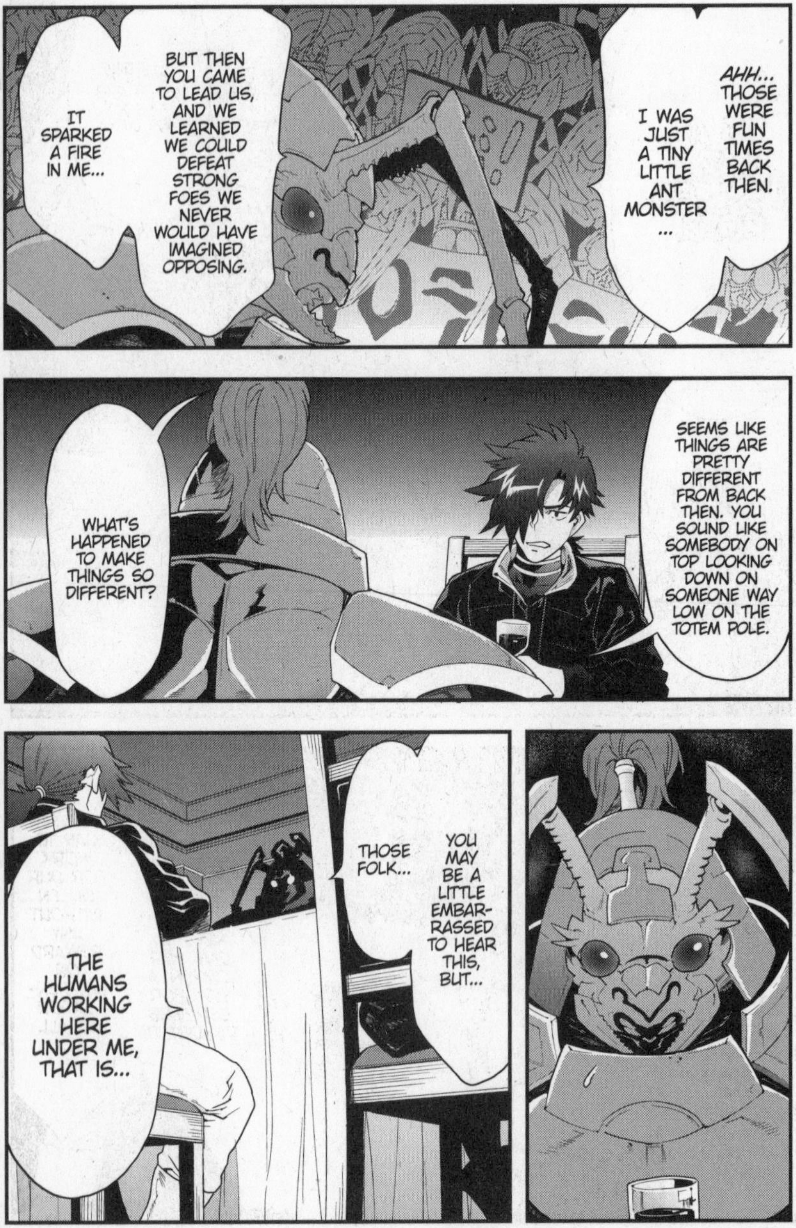
AHH... THOSE WERE FUN TIMES BACK THEN.
I WAS JUST A TINY LITTLE ANT MONSTER ...
BUT THEN YOU CAME TO LEAD US, AND WE LEARNED WE COULD DEFEAT STRONG FOES WE NEVER WOULD HAVE IMAGINED OPPOSING.
IT SPARKED A FIRE IN ME...
SEEMS LIKE THINGS ARE PRETTY DIFFERENT FROM BACK THEN. YOU SOUND LIKE SOMEBODY ON TOP LOOKING DOWN ON SOMEONE WAY LOW ON THE TOTEM POLE.
WHAT'S HAPPENED TO MAKE THINGS SO DIFFERENT?
YOU MAY BE A LITTLE EMBARRASSED TO HEAR THIS, BUT...
THOSE FOLK...
THE HUMANS WORKING HERE UNDER ME, THAT IS...

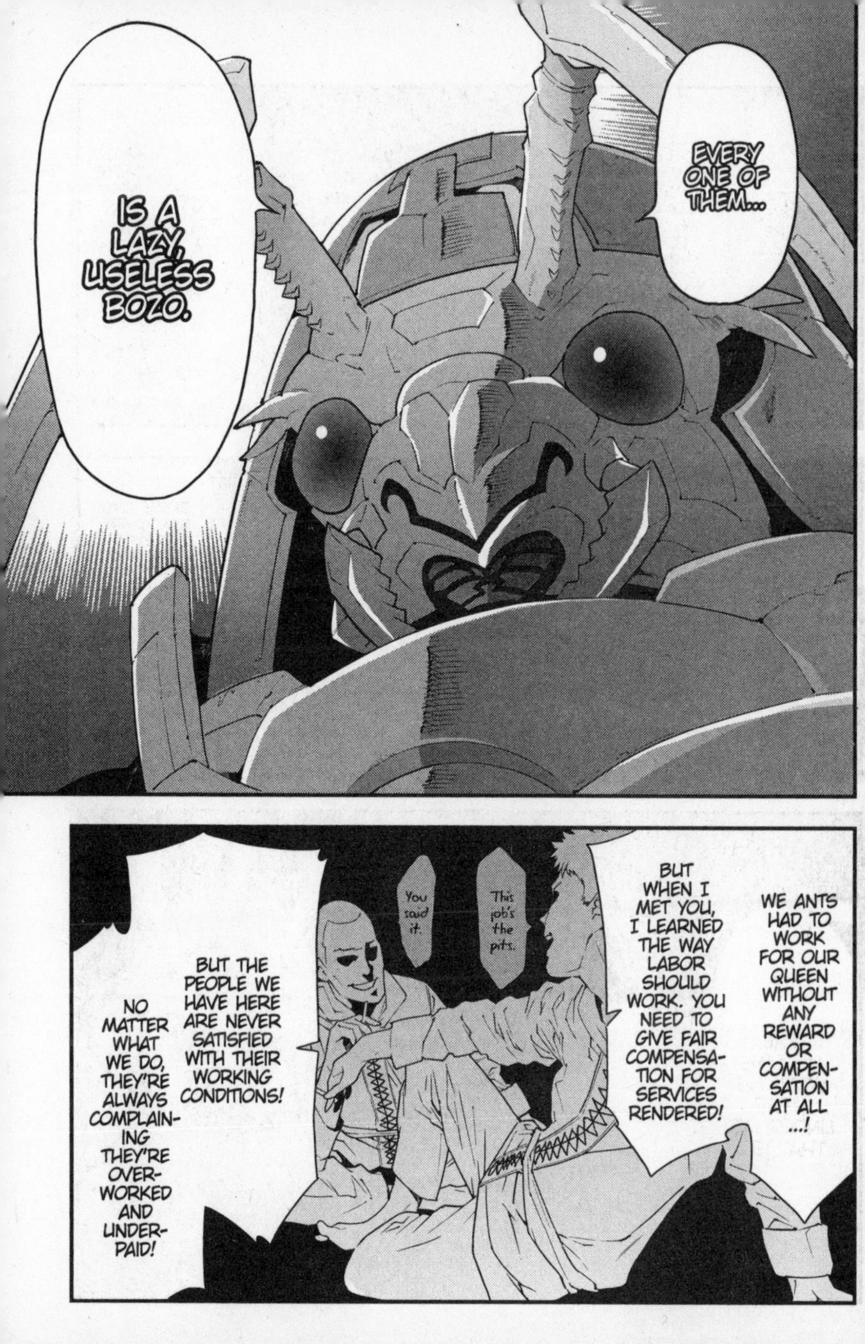
EVERY ONE OF THEM...
IS A LAZY, USELESS BOZO.
WE ANTS HAD TO WORK FOR OUR QUEEN WITHOUT ANY REWARD OR COMPENSATION AT ALL...!
BUT WHEN I MET YOU, I LEARNED THE WAY LABOR SHOULD WORK. YOU NEED TO GIVE FAIR COMPENSATION FOR SERVICES RENDERED!
This job's the pits.
You said it.
BUT THE PEOPLE WE HAVE HERE ARE NEVER SATISFIED WITH THEIR WORKING CONDITIONS!
NO MATTER WHAT WE DO, THEY'RE ALWAYS COMPLAINING THEY'RE OVERWORKED AND UNDERPAID!

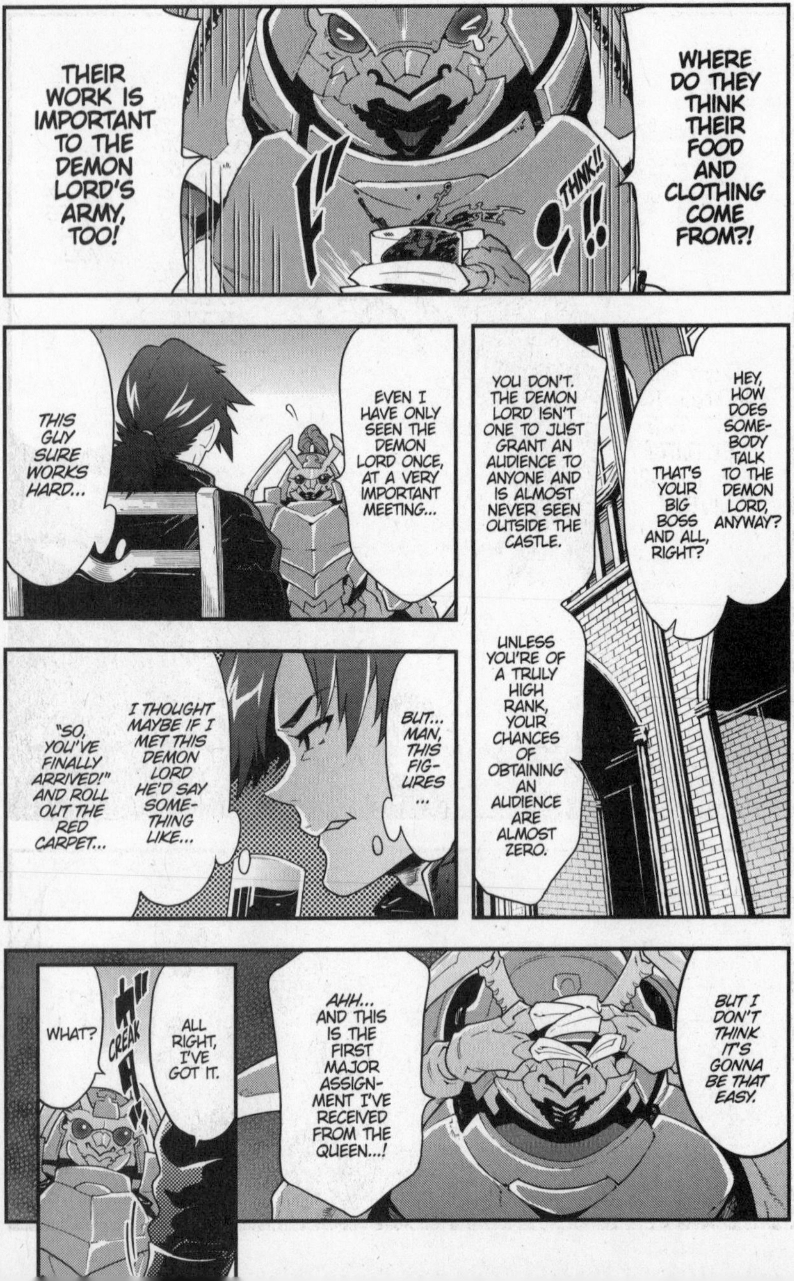
WHERE DO THEY THINK THEIR FOOD AND CLOTHING COME FROM?!
THINK!!
THEIR WORK IS IMPORTANT TO THE DEMON LORD'S ARMY, TOO!
HEY, HOW DOES SOMEBODY TALK TO THE DEMON LORD, ANYWAY?
THAT'S YOUR BIG BOSS AND ALL, RIGHT?
YOU DON'T. THE DEMON LORD ISN'T ONE TO JUST GRANT AN AUDIENCE TO ANYONE AND IS ALMOST NEVER SEEN OUTSIDE THE CASTLE.
UNLESS YOU'RE OF A TRULY HIGH RANK, YOUR CHANCES OF OBTAINING AN AUDIENCE ARE ALMOST ZERO.
EVEN I HAVE ONLY SEEN THE DEMON LORD ONCE, AT A VERY IMPORTANT MEETING...
THIS GUY SURE WORKS HARD...
BUT... MAN, THIS FIGURES...
I THOUGHT MAYBE IF I MET THIS DEMON LORD HE'D SAY SOMETHING LIKE...
"SO, YOU'VE FINALLY ARRIVED!" AND ROLL OUT THE RED CARPET...
BUT I DON'T THINK IT'S GONNA BE THAT EASY.
AHH... AND THIS IS THE FIRST MAJOR ASSIGNMENT I'VE RECEIVED FROM THE QUEEN...!
ALL RIGHT, I'VE GOT IT.
CREAK
WHAT?

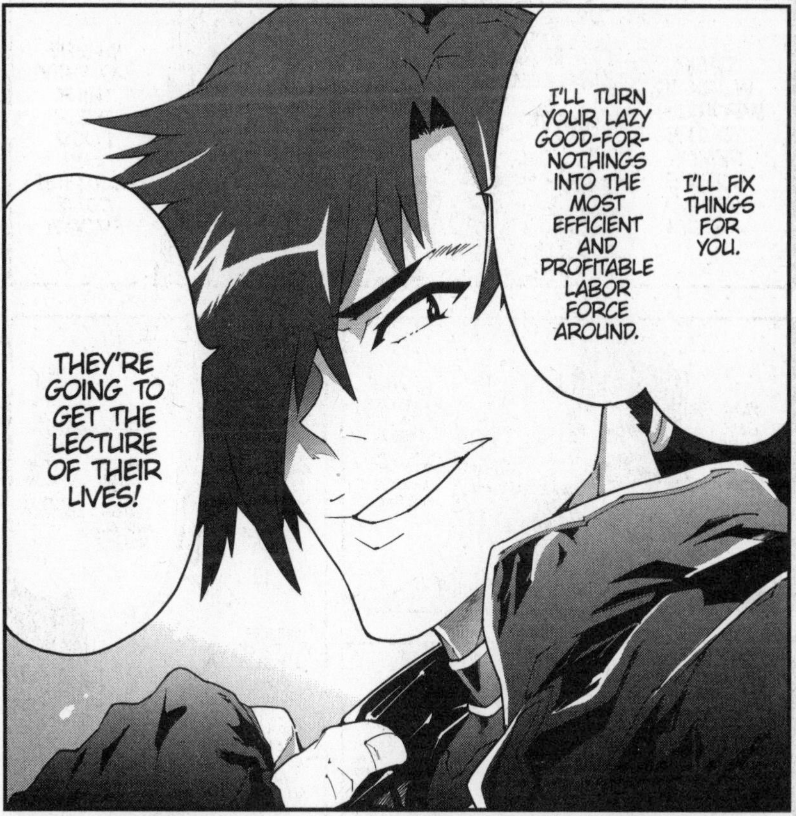
I'LL FIX THINGS FOR YOU.
I'LL TURN YOUR LAZY GOOD-FOR-NOTHINGS INTO THE MOST EFFICIENT AND PROFITABLE LABOR FORCE AROUND.
THEY'RE GOING TO GET THE LECTURE OF THEIR LIVES!
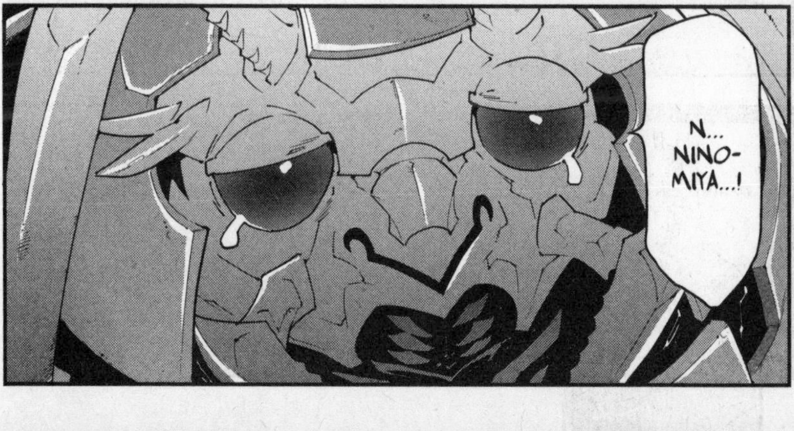
N... NINO-MIYA...!

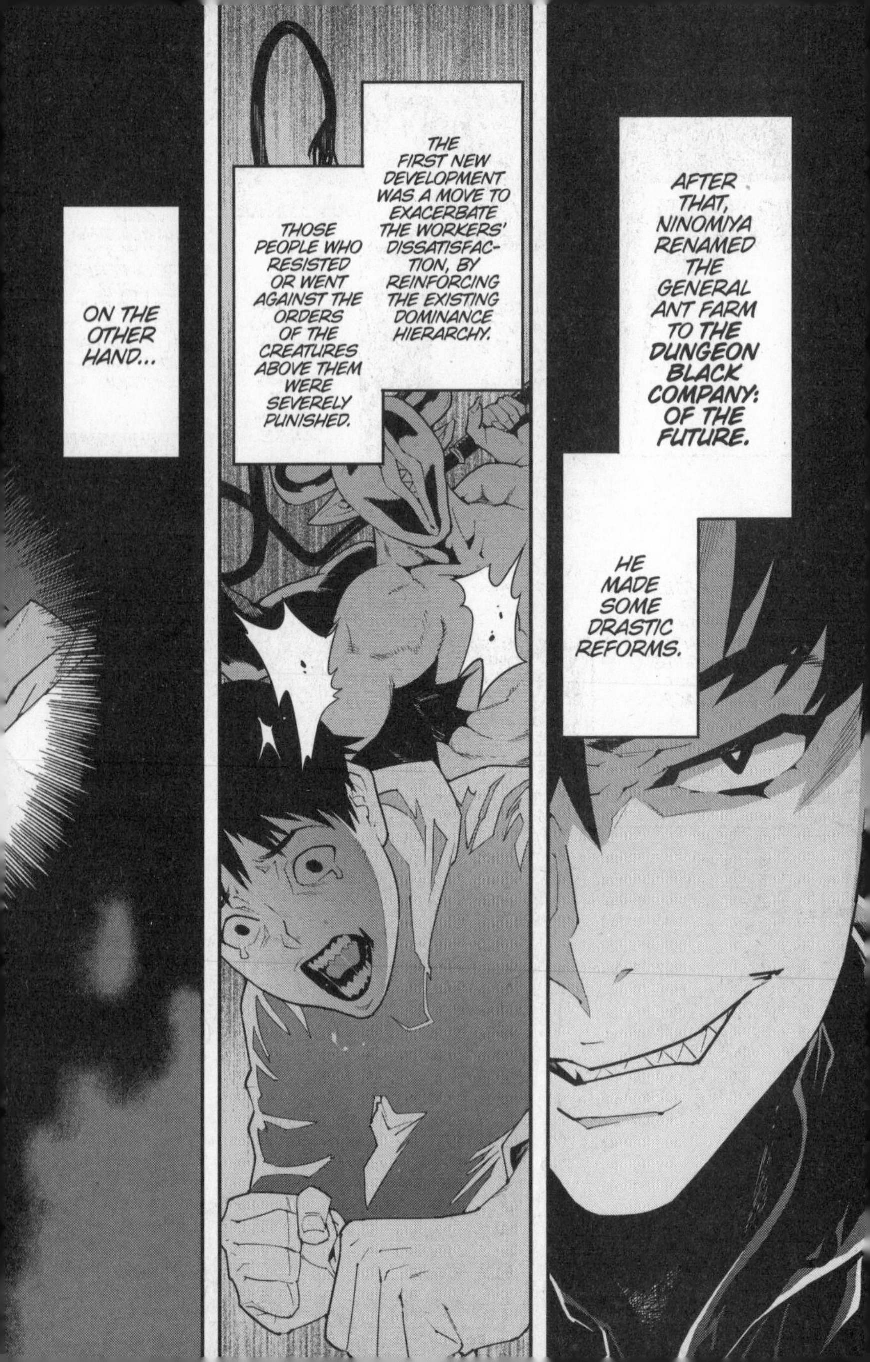
AFTER THAT, NINOMIYA RENAMED THE GENERAL ANT FARM TO THE DUNGEON BLACK COMPANY: OF THE FUTURE.
HE MADE SOME DRASTIC REFORMS.
THE FIRST NEW DEVELOPMENT WAS A MOVE TO EXACERBATE THE WORKERS' DISSATISFACTION, BY REINFORCING THE EXISTING DOMINANCE HIERARCHY.
THOSE PEOPLE WHO RESISTED OR WENT AGAINST THE ORDERS OF THE CREATURES ABOVE THEM WERE SEVERELY PUNISHED.
ON THE OTHER HAND...

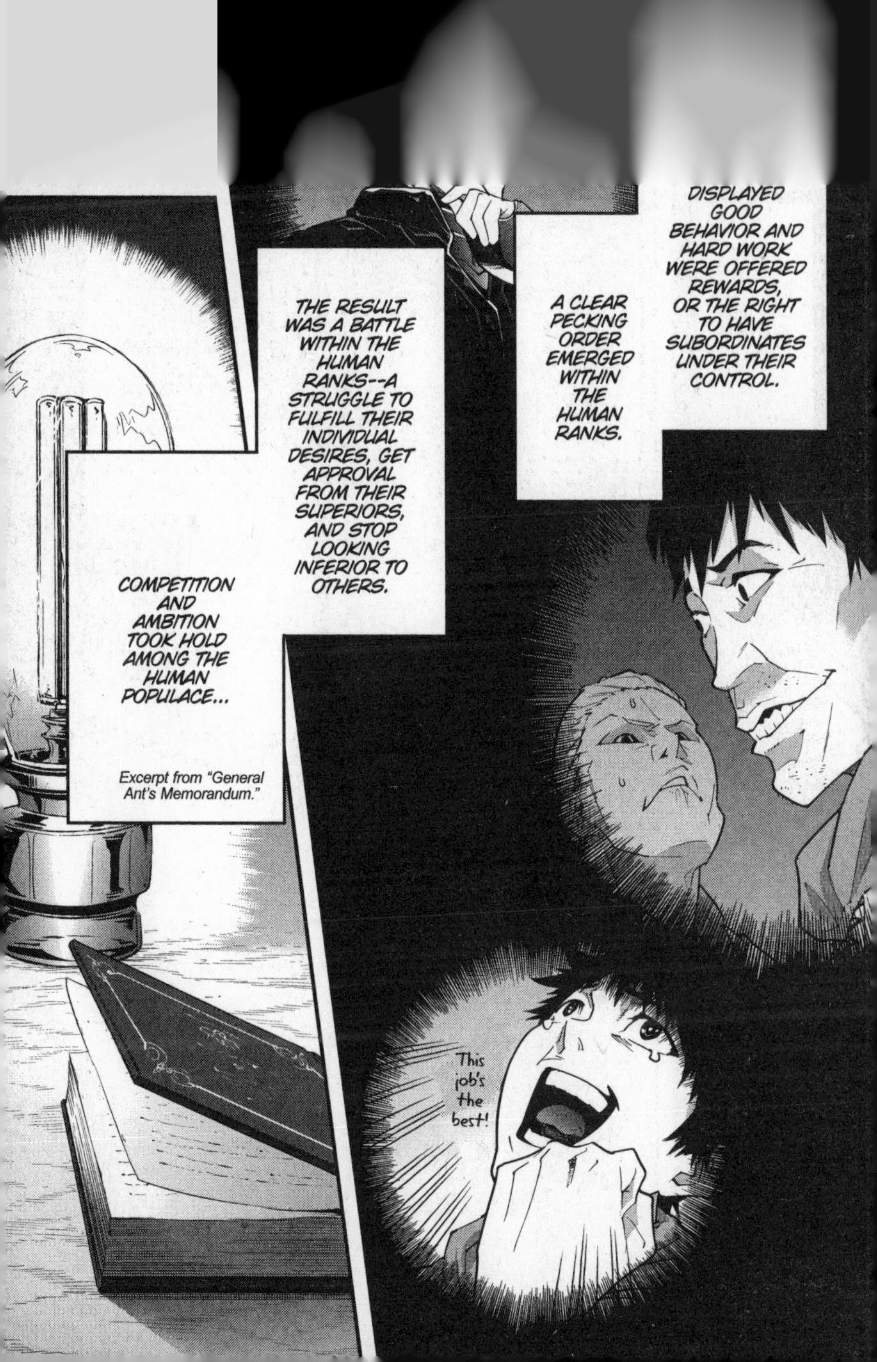
DISPLAYED GOOD BEHAVIOR AND HARD WORK WERE OFFERED REWARDS, OR THE RIGHT TO HAVE SUBORDINATES UNDER THEIR CONTROL.
A CLEAR PECKING ORDER EMERGED WITHIN THE HUMAN RANKS.
THE RESULT WAS A BATTLE WITHIN THE HUMAN RANKS--A STRUGGLE TO FULFILL THEIR INDIVIDUAL DESIRES, GET APPROVAL FROM THEIR SUPERIORS, AND STOP LOOKING INFERIOR TO OTHERS.
COMPETITION AND AMBITION TOOK HOLD AMONG THE HUMAN POPULACE...
Excerpt from "General Ant's Memorandum."
This job's the best!

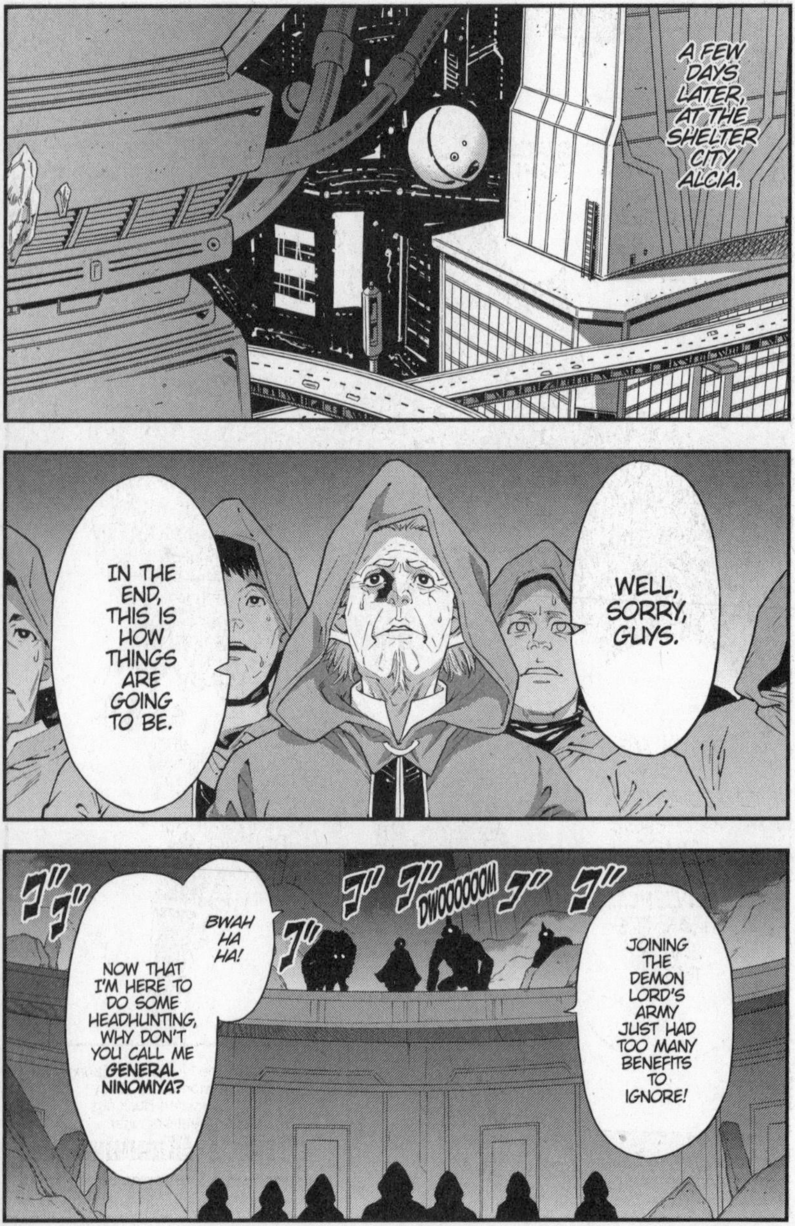
A FEW DAYS LATER, AT THE SHELTER CITY ALCIA.
WELL, SORRY, GUYS.
IN THE END, THIS IS HOW THINGS ARE GOING TO BE.
DWOOOOOOM
JOINING THE DEMON LORD'S ARMY JUST HAD TOO MANY BENEFITS TO IGNORE!
BWAH HA HA!
NOW THAT I'M HERE TO DO SOME HEADHUNTING, WHY DON'T YOU CALL ME GENERAL NINOMIYA?

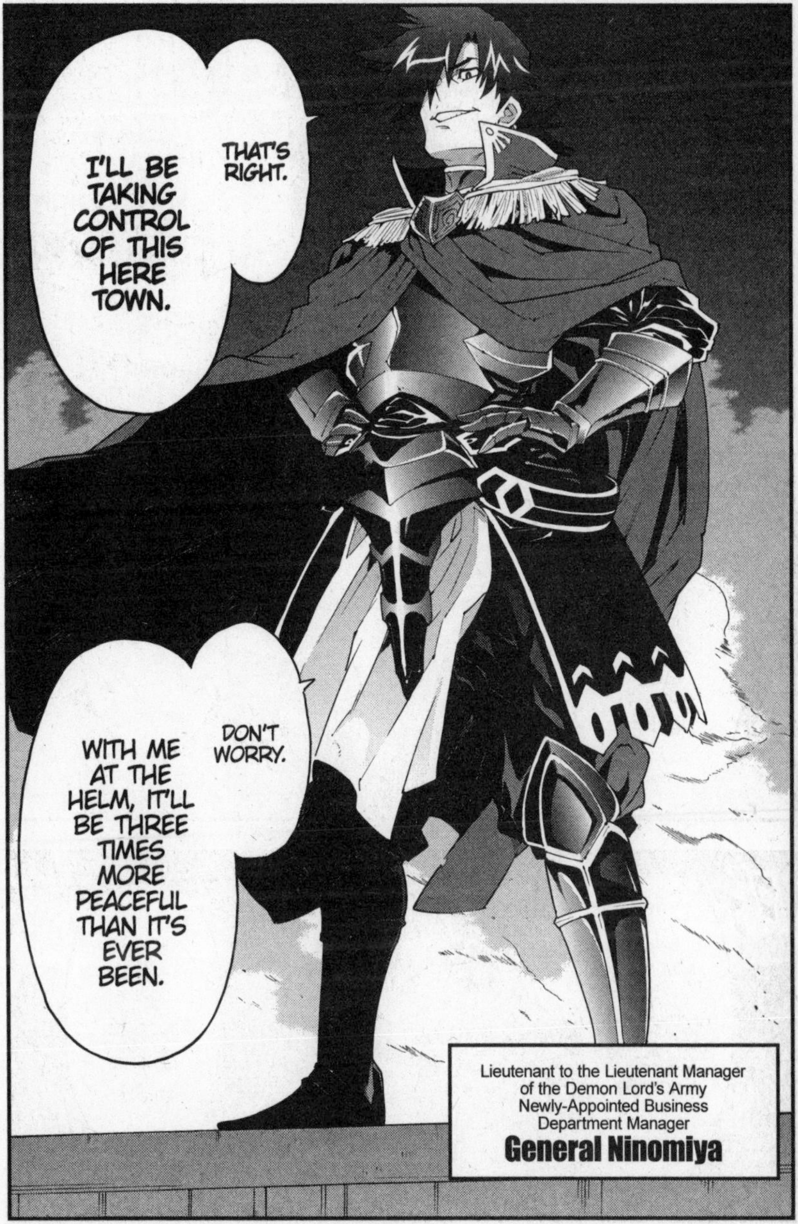
THAT'S RIGHT.
I'LL BE TAKING CONTROL OF THIS HERE TOWN.
DON'T WORRY.
WITH ME AT THE HELM, IT'LL BE THREE TIMES MORE PEACEFUL THAN IT'S EVER BEEN.
Lieutenant to the Lieutenant Manager of the Demon Lord's Army Newly-Appointed Business Department Manager
General Ninomiya

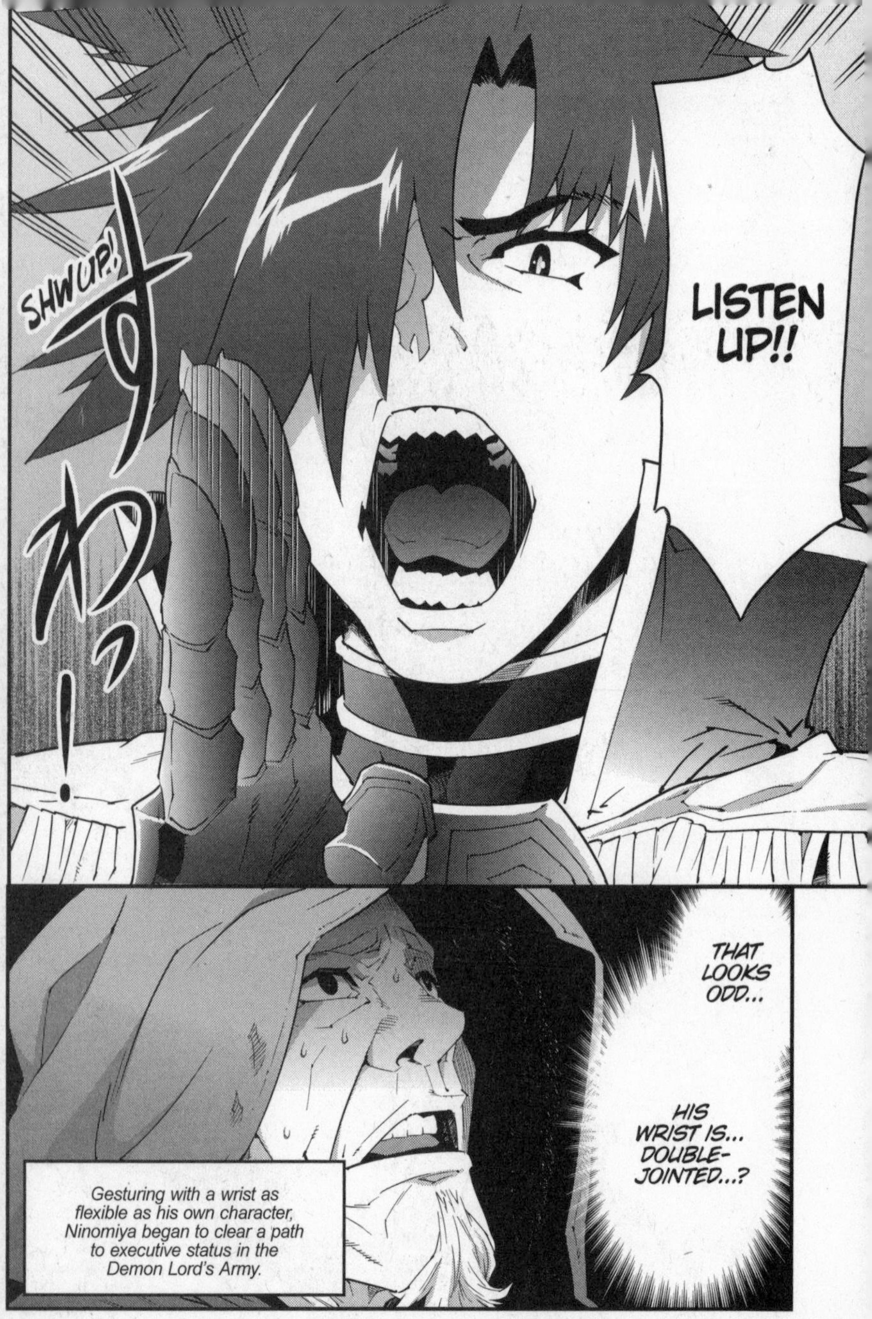
LISTEN UP!!
SHWUP!
すわっ!
THAT LOOKS ODD...
HIS WRIST IS... DOUBLE-JOINTED...?
Gesturing with a wrist as flexible as his own character, Ninomiya began to clear a path to executive status in the Demon Lord's Army.

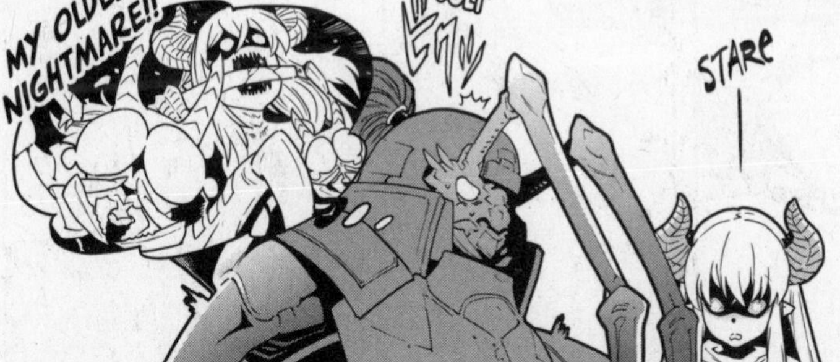
STARE
JOLT
MY OLDEST NIGHTMARE!!

THE DUNGEON OF
BLACK COMPANY

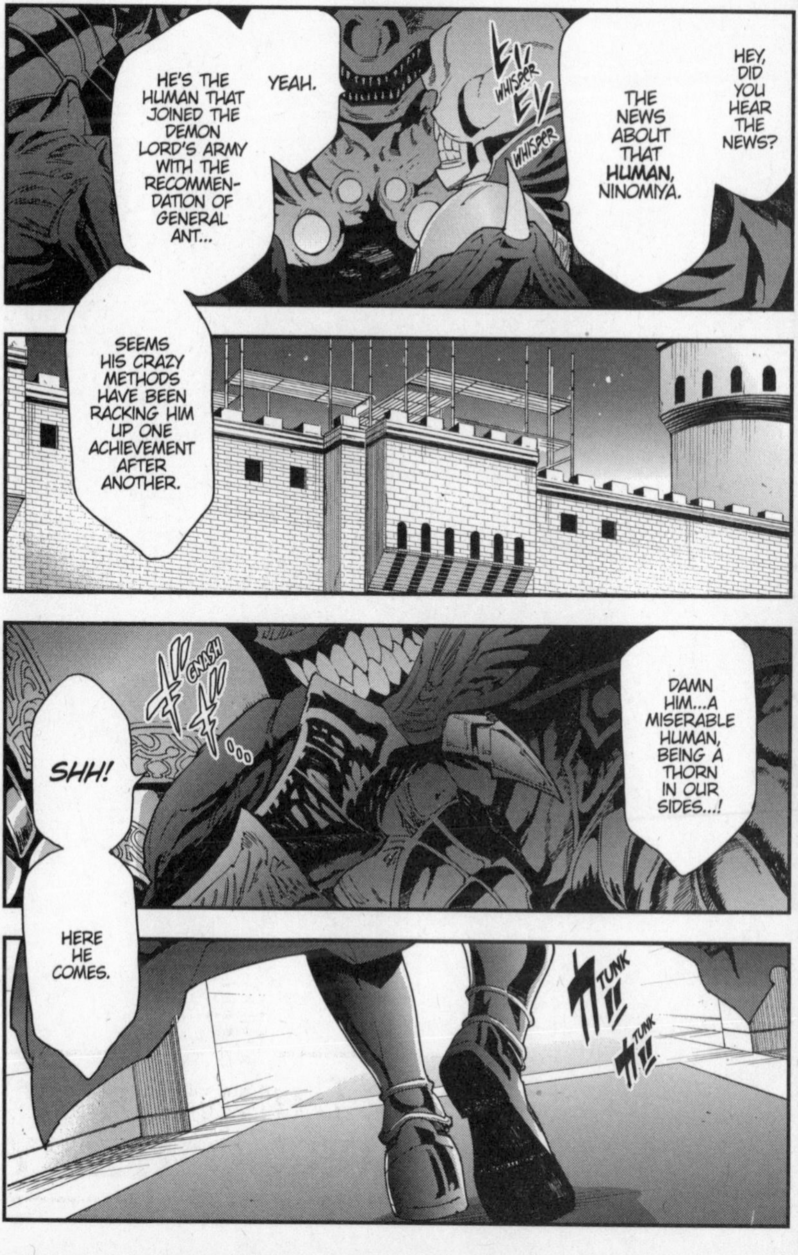
HEY, DID YOU HEAR THE NEWS?
THE NEWS ABOUT THAT **HUMAN**, NINOMIYA.
WHISPER
WHISPER
YEAH.
HE'S THE HUMAN THAT JOINED THE DEMON LORD'S ARMY WITH THE RECOMMENDATION OF GENERAL ANT...
SEEMS HIS CRAZY METHODS HAVE BEEN RACKING HIM UP ONE ACHIEVEMENT AFTER ANOTHER.
DAMN HIM...A MISERABLE HUMAN, BEING A THORN IN OUR SIDES...!
GNASH
SHH!
TUNK
TUNK
HERE HE COMES.

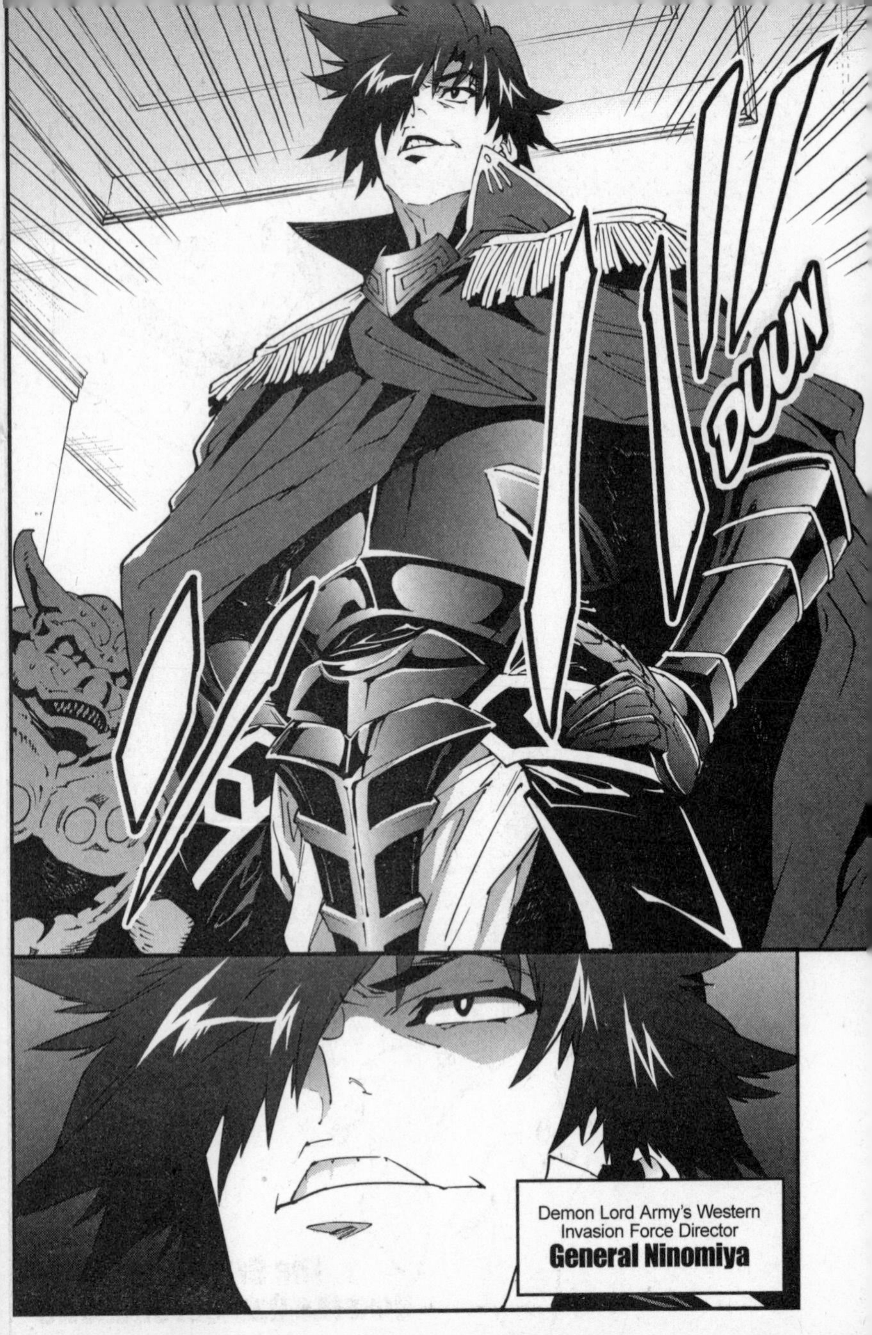
DUUN
Demon Lord Army's Western Invasion Force Director
General Ninomiya

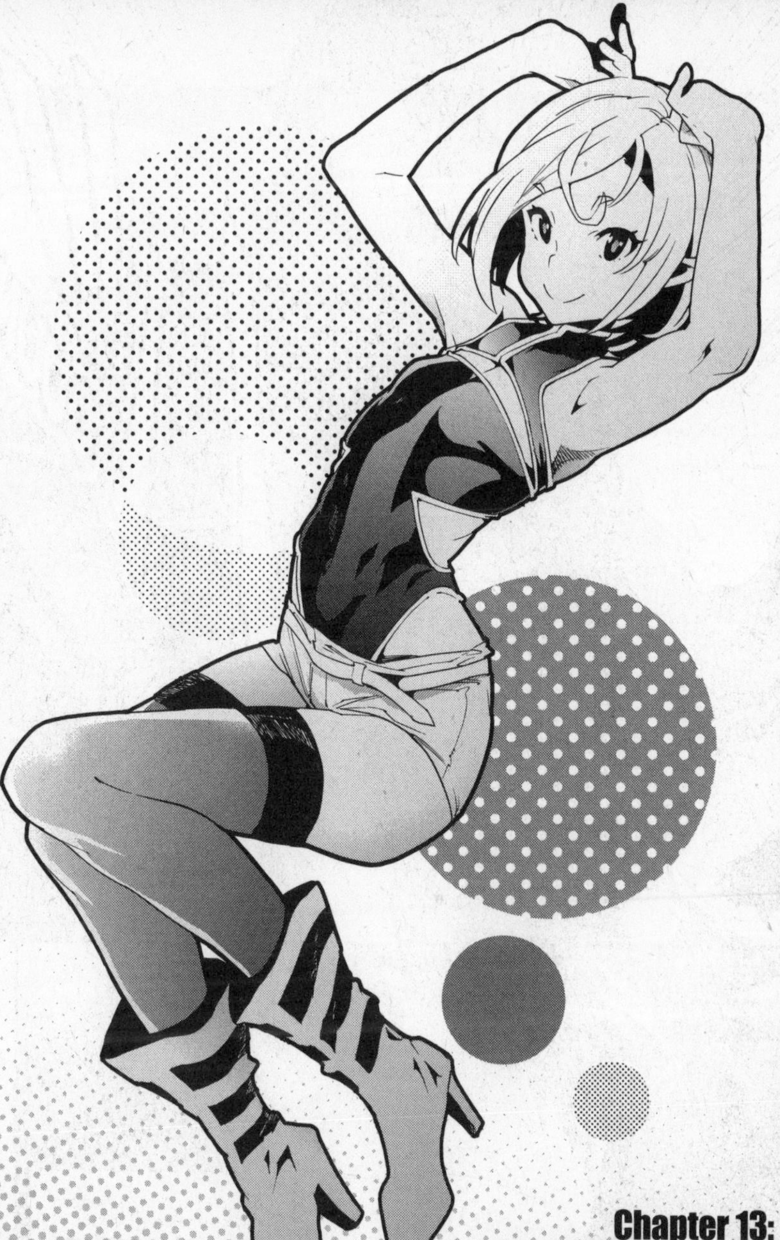

Chapter 13: The Brightest Lights Cast the Darkest Shadows

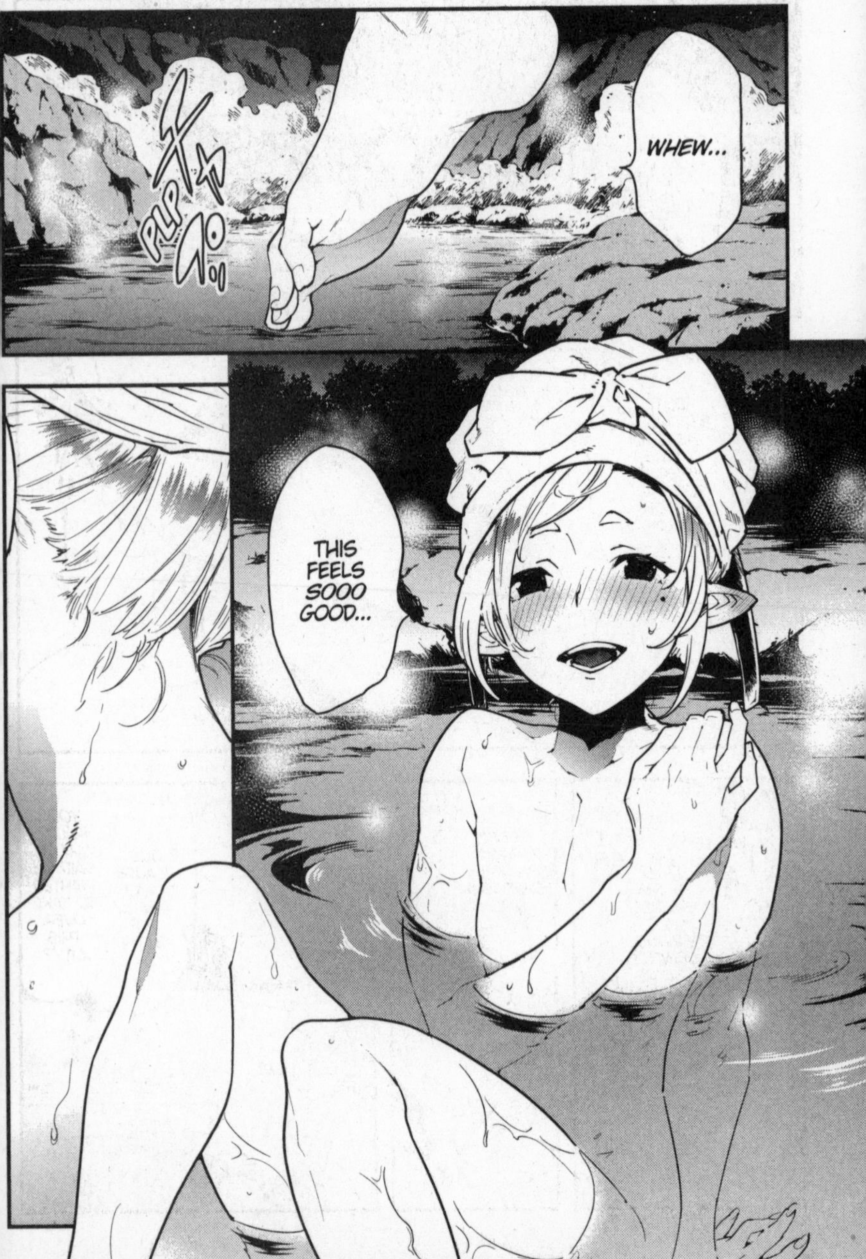
WHEW...
PLIP
THIS FEELS SOOO GOOD...

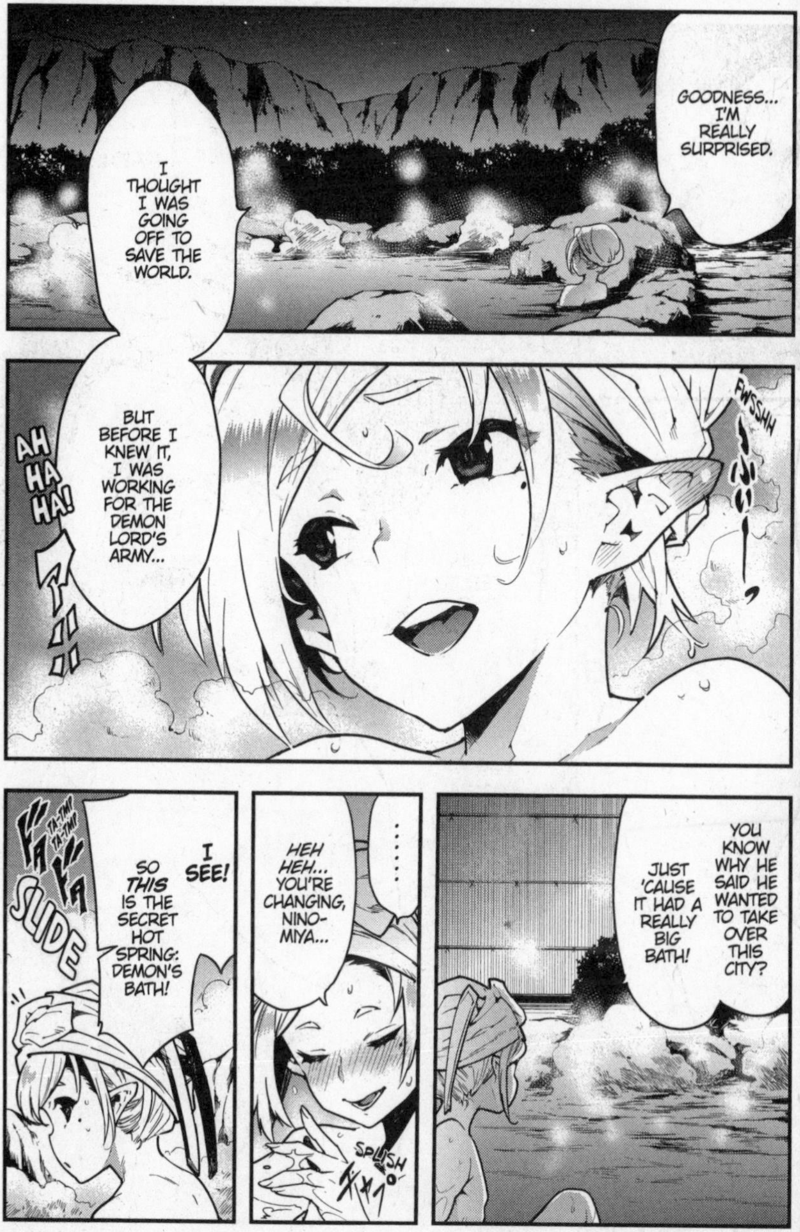
GOODNESS... I'M REALLY SURPRISED.
I THOUGHT I WAS GOING OFF TO SAVE THE WORLD.
FWSSHH
BUT BEFORE I KNEW IT, I WAS WORKING FOR THE DEMON LORD'S ARMY...
AH HA HA!
YOU KNOW WHY HE SAID HE WANTED TO TAKE OVER THIS CITY?
JUST 'CAUSE IT HAD A REALLY BIG BATH!
......
HEH HEH... YOU'RE CHANGING, NINO-MIYA...
SPLISH
I SEE!
SO *THIS* IS THE SECRET HOT SPRING: DEMON'S BATH!
TA-TMP TA-TMP
SLIDE

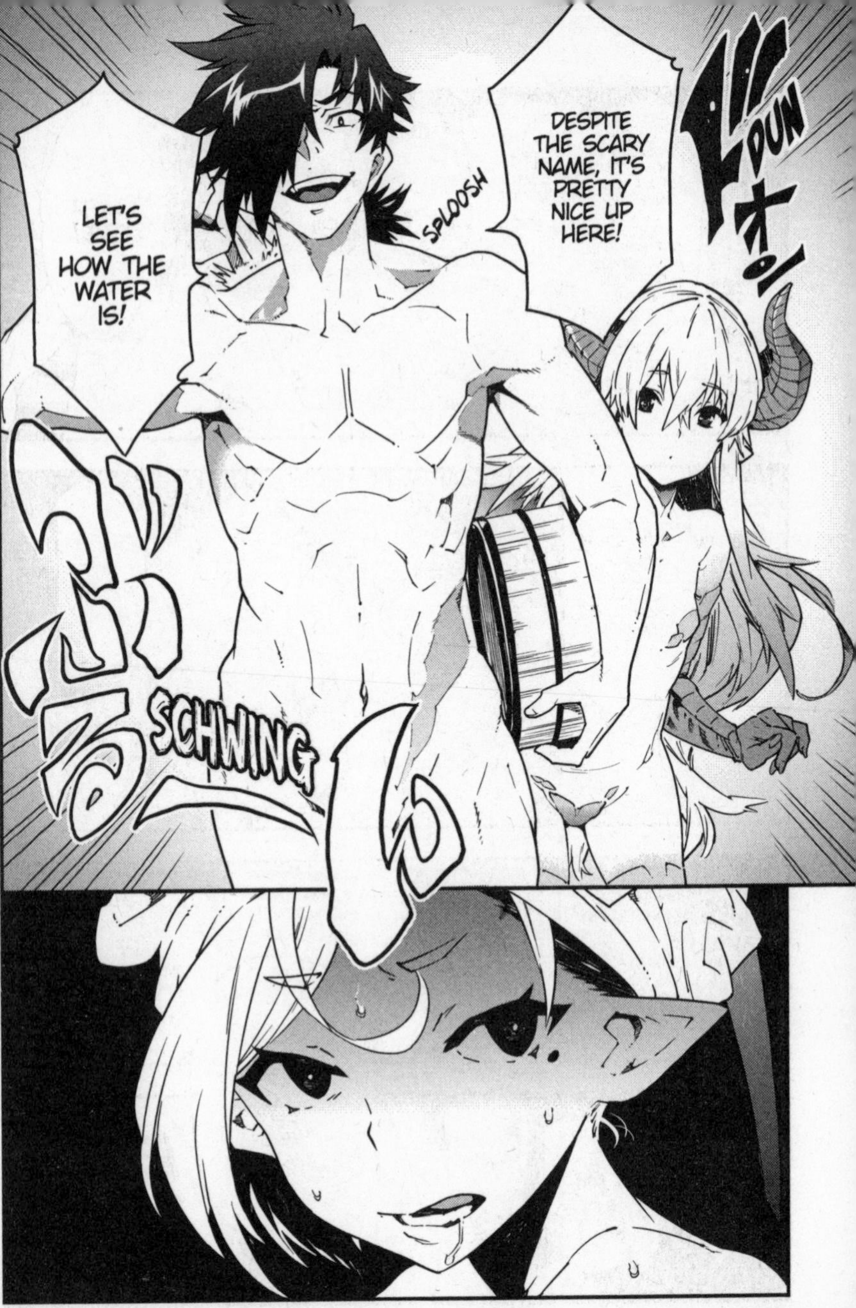
DUN
DESPITE THE SCARY NAME, IT'S PRETTY NICE UP HERE!
SPLOOSH
LET'S SEE HOW THE WATER IS!
SCHWING

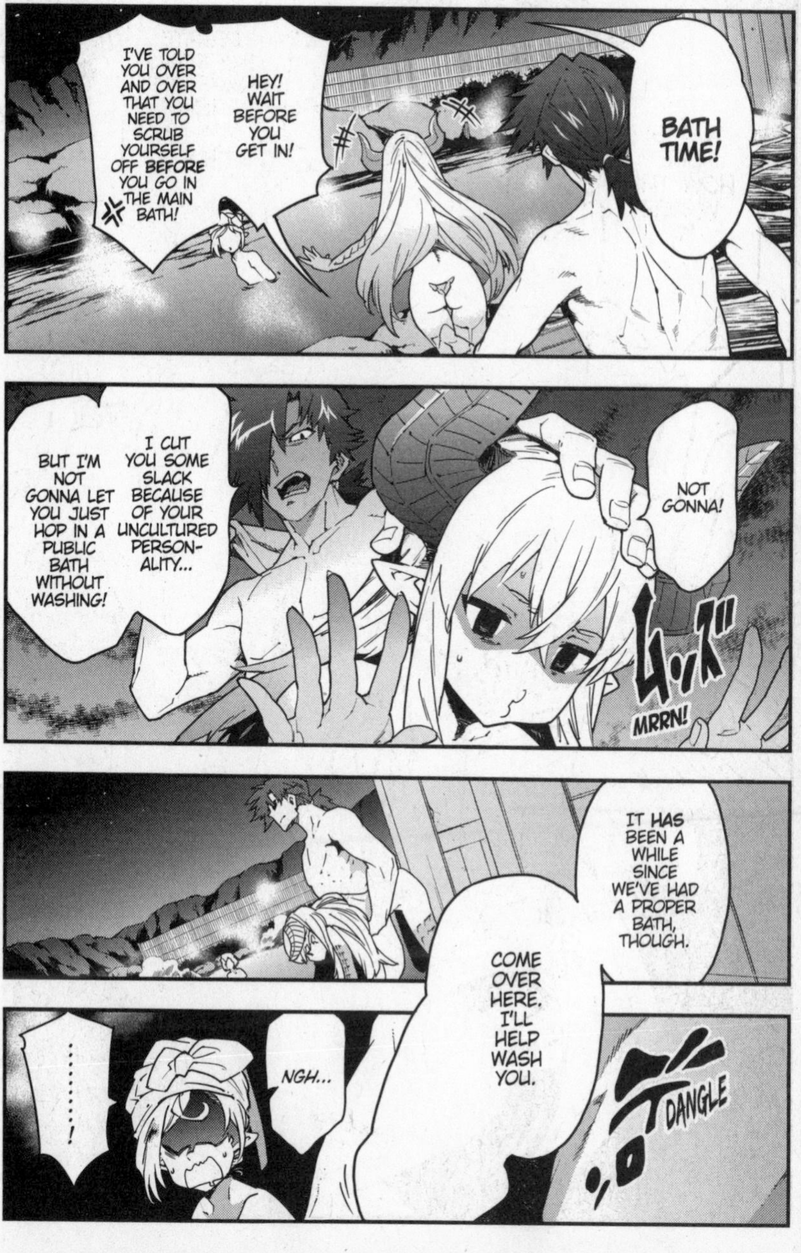
BATH TIME!
HEY! WAIT BEFORE YOU GET IN!
I'VE TOLD YOU OVER AND OVER THAT YOU NEED TO SCRUB YOURSELF OFF BEFORE YOU GO IN THE MAIN BATH!
NOT GONNA!
MRRN!
I CUT YOU SOME SLACK BECAUSE OF YOUR UNCULTURED PERSON-ALITY...
BUT I'M NOT GONNA LET YOU JUST HOP IN A PUBLIC BATH WITHOUT WASHING!
IT HAS BEEN A WHILE SINCE WE'VE HAD A PROPER BATH, THOUGH.
COME OVER HERE. I'LL HELP WASH YOU.
DANGLE
NGH...
......!

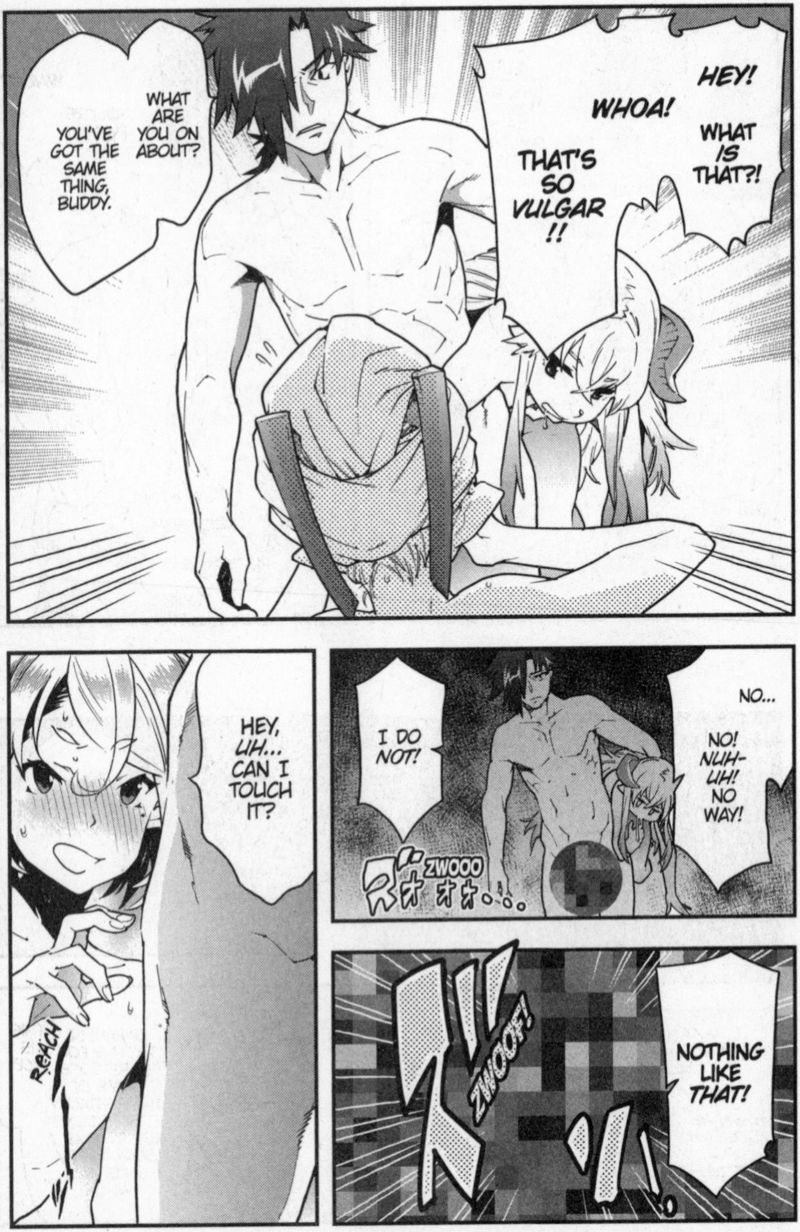
HEY! WHAT IS THAT?!
WHOA! THAT'S SO VULGAR!!
WHAT ARE YOU ON ABOUT?
YOU'VE GOT THE SAME THING, BUDDY.
NO... NO! NUH-UH! NO WAY!
I DO NOT!
ZWOOO
NOTHING LIKE THAT!
ZWOOF!
HEY, UH... CAN I TOUCH IT?
REACH

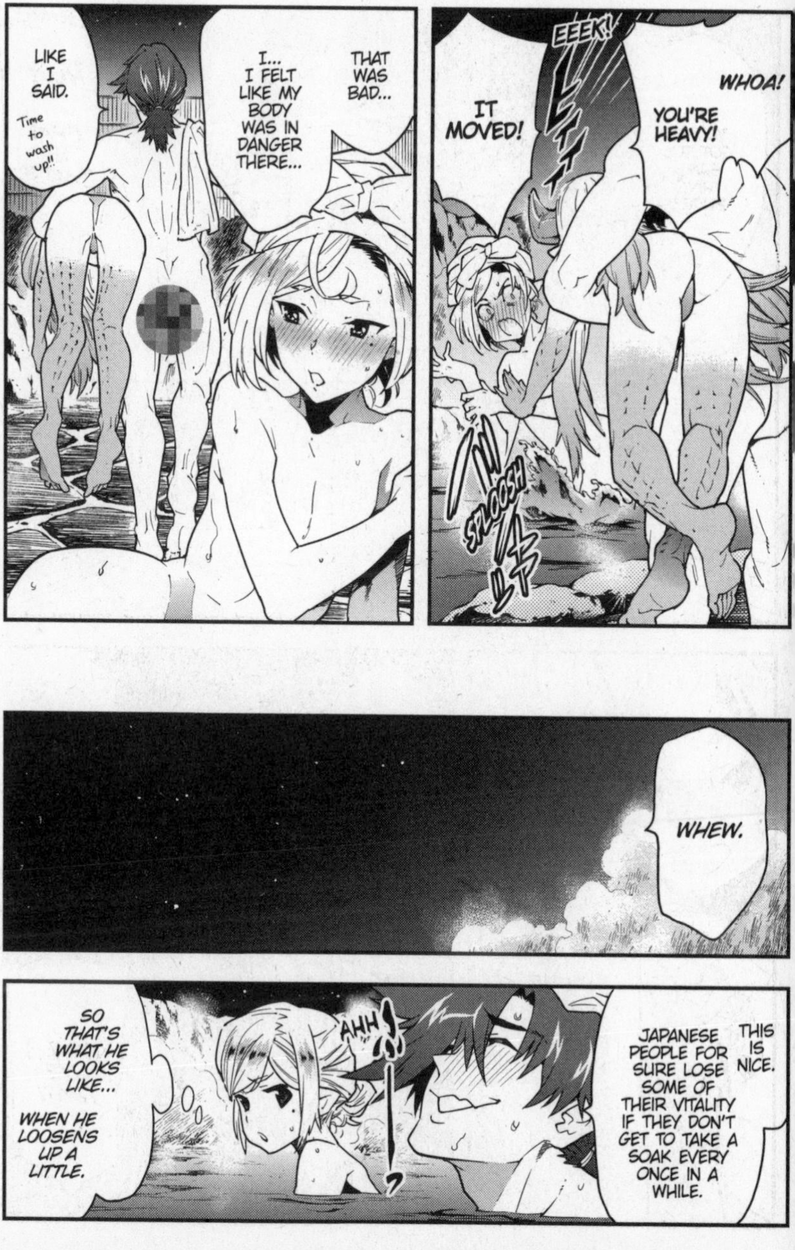
WHOA!
YOU'RE HEAVY!
EEEK!!
IT MOVED!
SPLOOSH
THAT WAS BAD...
I... I FELT LIKE MY BODY WAS IN DANGER THERE...
LIKE I SAID.
Time to wash up!!
WHEW.
THIS IS NICE.
JAPANESE PEOPLE FOR SURE LOSE SOME OF THEIR VITALITY IF THEY DON'T GET TO TAKE A SOAK EVERY ONCE IN A WHILE.
AHH!
SO THAT'S WHAT HE LOOKS LIKE...
WHEN HE LOOSENS UP A LITTLE.

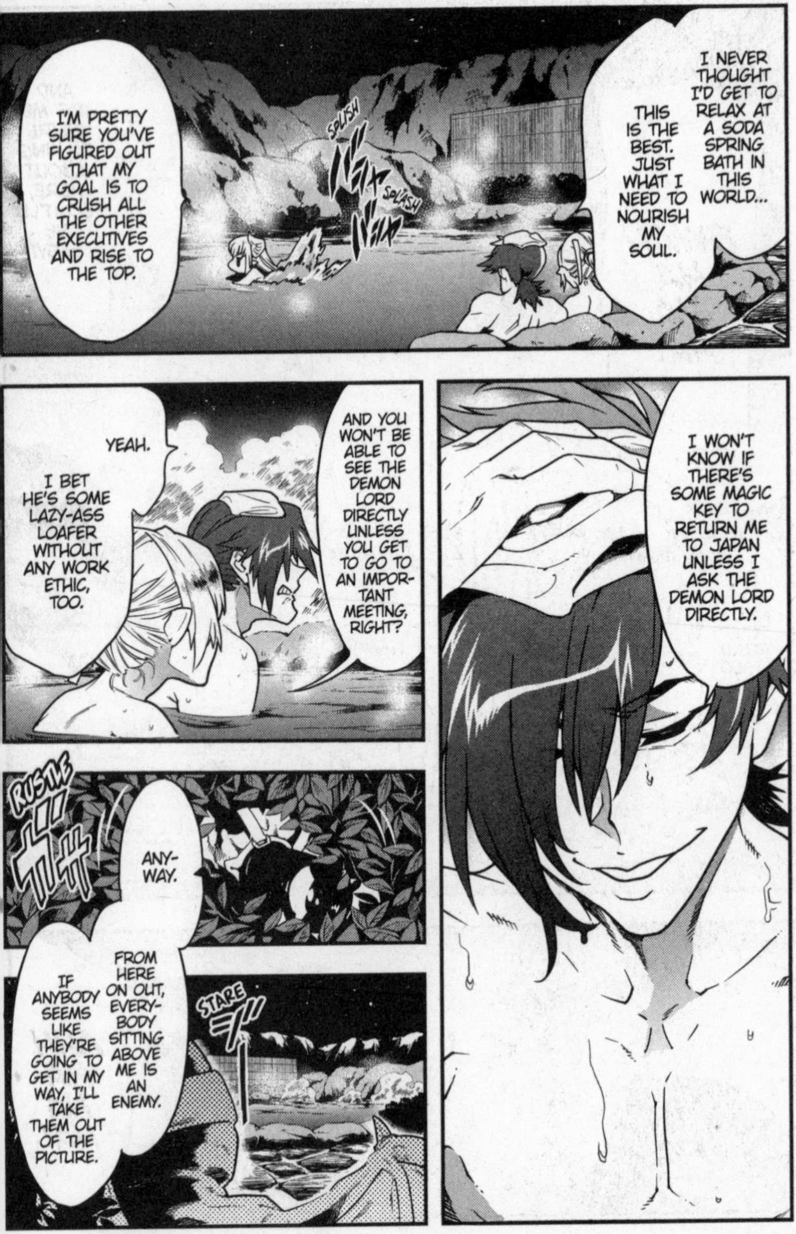
I NEVER THOUGHT I'D GET TO RELAX AT A SODA SPRING BATH IN THIS WORLD...
THIS IS THE BEST. JUST WHAT I NEED TO NOURISH MY SOUL.
SPLISH
SPLASH
I'M PRETTY SURE YOU'VE FIGURED OUT THAT MY GOAL IS TO CRUSH ALL THE OTHER EXECUTIVES AND RISE TO THE TOP.
I WON'T KNOW IF THERE'S SOME MAGIC KEY TO RETURN ME TO JAPAN UNLESS I ASK THE DEMON LORD DIRECTLY.
AND YOU WON'T BE ABLE TO SEE THE DEMON LORD DIRECTLY UNLESS YOU GET TO GO TO AN IMPOR-TANT MEETING, RIGHT?
YEAH.
I BET HE'S SOME LAZY-ASS LOAFER WITHOUT ANY WORK ETHIC, TOO.
ANY-WAY.
RUSTLE
STARE
FROM HERE ON OUT, EVERY-BODY SITTING ABOVE ME IS AN ENEMY.
IF ANYBODY SEEMS LIKE THEY'RE GOING TO GET IN MY WAY, I'LL TAKE THEM OUT OF THE PICTURE.

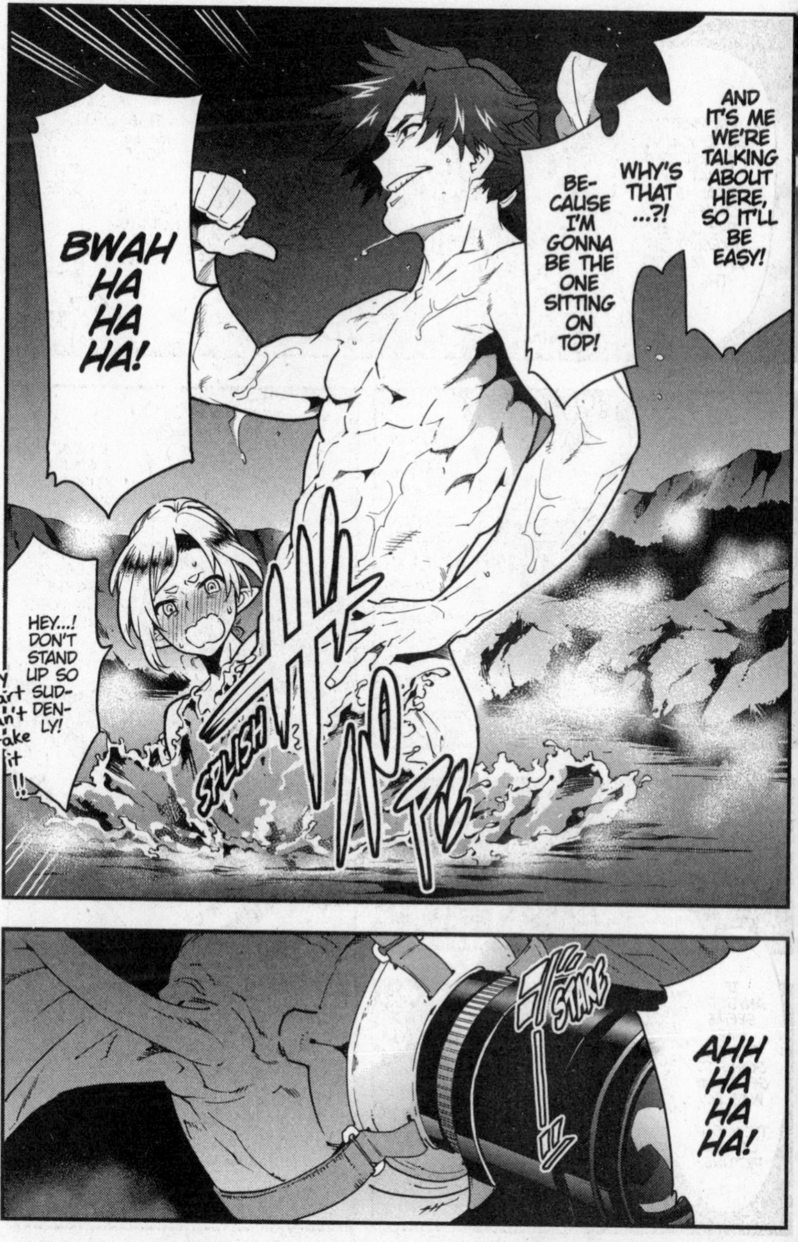
AND IT'S ME WE'RE TALKING ABOUT HERE, SO IT'LL BE EASY!
WHY'S THAT ...?!
BE-CAUSE I'M GONNA BE THE ONE SITTING ON TOP!
BWAH HA HA HA!
SPLISH
HEY...! DON'T STAND UP SO SUD-DEN-LY!
My heart can't take it !!
STARE
AHH HA HA HA!

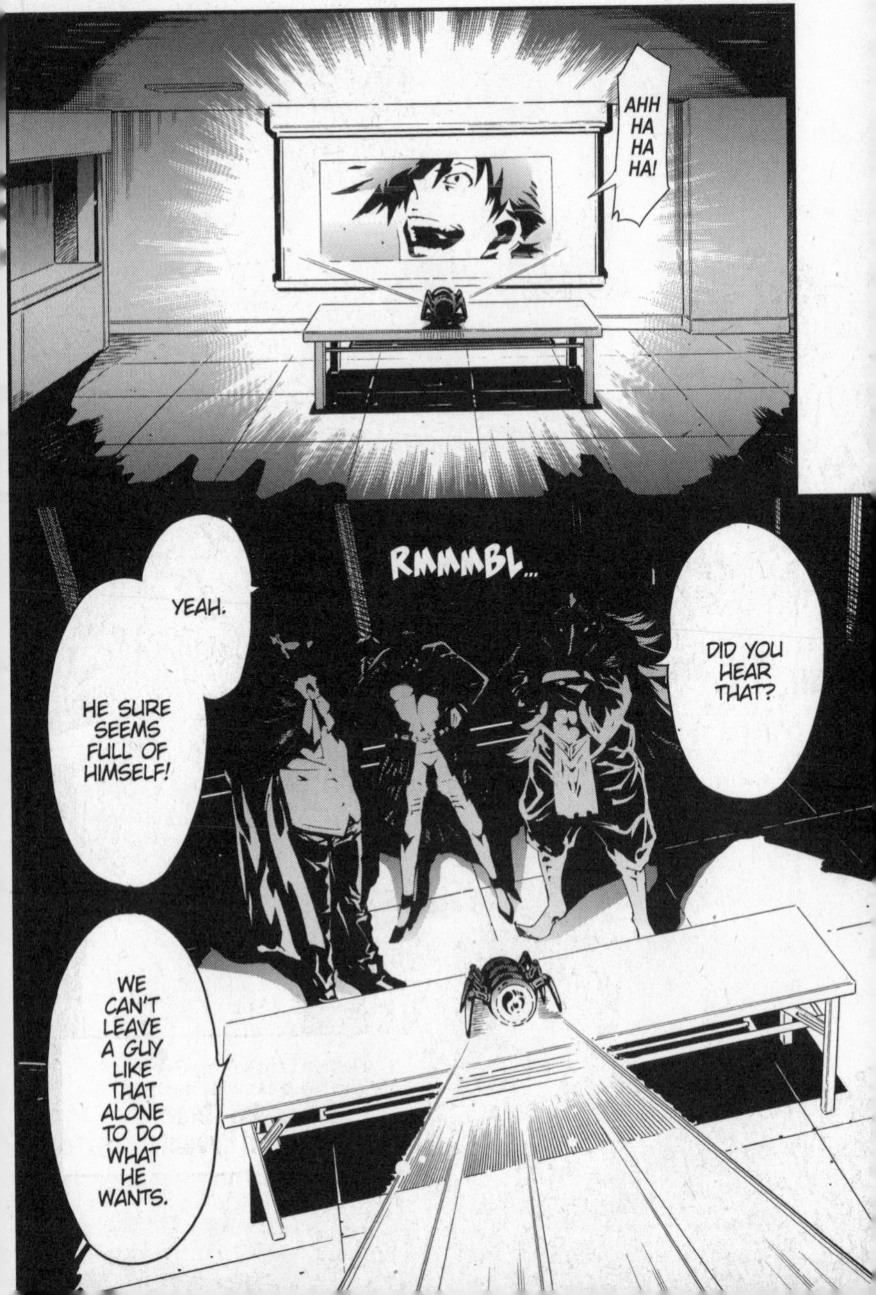
AHH HA HA HA!
RMMMBL...
DID YOU HEAR THAT?
YEAH.
HE SURE SEEMS FULL OF HIMSELF!
WE CAN'T LEAVE A GUY LIKE THAT ALONE TO DO WHAT HE WANTS.

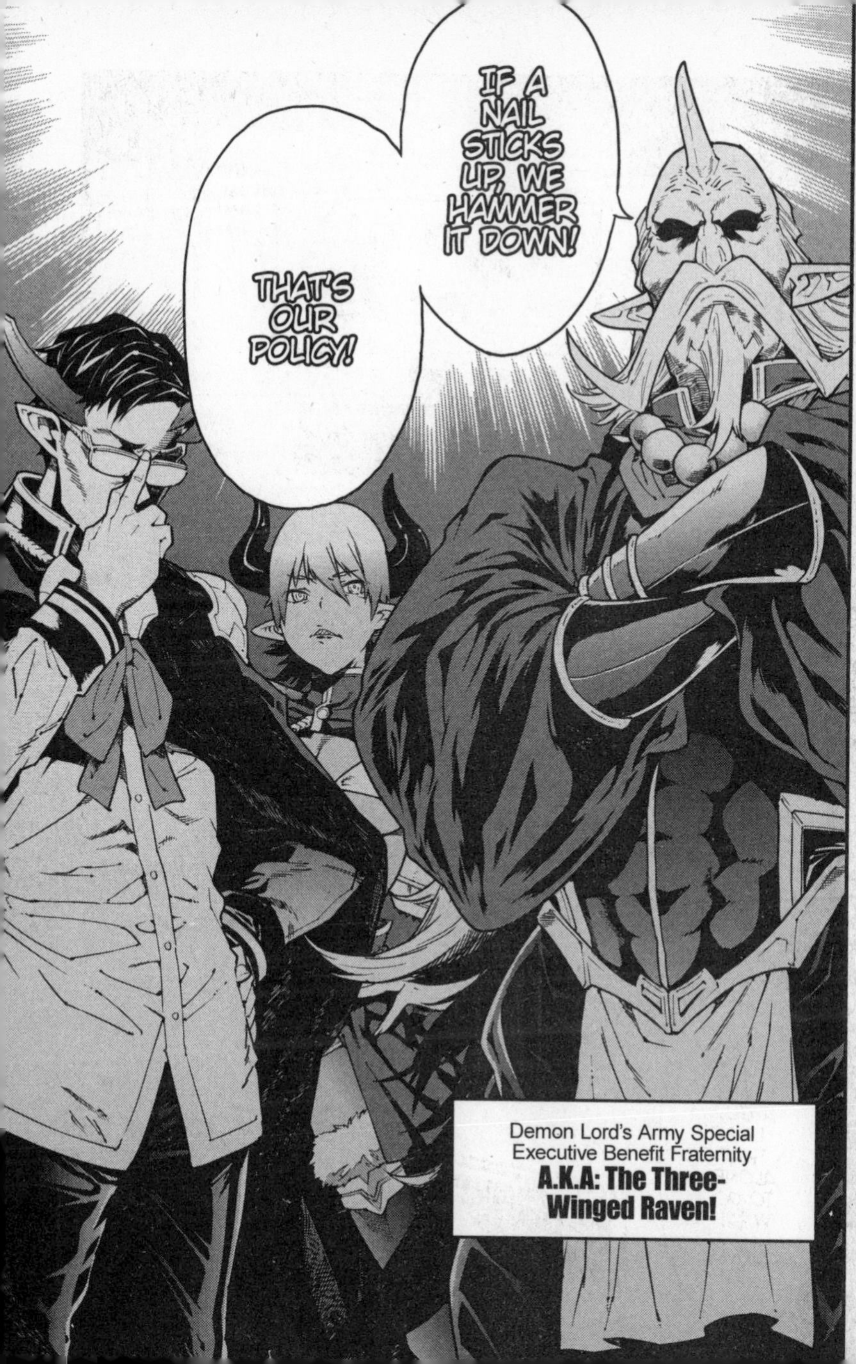
IF A NAIL STICKS UP, WE HAMMER IT DOWN!
THAT'S OUR POLICY!
Demon Lord's Army Special Executive Benefit Fraternity
A.K.A: The Three-Winged Raven!

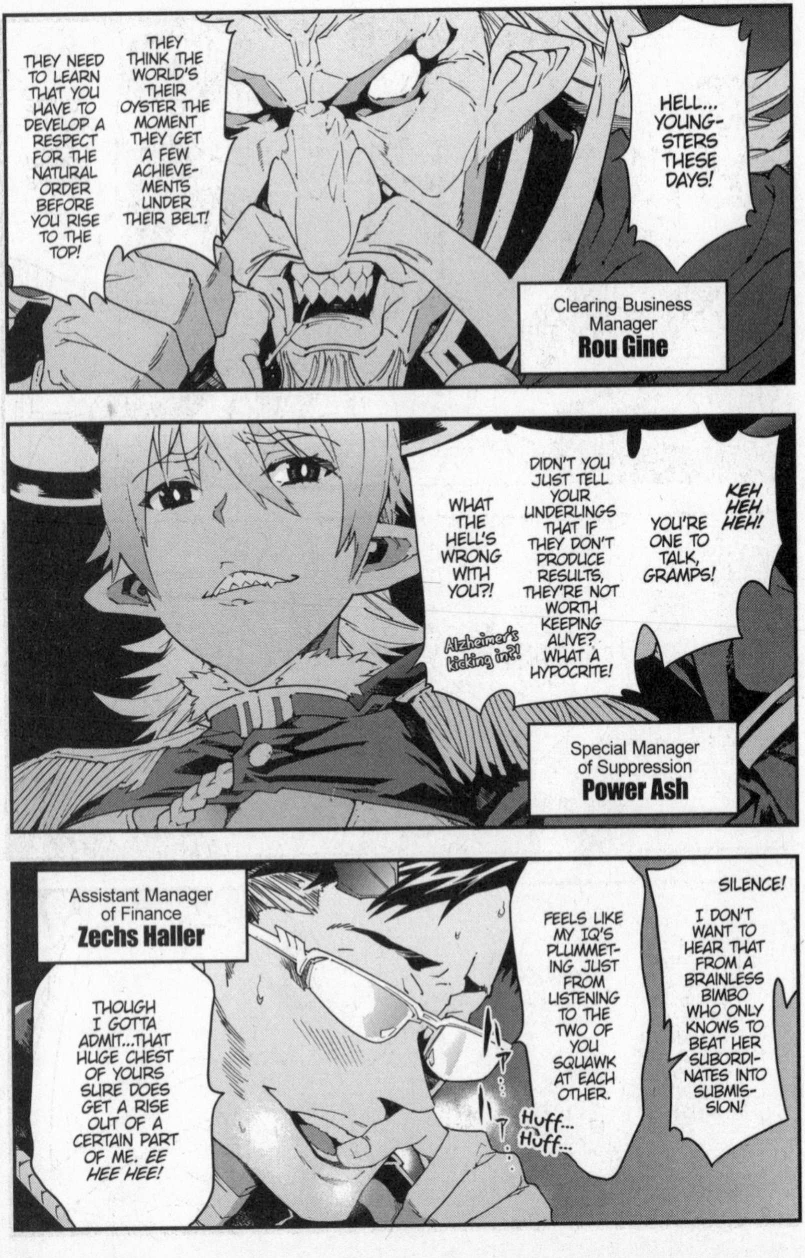
HELL... YOUNGSTERS THESE DAYS!
THEY THINK THE WORLD'S THEIR OYSTER THE MOMENT THEY GET A FEW ACHIEVEMENTS UNDER THEIR BELT!
THEY NEED TO LEARN THAT YOU HAVE TO DEVELOP A RESPECT FOR THE NATURAL ORDER BEFORE YOU RISE TO THE TOP!
Clearing Business Manager
Rou Gine
KEH HEH HEH!
YOU'RE ONE TO TALK, GRAMPS!
DIDN'T YOU JUST TELL YOUR UNDERLINGS THAT IF THEY DON'T PRODUCE RESULTS, THEY'RE NOT WORTH KEEPING ALIVE? WHAT A HYPOCRITE!
WHAT THE HELL'S WRONG WITH YOU?!
Alzheimer's kicking in?!
Special Manager of Suppression
Power Ash
SILENCE!
I DON'T WANT TO HEAR THAT FROM A BRAINLESS BIMBO WHO ONLY KNOWS TO BEAT HER SUBORDINATES INTO SUBMISSION!
FEELS LIKE MY IQ'S PLUMMETING JUST FROM LISTENING TO THE TWO OF YOU SQUAWK AT EACH OTHER.
Assistant Manager of Finance
Zechs Haller
Huff... Huff...
THOUGH I GOTTA ADMIT...THAT HUGE CHEST OF YOURS SURE DOES GET A RISE OUT OF A CERTAIN PART OF ME. EE HEE HEE!

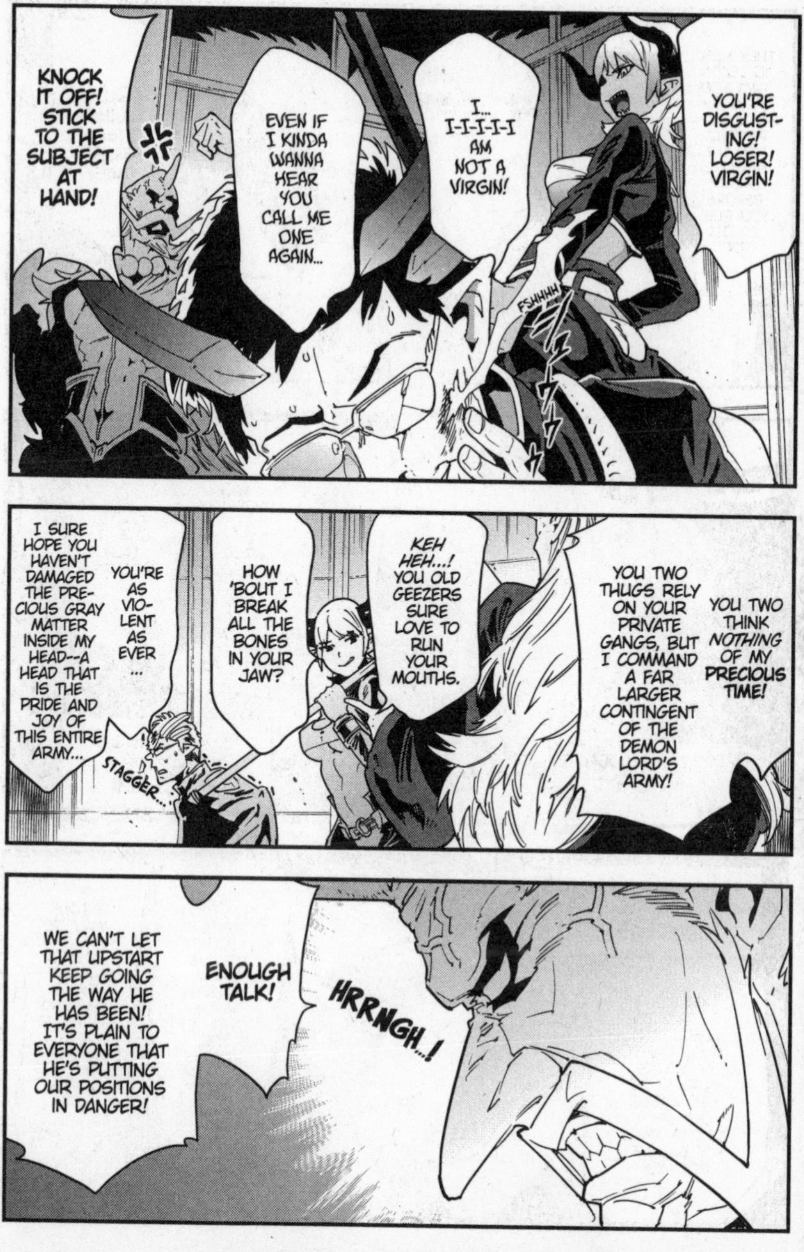
YOU'RE DISGUST-ING! LOSER! VIRGIN!
I... I-I-I-I-I AM NOT A VIRGIN!
EVEN IF I KINDA WANNA HEAR YOU CALL ME ONE AGAIN...
FSHHHH
KNOCK IT OFF! STICK TO THE SUBJECT AT HAND!
YOU TWO THINK *NOTHING* OF MY **PRECIOUS TIME!**
YOU TWO THUGS RELY ON YOUR PRIVATE GANGS, BUT I COMMAND A FAR LARGER CONTINGENT OF THE DEMON LORD'S ARMY!
KEH HEH...! YOU OLD GEEZERS SURE LOVE TO RUN YOUR MOUTHS.
HOW 'BOUT I BREAK ALL THE BONES IN YOUR JAW?
YOU'RE AS VIO-LENT AS EVER...
I SURE HOPE YOU HAVEN'T DAMAGED THE PRE-CIOUS GRAY MATTER INSIDE MY HEAD--A HEAD THAT IS THE PRIDE AND JOY OF THIS ENTIRE ARMY...
STAGGER...
HRRNGH...!
ENOUGH TALK!
WE CAN'T LET THAT UPSTART KEEP GOING THE WAY HE HAS BEEN! IT'S PLAIN TO EVERYONE THAT HE'S PUTTING OUR POSITIONS IN DANGER!

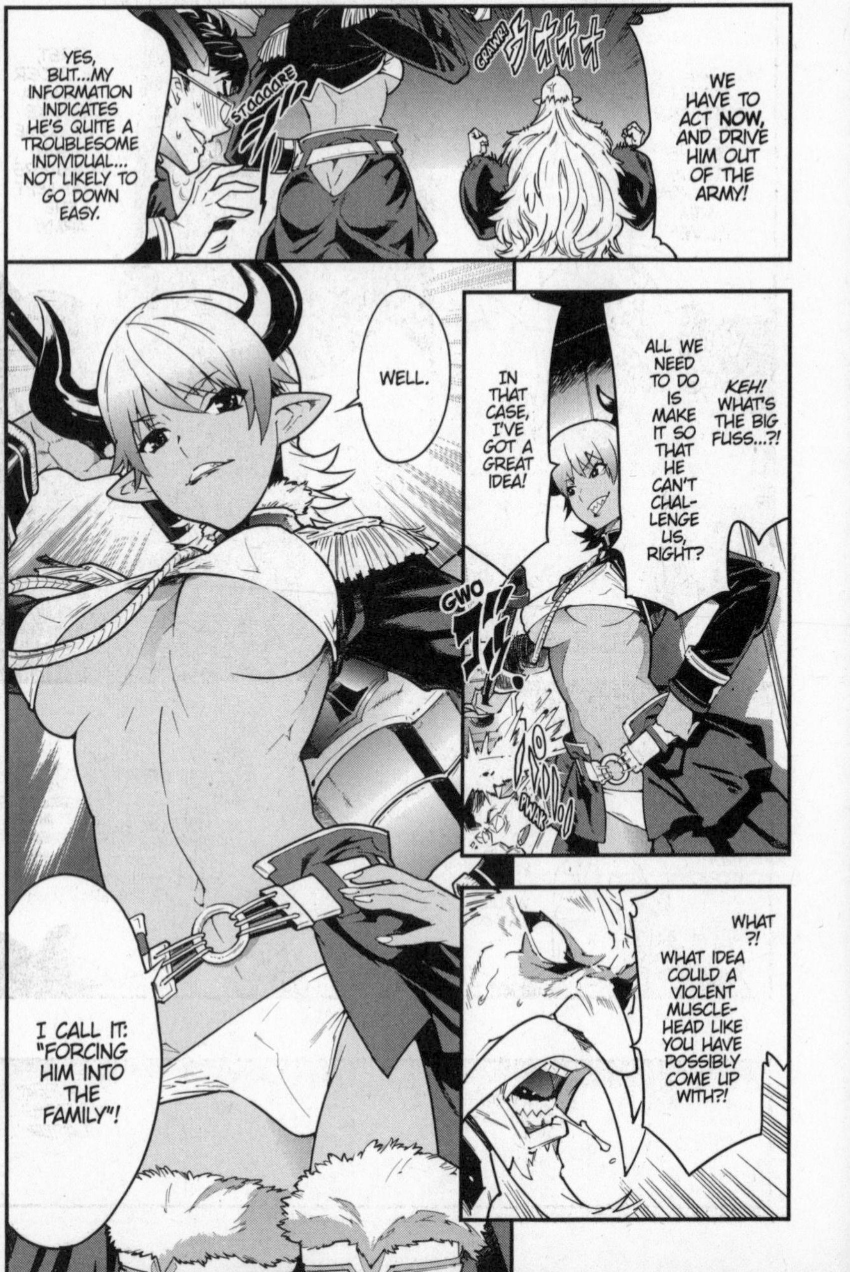
WE HAVE TO ACT NOW, AND DRIVE HIM OUT OF THE ARMY!
GRAWR!
STAAAARE
YES, BUT...MY INFORMATION INDICATES HE'S QUITE A TROUBLESOME INDIVIDUAL... NOT LIKELY TO GO DOWN EASY.
KEH! WHAT'S THE BIG FUSS...?!
ALL WE NEED TO DO IS MAKE IT SO THAT HE CAN'T CHAL-LENGE US, RIGHT?
IN THAT CASE, I'VE GOT A GREAT IDEA!
GWO
PWAK
WHAT ?!
WHAT IDEA COULD A VIOLENT MUSCLE-HEAD LIKE YOU HAVE POSSIBLY COME UP WITH?!
WELL.
I CALL IT: "FORCING HIM INTO THE FAMILY"!

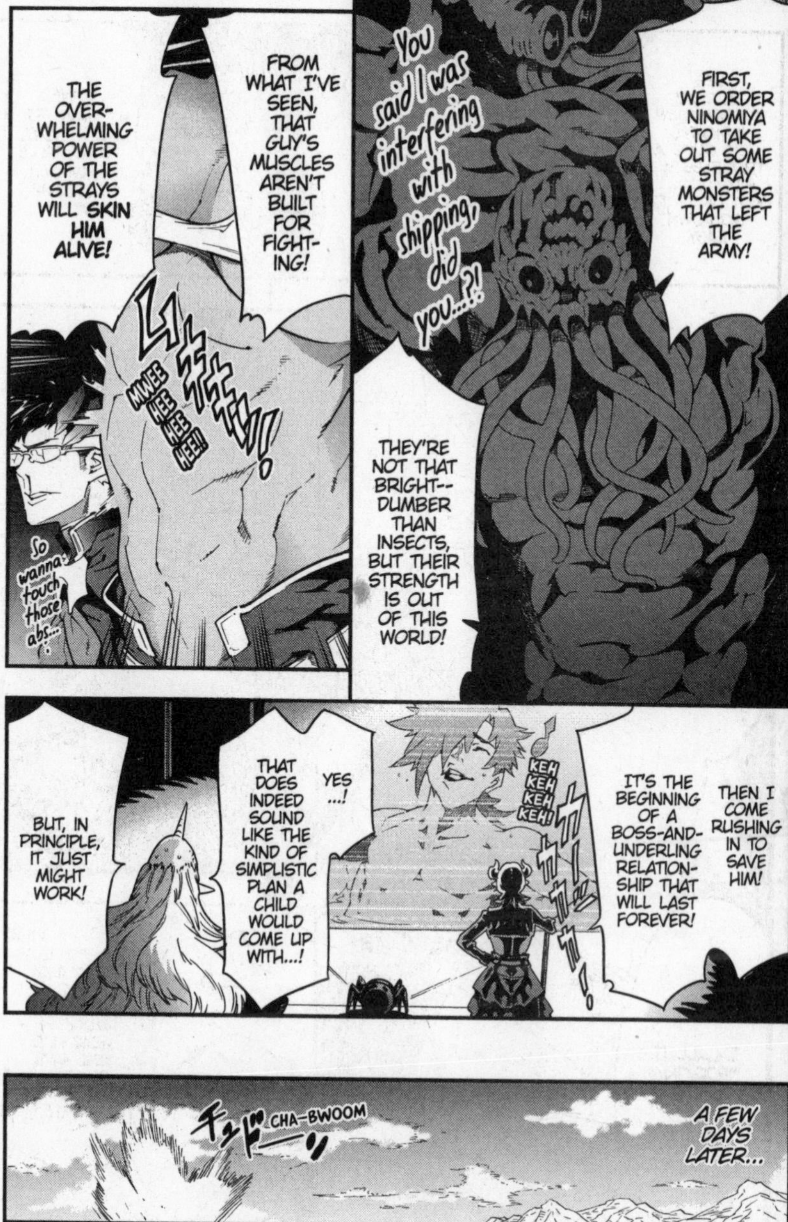
FIRST, WE ORDER NINOMIYA TO TAKE OUT SOME STRAY MONSTERS THAT LEFT THE ARMY!
You said I was interfering with shipping, did you...?!
THEY'RE NOT THAT BRIGHT-- DUMBER THAN INSECTS, BUT THEIR STRENGTH IS OUT OF THIS WORLD!
FROM WHAT I'VE SEEN, THAT GUY'S MUSCLES AREN'T BUILT FOR FIGHT-ING!
THE OVER-WHELMING POWER OF THE STRAYS WILL SKIN HIM ALIVE!
MWEE HEE HEE HEE!!
So wanna touch those abs...!
THEN I COME RUSHING IN TO SAVE HIM!
IT'S THE BEGINNING OF A BOSS-AND-UNDERLING RELATION-SHIP THAT WILL LAST FOREVER!
KEH KEH KEH KEH!
YES ...!
THAT DOES INDEED SOUND LIKE THE KIND OF SIMPLISTIC PLAN A CHILD WOULD COME UP WITH...!
BUT, IN PRINCIPLE, IT JUST MIGHT WORK!
A FEW DAYS LATER...
CHA-BWOOM

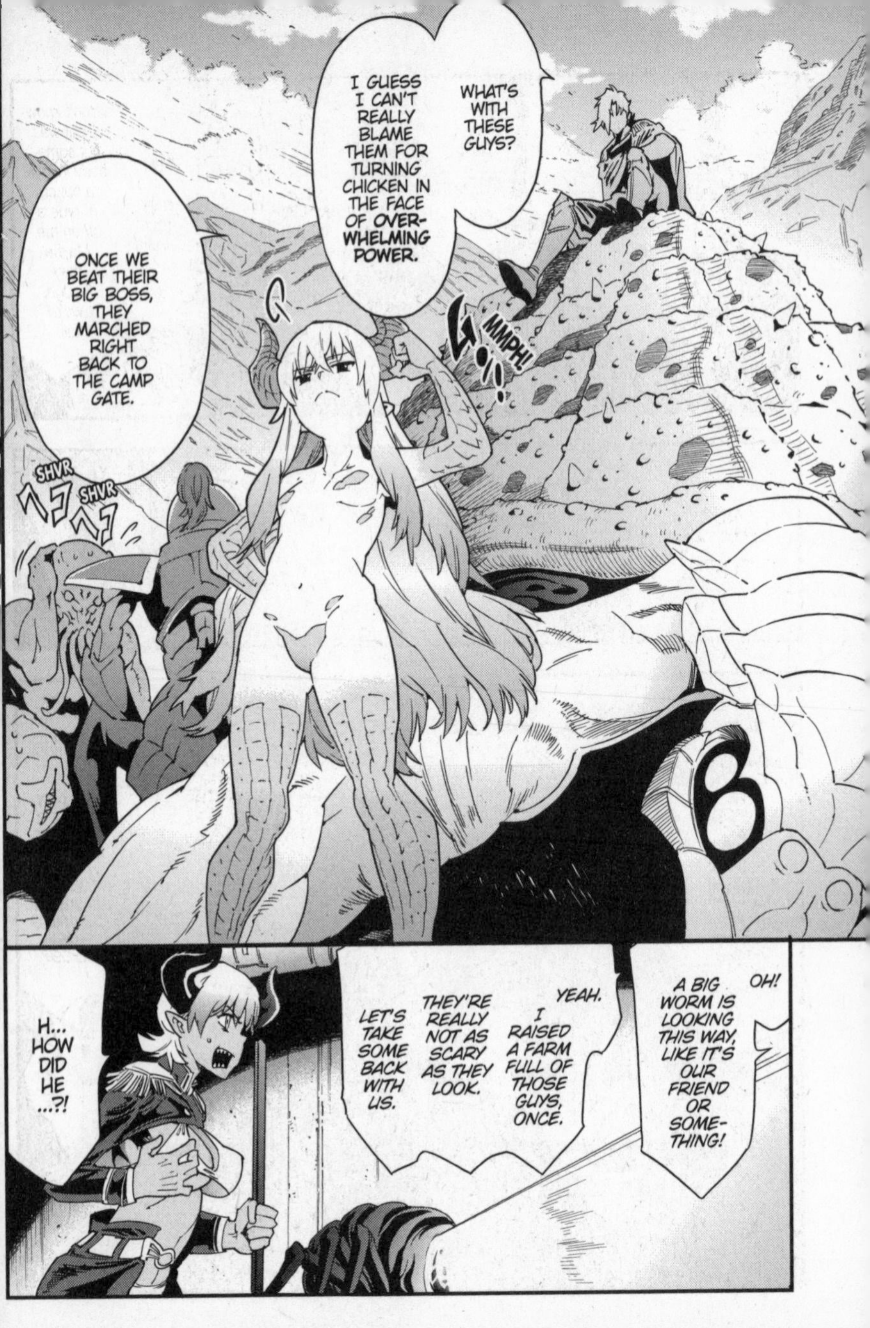
WHAT'S WITH THESE GUYS?
I GUESS I CAN'T REALLY BLAME THEM FOR TURNING CHICKEN IN THE FACE OF OVER-WHELMING POWER.
MMPH!
ONCE WE BEAT THEIR BIG BOSS, THEY MARCHED RIGHT BACK TO THE CAMP GATE.
SHVR
SHVR
OH!
A BIG WORM IS LOOKING THIS WAY, LIKE IT'S OUR FRIEND OR SOME-THING!
YEAH.
I RAISED A FARM FULL OF THOSE GUYS, ONCE.
THEY'RE REALLY NOT AS SCARY AS THEY LOOK.
LET'S TAKE SOME BACK WITH US.
H... HOW DID HE ...?!

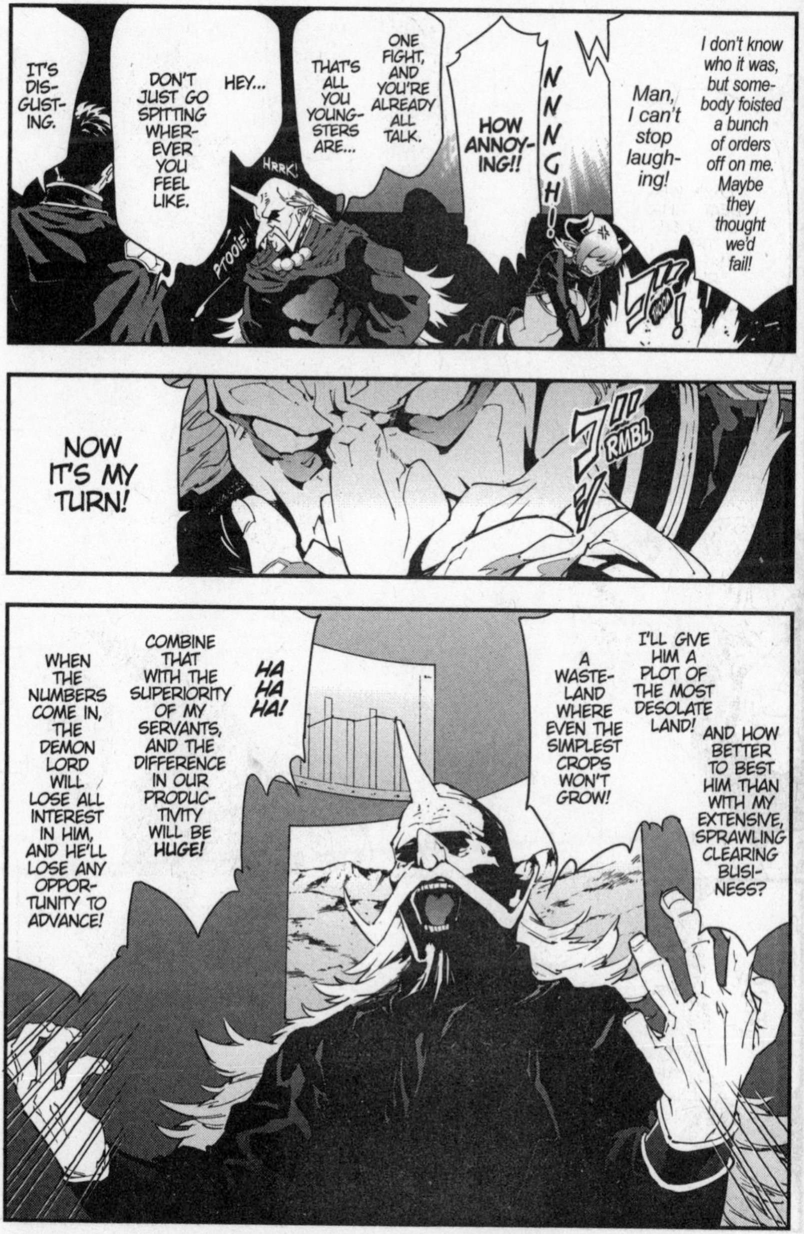
I don't know who it was, but somebody foisted a bunch of orders off on me. Maybe they thought we'd fail!
Man, I can't stop laughing!
NNNNGH!!
HOW ANNOYING!!
THOOM
ONE FIGHT, AND YOU'RE ALREADY ALL TALK.
THAT'S ALL YOU YOUNGSTERS ARE...
HRRK!
HEY...
DON'T JUST GO SPITTING WHEREVER YOU FEEL LIKE.
PTOOIE!
IT'S DISGUSTING.
RMBL
NOW IT'S MY TURN!
I'LL GIVE HIM A PLOT OF THE MOST DESOLATE LAND!
A WASTELAND WHERE EVEN THE SIMPLEST CROPS WON'T GROW!
AND HOW BETTER TO BEST HIM THAN WITH MY EXTENSIVE, SPRAWLING CLEARING BUSINESS?
HA HA HA!
COMBINE THAT WITH THE SUPERIORITY OF MY SERVANTS, AND THE DIFFERENCE IN OUR PRODUCTIVITY WILL BE HUGE!
WHEN THE NUMBERS COME IN, THE DEMON LORD WILL LOSE ALL INTEREST IN HIM, AND HE'LL LOSE ANY OPPORTUNITY TO ADVANCE!

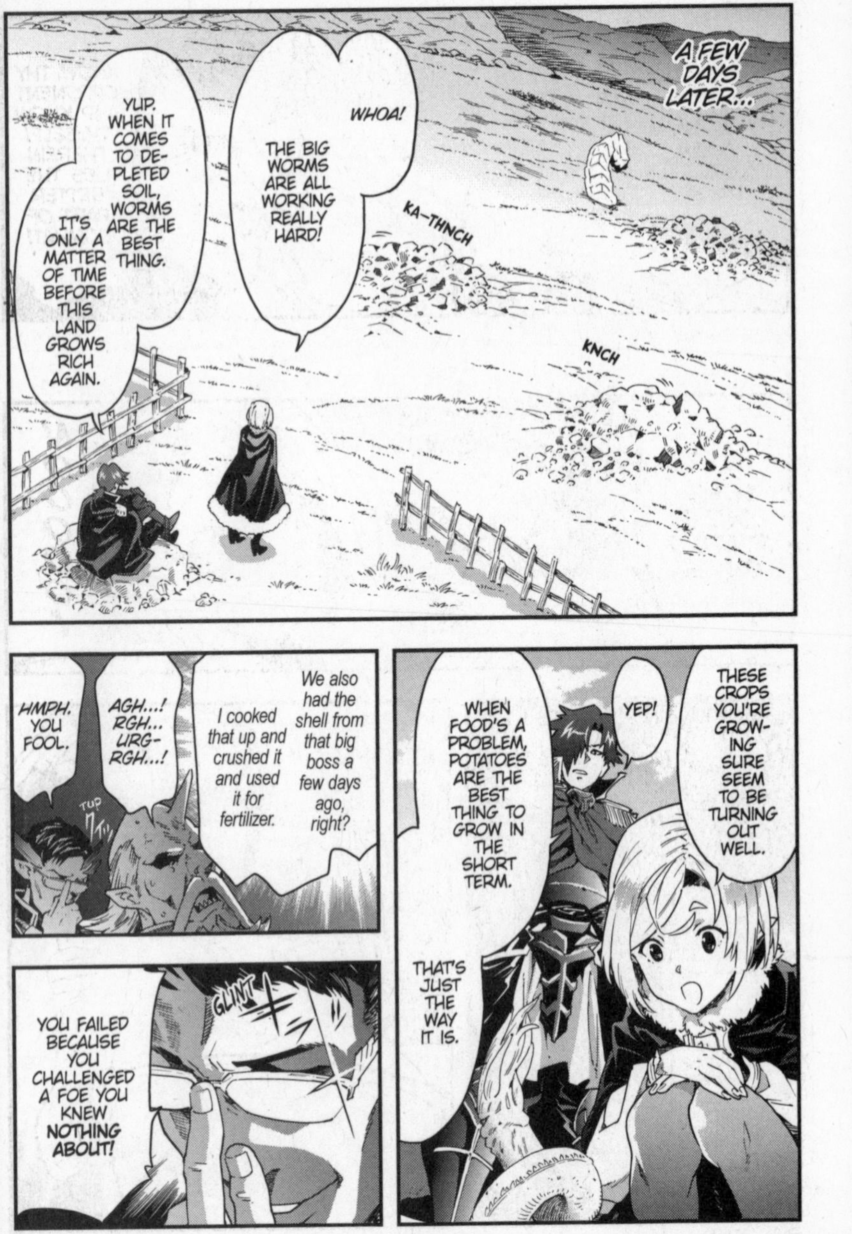
A FEW DAYS LATER...
WHOA!
THE BIG WORMS ARE ALL WORKING REALLY HARD!
KA-THNCH
KNCH
YUP. WHEN IT COMES TO DE-PLETED SOIL, WORMS ARE THE BEST THING.
IT'S ONLY A MATTER OF TIME BEFORE THIS LAND GROWS RICH AGAIN.
THESE CROPS YOU'RE GROW-ING SURE SEEM TO BE TURNING OUT WELL.
YEP!
WHEN FOOD'S A PROBLEM, POTATOES ARE THE BEST THING TO GROW IN THE SHORT TERM.
THAT'S JUST THE WAY IT IS.
We also had the shell from that big boss a few days ago, right?
I cooked that up and crushed it and used it for fertilizer.
AGH...! RGH... URG-RGH...!
TUP
HMPH. YOU FOOL.
GLINT
YOU FAILED BECAUSE YOU CHALLENGED A FOE YOU KNEW NOTHING ABOUT!

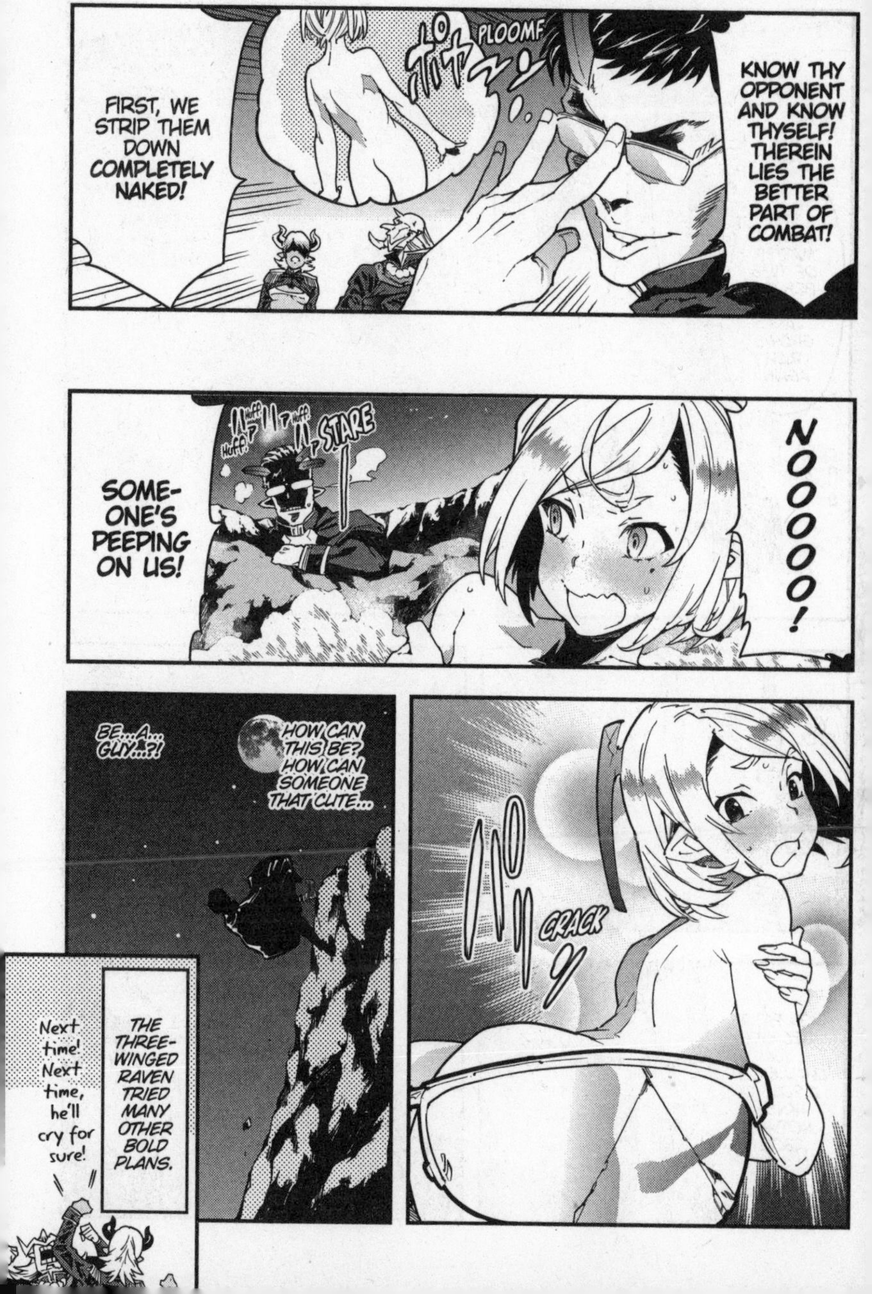
KNOW THY OPPONENT AND KNOW THYSELF! THEREIN LIES THE BETTER PART OF COMBAT!
PLOOMF
FIRST, WE STRIP THEM DOWN COMPLETELY NAKED!
NOOOOOO!
STARE
SOME-ONE'S PEEPING ON US!
CRACK
HOW CAN THIS BE? HOW CAN SOMEONE THAT CUTE...
BE...A... GUY...?!
THE THREE-WINGED RAVEN TRIED MANY OTHER BOLD PLANS.
Next time! Next time, he'll cry for sure!

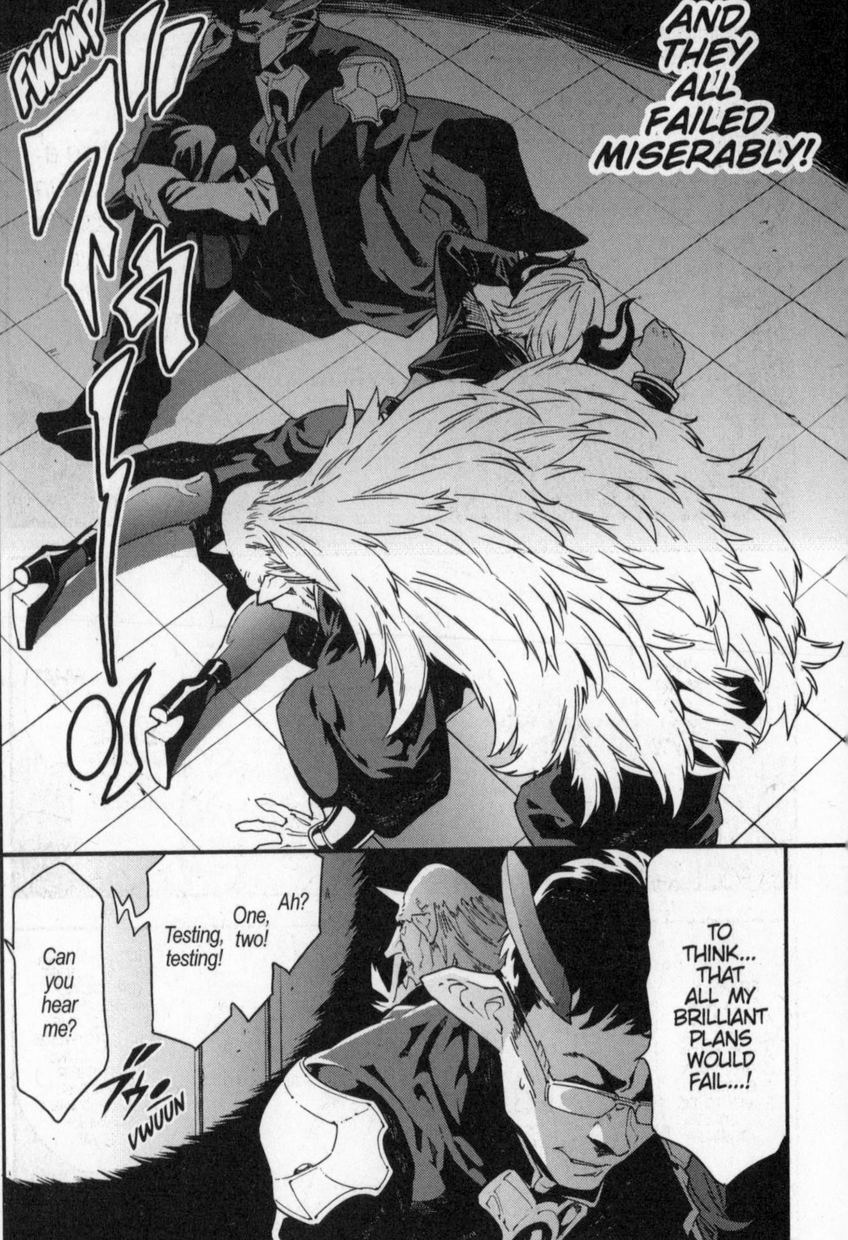
AND THEY ALL FAILED MISERABLY!
FWUMP
TO THINK... THAT ALL MY BRILLIANT PLANS WOULD FAIL...!
Ah?
One, two!
Testing, testing!
Can you hear me?
VWUUN

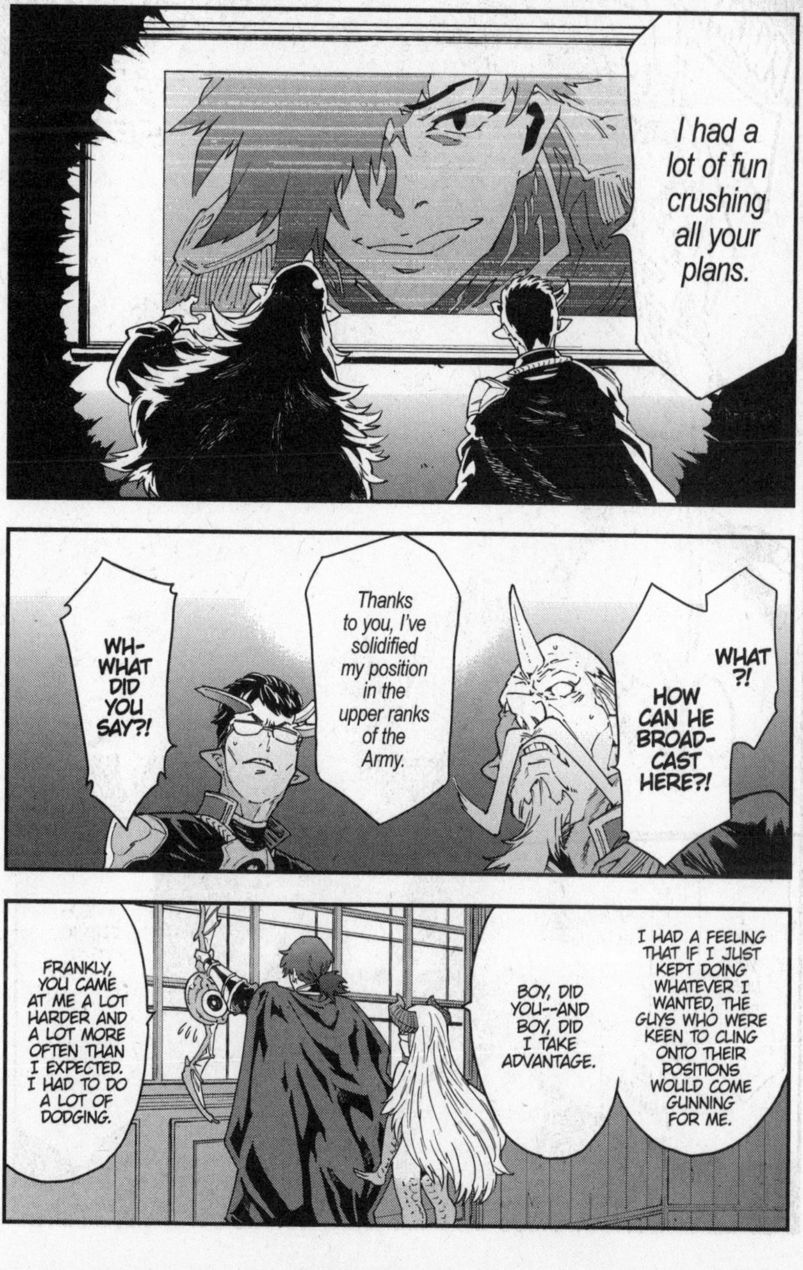
I had a lot of fun crushing all your plans.
WHAT?!
HOW CAN HE BROADCAST HERE?!
Thanks to you, I've solidified my position in the upper ranks of the Army.
WH-WHAT DID YOU SAY?!
I HAD A FEELING THAT IF I JUST KEPT DOING WHATEVER I WANTED, THE GUYS WHO WERE KEEN TO CLING ONTO THEIR POSITIONS WOULD COME GUNNING FOR ME.
BOY, DID YOU--AND BOY, DID I TAKE ADVANTAGE.
FRANKLY, YOU CAME AT ME A LOT HARDER AND A LOT MORE OFTEN THAN I EXPECTED. I HAD TO DO A LOT OF DODGING.

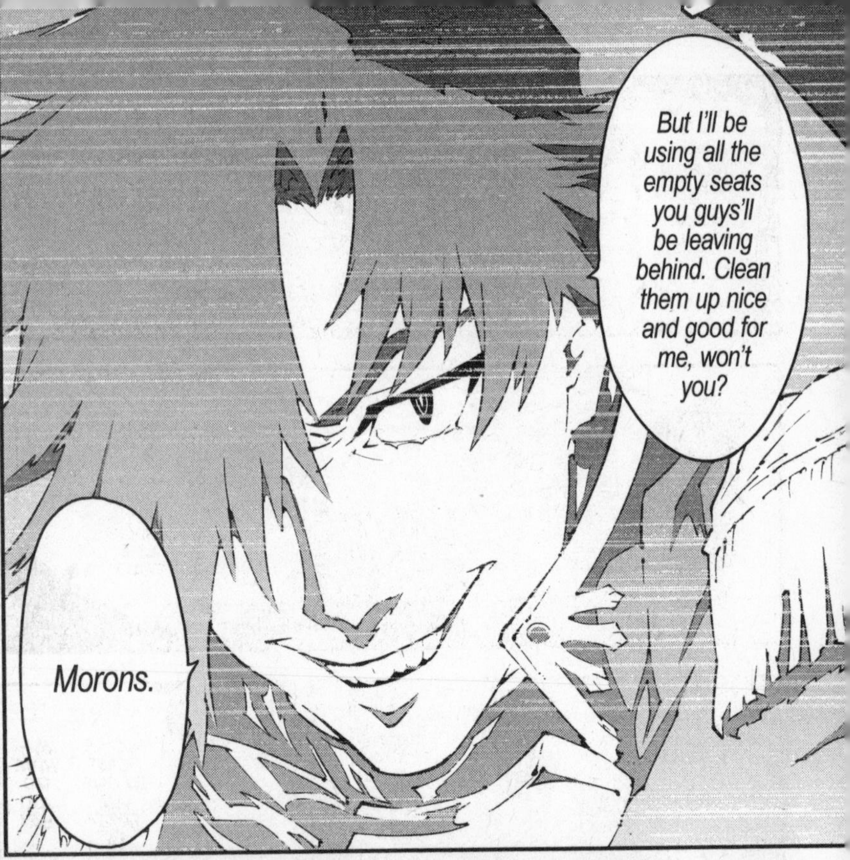
But I'll be using all the empty seats you guys'll be leaving behind. Clean them up nice and good for me, won't you?
Morons.

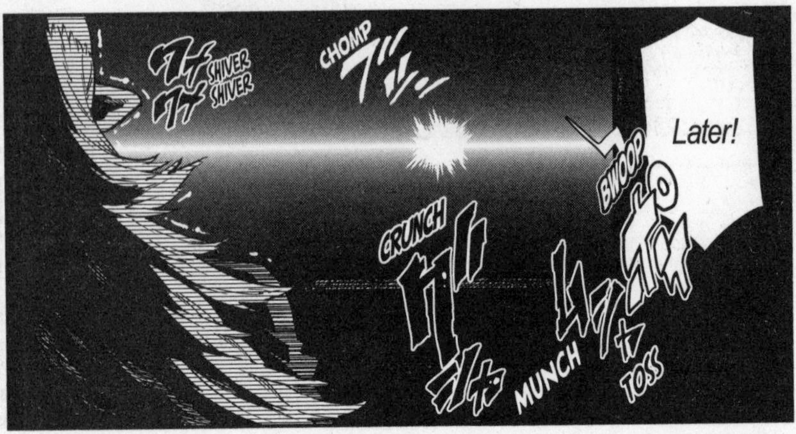
Later!
BWOOP
TOSS
MUNCH
CRUNCH
CHOMP
SHIVER SHIVER

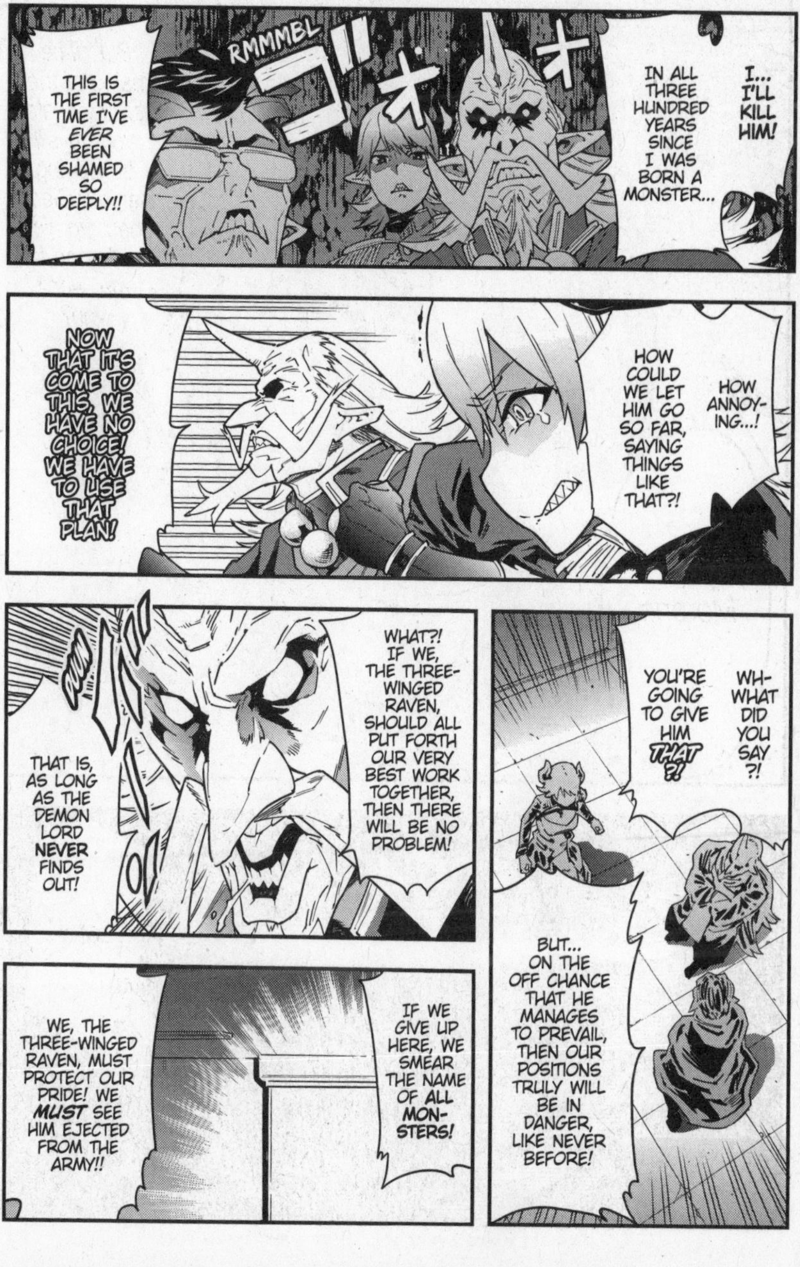
I... I'LL KILL HIM!
IN ALL THREE HUNDRED YEARS SINCE I WAS BORN A MONSTER...
RMMMBL
THIS IS THE FIRST TIME I'VE *EVER* BEEN SHAMED SO DEEPLY!!
HOW ANNOYING...!
HOW COULD WE LET HIM GO SO FAR, SAYING THINGS LIKE THAT?!
NOW THAT IT'S COME TO THIS, WE HAVE NO CHOICE! WE HAVE TO USE THAT PLAN!
WH-WHAT DID YOU SAY?!
YOU'RE GOING TO GIVE HIM *THAT*?!
BUT... ON THE OFF CHANCE THAT HE MANAGES TO PREVAIL, THEN OUR POSITIONS TRULY WILL BE IN DANGER, LIKE NEVER BEFORE!
WHAT?! IF WE, THE THREE-WINGED RAVEN, SHOULD ALL PUT FORTH OUR VERY BEST WORK TOGETHER, THEN THERE WILL BE NO PROBLEM!
THAT IS, AS LONG AS THE DEMON LORD **NEVER** FINDS OUT!
IF WE GIVE UP HERE, WE SMEAR THE NAME OF **ALL MONSTERS!**
WE, THE THREE-WINGED RAVEN, MUST PROTECT OUR PRIDE! WE ***MUST*** SEE HIM EJECTED FROM THE ARMY!!

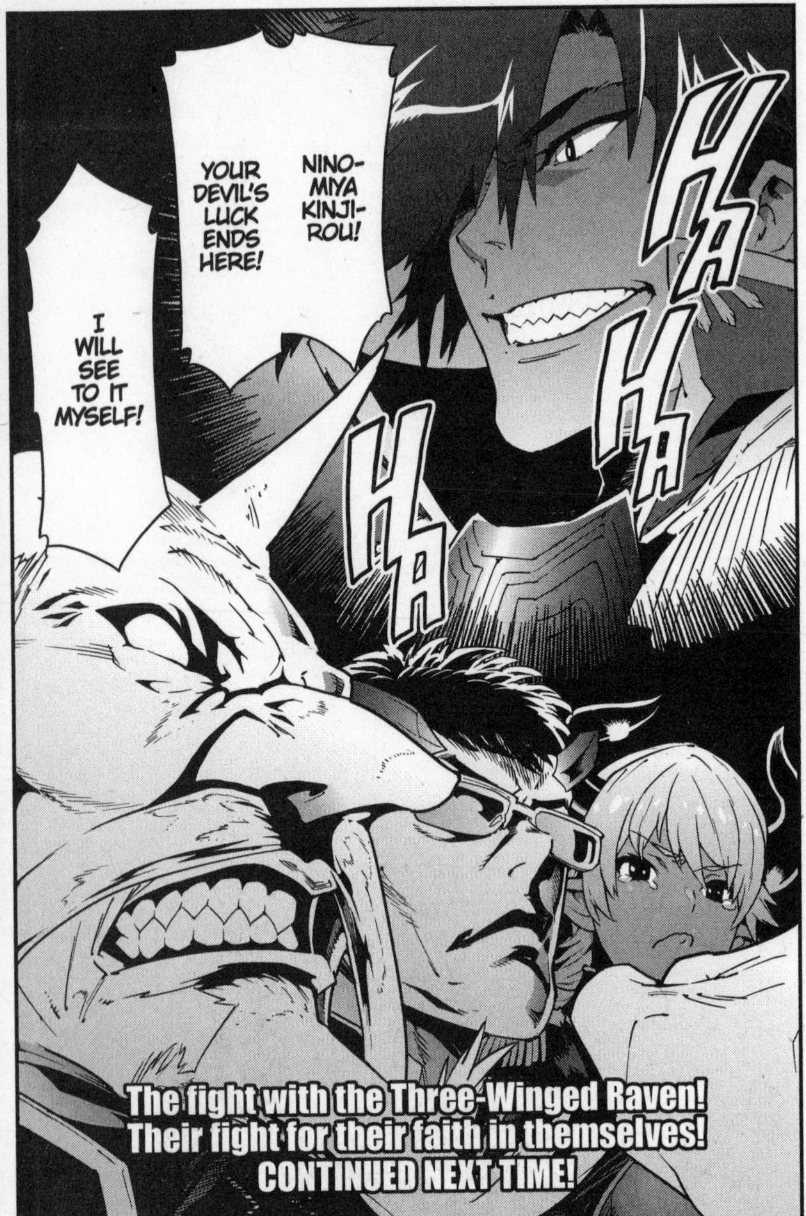
NINO-MIYA KINJI-ROU!
YOUR DEVIL'S LUCK ENDS HERE!
I WILL SEE TO IT MYSELF!
HAHAHA
The fight with the Three-Winged Raven!
Their fight for their faith in themselves!
CONTINUED NEXT TIME!

Actually, we never see these guys again.

3 FORMER EXECUTIVES

APPARENTLY, A HUNDRED
YEARS AGO, THEY WERE
QUITE THE SUPERSTARS...

THE DUNGEON OF
BLACK COMPANY

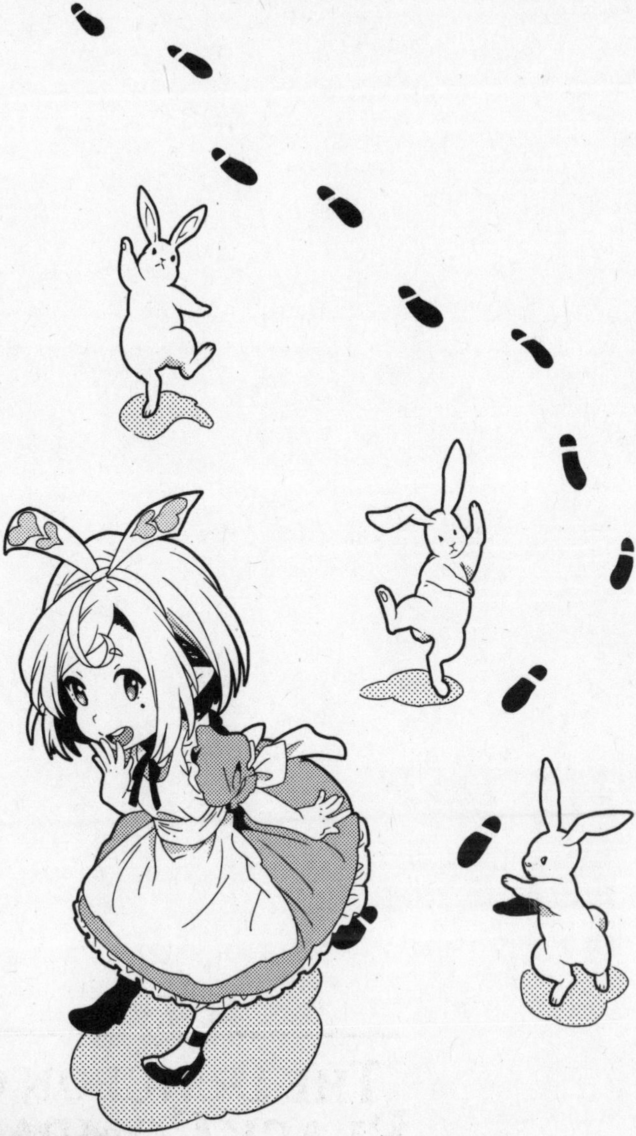

Chapter 14: Ranga in Angerworld

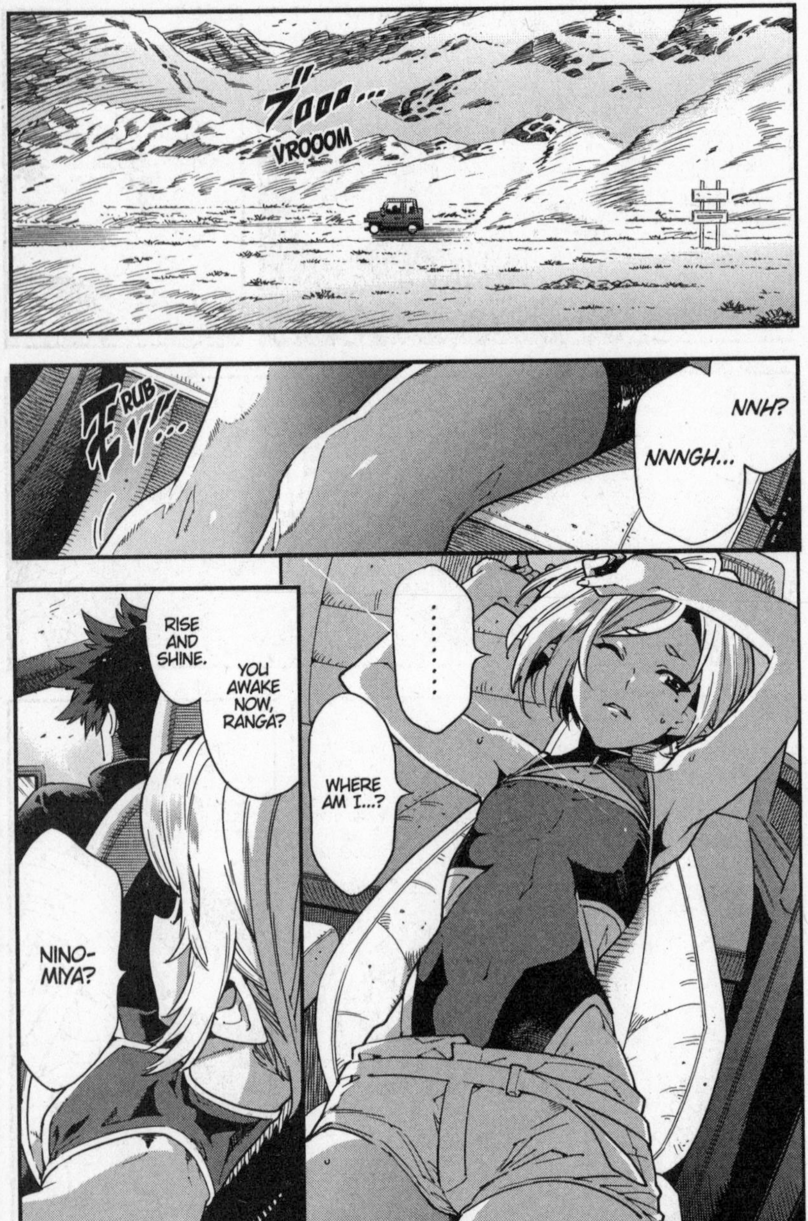
VROOOM
NNH?
NNNGH...
RUB
......
WHERE AM I...?
RISE AND SHINE.
YOU AWAKE NOW, RANGA?
NINO-MIYA?

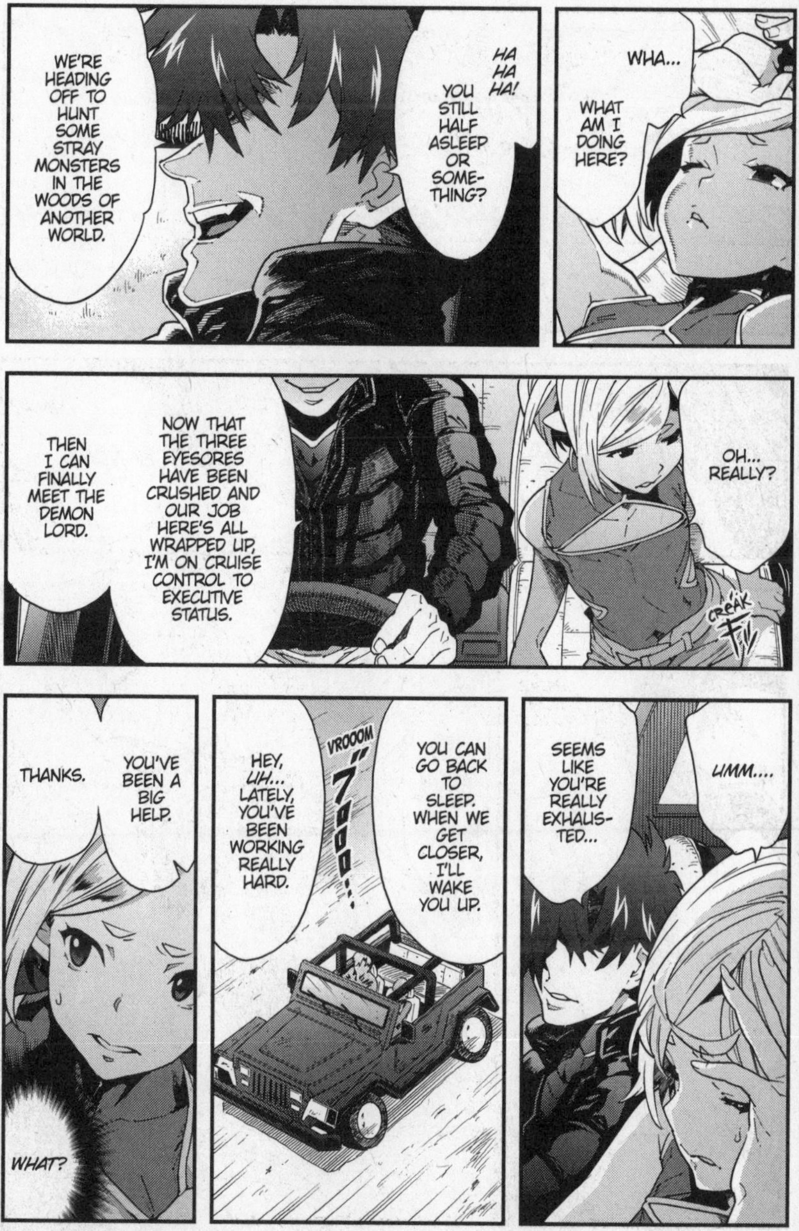
WHA...
WHAT AM I DOING HERE?
HA HA HA!
YOU STILL HALF ASLEEP OR SOME-THING?
WE'RE HEADING OFF TO HUNT SOME STRAY MONSTERS IN THE WOODS OF ANOTHER WORLD.
OH... REALLY?
CREAK
NOW THAT THE THREE EYESORES HAVE BEEN CRUSHED AND OUR JOB HERE'S ALL WRAPPED UP, I'M ON CRUISE CONTROL TO EXECUTIVE STATUS.
THEN I CAN FINALLY MEET THE DEMON LORD.
UMM....
SEEMS LIKE YOU'RE REALLY EXHAUS-TED...
YOU CAN GO BACK TO SLEEP. WHEN WE GET CLOSER, I'LL WAKE YOU UP.
VROOOM
HEY, UH... LATELY, YOU'VE BEEN WORKING REALLY HARD.
YOU'VE BEEN A BIG HELP.
THANKS.
WHAT?

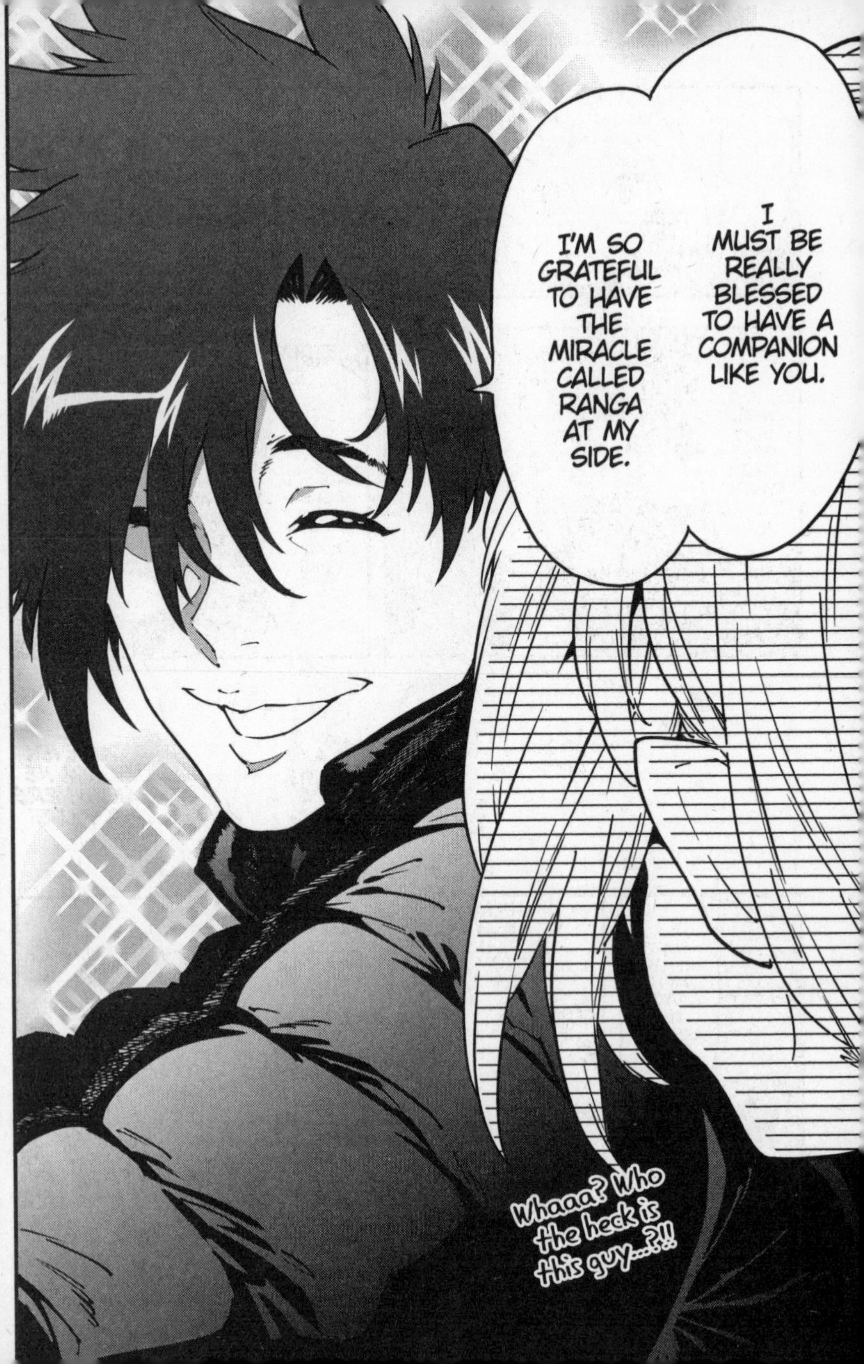
I MUST BE REALLY BLESSED TO HAVE A COMPANION LIKE YOU.
I'M SO GRATEFUL TO HAVE THE MIRACLE CALLED RANGA AT MY SIDE.
Whaaa? Who the heck is this guy...?!!

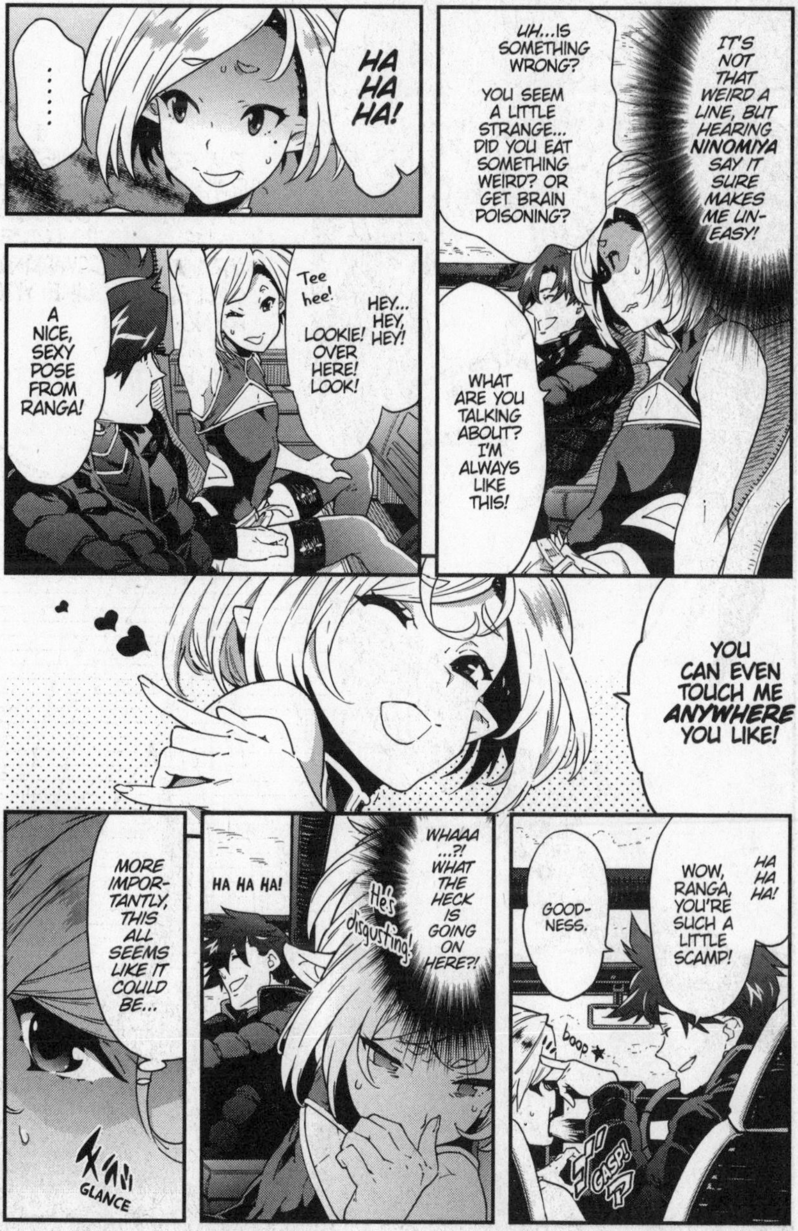
UH...IS SOMETHING WRONG?
YOU SEEM A LITTLE STRANGE... DID YOU EAT SOMETHING WEIRD? OR GET BRAIN POISONING?
IT'S NOT THAT WEIRD A LINE, BUT HEARING NINOMIYA SAY IT SURE MAKES ME UN-EASY!
WHAT ARE YOU TALKING ABOUT? I'M ALWAYS LIKE THIS!
......
HA HA HA!
HEY... HEY, HEY!
Tee hee!
LOOKIE! OVER HERE! LOOK!
A NICE, SEXY POSE FROM RANGA!
YOU CAN EVEN TOUCH ME ANYWHERE YOU LIKE!
HA HA HA!
WOW, RANGA, YOU'RE SUCH A LITTLE SCAMP!
GOOD-NESS.
boop★
GASP!
WHAAA ...?! WHAT THE HECK IS GOING ON HERE?!
He's disgusting!
HA HA HA!
MORE IMPOR-TANTLY, THIS ALL SEEMS LIKE IT COULD BE...
GLANCE

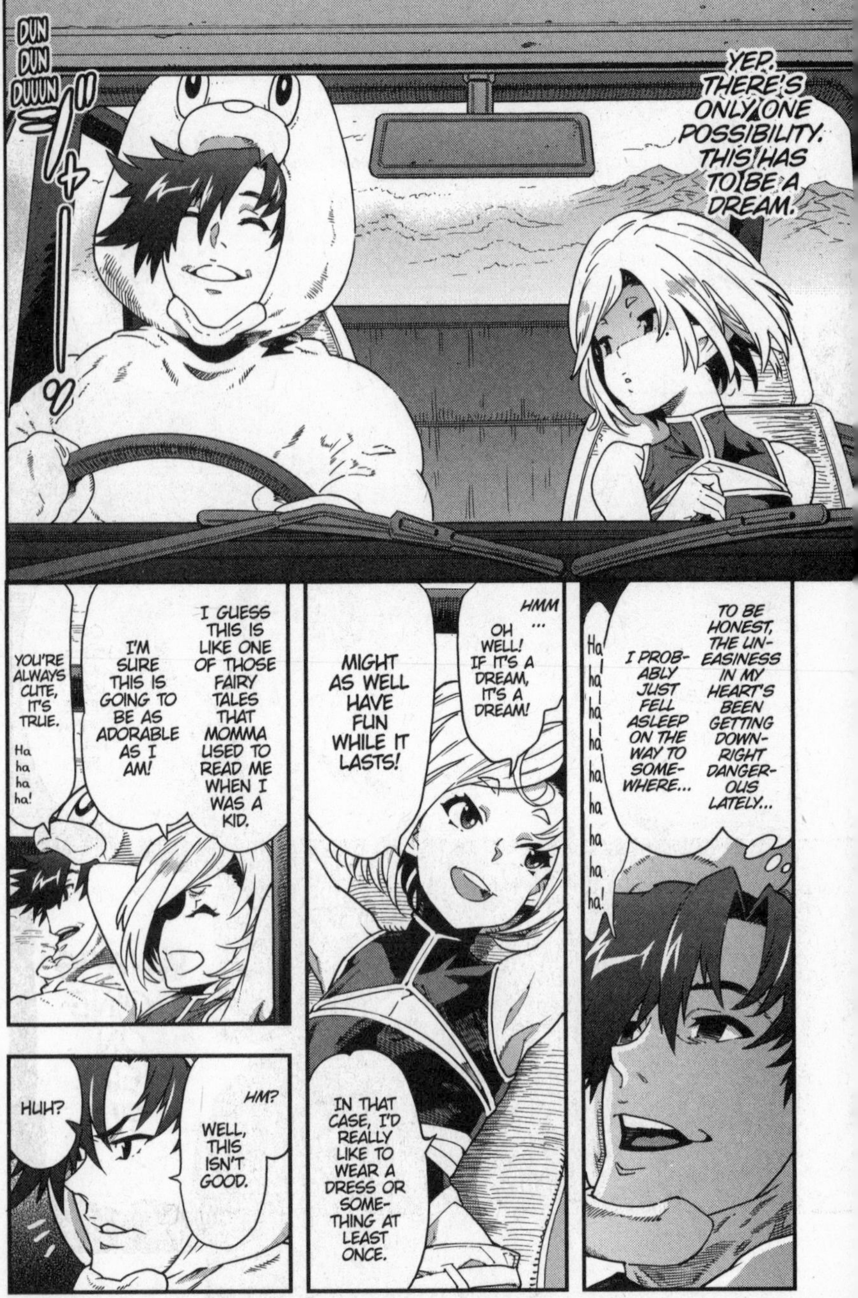
YEP. THERE'S ONLY ONE POSSIBILITY. THIS HAS TO BE A DREAM.
DUN DUN DUUUN
TO BE HONEST, THE UN-EASINESS IN MY HEART'S BEEN GETTING DOWN-RIGHT DANGER-OUS LATELY...
I PROB-ABLY JUST FELL ASLEEP ON THE WAY TO SOME-WHERE...
Ha ha ha ha ha ha ha ha ha ha!
HMM ...
OH WELL! IF IT'S A DREAM, IT'S A DREAM!
MIGHT AS WELL HAVE FUN WHILE IT LASTS!
IN THAT CASE, I'D REALLY LIKE TO WEAR A DRESS OR SOME-THING AT LEAST ONCE.
I GUESS THIS IS LIKE ONE OF THOSE FAIRY TALES THAT MOMMA USED TO READ ME WHEN I WAS A KID.
I'M SURE THIS IS GOING TO BE AS ADORABLE AS I AM!
YOU'RE ALWAYS CUTE, IT'S TRUE.
Ha ha ha ha!
HM?
WELL, THIS ISN'T GOOD.
HUH?

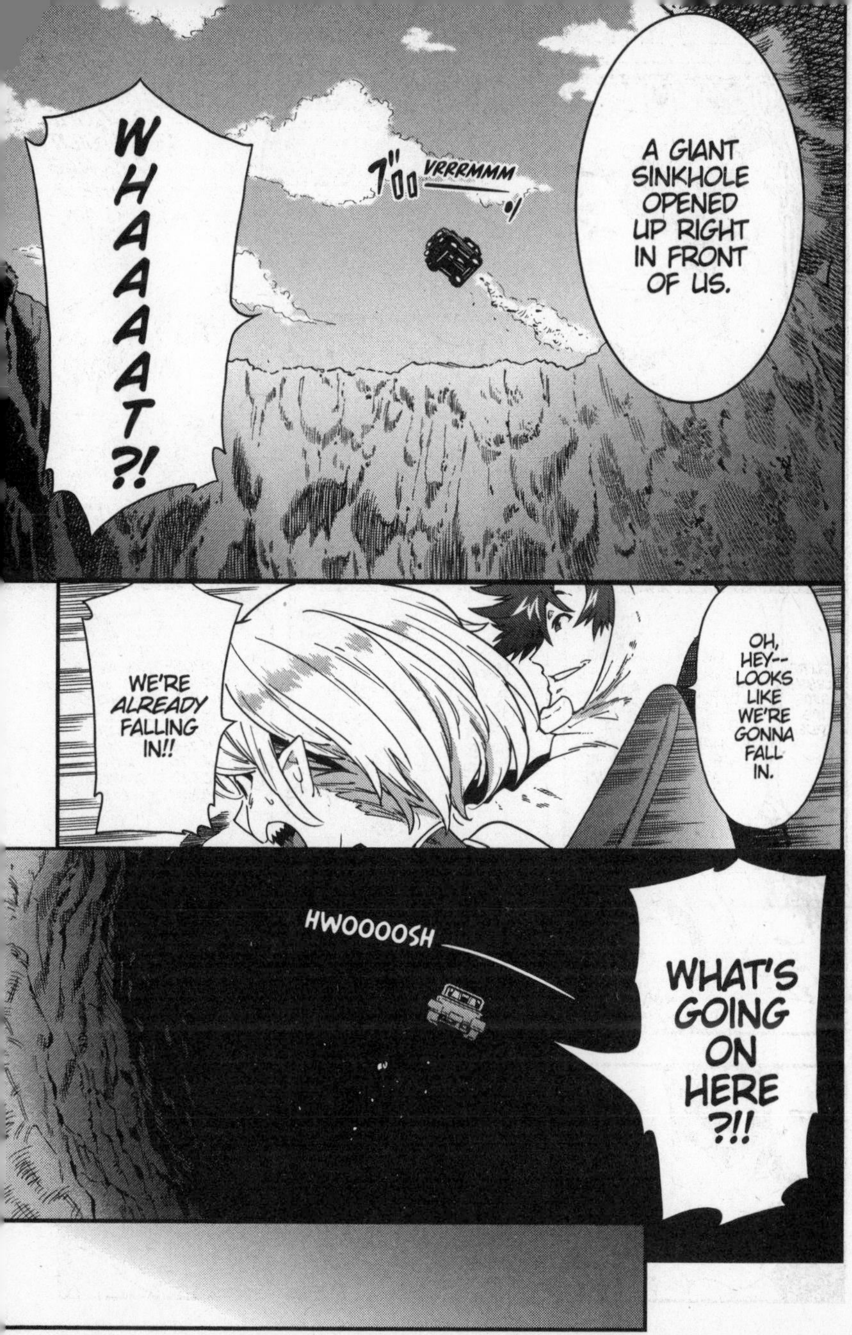
A GIANT SINKHOLE OPENED UP RIGHT IN FRONT OF US.
VRRRMMM
WHAAAAAT?!
OH, HEY-- LOOKS LIKE WE'RE GONNA FALL IN.
WE'RE ALREADY FALLING IN!!
WHAT'S GOING ON HERE?!!
HWOOOOSH

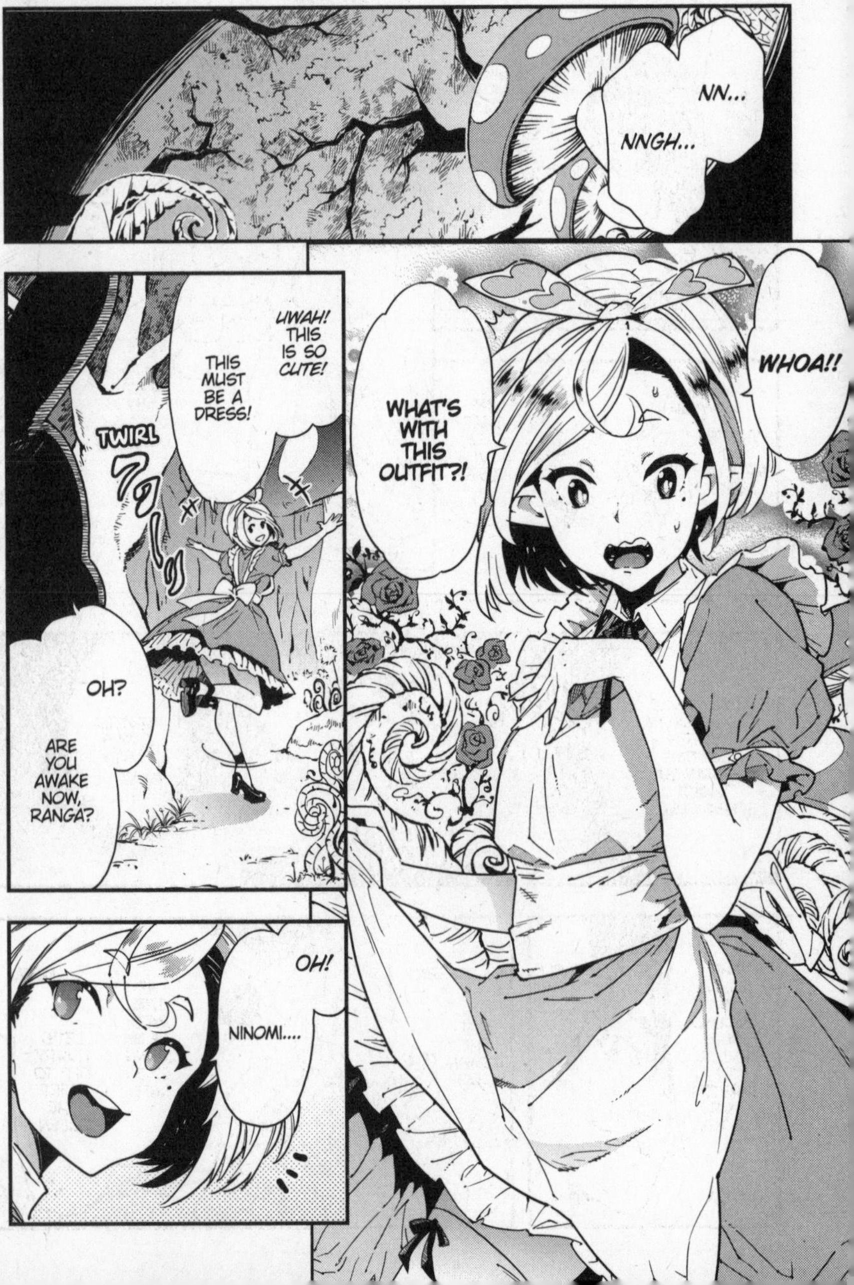
NN...
NNGH...
WHOA!!
WHAT'S WITH THIS OUTFIT?!
UWAH! THIS IS SO CUTE!
THIS MUST BE A DRESS!
TWIRL
OH?
ARE YOU AWAKE NOW, RANGA?
OH!
NINOMI....

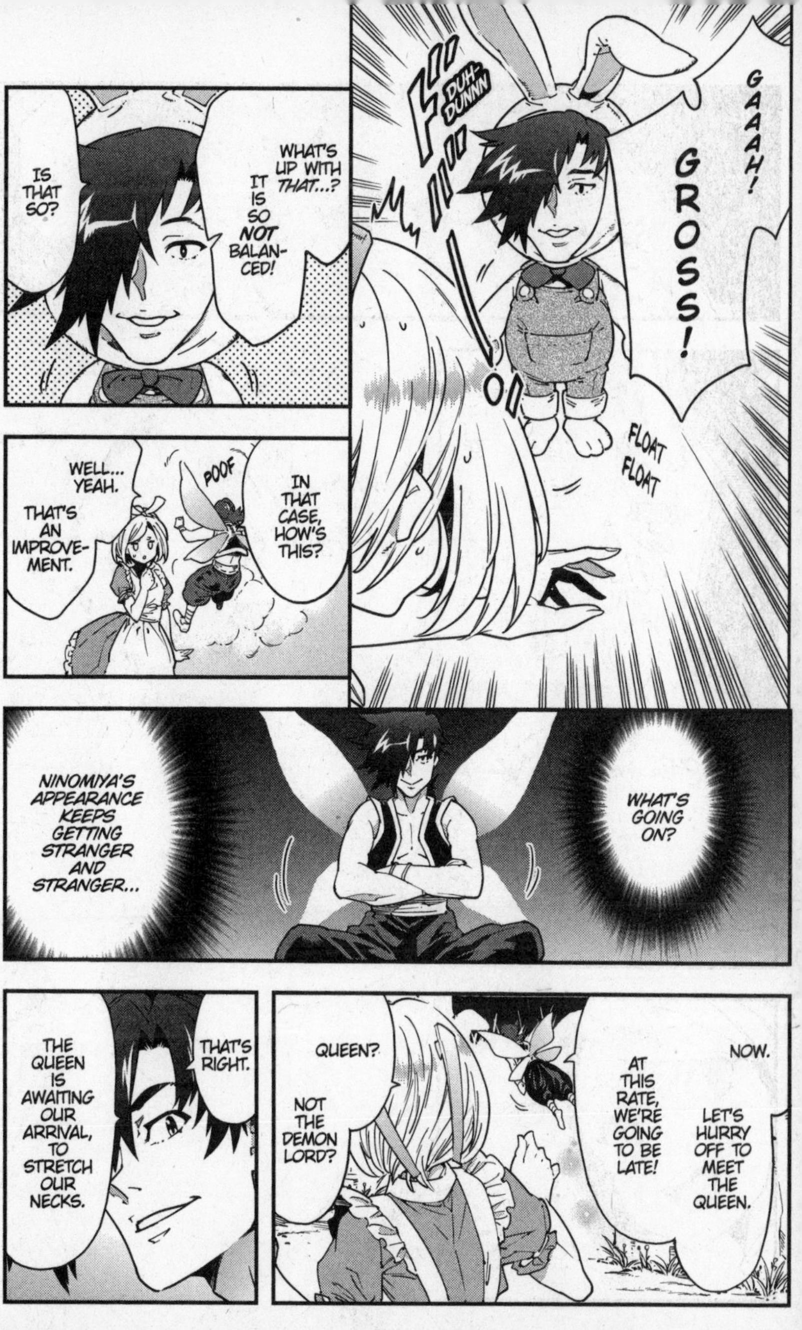
GAAAH!
GROSS!
DUH-DUNNN
FLOAT FLOAT
WHAT'S UP WITH THAT...?
IT IS SO NOT BALANCED!
IS THAT SO?
IN THAT CASE, HOW'S THIS?
POOF
WELL... YEAH.
THAT'S AN IMPROVEMENT.
WHAT'S GOING ON?
NINOMIYA'S APPEARANCE KEEPS GETTING STRANGER AND STRANGER...
NOW.
LET'S HURRY OFF TO MEET THE QUEEN.
AT THIS RATE, WE'RE GOING TO BE LATE!
QUEEN?
NOT THE DEMON LORD?
THAT'S RIGHT.
THE QUEEN IS AWAITING OUR ARRIVAL, TO STRETCH OUR NECKS.

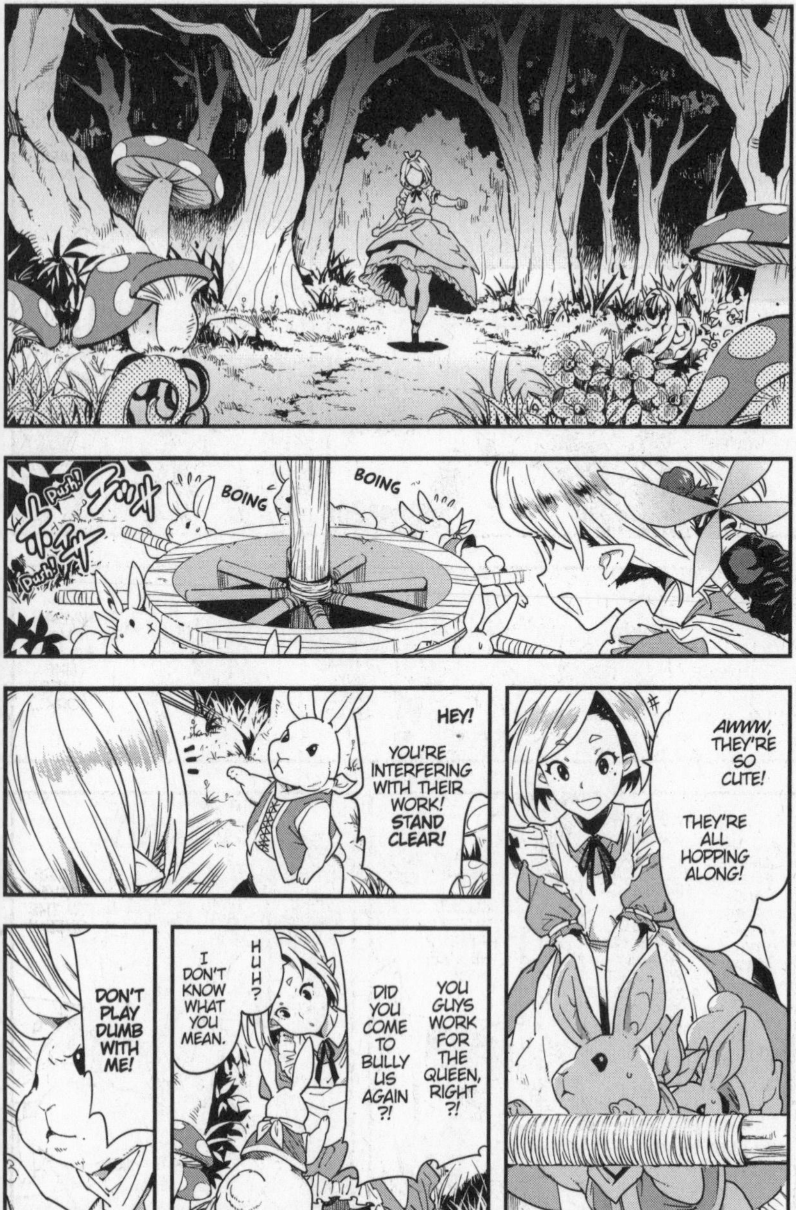
BOING
BOING
Push!
Push!
AWWW, THEY'RE SO CUTE!
THEY'RE ALL HOPPING ALONG!
HEY!
YOU'RE INTERFERING WITH THEIR WORK! STAND CLEAR!
YOU GUYS WORK FOR THE QUEEN, RIGHT?!
DID YOU COME TO BULLY US AGAIN?!
HUH?
I DON'T KNOW WHAT YOU MEAN.
DON'T PLAY DUMB WITH ME!

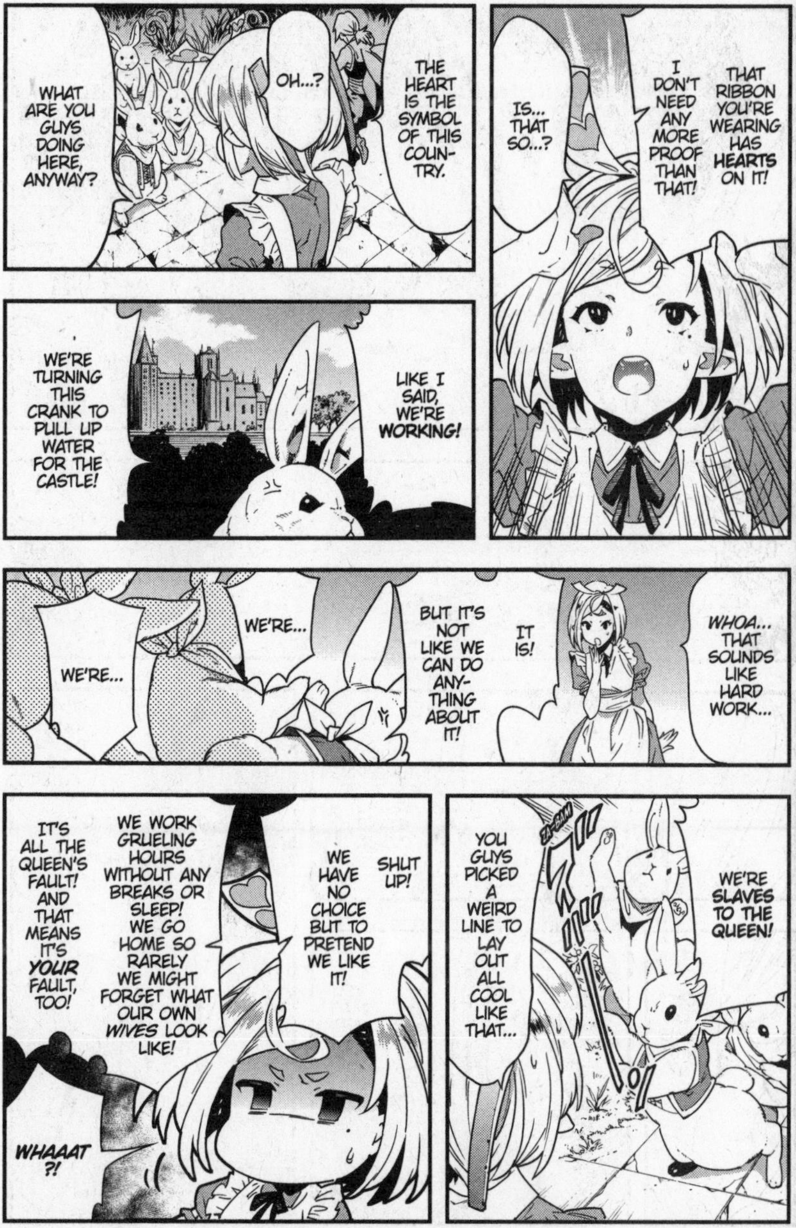
THAT RIBBON YOU'RE WEARING HAS HEARTS ON IT!
I DON'T NEED ANY MORE PROOF THAN THAT!
IS... THAT SO...?
THE HEART IS THE SYMBOL OF THIS COUN-TRY.
OH...?
WHAT ARE YOU GUYS DOING HERE, ANYWAY?
LIKE I SAID, WE'RE WORKING!
WE'RE TURNING THIS CRANK TO PULL UP WATER FOR THE CASTLE!
WHOA... THAT SOUNDS LIKE HARD WORK...
IT IS!
BUT IT'S NOT LIKE WE CAN DO ANY-THING ABOUT IT!
WE'RE...
WE'RE...
WE'RE SLAVES TO THE QUEEN!
YOU GUYS PICKED A WEIRD LINE TO LAY OUT ALL COOL LIKE THAT...
SHUT UP!
WE HAVE NO CHOICE BUT TO PRETEND WE LIKE IT!
WE WORK GRUELING HOURS WITHOUT ANY BREAKS OR SLEEP! WE GO HOME SO RARELY WE MIGHT FORGET WHAT OUR OWN WIVES LOOK LIKE!
IT'S ALL THE QUEEN'S FAULT! AND THAT MEANS IT'S YOUR FAULT, TOO!
WHAAAT ?!

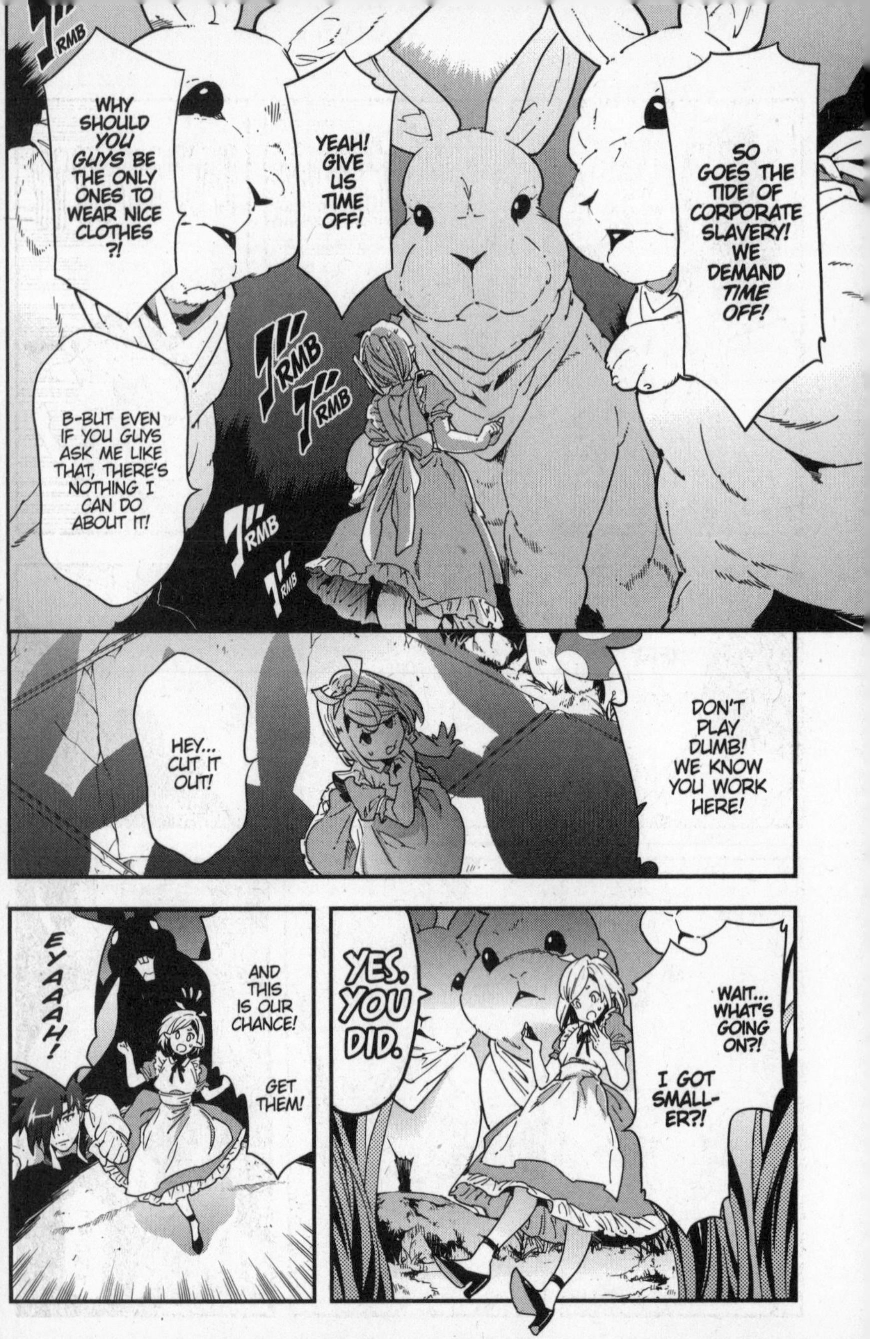
RMB
SO GOES THE TIDE OF CORPORATE SLAVERY! WE DEMAND TIME OFF!
YEAH! GIVE US TIME OFF!
WHY SHOULD YOU GUYS BE THE ONLY ONES TO WEAR NICE CLOTHES?!
RMB
RMB
B-BUT EVEN IF YOU GUYS ASK ME LIKE THAT, THERE'S NOTHING I CAN DO ABOUT IT!
RMB
RMB
DON'T PLAY DUMB! WE KNOW YOU WORK HERE!
HEY... CUT IT OUT!
WAIT... WHAT'S GOING ON?!
I GOT SMALLER?!
YES, YOU DID.
AND THIS IS OUR CHANCE!
GET THEM!
EYAAAH!

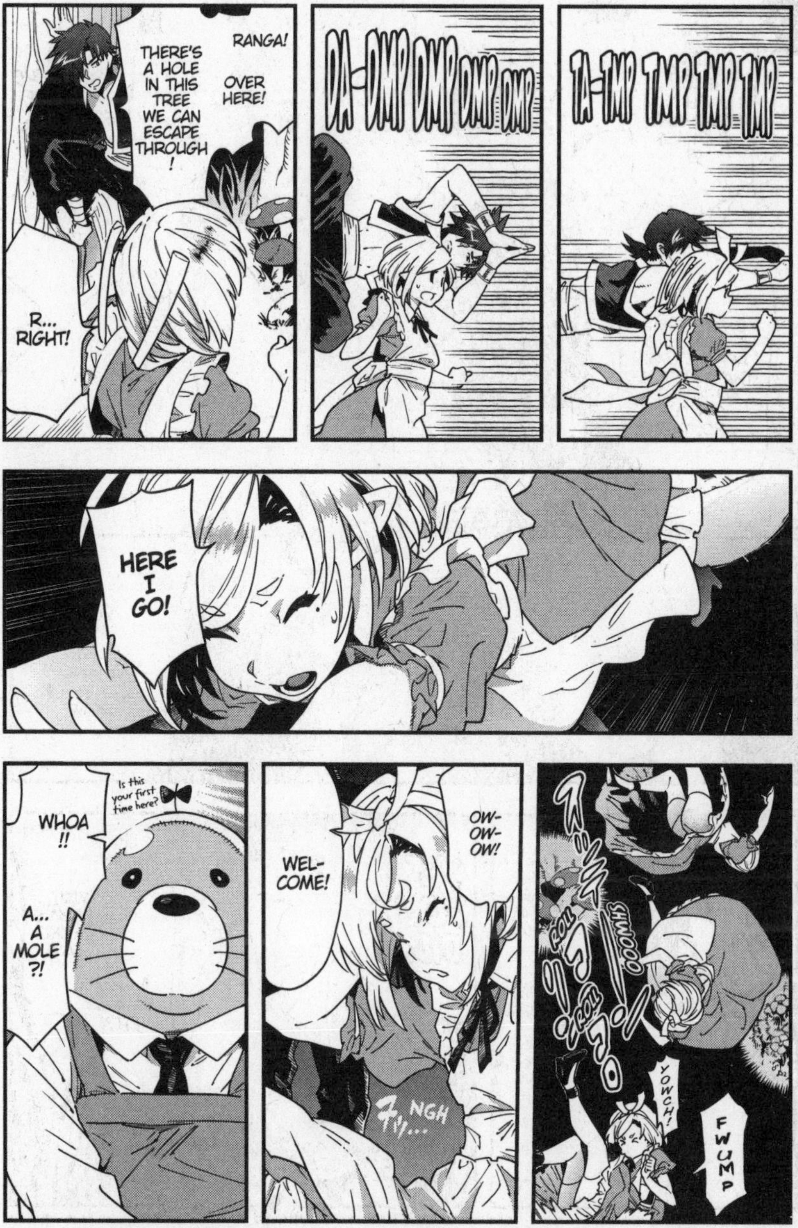
TA-TMP TMP TMP TMP
DA-DMP DMP DMP DMP DMP
RANGA!
OVER HERE!
THERE'S A HOLE IN THIS TREE WE CAN ESCAPE THROUGH!
R... RIGHT!
HERE I GO!
SHWOOOO
ROLL
ROLL
YOWCH!
FWUMP
OW-OW-OW!
WEL-COME!
NGH
Is this your first time here?
WHOA!!
A... A MOLE?!

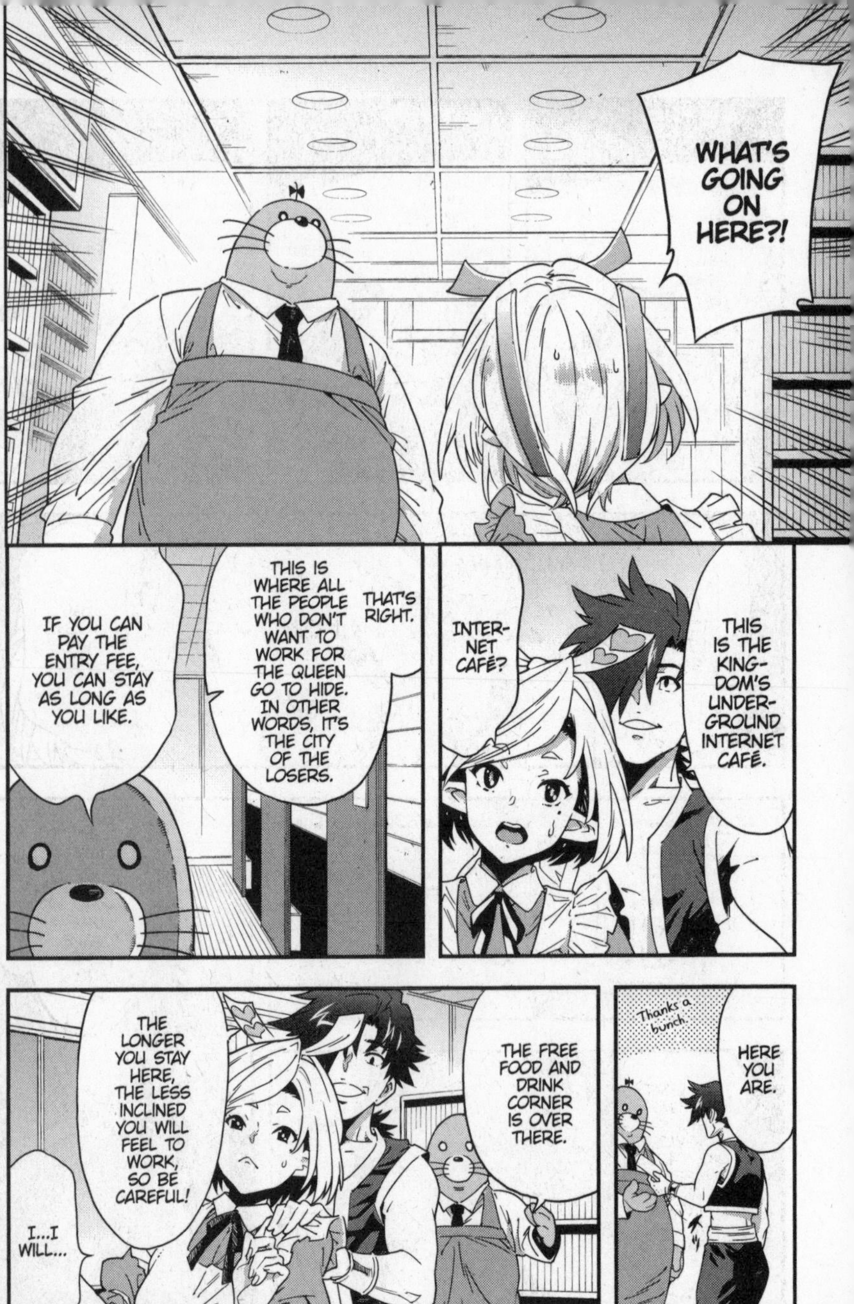

WHAT'S GOING ON HERE?!
THIS IS THE KING-DOM'S UNDER-GROUND INTERNET CAFÉ.
INTER-NET CAFÉ?
THAT'S RIGHT.
THIS IS WHERE ALL THE PEOPLE WHO DON'T WANT TO WORK FOR THE QUEEN GO TO HIDE. IN OTHER WORDS, IT'S THE CITY OF THE LOSERS.
IF YOU CAN PAY THE ENTRY FEE, YOU CAN STAY AS LONG AS YOU LIKE.
HERE YOU ARE.
Thanks a bunch.
THE FREE FOOD AND DRINK CORNER IS OVER THERE.
THE LONGER YOU STAY HERE, THE LESS INCLINED YOU WILL FEEL TO WORK, SO BE CAREFUL!
I...I WILL...

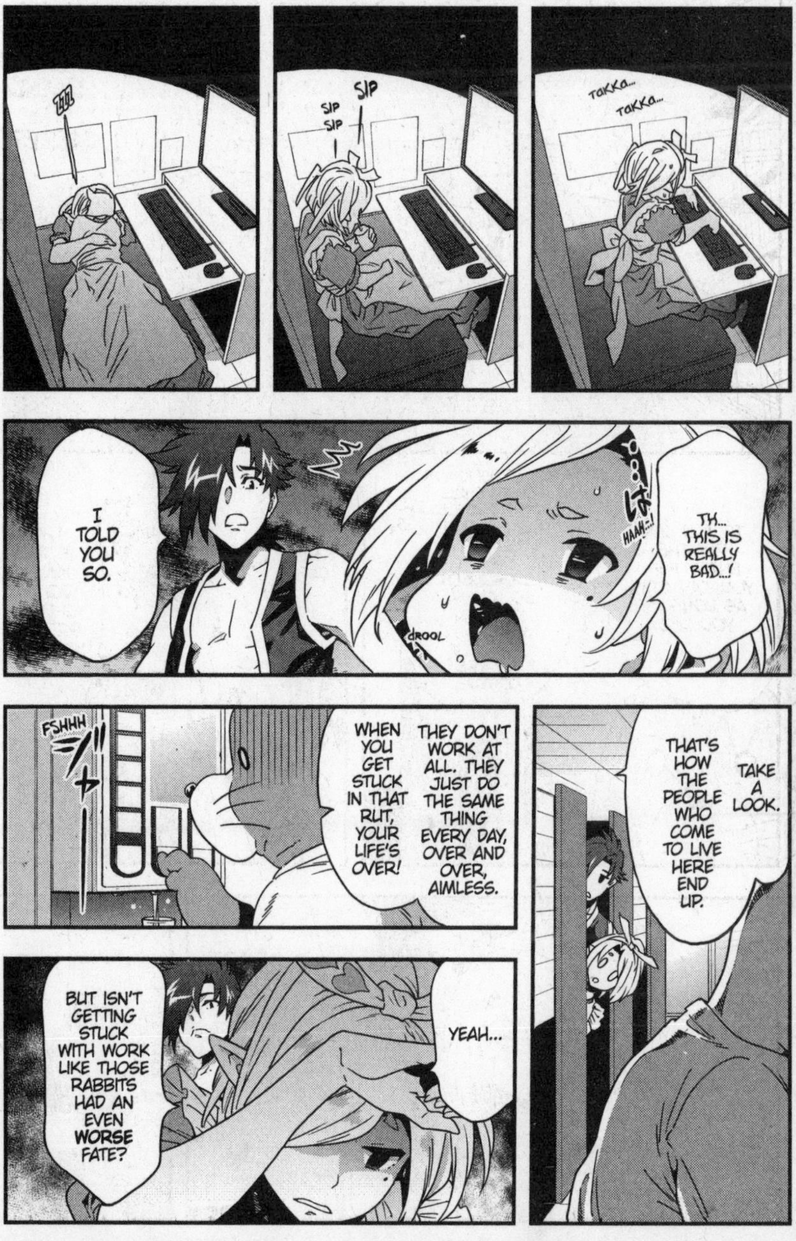
TaKKa...
TaKKa...
SIP
SIP
SIP
TK... THIS IS REALLY BAD...!
は HAAH...!
DROOL
I TOLD YOU SO.
TAKE A LOOK.
THAT'S HOW THE PEOPLE WHO COME TO LIVE HERE END UP.
THEY DON'T WORK AT ALL. THEY JUST DO THE SAME THING EVERY DAY, OVER AND OVER, AIMLESS.
WHEN YOU GET STUCK IN THAT RUT, YOUR LIFE'S OVER!
FSHHH
YEAH...
BUT ISN'T GETTING STUCK WITH WORK LIKE THOSE RABBITS HAD AN EVEN WORSE FATE?

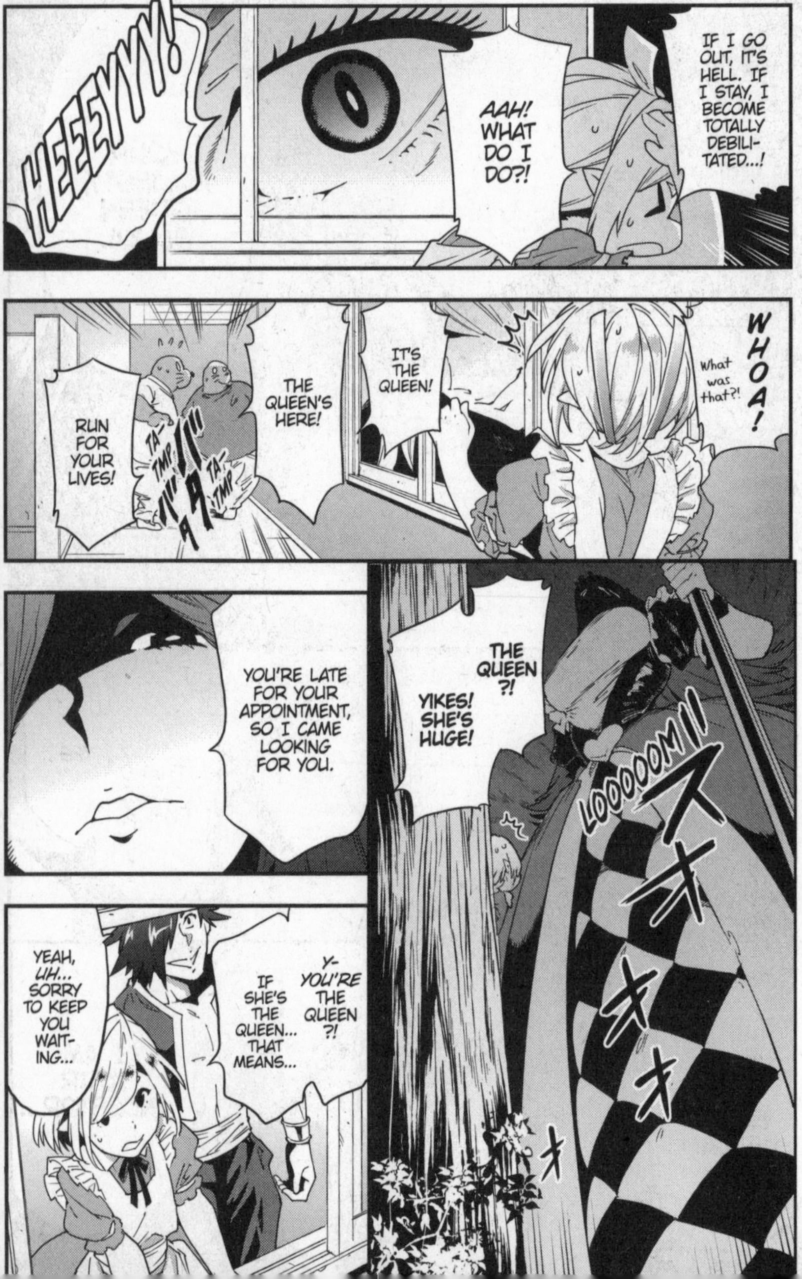
IF I GO OUT, IT'S HELL. IF I STAY, I BECOME TOTALLY DEBILITATED...!
AAH! WHAT DO I DO?!
HEEEYYY!
WHOA!
What was that?!
IT'S THE QUEEN!
THE QUEEN'S HERE!
RUN FOR YOUR LIVES!
TA-TMP
TA-TMP
THE QUEEN ?!
YIKES! SHE'S HUGE!
LOOOOOM
YOU'RE LATE FOR YOUR APPOINTMENT, SO I CAME LOOKING FOR YOU.
Y-YOU'RE THE QUEEN ?!
IF SHE'S THE QUEEN... THAT MEANS...
YEAH, UH... SORRY TO KEEP YOU WAIT-ING...

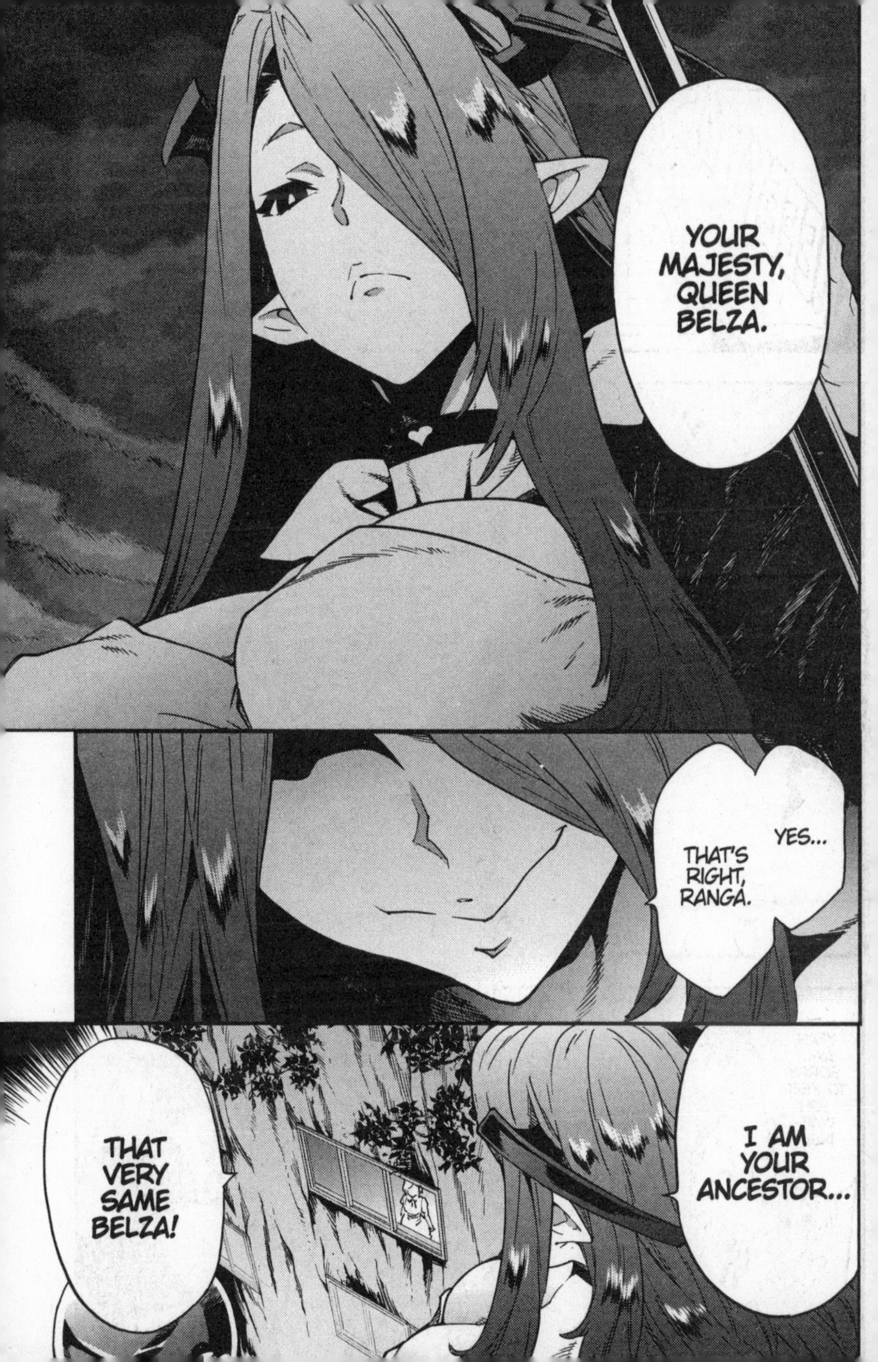
YOUR MAJESTY, QUEEN BELZA.
YES...
THAT'S RIGHT, RANGA.
I AM YOUR ANCESTOR...
THAT VERY SAME BELZA!

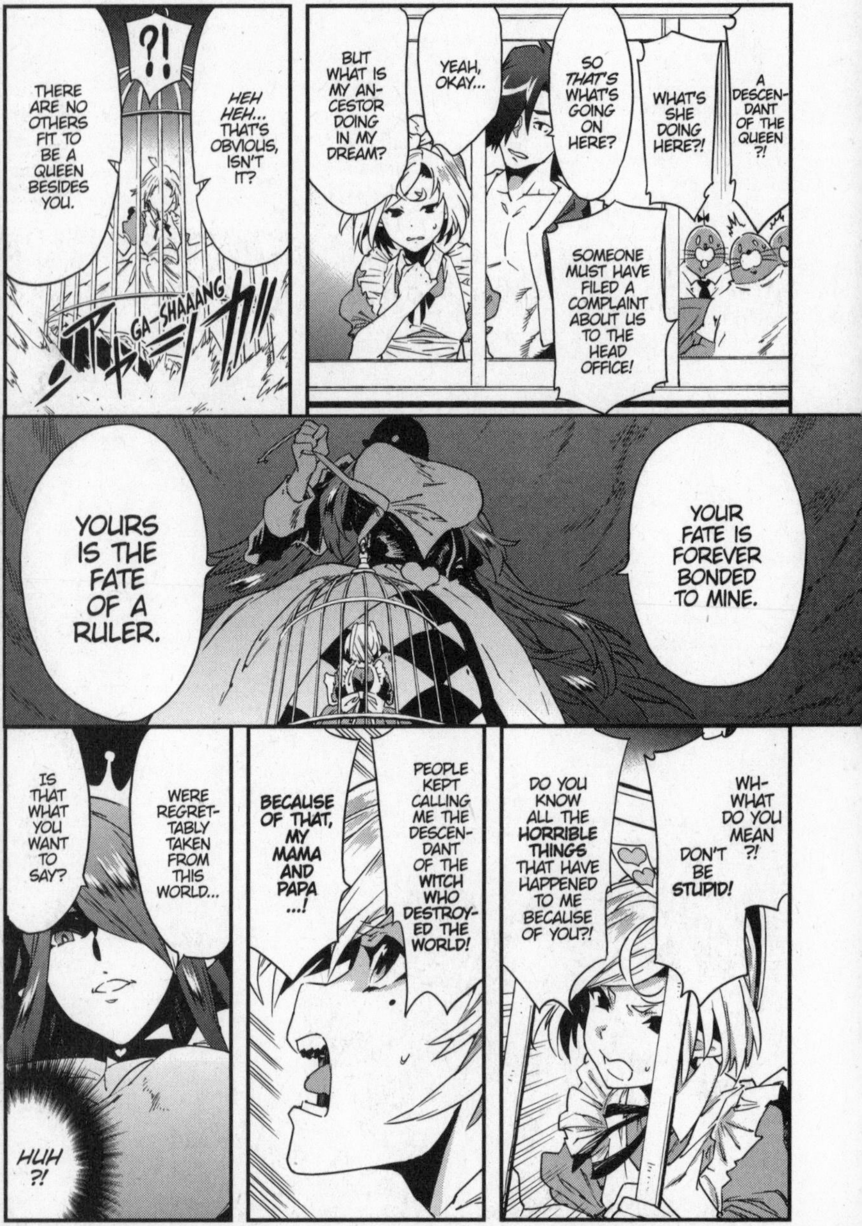
A DESCENDANT OF THE QUEEN?!
WHAT'S SHE DOING HERE?!
SO *THAT'S* WHAT'S GOING ON HERE?
SOMEONE MUST HAVE FILED A COMPLAINT ABOUT US TO THE HEAD OFFICE!
YEAH, OKAY...
BUT WHAT IS MY ANCESTOR DOING IN MY DREAM?
?!
HEH HEH... THAT'S OBVIOUS, ISN'T IT?
THERE ARE NO OTHERS FIT TO BE A QUEEN BESIDES YOU.
GA-SHAAANG
YOUR FATE IS FOREVER BONDED TO MINE.
YOURS IS THE FATE OF A RULER.
WH-WHAT DO YOU MEAN?!
DON'T BE **STUPID!**
DO YOU KNOW ALL THE **HORRIBLE THINGS** THAT HAVE HAPPENED TO ME BECAUSE OF YOU?!
PEOPLE KEPT CALLING ME THE DESCENDANT OF THE **WITCH** WHO **DESTROYED THE WORLD!**
BECAUSE OF THAT, MY MAMA AND PAPA ...!
WERE REGRETTABLY TAKEN FROM THIS WORLD...
IS THAT WHAT YOU WANT TO SAY?
HUH ?!

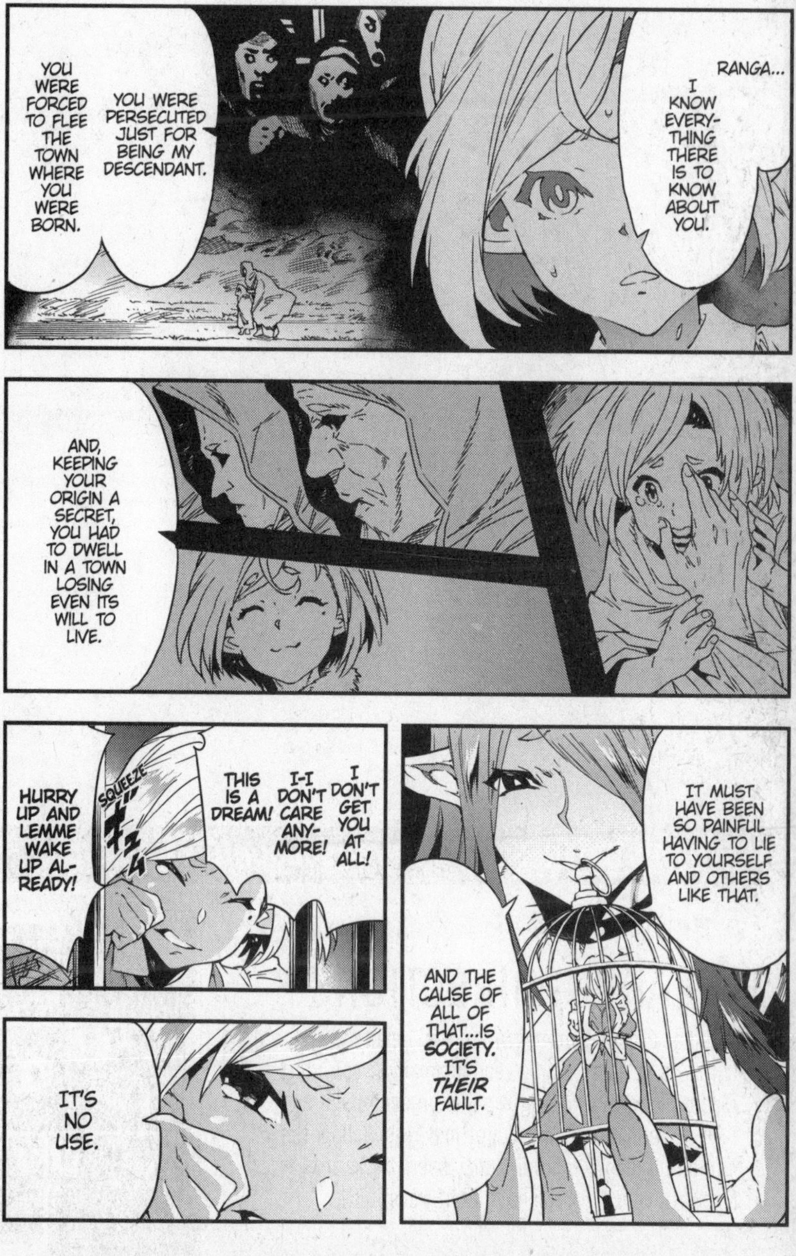
RANGA... I KNOW EVERY-THING THERE IS TO KNOW ABOUT YOU.
YOU WERE PERSECUTED JUST FOR BEING MY DESCENDANT.
YOU WERE FORCED TO FLEE THE TOWN WHERE YOU WERE BORN.
AND, KEEPING YOUR ORIGIN A SECRET, YOU HAD TO DWELL IN A TOWN LOSING EVEN ITS WILL TO LIVE.
IT MUST HAVE BEEN SO PAINFUL HAVING TO LIE TO YOURSELF AND OTHERS LIKE THAT.
AND THE CAUSE OF ALL OF THAT...IS **SOCIETY.** IT'S ***THEIR*** FAULT.
I DON'T GET YOU AT ALL!
I-I DON'T CARE ANY-MORE!
THIS IS A DREAM!
SQUEEZE
HURRY UP AND LEMME WAKE UP AL-READY!
IT'S NO USE.

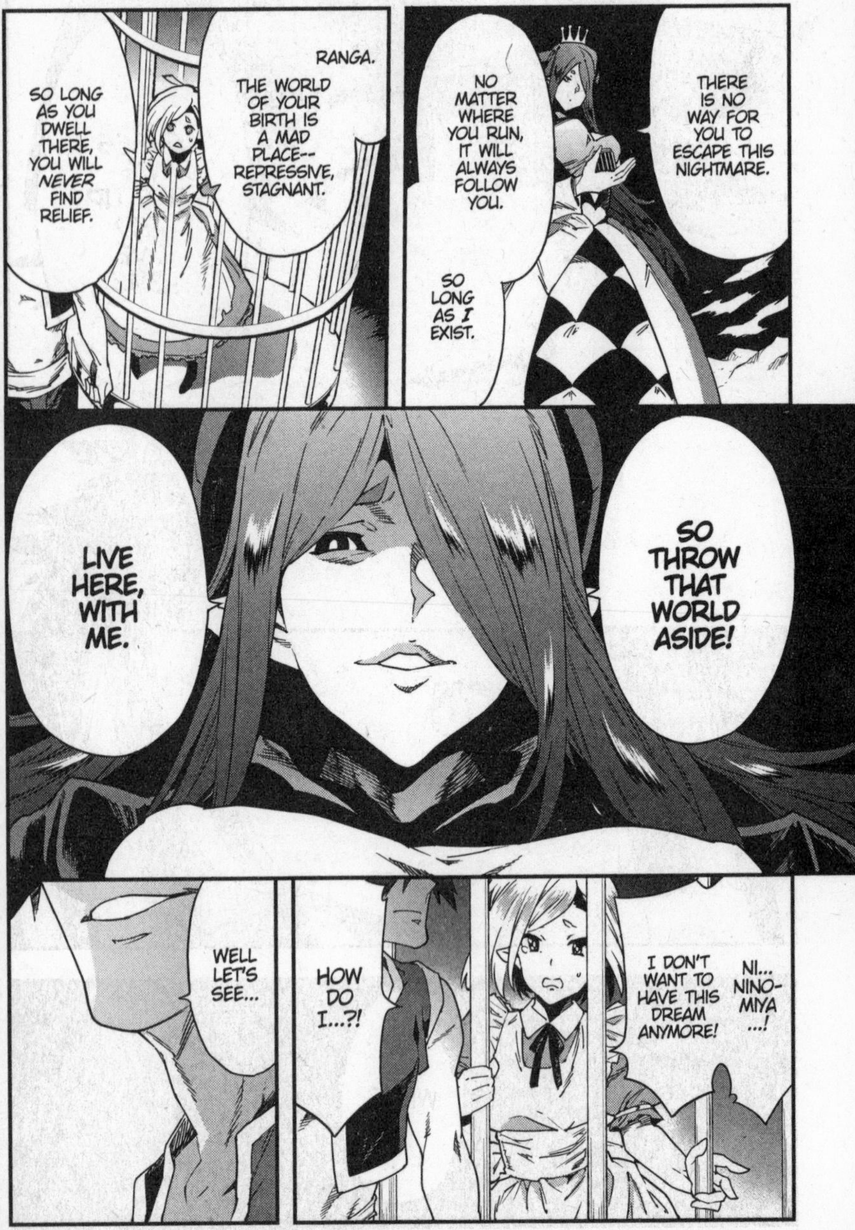
THERE IS NO WAY FOR YOU TO ESCAPE THIS NIGHTMARE.
NO MATTER WHERE YOU RUN, IT WILL ALWAYS FOLLOW YOU.
SO LONG AS *I* EXIST.
RANGA.
THE WORLD OF YOUR BIRTH IS A MAD PLACE-- REPRESSIVE, STAGNANT.
SO LONG AS YOU DWELL THERE, YOU WILL *NEVER* FIND RELIEF.
SO THROW THAT WORLD ASIDE!
LIVE HERE, WITH ME.
NI... NINO-MIYA...!
I DON'T WANT TO HAVE THIS DREAM ANYMORE!
HOW DO I...?!
WELL LET'S SEE...

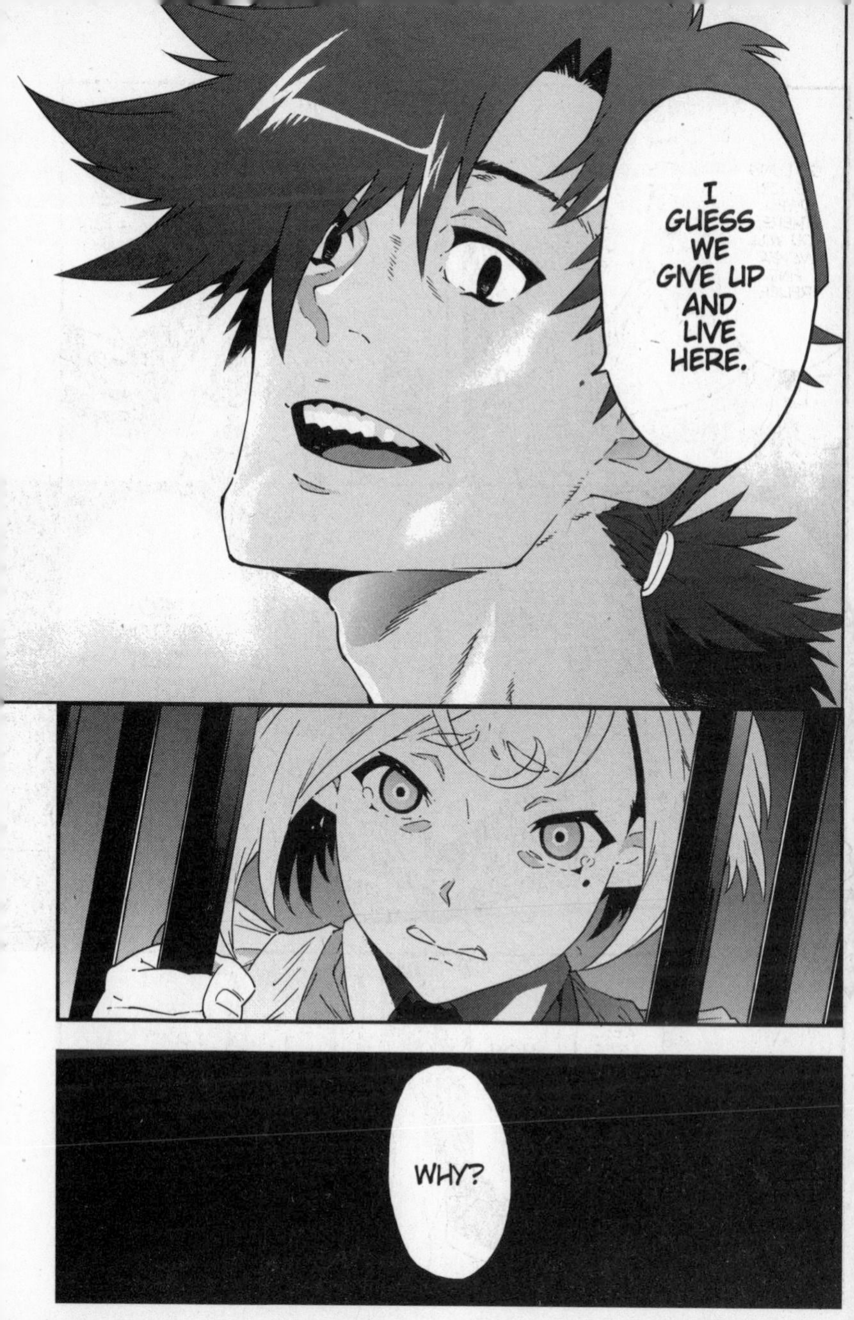
I GUESS WE GIVE UP AND LIVE HERE.
WHY?

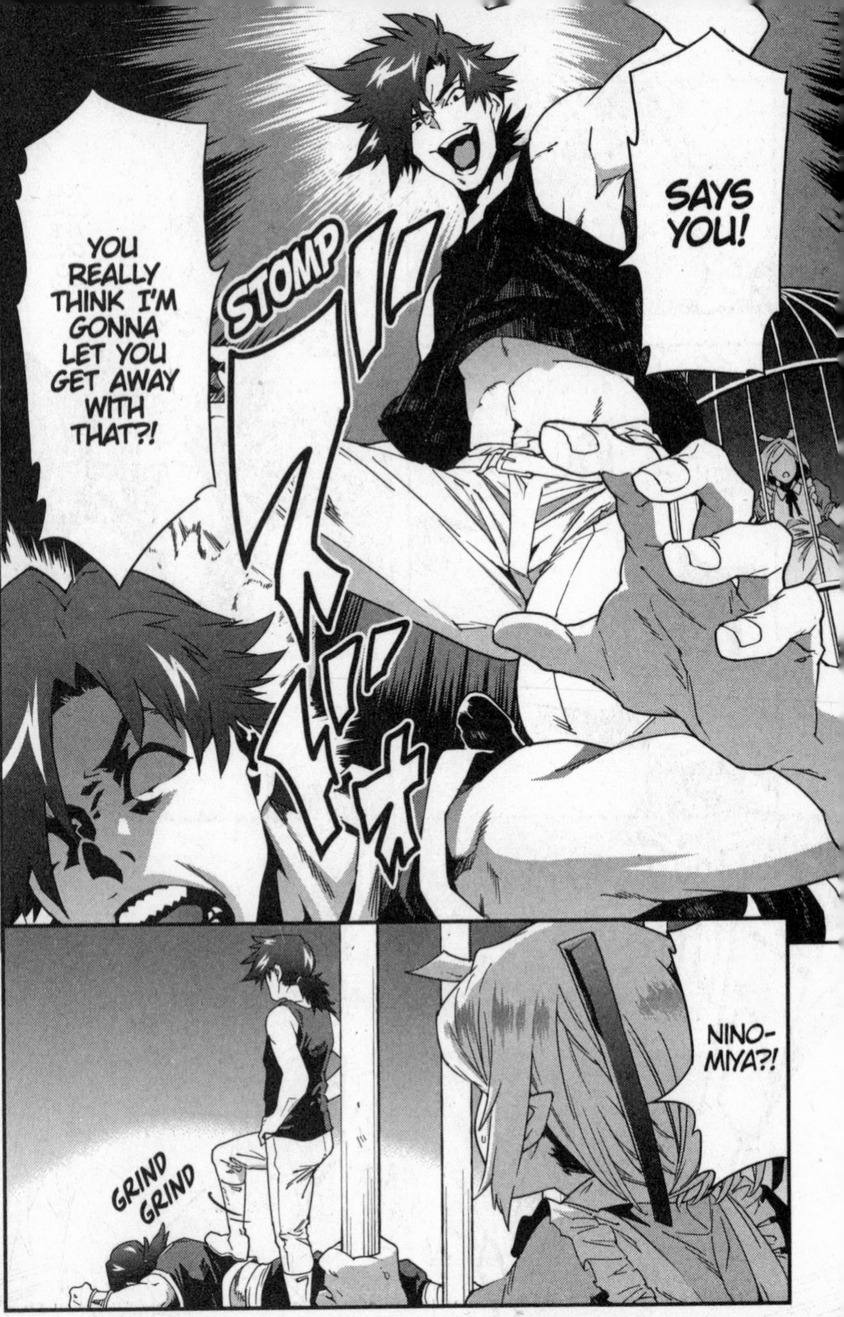
SAYS YOU!
STOMP
YOU REALLY THINK I'M GONNA LET YOU GET AWAY WITH THAT?!
NINO-MIYA?!
GRIND GRIND

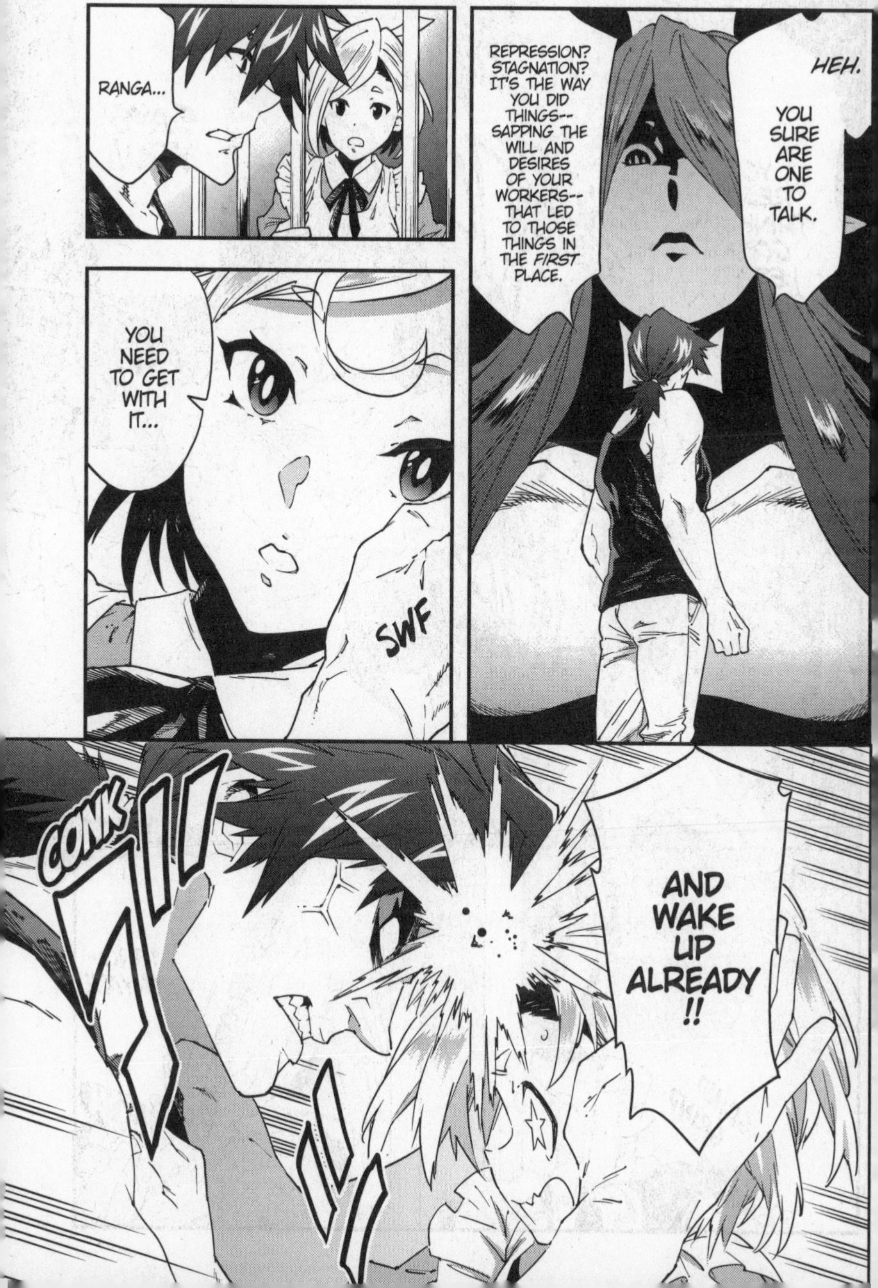
HEH.
YOU SURE ARE ONE TO TALK.
REPRESSION? STAGNATION? IT'S THE WAY YOU DID THINGS--SAPPING THE WILL AND DESIRES OF YOUR WORKERS--THAT LED TO THOSE THINGS IN THE *FIRST* PLACE.
RANGA...
YOU NEED TO GET WITH IT...
SWF
AND WAKE UP ALREADY!!
CONK!!

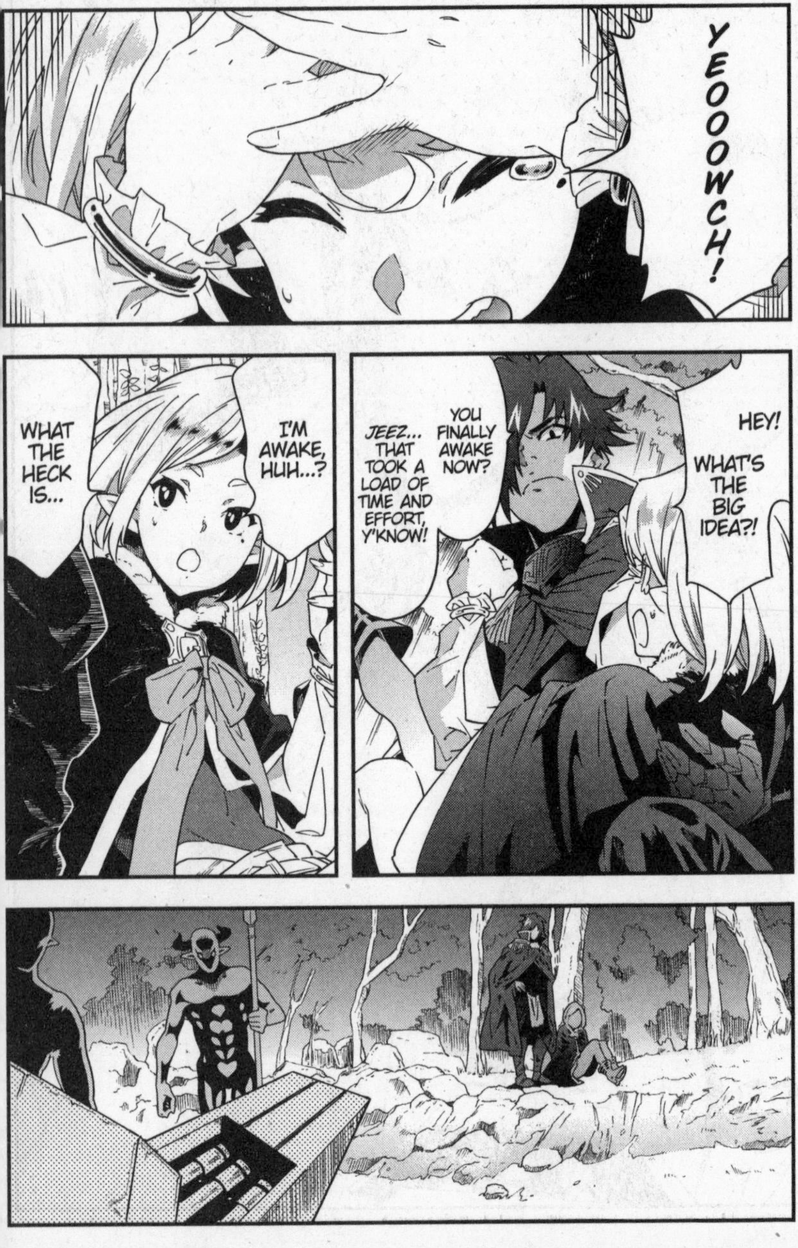
YEOOOWCH!
HEY! WHAT'S THE BIG IDEA?!
YOU FINALLY AWAKE NOW?
JEEZ... THAT TOOK A LOAD OF TIME AND EFFORT, Y'KNOW!
I'M AWAKE, HUH...?
WHAT THE HECK IS...

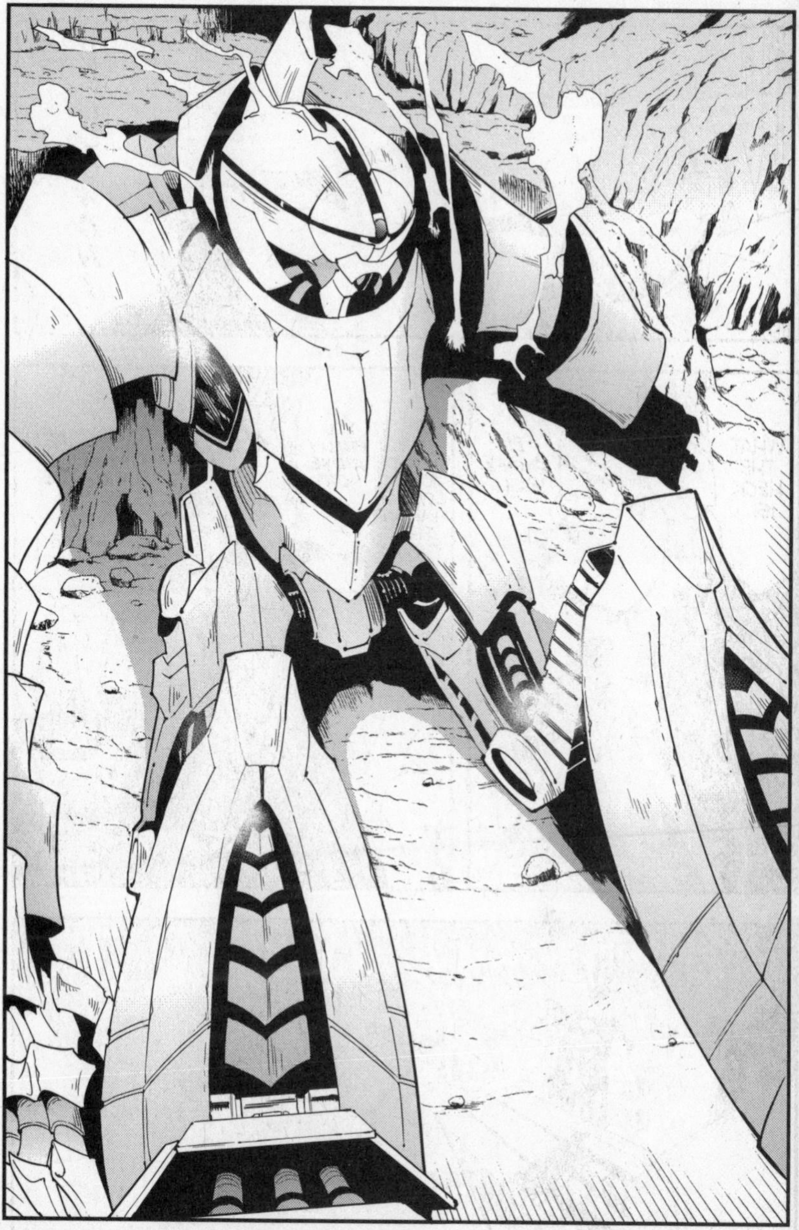

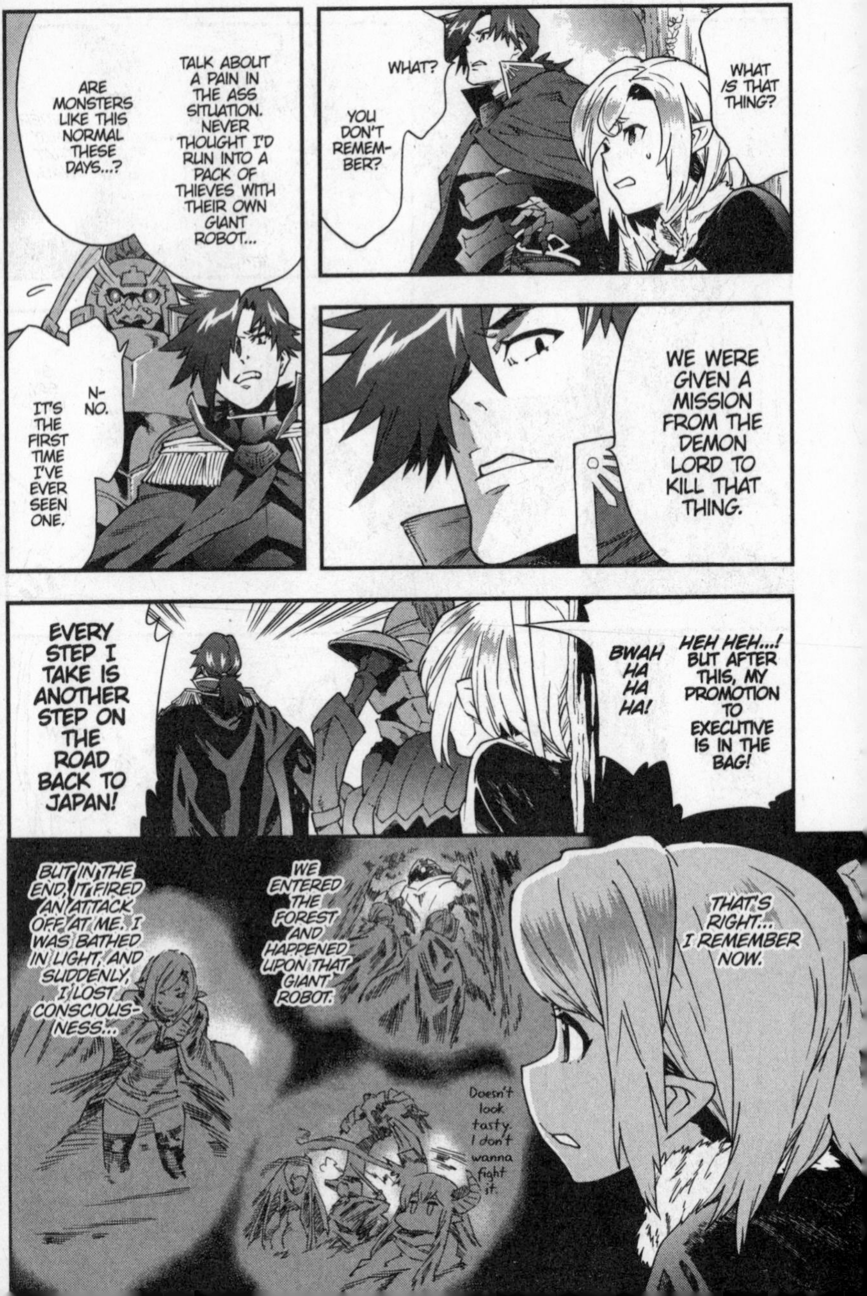
WHAT IS THAT THING?
WHAT?
YOU DON'T REMEMBER?
WE WERE GIVEN A MISSION FROM THE DEMON LORD TO KILL THAT THING.
TALK ABOUT A PAIN IN THE ASS SITUATION. NEVER THOUGHT I'D RUN INTO A PACK OF THIEVES WITH THEIR OWN GIANT ROBOT...
ARE MONSTERS LIKE THIS NORMAL THESE DAYS...?
N-NO.
IT'S THE FIRST TIME I'VE EVER SEEN ONE.
HEH HEH...! BUT AFTER THIS, MY PROMOTION TO EXECUTIVE IS IN THE BAG!
BWAH HA HA HA!
EVERY STEP I TAKE IS ANOTHER STEP ON THE ROAD BACK TO JAPAN!
THAT'S RIGHT... I REMEMBER NOW.
WE ENTERED THE FOREST AND HAPPENED UPON THAT GIANT ROBOT.
BUT IN THE END, IT FIRED AN ATTACK OFF AT ME. I WAS BATHED IN LIGHT, AND SUDDENLY, I LOST CONSCIOUSNESS...
Doesn't look tasty. I don't wanna fight it.

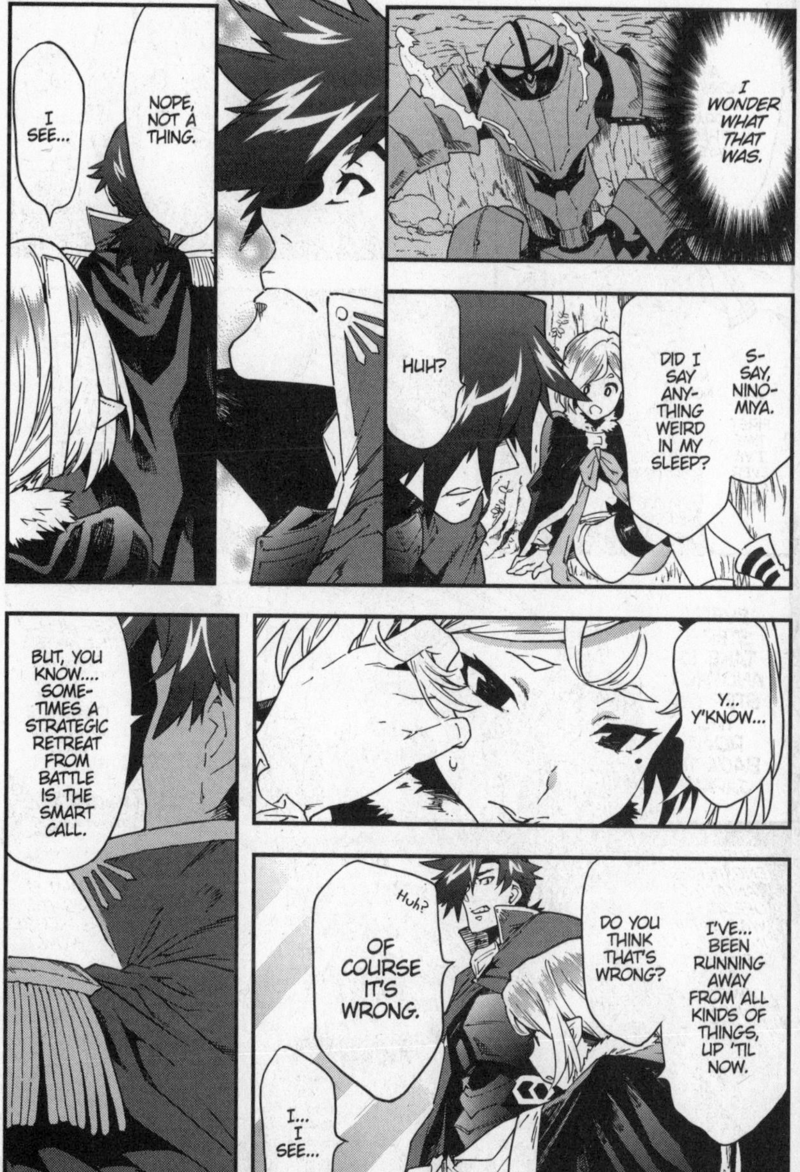
I WONDER WHAT THAT WAS.
S- SAY, NINOMIYA.
DID I SAY ANYTHING WEIRD IN MY SLEEP?
HUH?
NOPE, NOT A THING.
I SEE...
Y... Y'KNOW...
I'VE... BEEN RUNNING AWAY FROM ALL KINDS OF THINGS, UP 'TIL NOW.
DO YOU THINK THAT'S WRONG?
Huh?
OF COURSE IT'S WRONG.
I... I SEE...
BUT, YOU KNOW.... SOMETIMES A STRATEGIC RETREAT FROM BATTLE IS THE SMART CALL.

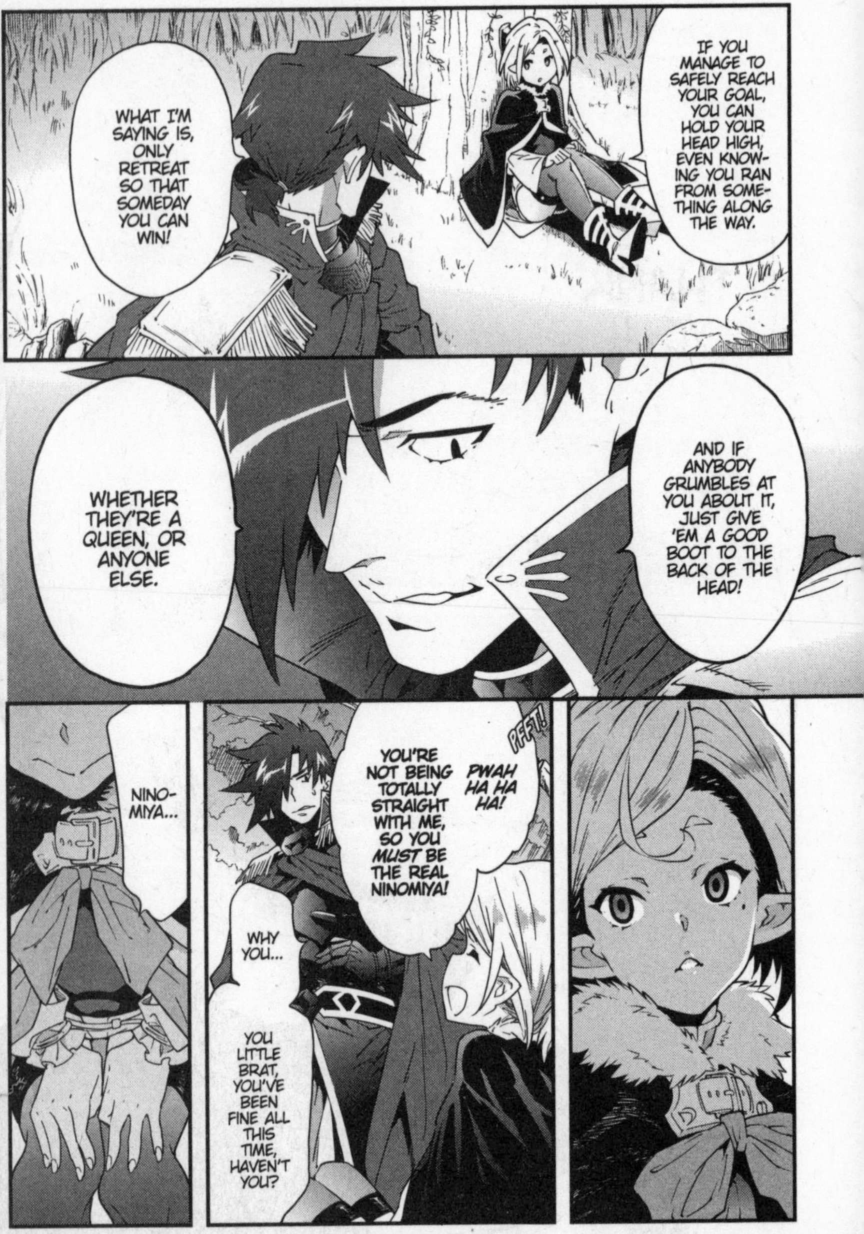
IF YOU MANAGE TO SAFELY REACH YOUR GOAL, YOU CAN HOLD YOUR HEAD HIGH, EVEN KNOWING YOU RAN FROM SOMETHING ALONG THE WAY.
WHAT I'M SAYING IS, ONLY RETREAT SO THAT SOMEDAY YOU CAN WIN!
AND IF ANYBODY GRUMBLES AT YOU ABOUT IT, JUST GIVE 'EM A GOOD BOOT TO THE BACK OF THE HEAD!
WHETHER THEY'RE A QUEEN, OR ANYONE ELSE.
PFFT!
PWAH HA HA HA!
YOU'RE NOT BEING TOTALLY STRAIGHT WITH ME, SO YOU *MUST* BE THE REAL NINOMIYA!
WHY YOU...
YOU LITTLE BRAT, YOU'VE BEEN FINE ALL THIS TIME, HAVEN'T YOU?
NINO-MIYA...

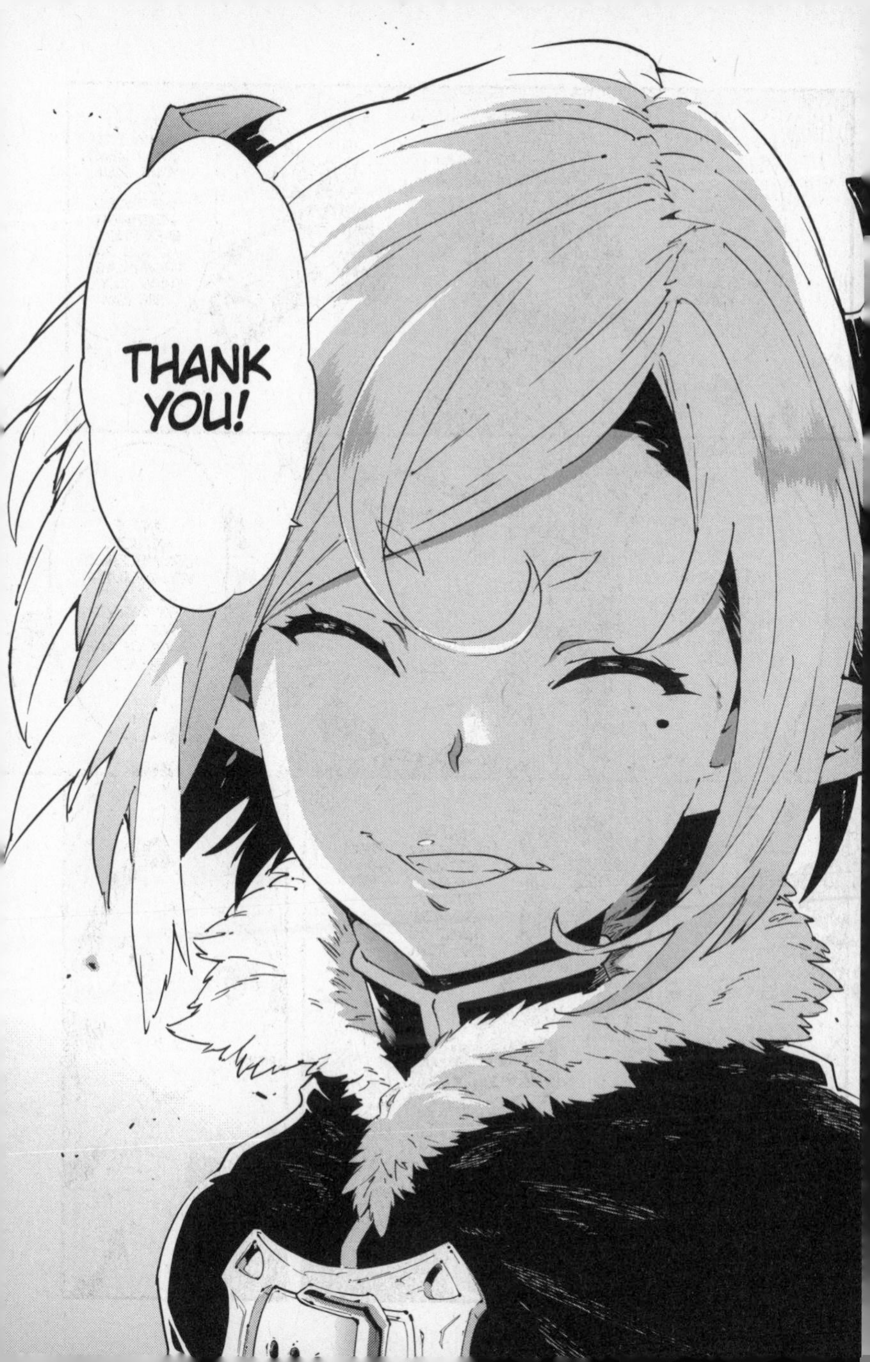
THANK YOU!

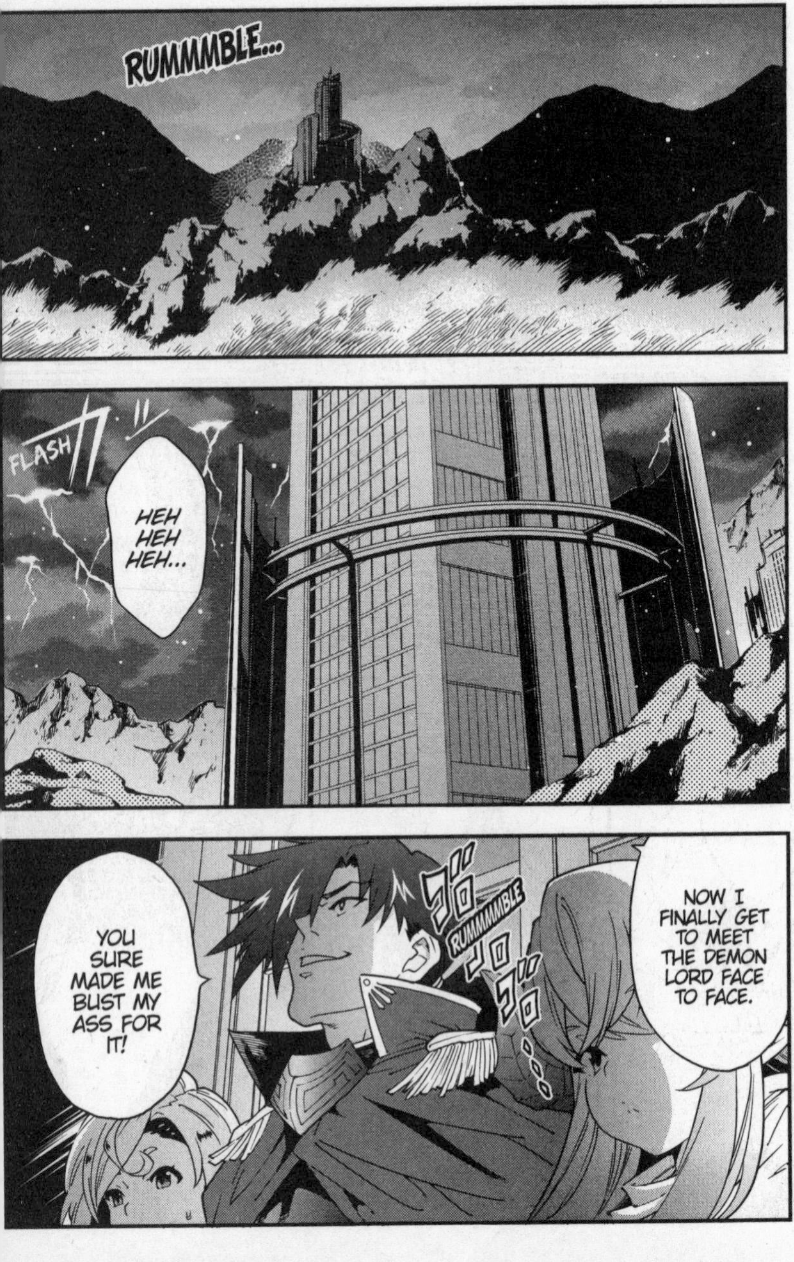
RUMMMBLE...
FLASH
HEH HEH HEH...
NOW I FINALLY GET TO MEET THE DEMON LORD FACE TO FACE.
RUMMMMMBLE
YOU SURE MADE ME BUST MY ASS FOR IT!

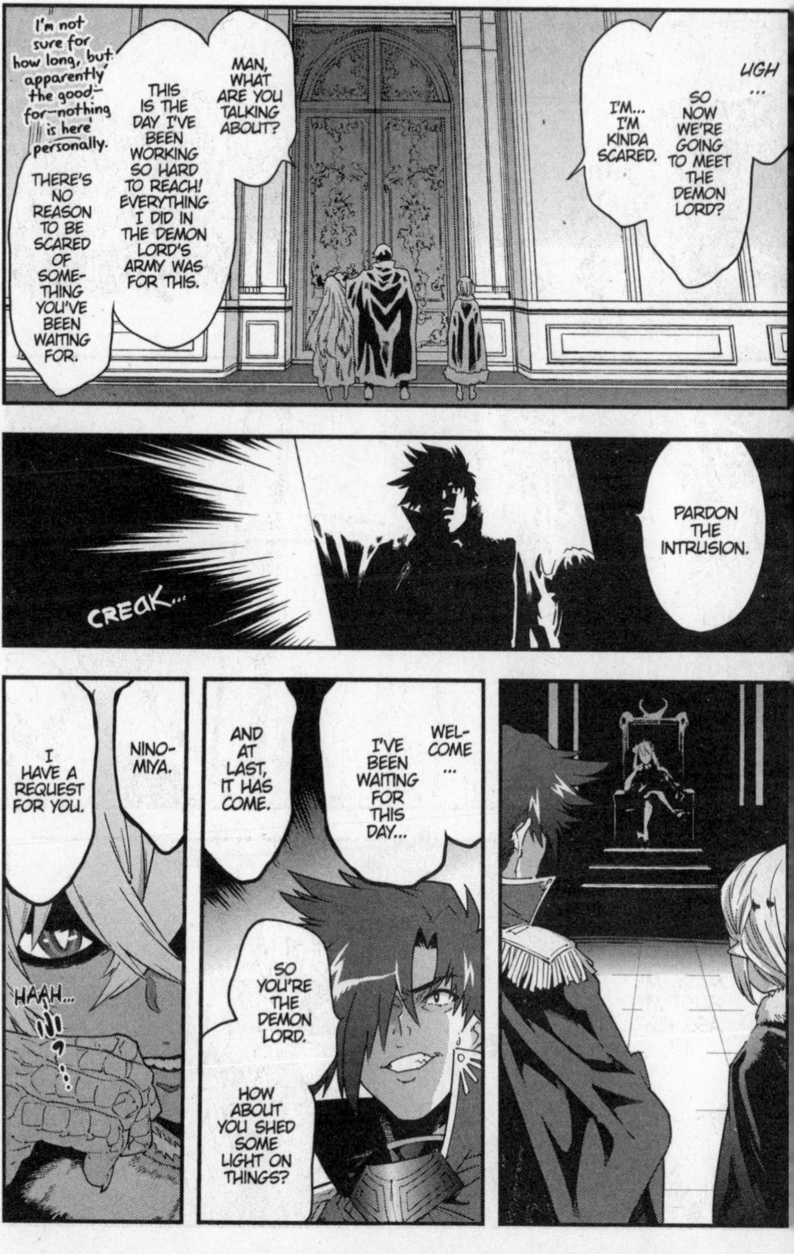
UGH ...
SO NOW WE'RE GOING TO MEET THE DEMON LORD?
I'M... I'M KINDA SCARED.
MAN, WHAT ARE YOU TALKING ABOUT?
THIS IS THE DAY I'VE BEEN WORKING SO HARD TO REACH! EVERYTHING I DID IN THE DEMON LORD'S ARMY WAS FOR THIS.
I'm not sure for how long, but apparently the good-for-nothing is here personally.
THERE'S NO REASON TO BE SCARED OF SOMETHING YOU'VE BEEN WAITING FOR.
PARDON THE INTRUSION.
CREAK...
WEL-COME ...
I'VE BEEN WAITING FOR THIS DAY...
AND AT LAST, IT HAS COME.
SO YOU'RE THE DEMON LORD.
HOW ABOUT YOU SHED SOME LIGHT ON THINGS?
NINO-MIYA.
I HAVE A REQUEST FOR YOU.
HAAH...

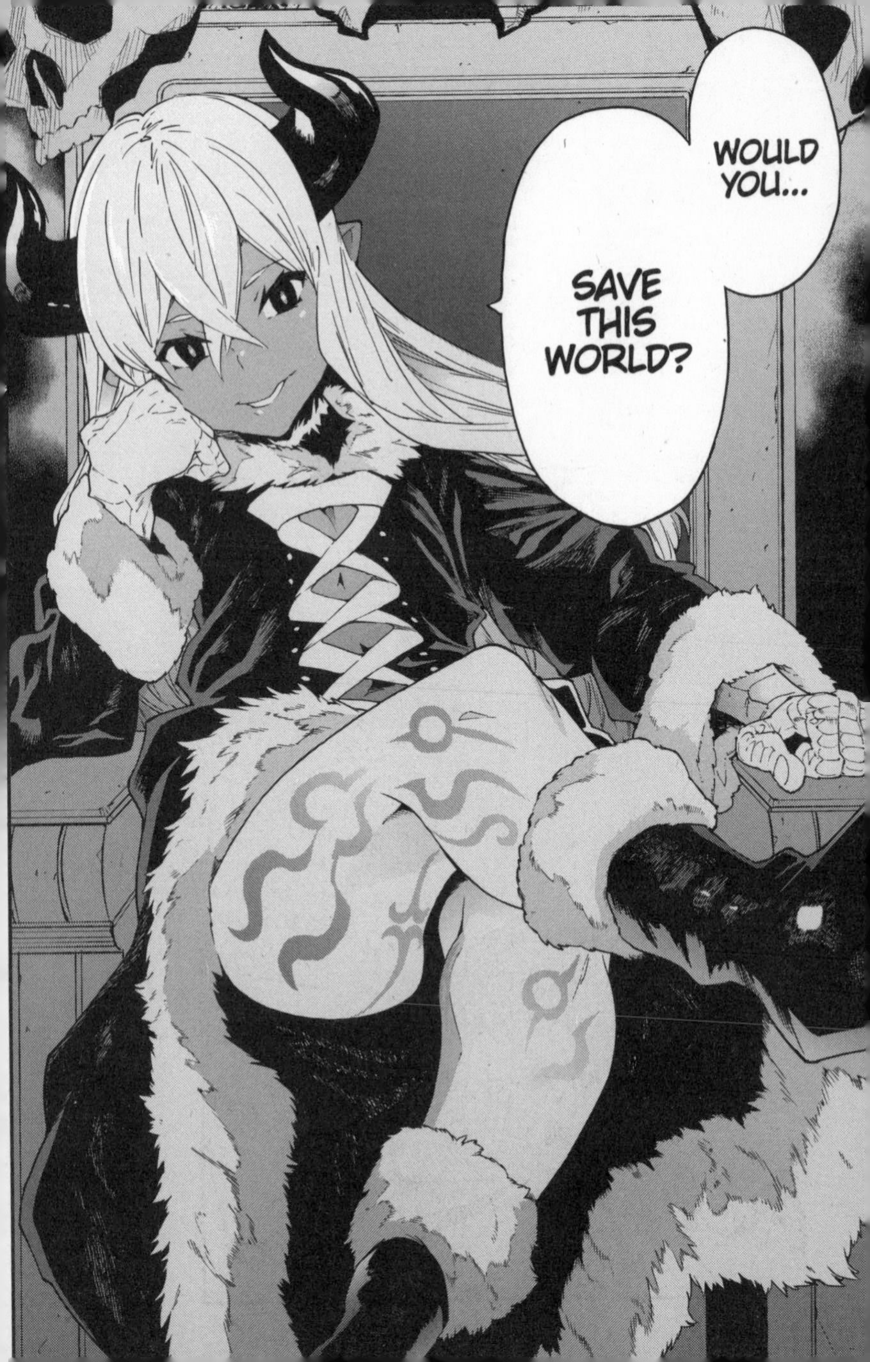
WOULD YOU...
SAVE THIS WORLD?

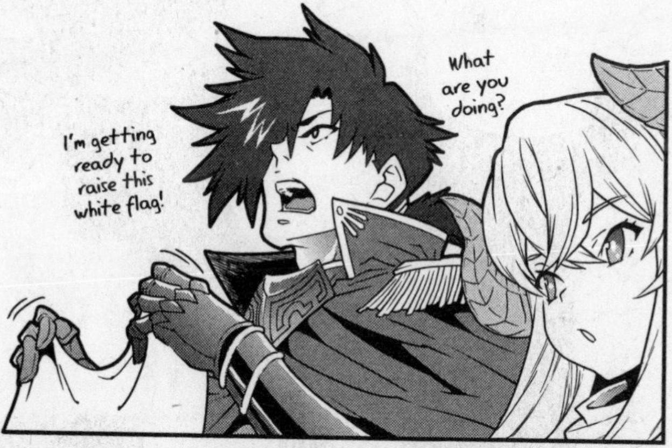
What are you doing?
I'm getting ready to raise this white flag!

THE DUNGEON OF
BLACK COMPANY

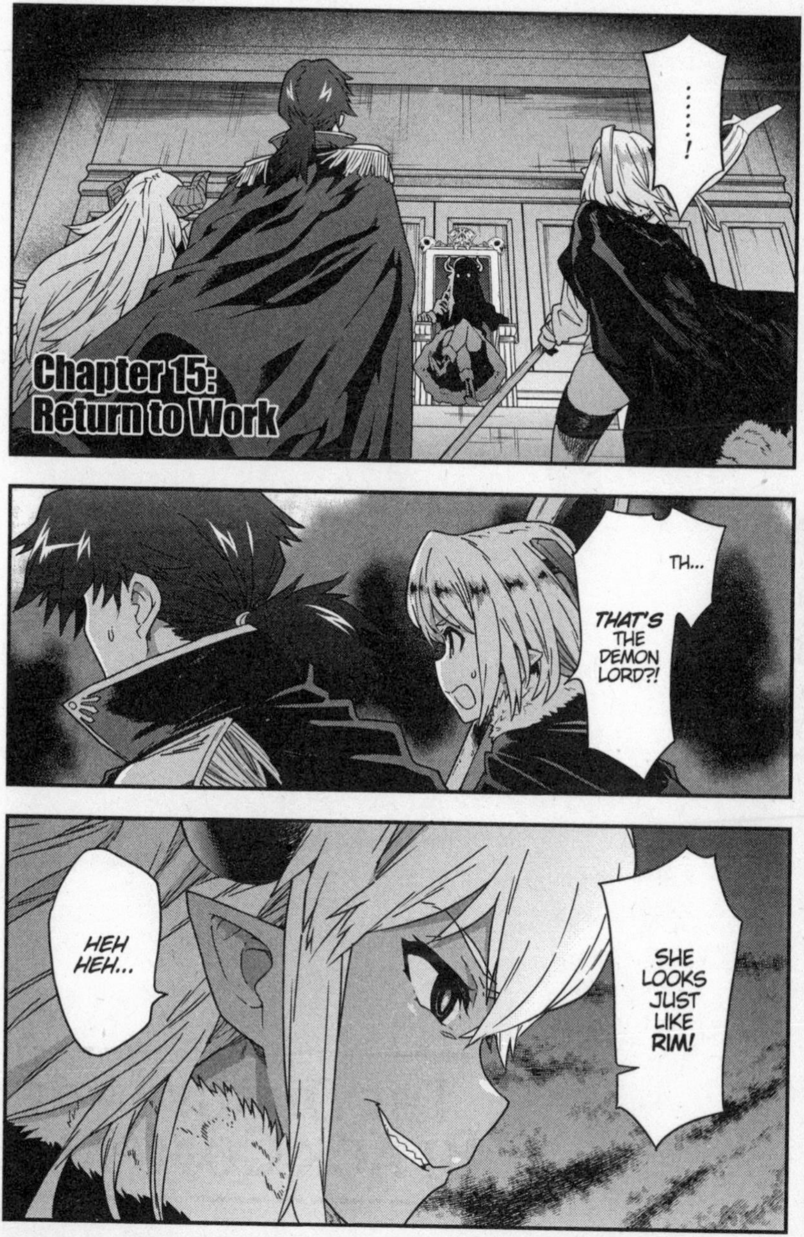
......!
Chapter 15: Return to Work
TH...
THAT'S THE DEMON LORD?!
SHE LOOKS JUST LIKE RIM!
HEH HEH...

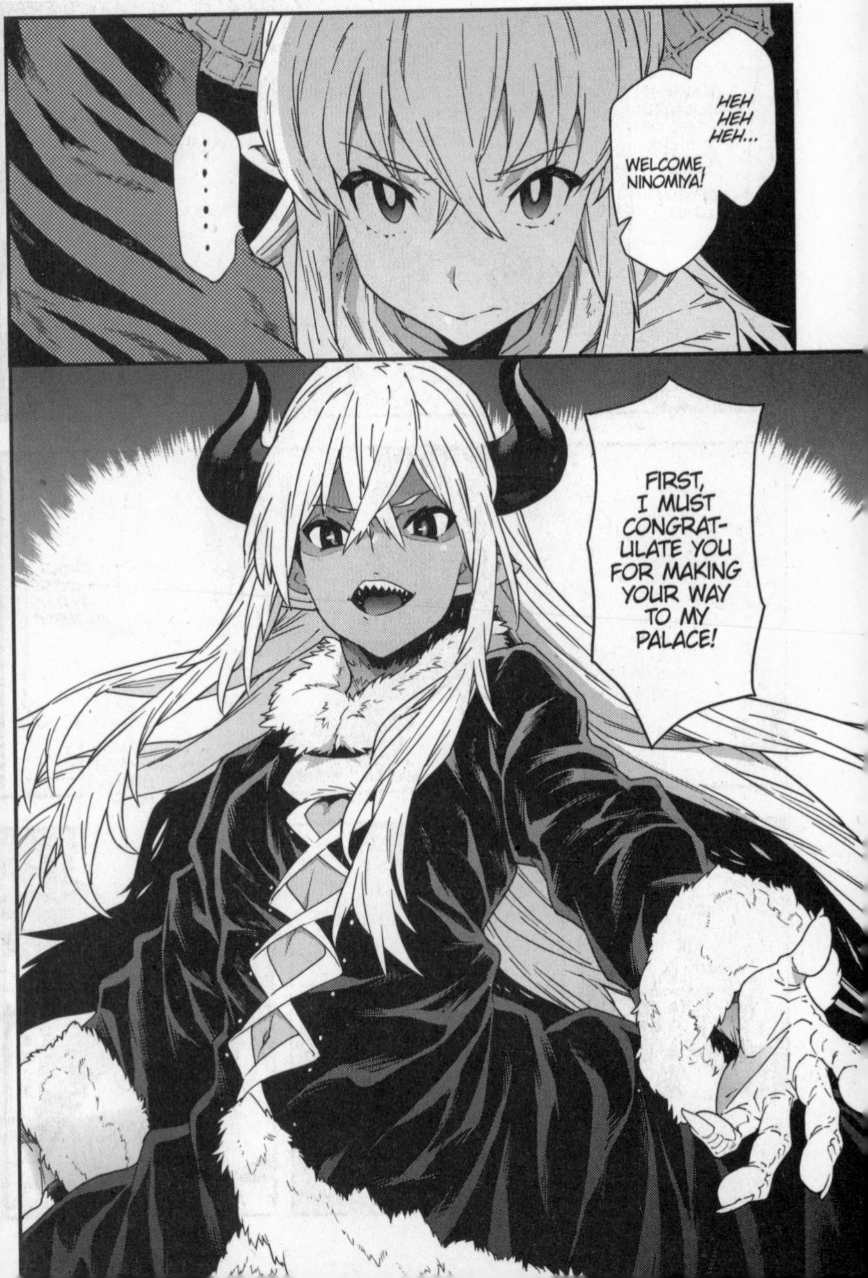
HEH HEH HEH...
WELCOME, NINOMIYA!
......
FIRST, I MUST CONGRAT-ULATE YOU FOR MAKING YOUR WAY TO MY PALACE!

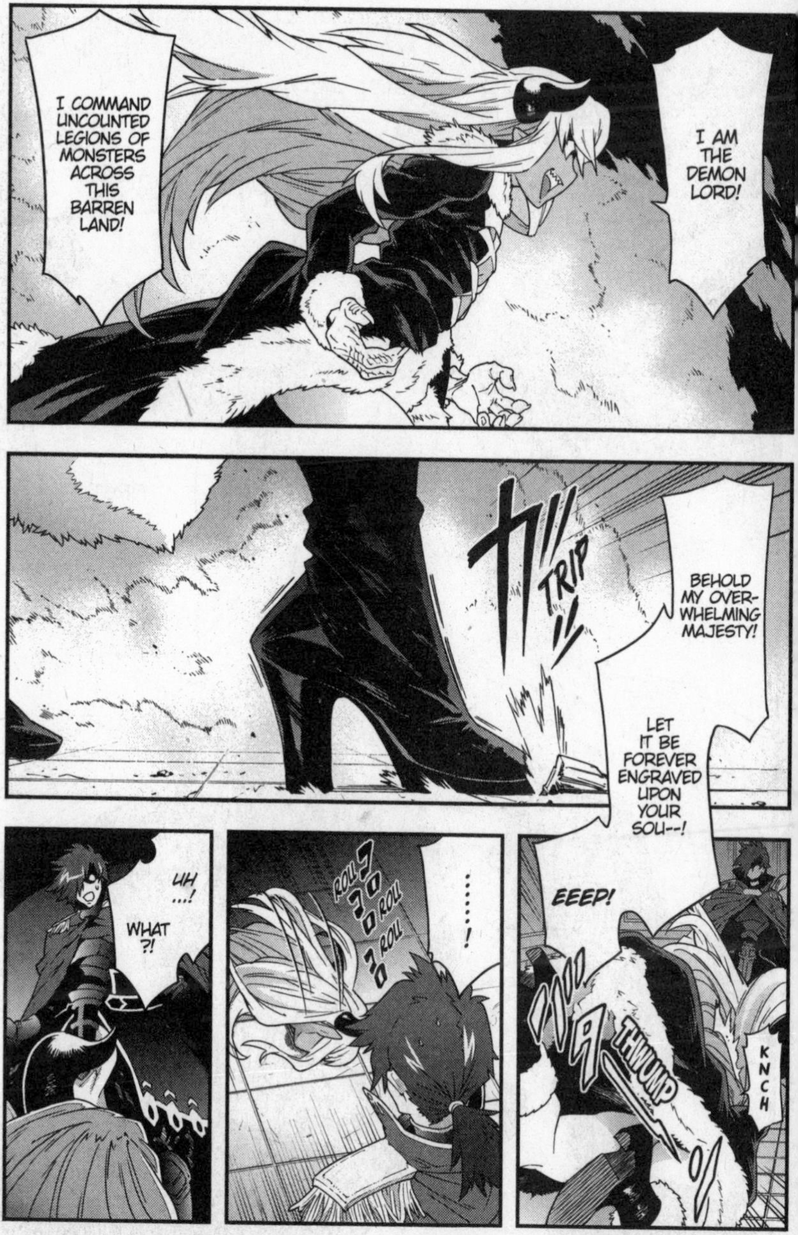
I AM THE DEMON LORD!
I COMMAND UNCOUNTED LEGIONS OF MONSTERS ACROSS THIS BARREN LAND!
BEHOLD MY OVER-WHELMING MAJESTY!
TRIP
LET IT BE FOREVER ENGRAVED UPON YOUR SOU--!
EEEP!
THWUMP
KNCH
ROLL ROLL ROLL
......!
UH ...!
WHAT ?!

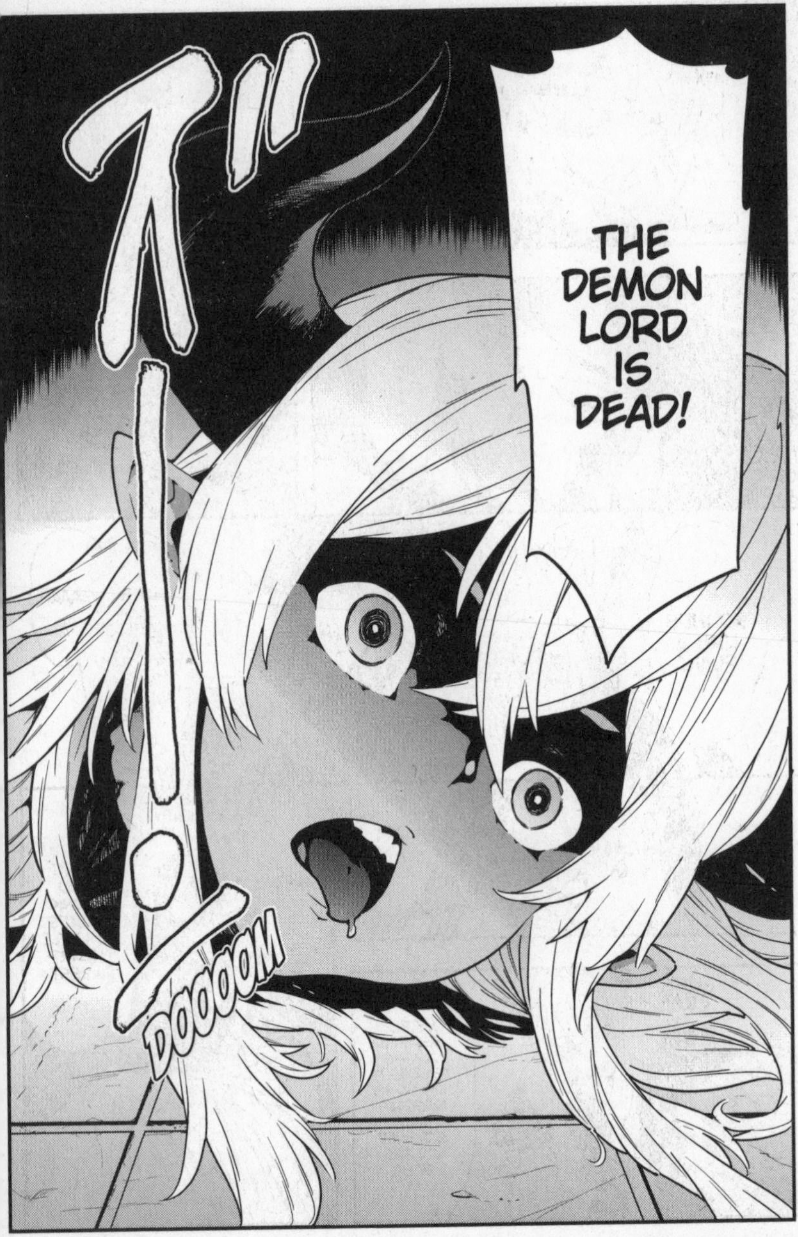
THE DEMON LORD IS DEAD!
DOOOOM

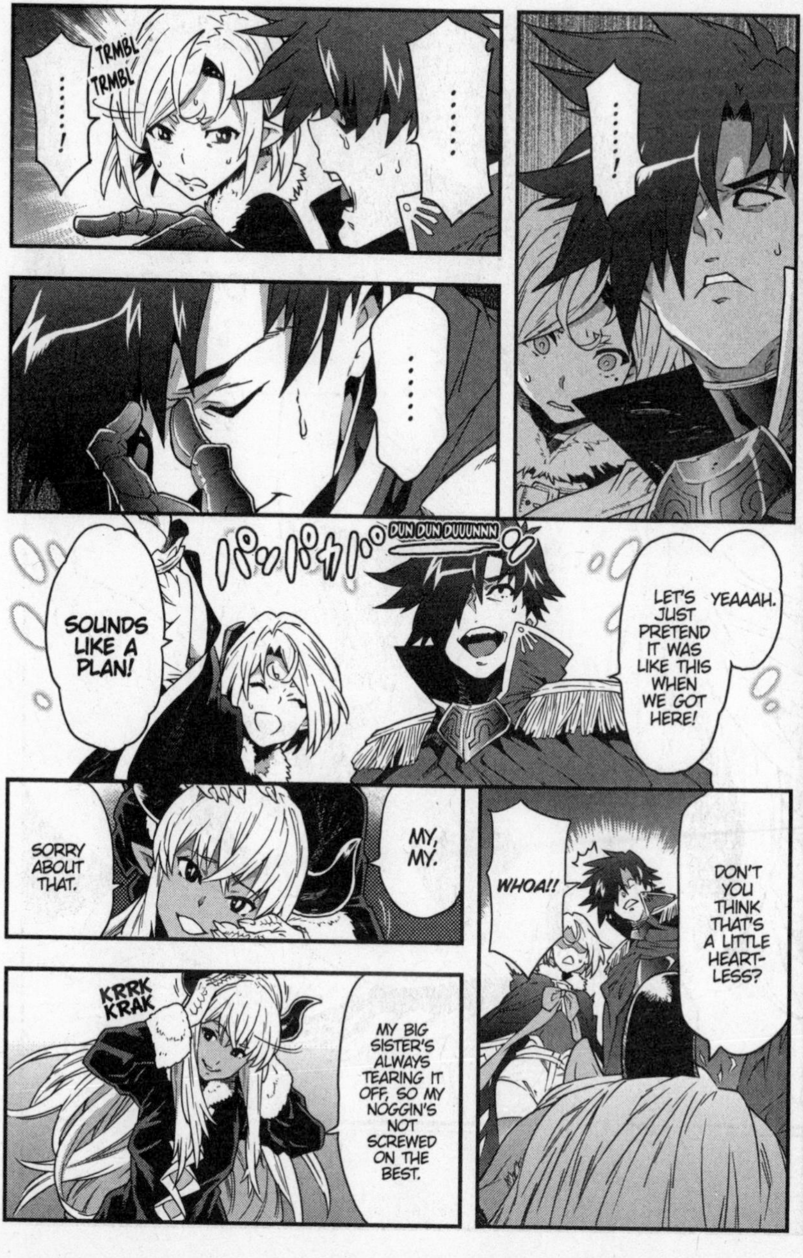
......!
......
TRMBL TRMBL
......!
......
YEAAAH.
LET'S JUST PRETEND IT WAS LIKE THIS WHEN WE GOT HERE!
DUN DUN DUUUNNN
パッパカパ
SOUNDS LIKE A PLAN!
DON'T YOU THINK THAT'S A LITTLE HEART-LESS?
WHOA!!
MY, MY.
SORRY ABOUT THAT.
MY BIG SISTER'S ALWAYS TEARING IT OFF, SO MY NOGGIN'S NOT SCREWED ON THE BEST.
KRRK KRAK

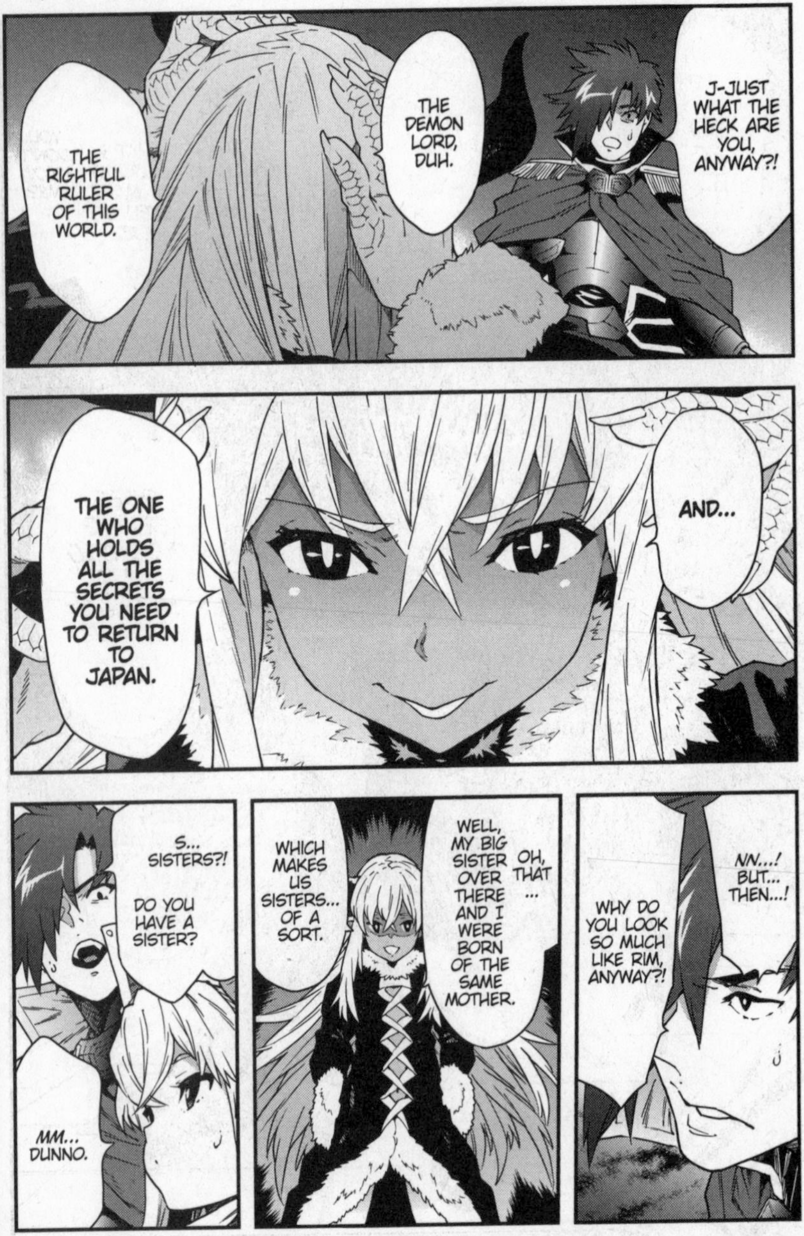
J-JUST WHAT THE HECK ARE YOU, ANYWAY?!
THE DEMON LORD, DUH.
THE RIGHTFUL RULER OF THIS WORLD.
AND...
THE ONE WHO HOLDS ALL THE SECRETS YOU NEED TO RETURN TO JAPAN.
NN...! BUT... THEN...!
WHY DO YOU LOOK SO MUCH LIKE RIM, ANYWAY?!
OH, THAT ...
WELL, MY BIG SISTER OVER THERE AND I WERE BORN OF THE SAME MOTHER.
WHICH MAKES US SISTERS... OF A SORT.
S... SISTERS?!
DO YOU HAVE A SISTER?
MM... DUNNO.

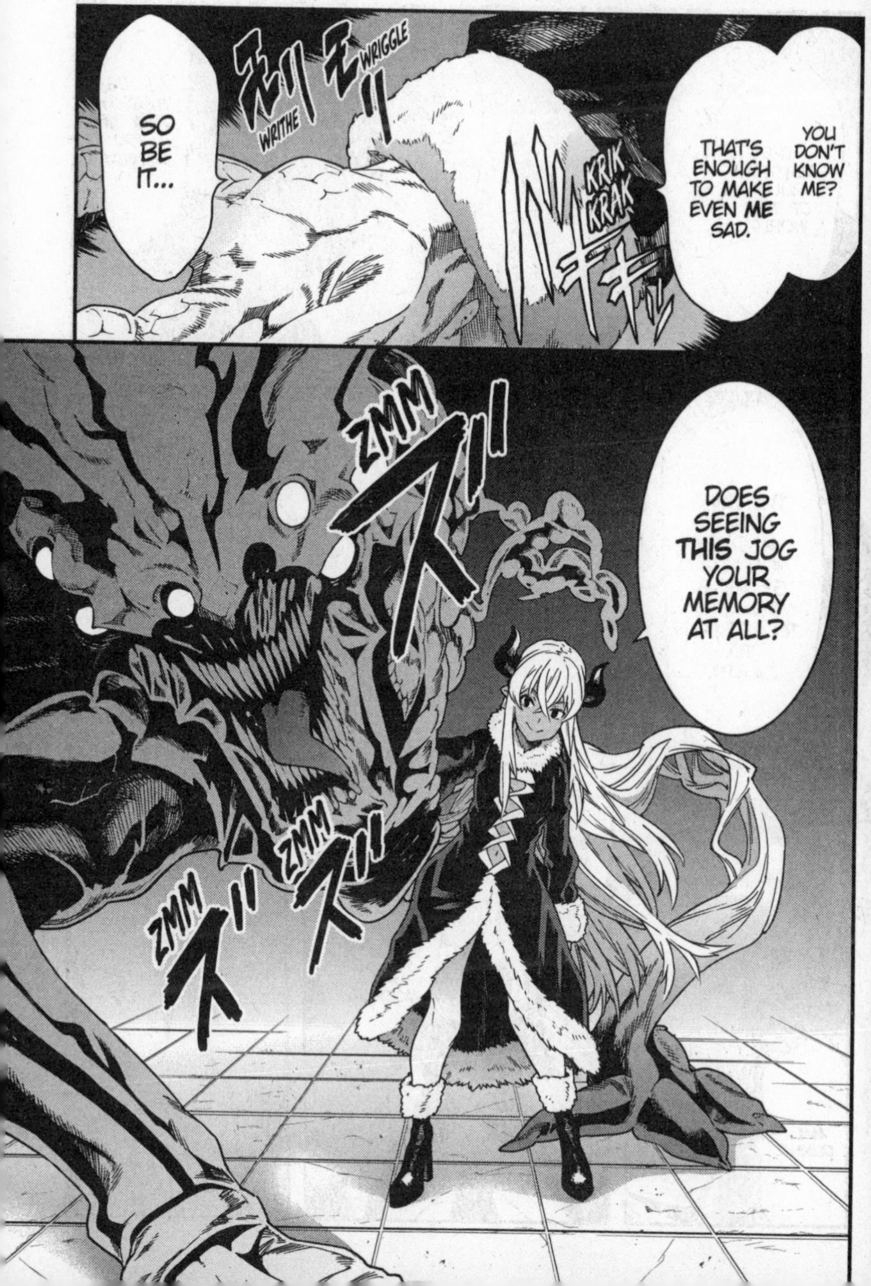
YOU DON'T KNOW ME?
THAT'S ENOUGH TO MAKE EVEN ME SAD.
KRIK KRAK
WRIGGLE
WRITHE
SO BE IT...
DOES SEEING THIS JOG YOUR MEMORY AT ALL?
ZMM
ZMM
ZMM

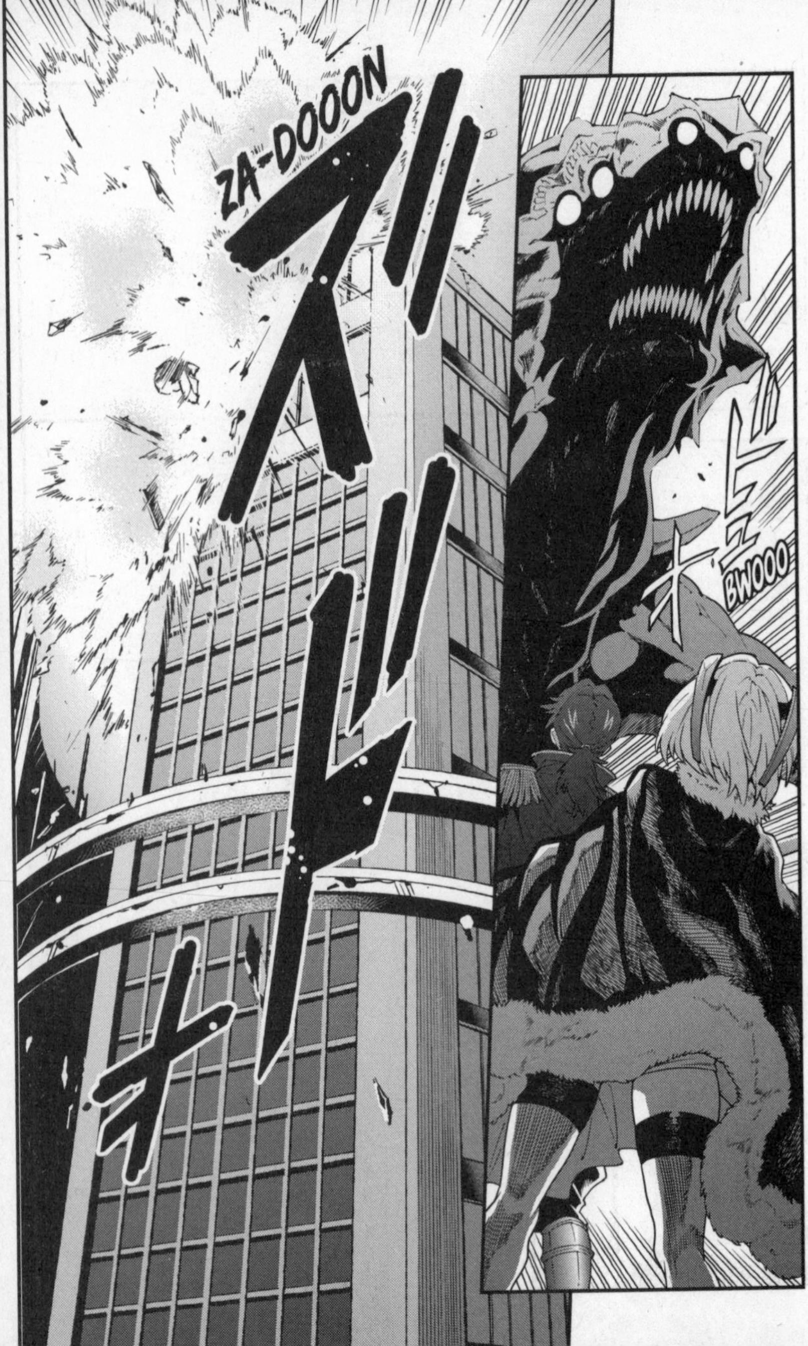
BWOOO
ZA-DOOON

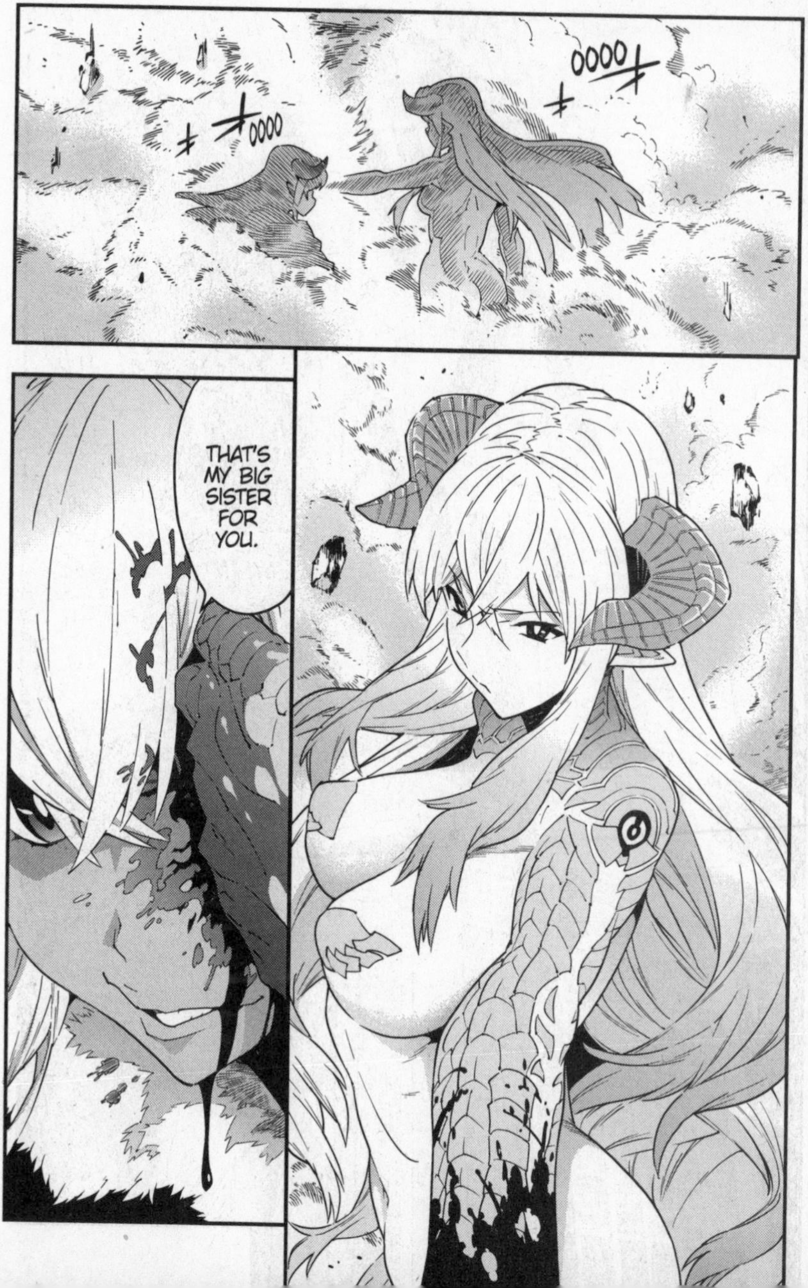
OOOO
OOOO
THAT'S MY BIG SISTER FOR YOU.

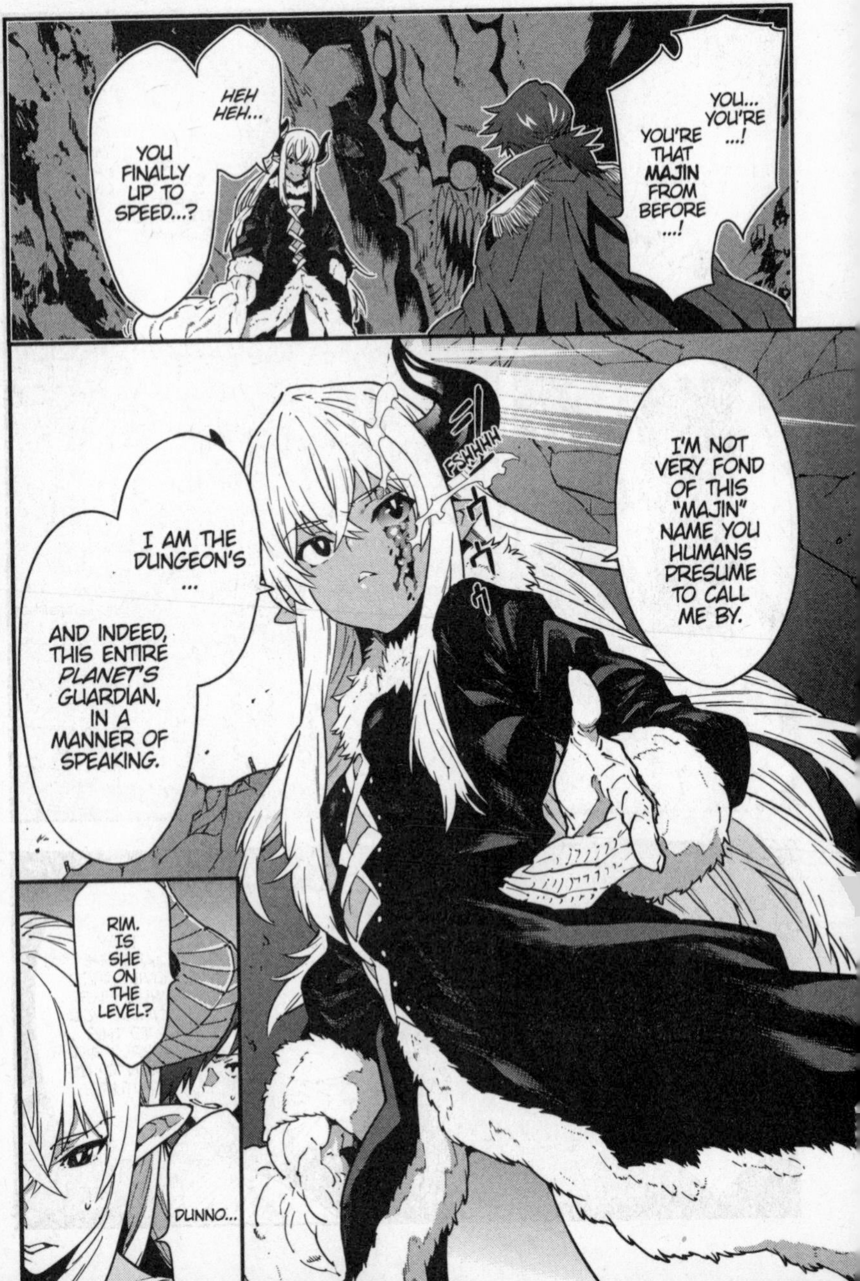
YOU... YOU'RE ...!
YOU'RE THAT MAJIN FROM BEFORE ...!
HEH HEH...
YOU FINALLY UP TO SPEED...?
I'M NOT VERY FOND OF THIS "MAJIN" NAME YOU HUMANS PRESUME TO CALL ME BY.
I AM THE DUNGEON'S ...
AND INDEED, THIS ENTIRE *PLANET'S* GUARDIAN, IN A MANNER OF SPEAKING.
RIM. IS SHE ON THE LEVEL?
DUNNO...

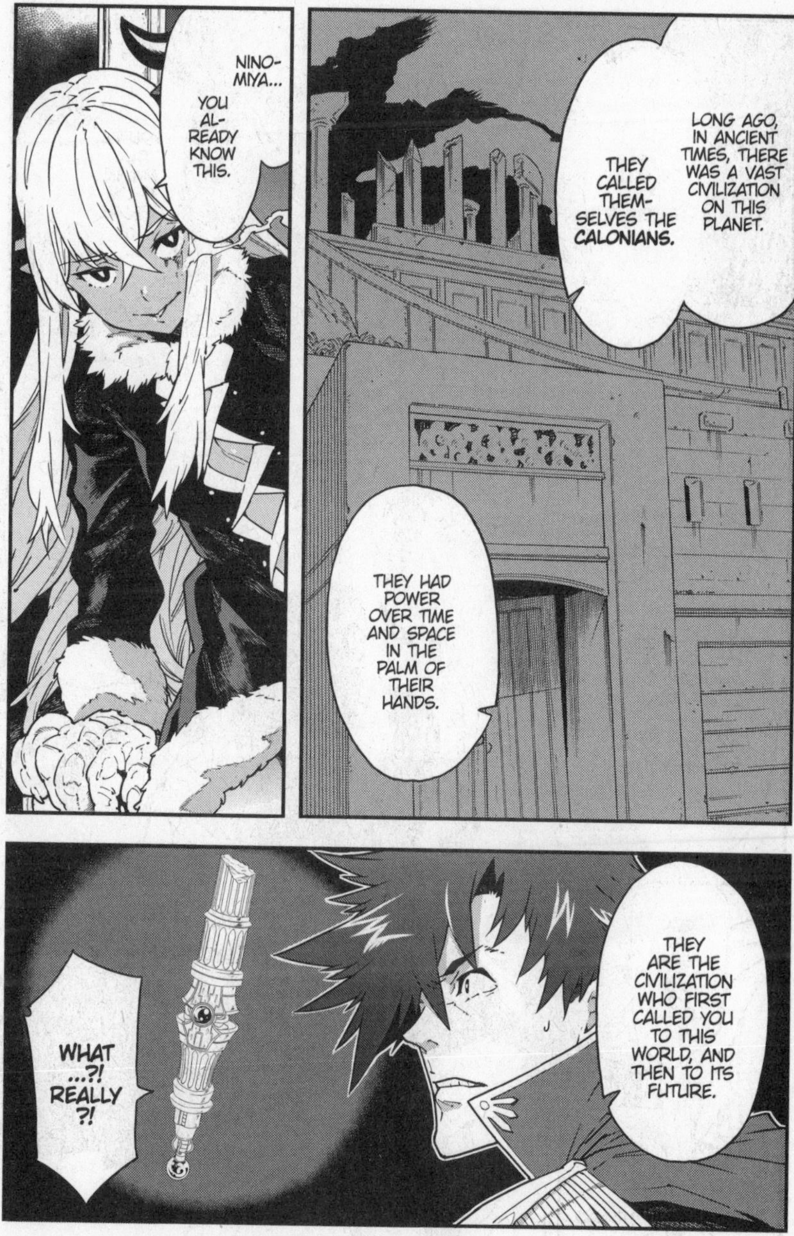
LONG AGO, IN ANCIENT TIMES, THERE WAS A VAST CIVILIZATION ON THIS PLANET.
THEY CALLED THEM-SELVES THE **CALONIANS.**
THEY HAD POWER OVER TIME AND SPACE IN THE PALM OF THEIR HANDS.
NINO-MIYA...
YOU AL-READY KNOW THIS.
THEY ARE THE CIVILIZATION WHO FIRST CALLED YOU TO THIS WORLD, AND THEN TO ITS FUTURE.
WHAT ...?! REALLY ?!

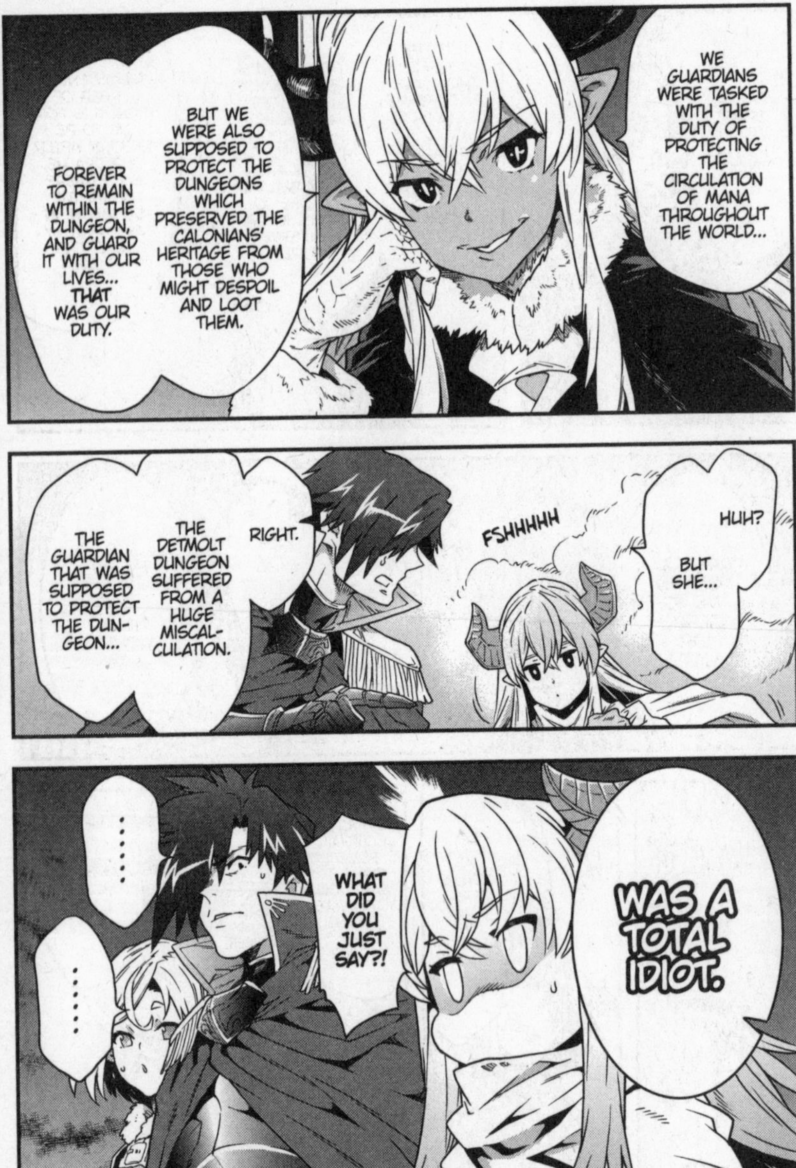
WE GUARDIANS WERE TASKED WITH THE DUTY OF PROTECTING THE CIRCULATION OF MANA THROUGHOUT THE WORLD...
BUT WE WERE ALSO SUPPOSED TO PROTECT THE DUNGEONS WHICH PRESERVED THE CALONIANS' HERITAGE FROM THOSE WHO MIGHT DESPOIL AND LOOT THEM.
FOREVER TO REMAIN WITHIN THE DUNGEON, AND GUARD IT WITH OUR LIVES... THAT WAS OUR DUTY.
HUH? BUT SHE...
FSHHHHH
RIGHT.
THE DETMOLT DUNGEON SUFFERED FROM A HUGE MISCALCULATION.
THE GUARDIAN THAT WAS SUPPOSED TO PROTECT THE DUNGEON...
WAS A TOTAL IDIOT.
WHAT DID YOU JUST SAY?!
......
......

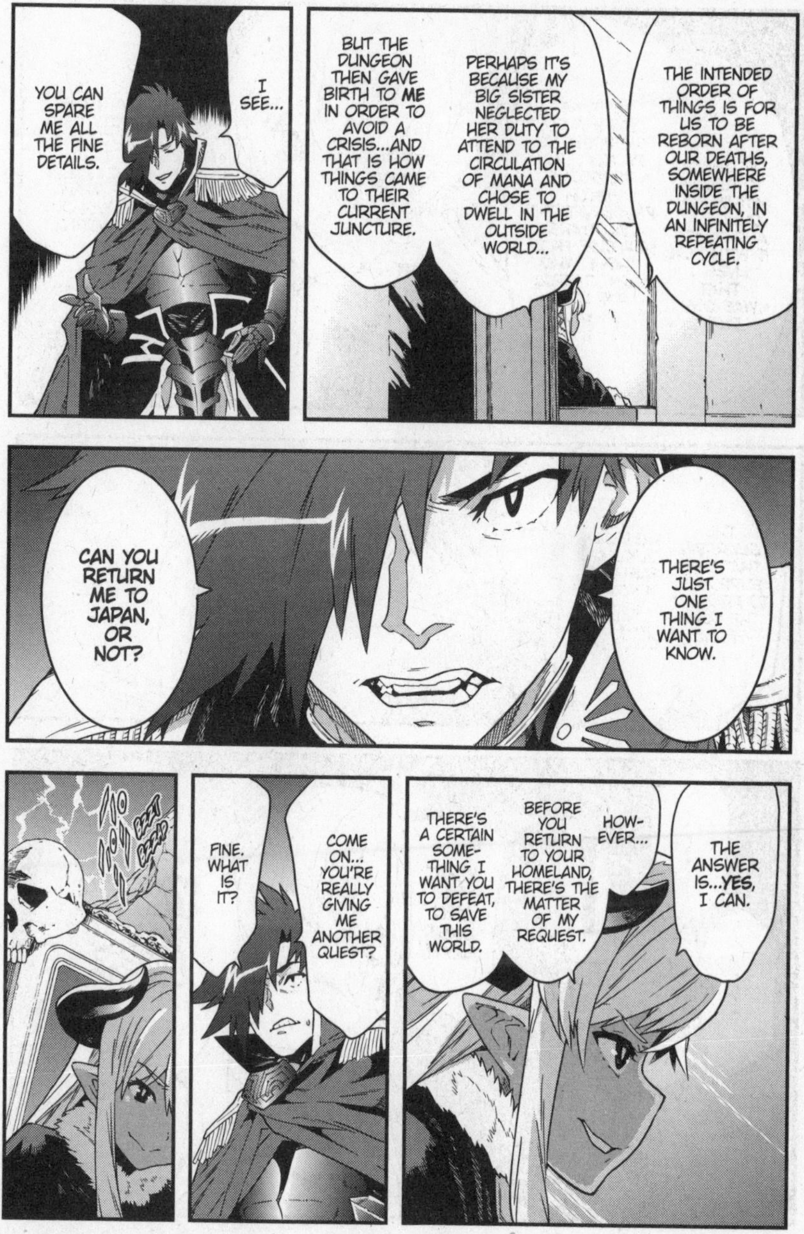
THE INTENDED ORDER OF THINGS IS FOR US TO BE REBORN AFTER OUR DEATHS, SOMEWHERE INSIDE THE DUNGEON, IN AN INFINITELY REPEATING CYCLE.
PERHAPS IT'S BECAUSE MY BIG SISTER NEGLECTED HER DUTY TO ATTEND TO THE CIRCULATION OF MANA AND CHOSE TO DWELL IN THE OUTSIDE WORLD...
BUT THE DUNGEON THEN GAVE BIRTH TO **ME** IN ORDER TO AVOID A CRISIS...AND THAT IS HOW THINGS CAME TO THEIR CURRENT JUNCTURE.
I SEE...
YOU CAN SPARE ME ALL THE FINE DETAILS.
THERE'S JUST ONE THING I WANT TO KNOW.
CAN YOU RETURN ME TO JAPAN, OR NOT?
THE ANSWER IS...**YES**, I CAN.
HOW-EVER...
BEFORE YOU RETURN TO YOUR HOMELAND, THERE'S THE MATTER OF MY REQUEST.
THERE'S A CERTAIN SOME-THING I WANT YOU TO DEFEAT, TO SAVE THIS WORLD.
COME ON... YOU'RE REALLY GIVING ME ANOTHER QUEST?
FINE. WHAT IS IT?
BZZT BZZAP

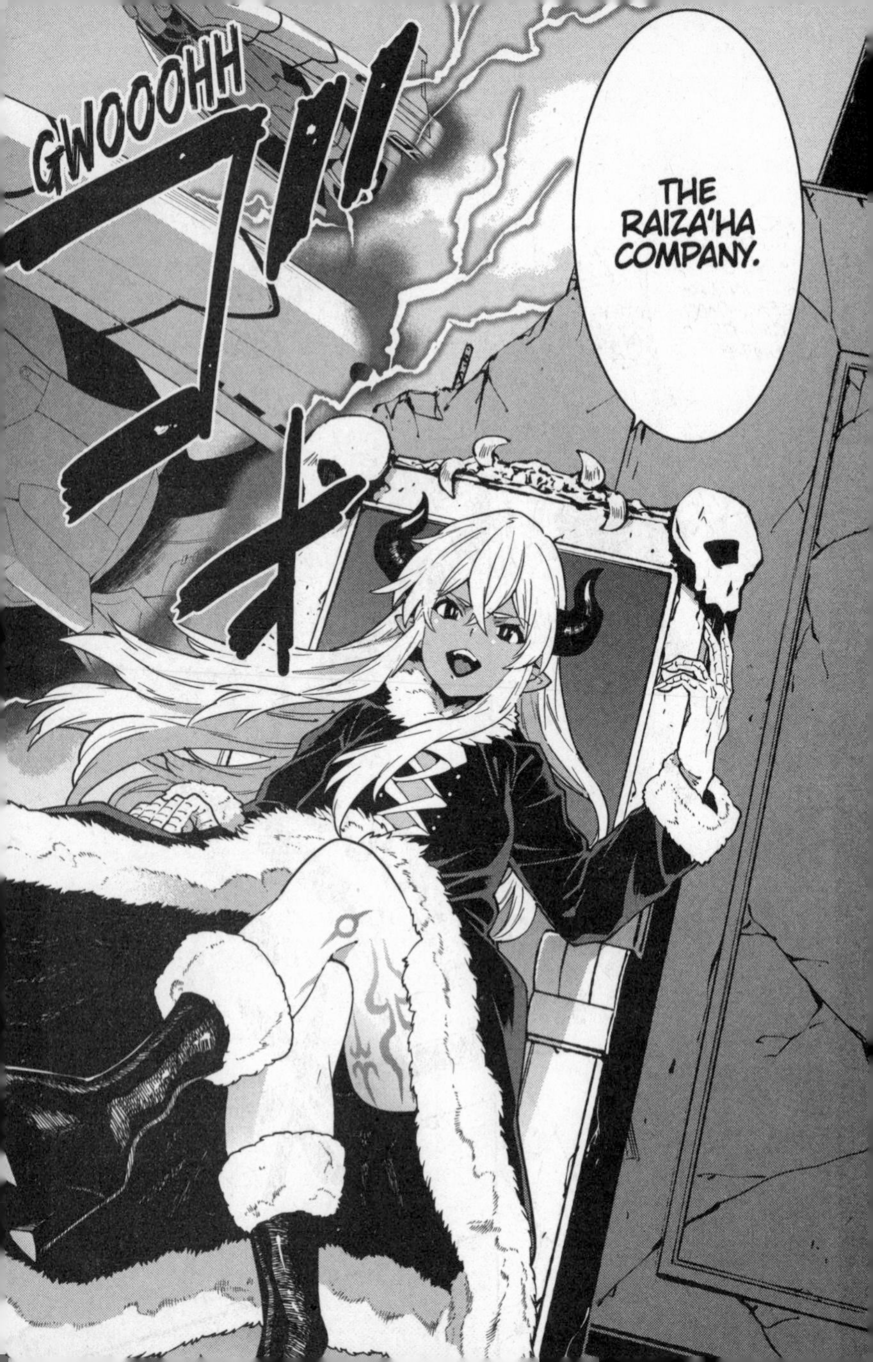
THE RAIZA'HA COMPANY.
GWOOOHH

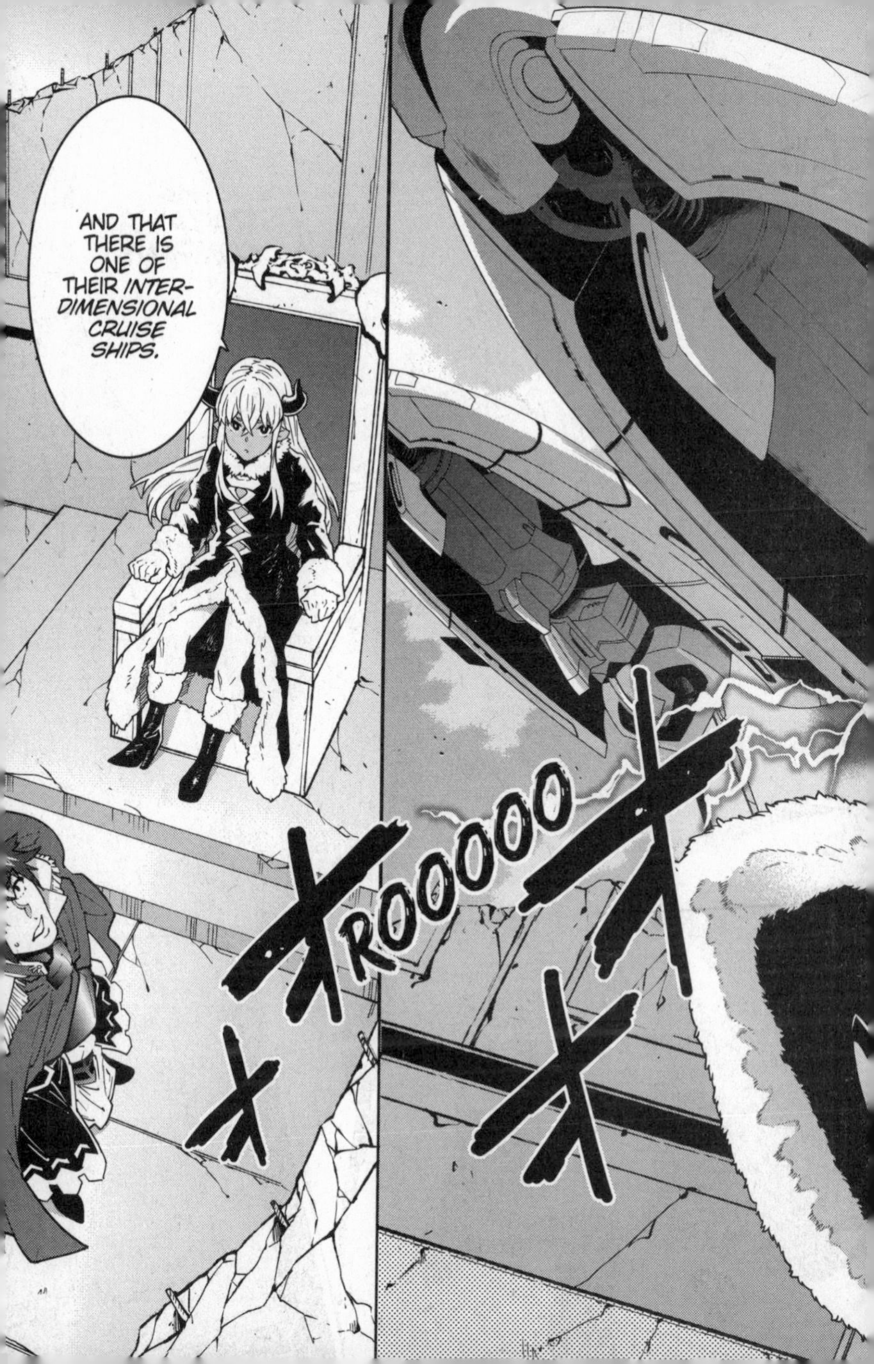
AND THAT THERE IS ONE OF THEIR INTER-DIMENSIONAL CRUISE SHIPS.
VROOOOOOM

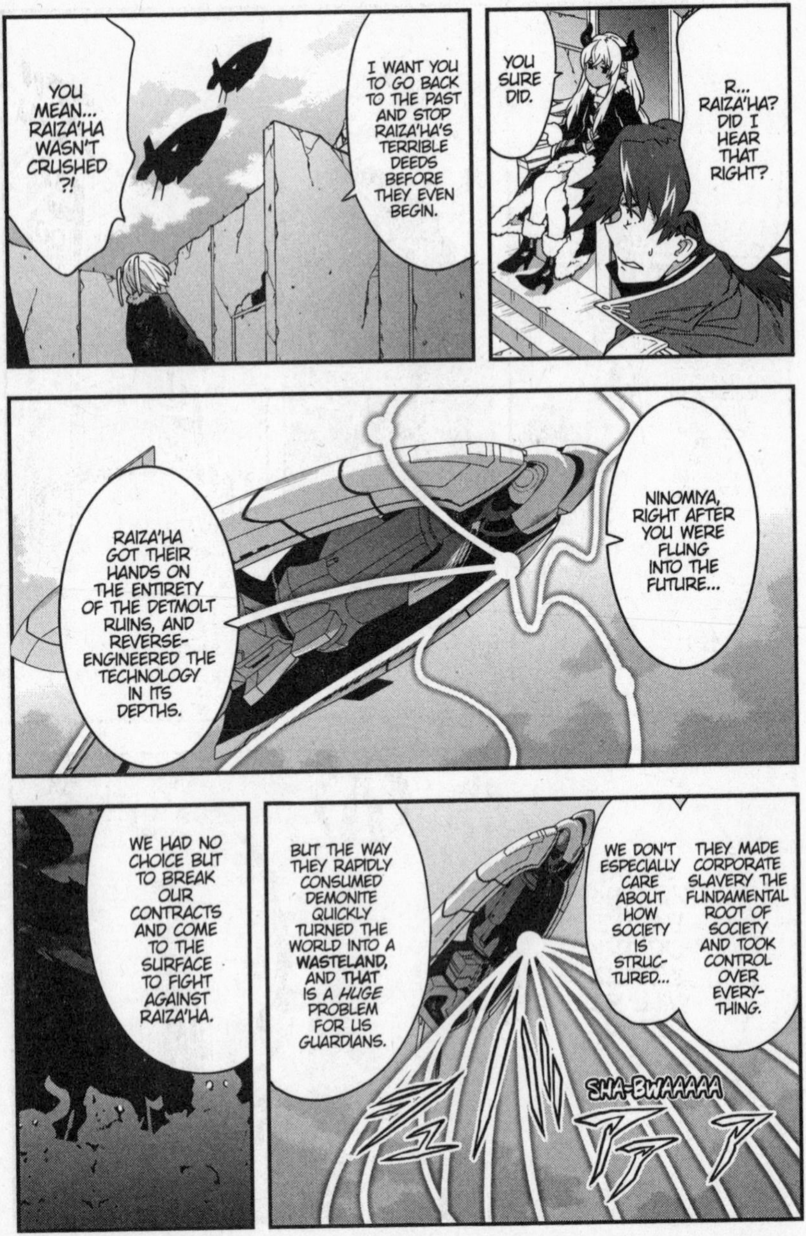
R... RAIZA'HA? DID I HEAR THAT RIGHT?
YOU SURE DID.
I WANT YOU TO GO BACK TO THE PAST AND STOP RAIZA'HA'S TERRIBLE DEEDS BEFORE THEY EVEN BEGIN.
YOU MEAN... RAIZA'HA WASN'T CRUSHED ?!
NINOMIYA, RIGHT AFTER YOU WERE FLUNG INTO THE FUTURE...
RAIZA'HA GOT THEIR HANDS ON THE ENTIRETY OF THE DETMOLT RUINS, AND REVERSE-ENGINEERED THE TECHNOLOGY IN ITS DEPTHS.
THEY MADE CORPORATE SLAVERY THE FUNDAMENTAL ROOT OF SOCIETY AND TOOK CONTROL OVER EVERY-THING.
WE DON'T ESPECIALLY CARE ABOUT HOW SOCIETY IS STRUC-TURED...
BUT THE WAY THEY RAPIDLY CONSUMED DEMONITE QUICKLY TURNED THE WORLD INTO A WASTELAND, AND THAT IS A *HUGE* PROBLEM FOR US GUARDIANS.
SHA-BWAAAAA
WE HAD NO CHOICE BUT TO BREAK OUR CONTRACTS AND COME TO THE SURFACE TO FIGHT AGAINST RAIZA'HA.

TCH!

THE STUFF THEY'VE GOT WITH THEM NOW LOOKS LIKE IT CAN BREAK MORE THAN A FEW BONES.

ONCE, WE WERE ABLE TO GET RAIZA'HA TO RETREAT BACK INTO THEIR EXTRA-DIMENSIONAL HOLDINGS...

BUT IT LOOKS LIKE WE'RE AT OUR LIMIT NOW.

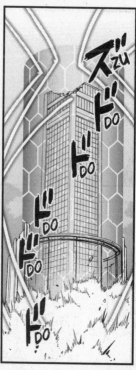

ズ
ZU
ド
DO
ド
DO
ド
DO
ド
DO
ド
DO

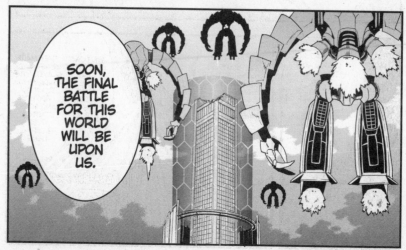

SOON, THE FINAL BATTLE FOR THIS WORLD WILL BE UPON US.

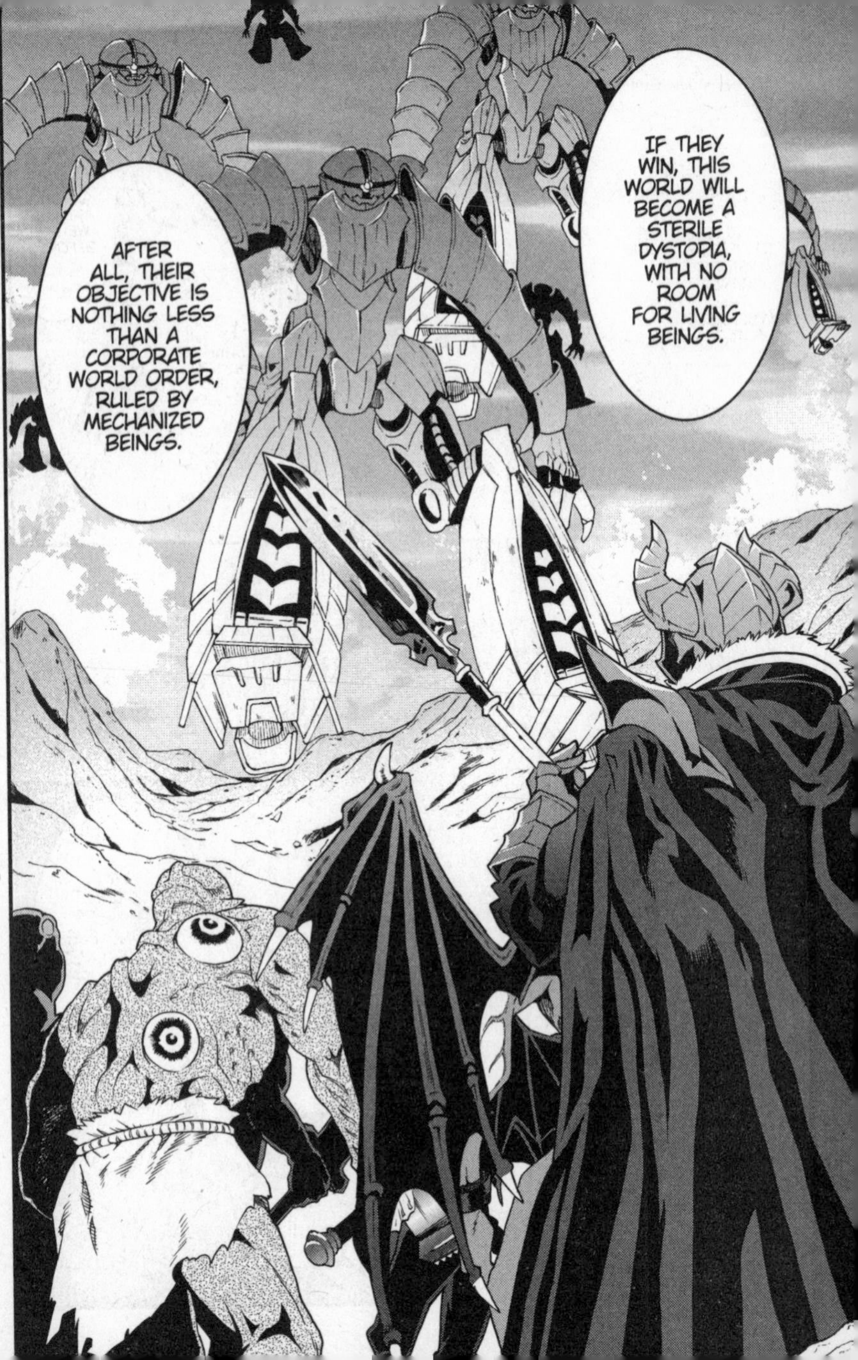
IF THEY WIN, THIS WORLD WILL BECOME A STERILE DYSTOPIA, WITH NO ROOM FOR LIVING BEINGS.
AFTER ALL, THEIR OBJECTIVE IS NOTHING LESS THAN A CORPORATE WORLD ORDER, RULED BY MECHANIZED BEINGS.

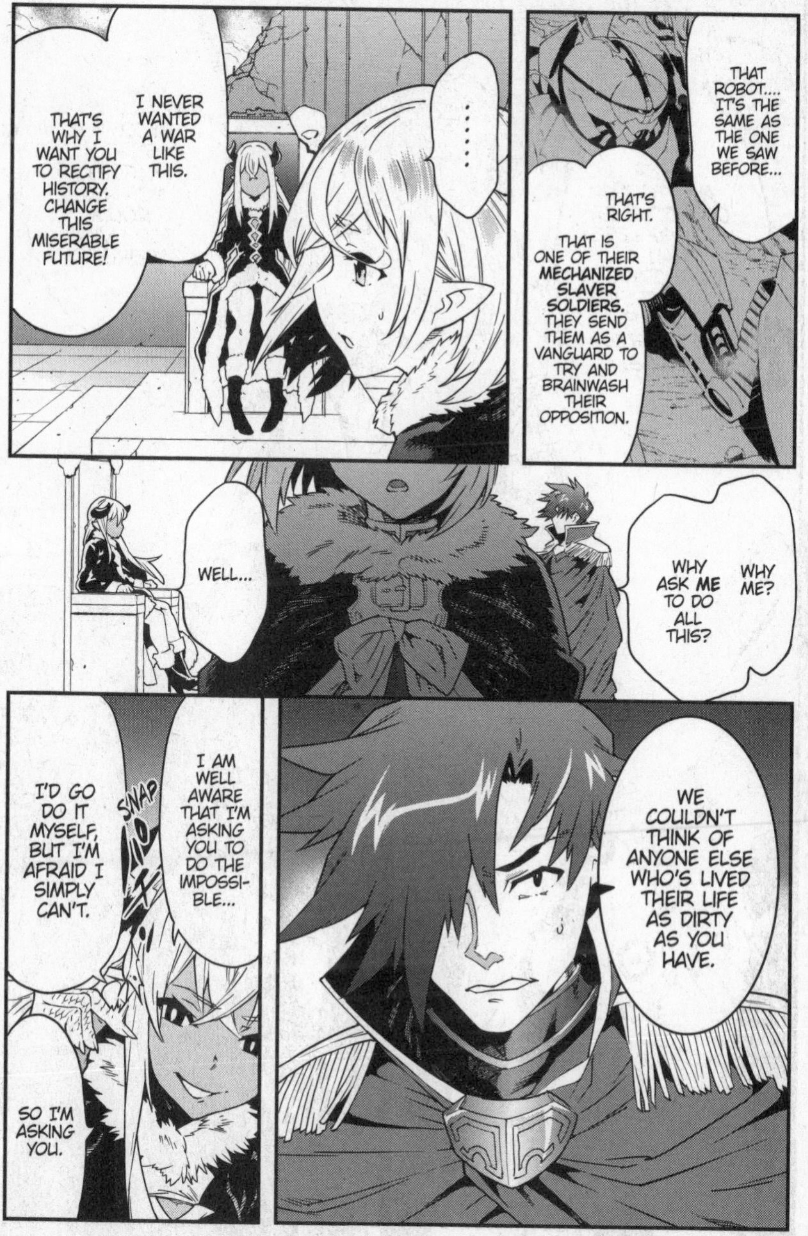
THAT ROBOT.... IT'S THE SAME AS THE ONE WE SAW BEFORE...
THAT'S RIGHT.
THAT IS ONE OF THEIR MECHANIZED SLAVER SOLDIERS. THEY SEND THEM AS A VANGUARD TO TRY AND BRAINWASH THEIR OPPOSITION.
......
I NEVER WANTED A WAR LIKE THIS.
THAT'S WHY I WANT YOU TO RECTIFY HISTORY. CHANGE THIS MISERABLE FUTURE!
WHY ME?
WHY ASK ME TO DO ALL THIS?
WELL...
WE COULDN'T THINK OF ANYONE ELSE WHO'S LIVED THEIR LIFE AS DIRTY AS YOU HAVE.
I AM WELL AWARE THAT I'M ASKING YOU TO DO THE IMPOSSIBLE...
SNAP
I'D GO DO IT MYSELF, BUT I'M AFRAID I SIMPLY CAN'T.
SO I'M ASKING YOU.

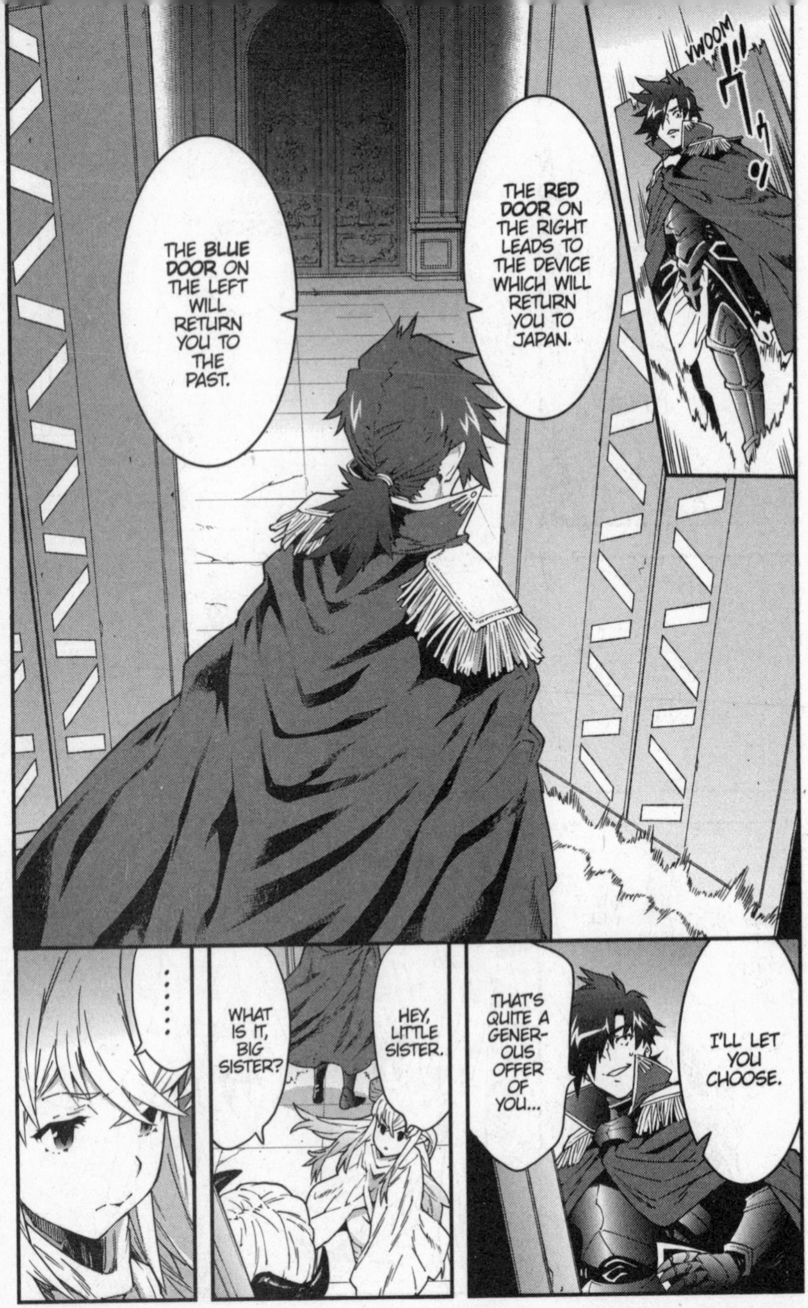
VWOOM
THE **RED DOOR** ON THE RIGHT LEADS TO THE DEVICE WHICH WILL RETURN YOU TO JAPAN.
THE **BLUE DOOR** ON THE LEFT WILL RETURN YOU TO THE PAST.
I'LL LET YOU CHOOSE.
THAT'S QUITE A GENER-OUS OFFER OF YOU...
HEY, LITTLE SISTER.
WHAT IS IT, BIG SISTER?
......

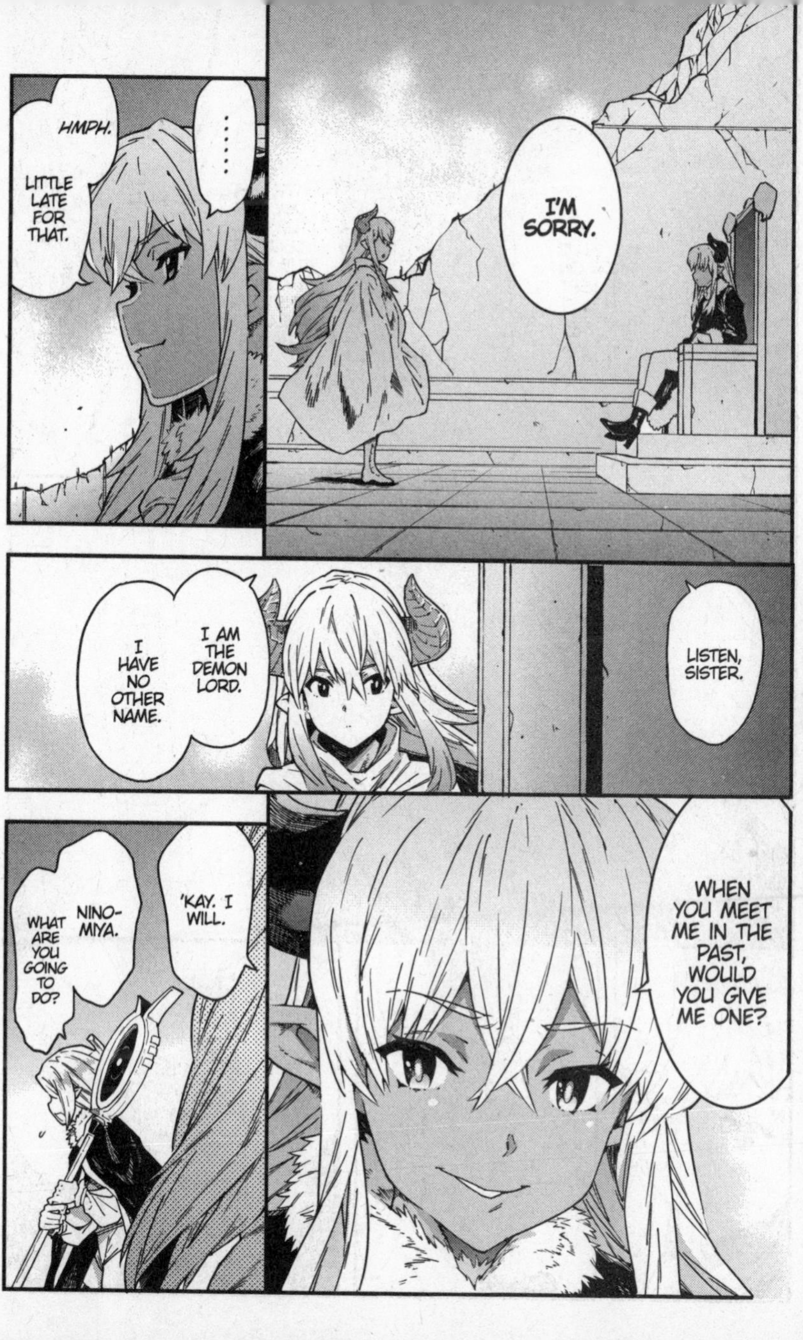
I'M SORRY.
......
HMPH.
LITTLE LATE FOR THAT.
LISTEN, SISTER.
I AM THE DEMON LORD.
I HAVE NO OTHER NAME.
WHEN YOU MEET ME IN THE PAST, WOULD YOU GIVE ME ONE?
'KAY. I WILL.
NINO-MIYA.
WHAT ARE YOU GOING TO DO?

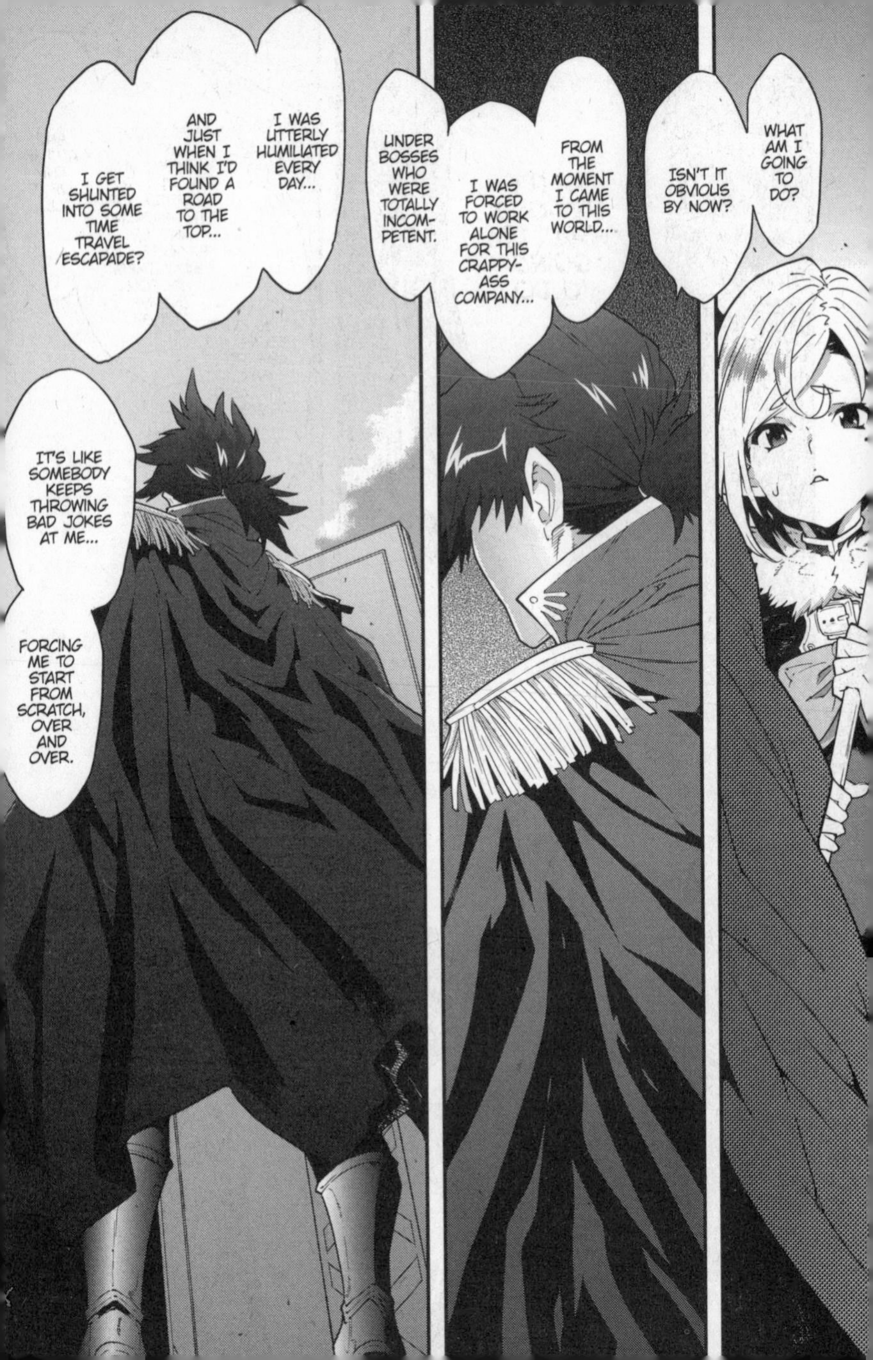
WHAT AM I GOING TO DO?
ISN'T IT OBVIOUS BY NOW?
FROM THE MOMENT I CAME TO THIS WORLD...
I WAS FORCED TO WORK ALONE FOR THIS CRAPPY-ASS COMPANY...
UNDER BOSSES WHO WERE TOTALLY INCOM-PETENT.
I WAS UTTERLY HUMILIATED EVERY DAY...
AND JUST WHEN I THINK I'D FOUND A ROAD TO THE TOP...
I GET SHUNTED INTO SOME TIME TRAVEL ESCAPADE?
IT'S LIKE SOMEBODY KEEPS THROWING BAD JOKES AT ME...
FORCING ME TO START FROM SCRATCH, OVER AND OVER.

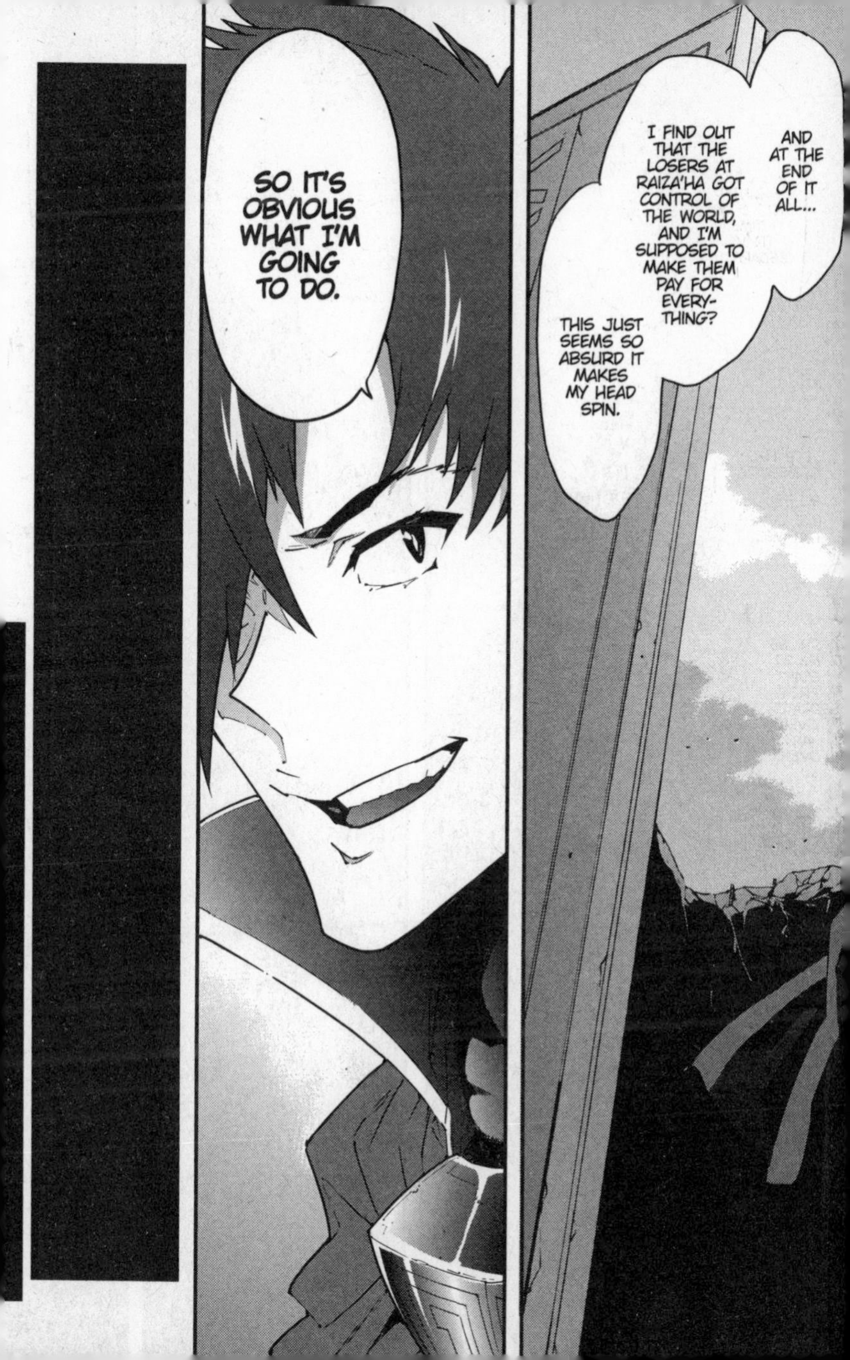
AND AT THE END OF IT ALL...
I FIND OUT THAT THE LOSERS AT RAIZA'HA GOT CONTROL OF THE WORLD, AND I'M SUPPOSED TO MAKE THEM PAY FOR EVERY-THING?
THIS JUST SEEMS SO ABSURD IT MAKES MY HEAD SPIN.
SO IT'S OBVIOUS WHAT I'M GOING TO DO.

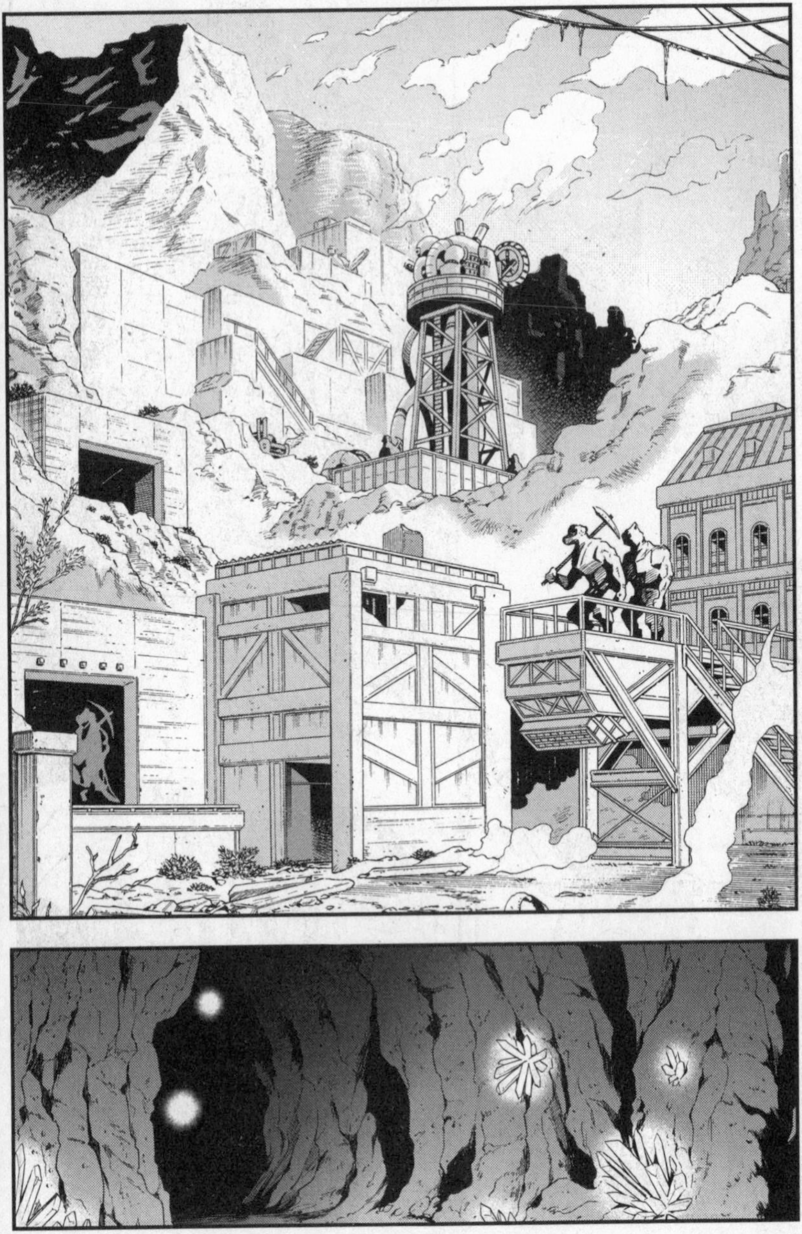

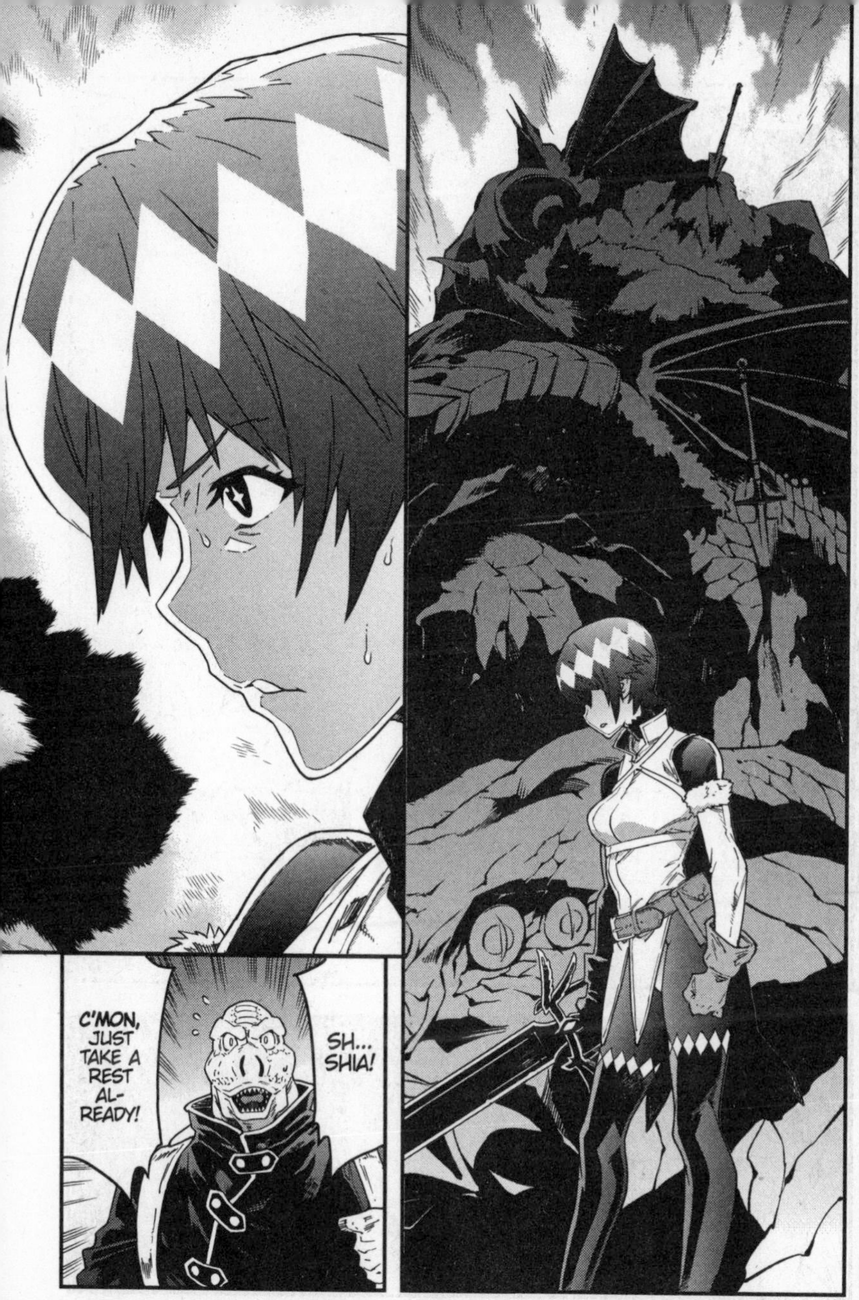
SH... SHIA!
C'MON, JUST TAKE A REST AL-READY!

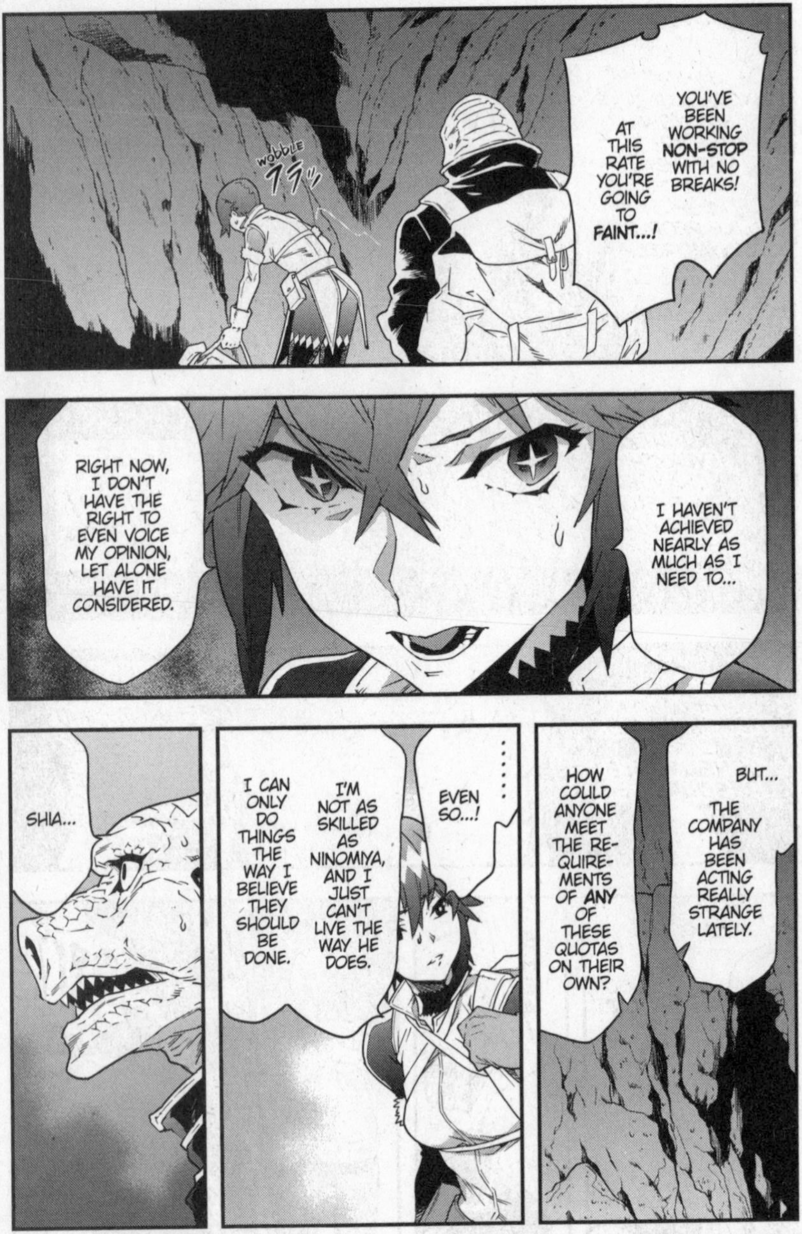

YOU'VE BEEN WORKING NON-STOP WITH NO BREAKS!
AT THIS RATE YOU'RE GOING TO FAINT...!
wobble
フラッ
I HAVEN'T ACHIEVED NEARLY AS MUCH AS I NEED TO...
RIGHT NOW, I DON'T HAVE THE RIGHT TO EVEN VOICE MY OPINION, LET ALONE HAVE IT CONSIDERED.
BUT...
THE COMPANY HAS BEEN ACTING REALLY STRANGE LATELY.
HOW COULD ANYONE MEET THE RE-QUIRE-MENTS OF ANY OF THESE QUOTAS ON THEIR OWN?
......
EVEN SO...!
I'M NOT AS SKILLED AS NINOMIYA, AND I JUST CAN'T LIVE THE WAY HE DOES.
I CAN ONLY DO THINGS THE WAY I BELIEVE THEY SHOULD BE DONE.
SHIA...

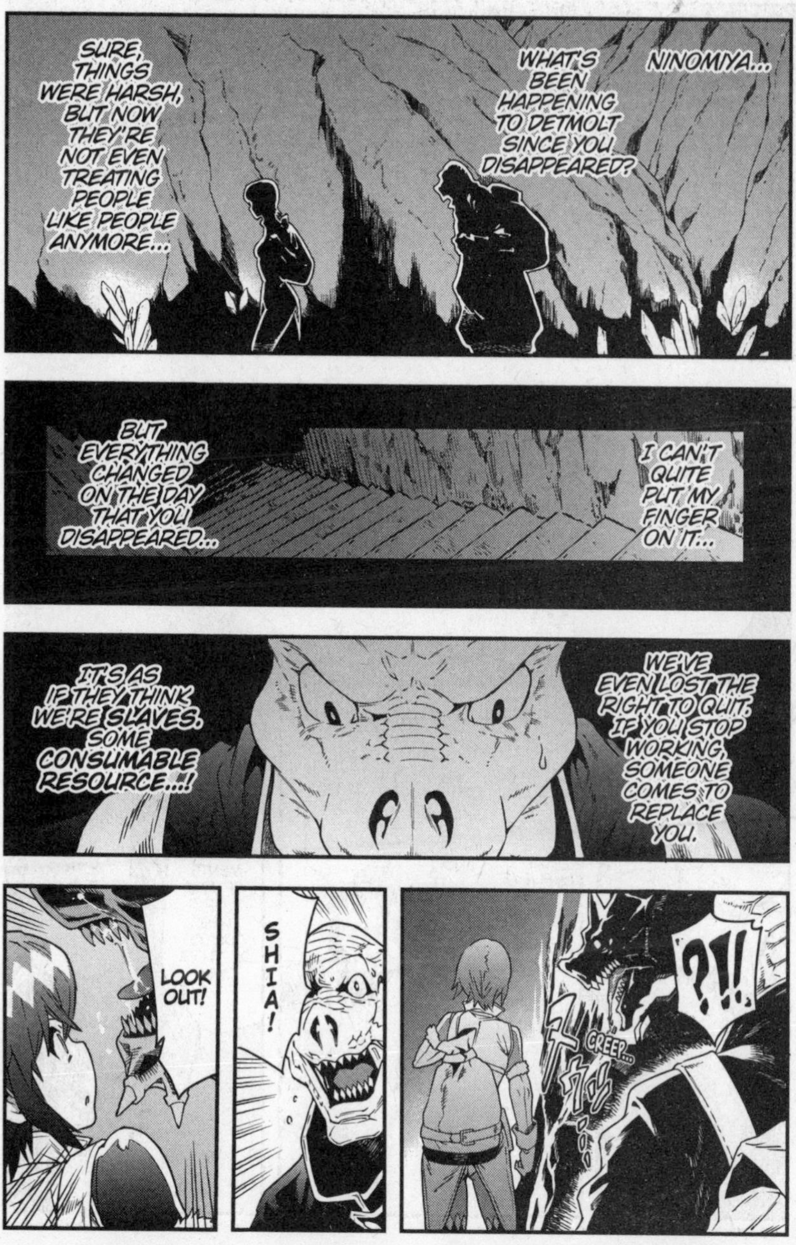
NINOMIYA...
WHAT'S BEEN HAPPENING TO DETMOLT SINCE YOU DISAPPEARED?
SURE, THINGS WERE HARSH, BUT NOW THEY'RE NOT EVEN TREATING PEOPLE LIKE PEOPLE ANYMORE...
I CAN'T QUITE PUT MY FINGER ON IT...
BUT EVERYTHING CHANGED ON THE DAY THAT YOU DISAPPEARED...
WE'VE EVEN LOST THE RIGHT TO QUIT. IF YOU STOP WORKING, SOMEONE COMES TO REPLACE YOU.
IT'S AS IF THEY THINK WE'RE SLAVES. SOME CONSUMABLE RESOURCE...!
?!!
CREEP...
SHIA!
LOOK OUT!

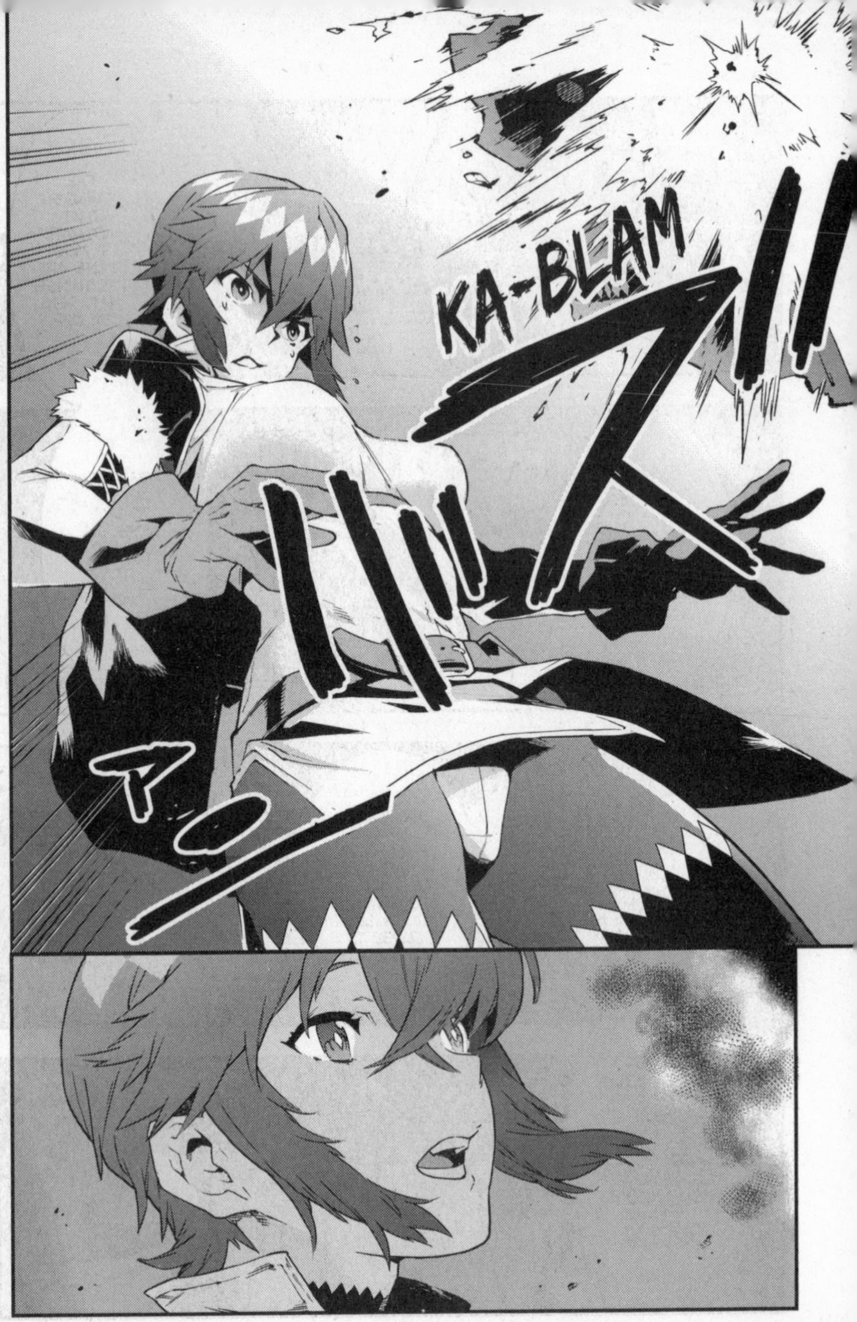
KA-BLAM

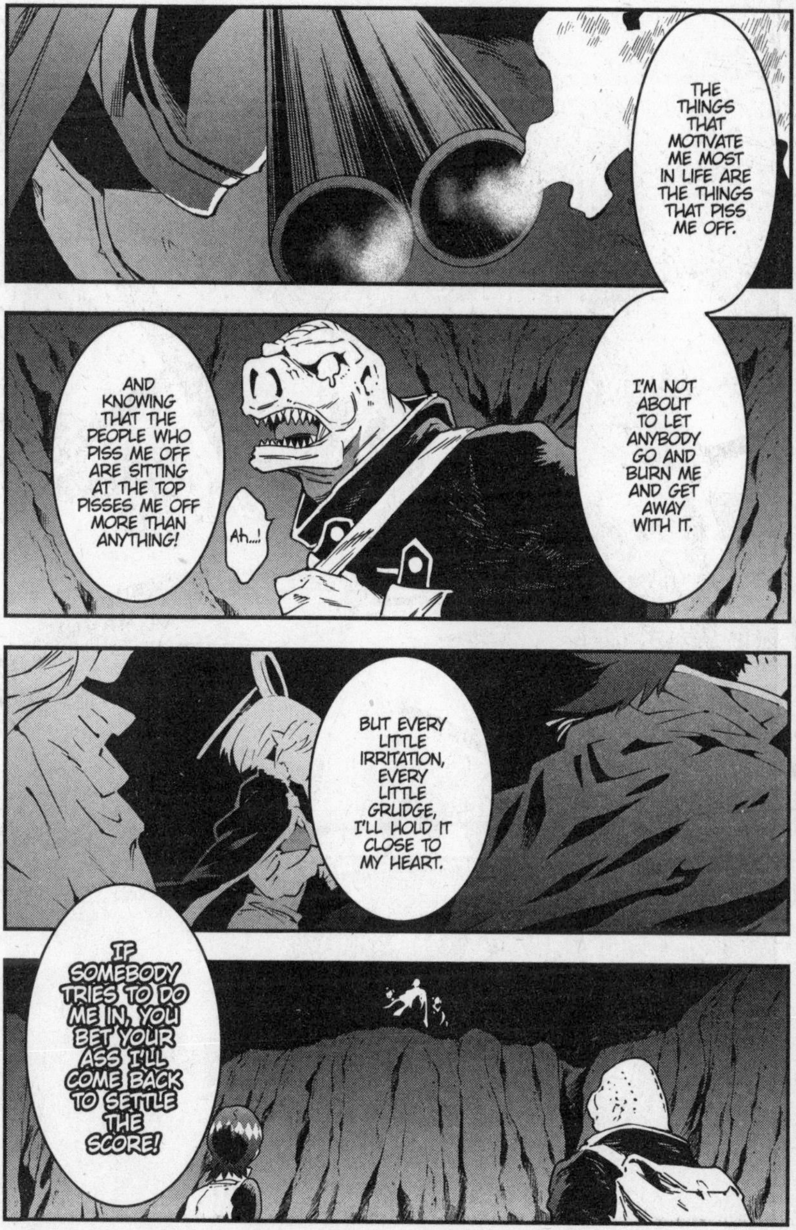
THE THINGS THAT MOTIVATE ME MOST IN LIFE ARE THE THINGS THAT PISS ME OFF.
I'M NOT ABOUT TO LET ANYBODY GO AND BURN ME AND GET AWAY WITH IT.
Ah...!
AND KNOWING THAT THE PEOPLE WHO PISS ME OFF ARE SITTING AT THE TOP PISSES ME OFF MORE THAN ANYTHING!
BUT EVERY LITTLE IRRITATION, EVERY LITTLE GRUDGE, I'LL HOLD IT CLOSE TO MY HEART.
IF SOMEBODY TRIES TO DO ME IN, YOU BET YOUR ASS I'LL COME BACK TO SETTLE THE SCORE!

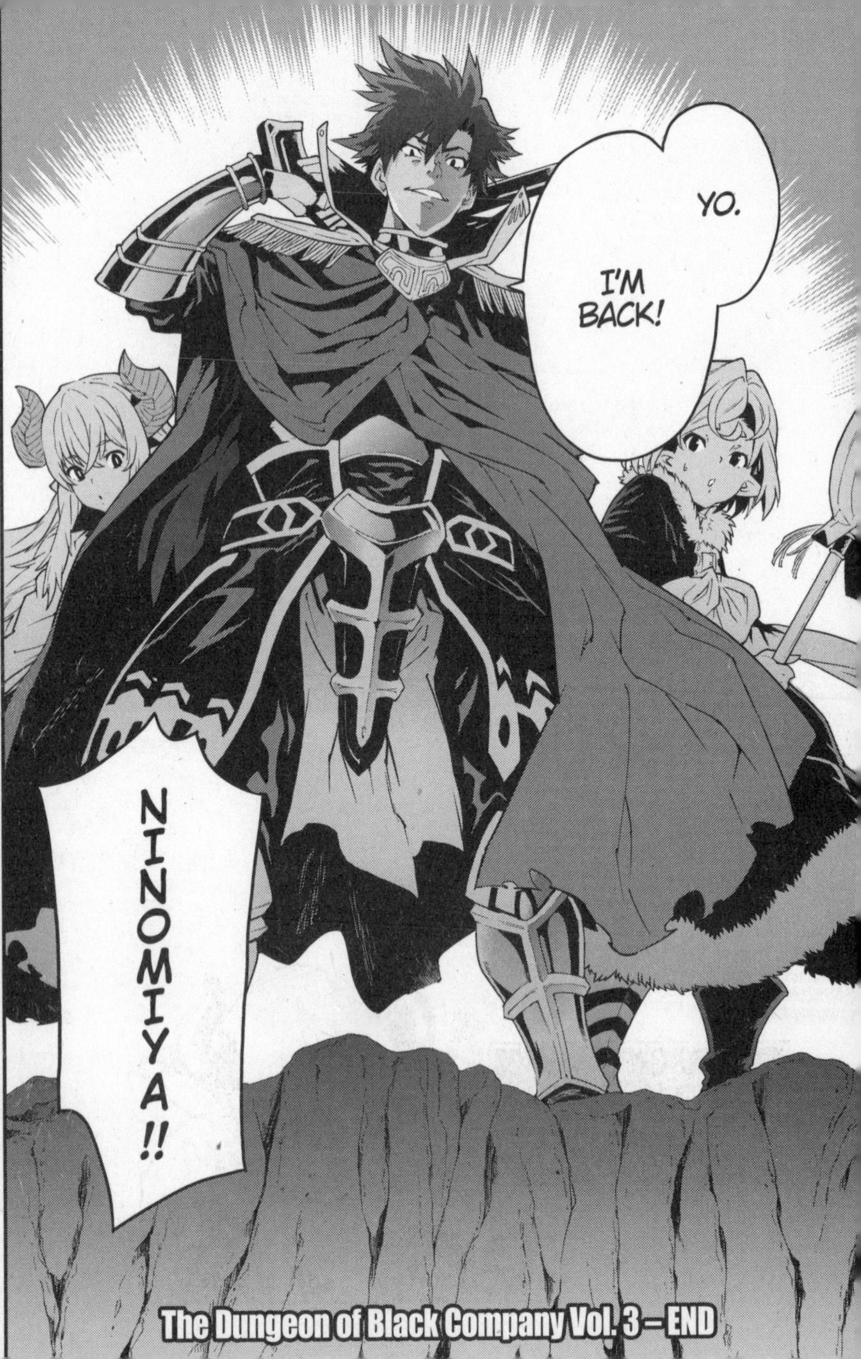
YO.
I'M BACK!
NINOMIYA!!
The Dungeon of Black Company Vol. 3 – END